METAPHYSICS . COSMOLOGY . TRADITION .

STUDIES IN COMPARATIVE RELIGION

The First English Journal on Traditional Studies — established **1963**

Studies in Comparative Religion is devoted to the exposition of the teachings, spiritual methods, symbolism, and other facets of the religious traditions of the world, together with the traditional arts and sciences which have sprung from those religions. It is not sectarian and, inasmuch as it is not tied to the interests of any particular religion, it is free to lay stress on the common spirit underlying the various religious forms.

One of our primary aims is to meet the need for accurate information created by the now world-wide interest in the question of "ecumenical relations" between the great religions, by providing a forum where writers of proven authority can exchange views on various aspects of religious life, doctrinal, historical, artistic and mystical, not forgetting the element of personal experience and reminiscence.

By collecting accurate information about the great religions under their many aspects and rendering them available to interested readers we feel we are fulfilling a very pressing need of our time and also contributing in a practical manner to the cause of inter-religious understanding. If there is to be an effective measure of this understanding at any level this can only be on the basis of accurate presentation both of teachings and facts. An ill-informed benevolence is no substitute for genuine insight, based on information that is neither willfully distorted nor confined to the surface of things.

In this manner we think that we are best serving the interest of our readers in their search for truth.

(*Excerpt from the Introduction to our first publication, almost fifty years ago*)

World Wisdom

Psychology and the Perennial Philosophy

Studies in Comparative Religion

Edited by
Samuel Bendeck Sotillos

World Wisdom

Psychology and the Perennial Philosophy:
Studies in Comparative Religion
© 2013 World Wisdom, Inc.

Publisher's Note:
Studies in Comparative Religion has published articles from over 400 different authors. The original editors of *Studies* did not insist upon a common convention for the transliteration of foreign terms; consequently a variety of different systems of diacritical mark usage can be found in any given issue of *Studies*. The current publisher has chosen to continue this policy and will thus remain faithful to the original transliteration convention used by each of its contributors.

Library of Congress Cataloging-in-Publication Data

Psychology and the perennial philosophy : studies in comparative religion / edited by Samuel Bendeck Sotillos.
     pages cm. -- (Studies in comparative religion series)
  Includes bibliographical references.
  ISBN 978-1-936597-20-8 (pbk. : alk. paper) 1. Psychology, Religious. 2. Philosophy and religion. I. Bendeck Sotillos, Samuel, 1972- editor of compilation.
  BL53.P82455 2013
  201'.615--dc23

                                                                         2012047743

Printed on acid-free paper in the USA.

For information address World Wisdom, Inc.
P.O. Box 2682, Bloomington, Indiana 47402-2682
www.worldwisdom.com

CONTENTS

Book Reviews

Psychology and the Perennial Philosophy

Editorial

As for modern Western psychology, it deals only with quite a restricted portion of the human individuality, where the mental faculty is in direct relationship with the corporeal modality, and, given the methods it employs, it is incapable of going any further. In any case the very objective which it sets before itself and which is exclusively the study of mental phenomena [of the ego], limits it strictly to the realm of the individuality, so that the state which we are now discussing [*Ātmā* or the Self] necessarily eludes its investigations.[1]

René Guénon

The health envisaged by the [modern] empirical psychotherapy is a freedom from particular pathological conditions; that envisaged by the other [traditional or perennial psychology] is a freedom from all conditions and predicaments. . . . Furthermore, the pursuit of the greater freedom necessarily involves that attainment of the lesser; psycho-physical health being a manifestation and consequence of spiritual wellbeing.[2]

Ananda Kentish Coomaraswamy

There is no science of the soul [psyche] without a metaphysical basis to it and without spiritual remedies at its disposal.[3]

Frithjof Schuon

[The spiritual] psychology [of the perennial philosophy] does not separate the soul either from the metaphysical or from the cosmic order. The connection with the metaphysical order provides spiritual psychology with qualitative criteria such as are wholly lacking in profane [modern] psychology, which studies only the dynamic character of phenomena of the psyche and their proximate causes.[4]

Titus Burckhardt

Without question, modern psychology has shaped and impacted the twentieth century in an unprecedented manner, though curiously this influence still appears to be unnoticed by the majority of present-day individuals. Yet the point cannot be overly emphasized that modern

---

[1] René Guénon, "The State of Deep Sleep or the Condition of *Prājna*," in *Man and His Becoming According to the Vedanta*, trans. Richard C. Nicholson (New York: The Noonday Press, 1958), p. 104.

[2] Ananda K. Coomaraswamy, "On the Indian and Traditional Psychology, or rather Pneumatology," in *Coomaraswamy, Vol. 2: Selected Papers, Metaphysics*, ed. Roger Lipsey (Princeton, NJ: Princeton University Press, 1977), p. 335.

[3] Frithjof Schuon, "The Contradiction of Relativism," in *Logic and Transcendence*, trans. Peter N. Townsend (London: Perennial Books, 1984), p. 14.

[4] Titus Burckhardt, "The Branches of the Doctrine," in *Introduction to Sufi Doctrine*, trans. D.M. Matheson (Bloomington, IN: World Wisdom, 2008), pp. 26-27.

psychology, as a derivative and stronghold of scientific materialism, can be credited as one of the leading and contributing factors that has destabilized the spiritual and correspondingly the psychological apparatus of traditional man.[5] This point is alluded to by Sigmund Freud (1856-1939): "No, our science [of psychology] is no illusion. But an illusion it would be to suppose that what [materialistic] science cannot give us we can get elsewhere."[6] This endemic scientism is observable throughout modern psychology. While most apparent in behaviorism and psychoanalysis, it is nonetheless also present in humanistic and transpersonal psychology, as these are both continuations and expansions of the two earlier "forces." This influence is aptly summarized by Gill Edwards:

> [Modern] science has claimed a monopoly on truth, seeing the scientific method as the only valid path towards knowledge. . . . [A]s recent products of their culture, modern psychology and psychotherapy were built upon the shifting sands of Cartesian-Newtonian assumptions—with devastating consequences . . . [and] many therapists are still clinging to the scientific tradition . . . and refusing to open their eyes. . . . [T]he old paradigm gave birth to a positivist, materialist psychology which values objectivity, rationality and empiricism. . . . The mechanistic, reductionist, determinist assumptions of the Cartesian-Newtonian world view are endemic in psychology and psychotherapy.[7]

The very notion of a scientific foundation underlying modern psychology has been brought into question by William James (1842-1910), a key pioneer within humanistic and transpersonal psychology, in saying that "This is no science, it is only the hope of a science."[8] The complex events that have altered the human outlook not only of the cosmos but of man's true identity during the Renaissance and the so-called Age of Enlightenment are often described as blows to man's narcissism, particularly the Copernican revolution, the Darwinian revolution, and the Psychoanalytic revolution:

> [T]he human individual has been successively reduced and dethroned by the discoveries of [modern] Western science—removed from his honored place in the center of the heavenly bodies by Copernicus and others, removed from his special position as king and curator of the animal kingdom by Darwin, removed even from command of his own acts by Freud and the behaviorists, thus rendered puny, insignificant, and impotent, vulnerable to further reduction with each further discovery.[9]

---

[5] "[P]sychoanalysis is one of those mass movements which are both a cause and consequence of spiritual decay" (Werner Kraft, quoted in Thomas Szasz, "Karl Kraus Today," in *Karl Kraus and the Soul-Doctors: A Pioneer Critic and his Criticism of Psychiatry and Psychoanalysis*, p. 93).

[6] Sigmund Freud, *The Future of an Illusion*, trans. and ed. James Strachey (New York: W.W. Norton & Company, 1989), p. 71.

[7] Gill Edwards, "Does Psychotherapy Need a Soul?" in *Psychotherapy and Its Discontents*, eds. Windy Dryden and Colin Feltham (Buckingham, UK: Open University Press, 1998), pp. 194-199.

[8] William James, "Psychology and Philosophy," in *Psychology: The Briefer Course* (New York: Dover Publications, 2001), p. 335.

[9] George B. Leonard, "A Morning on Mt. Tam," in *The Transformation: A Guide to the Inevitable Changes in Hu-*

These pernicious fissures or "blows," which began in the West and have since encroached upon the rest of the world via globalization, have devastated the traditional societies of both East and West, to the point where they may perhaps never recover. As René Guénon (1886-1951) has remarked: "[W]hile nineteenth century materialism closed the mind of man to what is above him, twentieth century [modern] psychology opened it to what is below him."[10]

The destabilization of the traditional societies has led to the simultaneous desacralization of the shamanic or primordial peoples that were once everywhere, for the origin and center of traditional man is anchored in the sacred, as was the case until the post-medieval West.[11] Traditional man, who is inherently *Homo religiosus* or *Homo spiritualis*, was always and continues until this day to be contextualized within the spiritual domain.

> In one manner or another all life is seen to participate in the sacred, all cultural forms express the sacred, so that inevitably within this context the lives of those peoples who live close to their sacred traditions may be called religious, and they are thus beings who are religiously human.[12]

"The problems faced by modern man," says Seyyed Hossein Nasr (b. 1933), "all point to the same cause, namely to man's living below his own possibilities and to the forgetfulness of who he is [*in divinis*]."[13] The idea of addressing the needs of the human psyche by what lies outside or rather below the spiritual domain—in isolation from the sacred principles that can provide authentic efficacy—is based on a radical misunderstanding of the unitive principles that facilitate a true and complete psychology of man. "Psychology, we must remember, is the study of the soul [psyche], therefore the discipline closest to the religious life. An authentic psychology discards none of the insights gained from spiritual disciplines."[14]

Paradoxically, the perennial psychologies of man, which have been applied since the dawn of civilization, were in essence rejected in an ideological *coup d'état* by a secular and materialistic worldview that was designed and endorsed by the same tendencies that manufactured the plethora of ills that are so prevalent in this turbulent epoch: "Psychoanalysis is the disease of which it pretends to be the cure."[15] It has been emphasized that "in a traditional society there

---

mankind (New York: Delacorte Press, 1972), p. 12.

[10] René Guénon, quoted in Ananda K. Coomaraswamy, "The Doctrine," in *Hinduism and Buddhism* (New York: Philosophical Library, 1943), p. 61.

[11] See Frithjof Schuon, "The Ancient Worlds in Perspective," in *Light on the Ancient Worlds*, trans. Lord Northbourne (Bloomington, IN: World Wisdom Books, 1984), p. 7.

[12] Joseph Epes Brown, "On Being Human," in *The Spiritual Legacy of the American Indian: Commemorative Edition with Letters While Living with Black Elk*, eds. Marina Brown Weatherly, Elenita Brown, and Michael Oren Fitzgerald (Bloomington, IN: World Wisdom, 2007), p. 93.

[13] Seyyed Hossein Nasr, "One Is the Spirit and Many Its Human Reflections—Thoughts on the Human Condition Today," in *The Need for a Sacred Science* (Albany, NY: State University of New York Press, 1993), p. 48.

[14] Theodore Roszak, "The Visionary Commonwealth," in *Where the Wasteland Ends: Politics and Transcendence in Postindustrial Society* (Garden City, NY: Doubleday & Company, 1972), p. 414.

[15] Thomas Szasz, "Kraus and Freud: Unmasking the Unmasker," in *Karl Kraus and the Soul-Doctors: A Pioneer Critic and his Criticism of Psychiatry and Psychoanalysis* (Baton Rouge, LA: Louisiana State University Press, 1976), p. 24.

is little or nothing that can properly be called secular,"[16] which is to say, "The fact is that every *bona fide* pre-modern science is rooted in an integral sapiential tradition [of the *philosophia perennis*]."[17] One cannot take lightly the following Promethean epigram that Freud borrowed from Virgil's *Aeneid*, which speaks to the nefarious quality of a science broken away from its sacred source: "If I cannot bend the higher powers [the gods or the spiritual domain], I shall stir up Hell"[18]—signifying that if modern psychology cannot gain access to what is above or transcendent it will unleash the subterranean forces of what is below or infernal in order to access power and legitimacy. For this reason it has been affirmed that "psychotherapy stirred up a hornets' nest of the first magnitude."[19]

Under the hypnotic guise of modernism and postmodernism, and filled with all the technological advancements of so-called "progress," the contemporary outlook is incapable of addressing the core symptoms or issues since it *a priori* excludes and even undermines the significance of the spiritual domain. It has been astutely illustrated that no matter how many attempts be made, they are doomed to fail as "the psychic cannot be treated by the psychic."[20] What has taken the place of the spiritual psychologies of man, based on the tripartite structure of the human microcosm—Spirit/Intellect, soul, and body—is a truncated, profane psychology that only addresses the psychic and the physical while abrogating the spirit, which is at once above man and also his center, both transcendent and immanent.

That modern psychology has become a substitute for the spiritual traditions is all-too-clear given the militantly secular milieu of today's world.[21] But what led to the undermining of the traditional civilizations of the world that were rooted in the metaphysical principles of the perennial philosophy? According to the perennial philosophy, the widespread disequilibrium and systematic dehumanization we see today are associated with the loss of authentic spiritual traditions. It can thus be confidently stated, in complete contrast to the modern and postmodern outlook, that "A civilization is integrated and healthy to the extent that it is founded on the 'invisible' or 'underlying' religion, the *religio perennis*."[22]

This issue of *Studies in Comparative Religion*, focused on "Psychology and the Perennial Philosophy," offers for the first time the distinctive and imperative perspective on the human psyche and the fullness of human condition in light of the timeless truths at the heart of the

---

[16] Rama P. Coomaraswamy (ed.), *The Essential Ananda K. Coomaraswamy* (Bloomington, IN: World Wisdom, 2004), p. 159.

[17] Wolfgang Smith, "*Sophia Perennis* and Modern Science," in *The Wisdom of Ancient Cosmology: Contemporary Science in Light of Tradition* (Oakton, VA: Foundation for Traditional Studies, 2003), p. 21.

[18] "*Flectere si nequeo superos, Acheronta movebo*": this motto was prefixed in Sigmund Freud, *The Interpretation of Dreams*, trans. A.A. Brill (London: George Allen & Unwin, 1913).

[19] C.G. Jung, "Psychotherapy and a Philosophy of Life," in *Essays on Contemporary Events: The Psychology of Nazism*, trans. R.F.C. Hull (Princeton, NJ: Princeton University Press, 1989), p. 43.

[20] Titus Burckhardt, "Traditional Cosmology and Modern Science: Modern Psychology," in *Mirror of the Intellect: Essays on Traditional Science and Sacred Art*, trans. and ed. William Stoddart (Albany, NY: State University of New York Press, 1987), p. 50.

[21] "The loss of religion as Center in the world has left a hole which [modern] psychology is trying to fill" (Whitall N. Perry, "The Zodiac of the Soul: Observation on the Differences between Traditional and Empirical Psychology," in *Challenges to a Secular Society* [Oakton, VA: Foundation for Traditional Studies, 1996], p. 200).

[22] Frithjof Schuon, "*Religio Perennis*," in *Light on the Ancient Worlds*, p. 143.

world's sapiential traditions. Its intent is to reclaim the sacred psychology that was known at all times and places before the emergence of the modern world. The theme is organized under three essential rubrics: "I. Critique," encompasses the core challenges and limitations that modern psychology in all of its schools and "forces" faces; "II. *Theoria*" provides further contemplations on the principial understanding of what is meant by psychology, or the "science of the soul," when contextualized within the integral metaphysics of the perennial philosophy; "III. *Praxis*" presents the direct application of the plenary principles, not only for psychological health and well-being, but in its often forgotten primary function: the facilitation of self-realization *in divinis*, in order to know what it means to be truly human. This after all is the *raison d'être* for psychology in the first place.

Samuel Bendeck Sotillos

I
CRITIQUE

The Psychological Imposture

Frithjof Schuon

What we term "psychologism" is the tendency to reduce everything to psychological factors and to call into question not only what is intellectual or spiritual—the first being related to truth and the second to life in and by truth—but also the human intelligence as such, and hence its capacity for adequation and, quite evidently, its inward boundlessness or its transcendence. The same belittling and truly subversive tendency has invaded all the domains that "scientism" claims to embrace, but its most acute expression is incontestably to be found in psychoanalysis. As is always the case with profane ideologies, psychoanalysis is at once an endpoint and a cause, like materialism and evolutionism, of which it is finally a logical and fatal ramification and a natural ally.

Psychoanalysis is doubly deserving of being termed an imposture, firstly because it pretends to have discovered facts which have always been known and could never not have been so, and secondly—and chiefly—because it arrogates to itself functions that in reality are spiritual, and thus, for all practical purposes, takes on the role of a religion. What is called "examination of conscience", or by the Muslims, "the science of thoughts" (*'ilm al-khawātir*), or, by the Hindus, "investigation" (*vichara*)—with somewhat different nuances in each case—is nothing other than an objective analysis of the proximate and remote causes of our ways of acting and reacting that we repeat automatically without being aware of their real motives, or without our discerning the real character of those motives. It may happen that a man habitually, and blindly, commits the same errors in the same circumstances, because he carries within himself, in his subconscious, errors founded on self-regard or traumas. Now to be healed, he must detect these complexes and translate them into clear formulas; he must therefore become conscious of subconscious errors and neutralize them by means of contrary affirmations; if he succeeds, his virtues will be all the more lucid. It is in this sense that Lao Tzu said: "To be aware of an illness is no longer to have it"; and the Law of Manu says: "There is no lustral water like unto knowledge", that is, like unto objectification by the intelligence.

What is new in psychoanalysis, and what gives it its sinister originality, is its determination to ascribe trivial causes for every reflex and every disposition of the soul and to exclude spiritual factors, whence its well-known tendency to see health in what is banal and vulgar, and neurosis in what is noble and profound. Man cannot escape in this world from trials and temptations; his soul is therefore inevitably marked by some sort of turmoil, unless it be of an angelic serenity—which occurs in highly religious surroundings—or, on the contrary, unless it be of an unshakable inertia, which occurs everywhere. But psychoanalysis, instead of allowing man to make the best of his natural, and in a sense providential, disequilibrium—and this best is whatever is beneficial for his ultimate fate—tends on the contrary to bring him back to an amorphous equilibrium, much as if one wished to spare a young bird the agonies of apprenticeship by clipping its wings. Analogically speaking, if a man is distressed by a flood and seeks a way to escape from it, psychoanalysis will dissolve the distress and let the patient drown; or again, instead of abolishing sin, it abolishes the sense of guilt, thus allowing the patient to go serenely to hell. This is not to say that a psychoanalyst might not occasionally discover and dissolve a dangerous complex without at the same time ruining the patient; but what matters here is the principle whereby the perils and errors involved infinitely outweigh whatever dubious advantages and fragmentary truths there may be.

As a result, for the average psychoanalyst a complex is bad because it is a complex; he refuses to see that there are complexes that do honor to man or that are natural to him by virtue of his deiformity, and consequently that there are disequilibriums that are necessary, and that can only be resolved from above ourselves and not from below.[1] There is another error that is fundamentally the same: this is to consider an equilibrium as being something good because it is an equilibrium, as if there were not equilibriums consisting of insensitivity or of perversion. Our human state itself is a disequilibrium, since we are existentially suspended between earthly contingencies and the summons of the Absolute innate to our nature; getting rid of a psychic knot is not the whole question, one must also know how and why it should be gotten rid of. We are not amorphous substances, we are movements that are in principle ascensional; our happiness must be proportioned to our total nature, on pain of lowering us to animality, for a happiness without God is precisely what man cannot withstand without becoming lost. And that is why a physician of the soul must be a *pontifex*, and thus a spiritual master in the proper and traditional sense of the word; a profane professional has neither the capacity nor, consequently, the right to interfere with the soul beyond such elementary difficulties as simple common sense can resolve.

The spiritual and social crime of psychoanalysis therefore is its usurpation of the place of religion or of the wisdom that is the wisdom of God, and the eliminating from its procedures all considerations regarding our ultimate destiny; it is as if, being unable to fight against God, one were to attack the human soul which belongs to Him and is destined for Him, by debasing the divine image instead of its Prototype. Like every solution that avoids the supernatural, psychoanalysis replaces in its own way what it abolishes: the void psychoanalysis produces by its intentional or unintentional destructions inflates it, and condemns it to postulate a false infinite or to function as a pseudo-religion.

In order to grow, psychoanalysis needed a favorable soil, not only from the point of view of ideas, but also from that of psychological phenomena: this means that Europeans, who have always been cerebral, have become infinitely more so in the last two centuries roughly speaking; now, this concentration of the entire intelligence in the head is something excessive and abnormal, and the hypertrophic developments accruing from this do not constitute a superiority, despite their efficacy in certain domains.

Normally intelligence ought to reside, not in the mind alone, but also in the heart, and it should also be spread throughout the body, as is especially the case with men who are termed "primitive" but who are undeniably superior in certain respects to the ultra-civilized; be that as it may, the point we wish to make is that psychoanalysis is to a great extent the result of a mental disequilibrium that prevails more or less generally in a world in which the machine dictates to man the rhythm of his life, and, what is more serious still, dictates even what his soul and his mind are to be.

* * *

[1] ". . . for it is profitable for thee that one of thy members should perish, and not that thy whole body should be cast into hell" (Matt. 5:29).

Psychoanalysis has made its more or less official entry into the world of "believers", which indeed is a sign of the times; this has led to the introduction into so-called "spirituality" of a method totally incompatible with human dignity, and at the same time one that stands strangely in contradiction with the pretension of being "adult" and "emancipated". People act as demigods and at the same time deem themselves to be irresponsible; for the slightest depression, caused either by too hectic an ambience, or by a manner of life too far contrary to good sense, people run to the psychiatrist, whose work consists then in instilling into them some false optimism or in recommending some "liberating" sin. Nobody seems to have even an inkling of the fact that there is but one equilibrium, namely that which fixes us in our real center and in God.

One of the most odious effects of the adoption of the psychoanalytical approach by "believers" is how the cult of the Holy Virgin has fallen into disfavor; only a barbarous mentality that wants to be "adult" at all costs and that no longer believes in anything but the trivial could be embarrassed by this cult. The answer to the reproach of "gynecolatry" or of the "Oedipus complex" is that, like every other psychoanalytical argument, it misses the point; for the real question is not what the psychological conditioning of an attitude may be but, on the contrary, what its results are. When for instance one is told that someone has chosen metaphysics as a means of "escapism" or "sublimation" and done so owing to an "inferiority complex" or a "repression", all this is of no importance whatsoever, for blessed be the complex that is the occasional cause of an acceptance of the true and the good! But there is also this: the moderns, tired as they are of the artificial comforts which their culture and their religiosity is laden with since the baroque period, displace their aversion—as is their habit—to the very notion of comfort, and thus shut themselves off, either from an entire spiritual dimension, if they are "believers", or even from all genuine humanity, as is shown by a kind of infantile cult of grossness and cacophony.

And besides, it is not enough to ask what the value of a particular devotion is in the consciousness of this or that soul, one must also ask what is to replace it; for the space of a devotion suppressed never remains empty.

*   *   *

"Know thyself" (Hellenism) says Tradition, and also "He who knows his own soul knows his Lord" (Islam). The traditional model of what psychoanalysis ought to be, or claims to be, is the science of virtues and vices; the fundamental virtue is sincerity and it coincides with humility; he who plunges the probe of truth and rectitude into his soul ends by detecting the subtlest knots of the unconscious. It is useless to seek to heal the soul without healing the mind: what matters then is first to clear the intelligence of the errors perverting it, and thus create a foundation in view of the soul's return to equilibrium; not to just any equilibrium, but to the equilibrium of which the soul bears within itself the principle.

For Saint Bernard the passionate soul is a "contemptible thing", and Meister Eckhart enjoins us to "hate" it. This means that the great remedy for all our inward miseries is objectivity towards ourselves; now the source, or starting point, of this objectivity is situated above ourselves, in God. That which is in God is likewise mirrored in our own transpersonal center which is the pure Intellect; in other words, the Truth that saves us is part of our inmost and realest substance. Error, or impiety, is the refusal to be what one is.

Translated by Mark Perry

5

The Confusion of the Psychic and the Spiritual

René Guénon

The account given above,[1] dealing with some of the psychological explanations that have been applied to traditional doctrines, covers only a particular case of a confusion that is very widespread in the modern world, namely, the confusion of the psychic and the spiritual domains. Even when it is not carried to such a point as to produce a subversion like that of psychoanalysis, this confusion assimilates the spiritual to all that is most inferior in the psychic order; it is therefore extremely serious in every case. In a sense it follows as a natural result of the fact that Westerners have for a very long time past no longer known how to distinguish the "soul" from the "spirit" (Cartesian dualism being to a great extent responsible for this, merging as it does into one and the same category everything that is not the body, and designating this one vague and ill-defined category indifferently by either name); and the confusion never ceases to be apparent even in current language: the word "spirits" is popularly used for psychic entities that are anything but "spiritual", and the very name "spiritualism" is derived from that usage; this mistake, together with another consisting in using the word "spirit" for something that is really only mental, will be enough by way of example for the present. It is all too easy to see the gravity of the consequences of any such state of affairs: anyone who propagates this confusion, whether intentionally or otherwise and especially under present conditions, is setting beings on the road to getting irremediably lost in the chaos of the "intermediary world", and thereby, though often unconsciously, playing the game of the "satanic" forces that rule over what has been called the "counter-initiation".

It is important at this point to be very precise if misunderstanding is to be avoided: it cannot be said that a particular development of the possibilities of a being, even in the comparatively low order represented by the psychic domain, is essentially "malefic" in itself; but it is necessary not to forget that this domain is above all that of illusions, and it is also necessary to know how to situate each thing in the place to which it normally belongs; in short, everything depends on the use made of any such development; the first thing to be considered is therefore whether it is taken as an end in itself, or on the other hand as a mere means for the attainment of a goal of a superior order. Anything whatever can in fact serve, according to the circumstances of each case, as an opportunity or "support" to one who has entered upon the way that is to lead him toward a spiritual "realization"; this is particularly true at the start, because of the diversity of individual natures, which exercises its maximum influence at that point, but it is still true to a certain extent for so long as the limits of the individuality have not been completely left behind. But on the other hand, anything whatever can just as well be an obstacle as a "support", if the being does not pass beyond it but allows itself to be deluded and led astray by appearances of realization that have no inherent value and are only accidental and contingent results—if indeed they can justifiably be regarded as results from any point of view. The danger of going astray is always present for exactly as long as the being is within the order of individual possibilities; it is without question greatest wherever psychic possibilities are involved, and is naturally greater still when those possibilities are of a very inferior order.

---

[1] Editor's Note: The author is referring to the previous chapter, entitled "The Misdeeds of Psycho-Analysis," from his book *The Reign of Quantity and the Signs of the Times.*

The danger is certainly much less when possibilities confined to the corporeal and physiological order alone are involved, as they are in the case of the aforementioned error of some Westerners who take *Yoga*, or at least the little they know of its preparatory procedures, to be a sort of method of "physical culture"; in cases of that kind, almost the only risk incurred is that of obtaining, by "practices" accomplished ill-advisedly and without control, exactly the opposite result to that desired, and of ruining one's health while seeking to improve it. Such things have no interest here save as examples of a crude deviation in the employment of these "practices", for they are really designed for quite a different purpose, as remote as possible from the physiological domain, and natural repercussions occurring in that domain constitute but a mere "accident" not to be credited with the smallest importance. Nevertheless it must be added that these same "practices" can also have repercussions in the subtle modalities of the individual unsuspected by the ignorant person who undertakes them as he would a kind of "gymnastics", and this considerably augments their danger. In this way the door may be quite unwittingly opened to all sorts of influences (those to take advantage of it in the first place being of course always of the lowest quality), and the less suspicion the victim has of the existence of anything of the kind the less is he prepared against them, and still less is he able to discern their real nature; there is in any event nothing in all this that can claim to be "spiritual" in any sense.

The state of affairs is quite different in cases where there is a confusion of the psychic properly so called with the spiritual. This confusion moreover appears in two contrary forms: in the first, the spiritual is brought down to the level of the psychic, and this is what happens more particularly in the kind of psychological explanations already referred to; in the second, the psychic is on the other hand mistaken for the spiritual; of this the most popular example is spiritualism, though the other more complex forms of "neo-spiritualism" all proceed from the very same error. In either case it is clearly the spiritual that is misconceived; but the first case concerns those who simply deny it, at least in practice if not always explicitly, whereas the second concerns those who are subject to the delusion of a false spirituality; and it is this second case that is now more particularly in view. The reason why so many people allow themselves to be led astray by this delusion is fundamentally quite simple: some of them seek above all for imagined "powers", or broadly speaking and in one form or another, for the production of more or less extraordinary "phenomena"; others constrain themselves to "centralize" their consciousness on inferior "prolongations" of the human individuality, mistaking them for superior states simply because they are outside the limits within which the activities of the "average" man are generally enclosed, the limits in question being, in the state corresponding to the profane point of view of the present period, those of what is commonly called "ordinary life", into which no possibility of an extra-corporeal order can enter. Even within the latter group it is the lure of the "phenomenon", that is to say in the final analysis the "experimental" tendency in the modern spirit, which is most frequently at the root of the error; what these people are in fact trying to obtain is always results that are in some way "sensational", and they mistake such results for "realization"; but this again amounts to saying that everything belonging to the spiritual order escapes them completely, that they are unable even to conceive of anything of the kind, however remotely; and it would be very much better for them, since they are entirely lacking in spiritual "qualification", if they were content to remain enclosed in the commonplace and mediocre security of "ordinary life". Of course there can be no question of denying the reality as such of the "phenomena" concerned; in fact they can be said to be only too real, and for that reason all the more dangerous. What is now being formally contested is their value and their interest, particularly from the point of view of spiritual development, and the delusion itself concerns the very nature of spiritual development. Again, if no more than a mere waste of time and effort were involved, the harm would not after all be so very great, but generally speaking the being that becomes attached to such things soon becomes incapable of releasing itself from them or passing beyond them, and its deviation is then beyond remedy; the occurrence of cases of this kind is well known in all the Eastern traditions, where the individuals affected become mere producers of "phenomena" and will never attain the least degree of spirituality. But there is still something more, for a sort of "inverted" development can take place, not only conferring no useful advantage, but taking the being ever further away from spiritual "realization", until it is irretrievably astray in the inferior "prolongations" of its individuality recently mentioned, and through these it can only come into contact with the "infra-human". There is then no escape from its situation, or at least there is only one, and that is the total disintegration of the conscious being; such a disintegration is strictly equivalent in the case of the individual to final dissolution in the case of the totality of the manifested "cosmos".

For this reason, perhaps more than for any other, it is impossible to be too mistrustful of every appeal to the "subconscious", to "instinct", and to sub-rational "intuition", no less than to a more or less ill-defined "vital force"—in a word to all those vague and obscure things that tend to exalt the new philosophy and psychology, yet lead more or less directly to a contact with inferior states. There is therefore all the more reason to exercise extreme vigilance (for the enemy knows only too well how to take on the most insidious disguises) against anything that may lead the being to become "fused" or preferably and more accurately "confused" or even "dissolved" in a sort of "cosmic consciousness" that shuts out all "transcendence" and so also shuts out all effective spirituality. This is the ultimate consequence of all the anti-metaphysical errors known more especially in their philosophical aspect by such names as "pantheism", "immanentism", and "naturalism", all of which are closely interrelated, and many people would doubtless recoil before such a consequence if they could know what it is that they are really talking about. These things do indeed quite literally amount to an "inversion" of spirituality, to a substitution for it of what is truly its opposite, since they inevitably lead to its final loss, and this constitutes "satanism" properly so called. Whether it be conscious or unconscious in any particular case makes little difference to the result, for it must not be forgotten that the "unconscious satanism" of some people, who are more numerous than ever in this period in which disorder has spread into every domain, is really in the end no more than an instrument in the service of the "conscious satanism" of those who represent the "counter-initiation".

There has been occasion elsewhere to call attention to the initiatic symbolism of a "navigation" across the ocean (representing the psychic domain), which must be crossed while avoiding all its dangers in order to reach the goal;[2] but what is to be said of someone who flings himself into the ocean and has no aspiration but to drown himself in it? This is very precisely the significance of a so-called "fusion" with a "cosmic consciousness" that is really nothing but the confused and indistinct assemblage of all the psychic influences; and, whatever some people may imagine, these influences have absolutely nothing in common with spiritual influences, even if they may happen to imitate them to a certain extent in some of their outward manifestations (for in this domain "counterfeit" comes into play in all its fullness, and this is

---

[2] See René Guénon, *The King of the World* and *Spiritual Authority & Temporal Power*.

why the "phenomenal" manifestations so eagerly sought for never by themselves prove anything, for they can be very much the same in a saint as in a sorcerer). Those who make this fatal mistake either forget about or are unaware of the distinction between the "upper waters" and the "lower waters"; instead of raising themselves toward the "ocean above", they plunge into the abyss of the "ocean below"; instead of concentrating all their powers so as to direct them toward the formless world, which alone can be called "spiritual", they disperse them in the endlessly changeable and fugitive diversity of the forms of subtle manifestation (this diversity corresponding as nearly as possible to the Bergsonian conception of "reality") with no suspicion that they are mistaking for a fullness of "life" something that is in truth the realm of death and of a dissolution without hope of return.

Translated by Lord Northbourne

Modern Psychology

Titus Burckhardt

"The object of psychology is the psychic; unfortunately it is also its subject." Thus wrote a famous psychologist of our time.[1] According to this opinion, every psychological judgment inevitably participates in the essentially subjective, not to say passionate and tendentious, nature of its object; for, according to this logic, no one understands the soul except by means of his own soul, and the latter, for the psychologist, is, precisely, purely psychic, and nothing else. Thus no psychologist, whatever be his claim to objectivity, escapes this dilemma, and the more categorical and general his affirmations in this realm are, the more they are suspect; such is the verdict that modern psychology pronounces in its own cause, when it is being sincere towards itself. But whether it be sincere or not, the relativism expressed in the words just quoted is always inherent in it. This relativism is also a kind of Prometheanism that would make of the psychic element the ultimate reality of man. It is the root of the numerous divergences within this discipline, and it dominates it to the point of contaminating everything that it touches: history, philosophy, art, and religion; all of them become psychological at its touch, and thereby also subjective, and thus devoid of objective and immutable certainties.[2]

But all *a priori* relativism is inconsequential towards itself. Despite the admitted precariousness of its point of view, modern psychology behaves like every other science: it passes judgments and believes in their validity, and in this connection it leans unwittingly, and without admitting it, on an innate certainty: indeed, if we can observe that the psychic is "subjective", in the sense of being dominated by a certain egocentric bias that imposes on it certain limits, or by a particular "coloring", this is because there is something in us which is not subject to these limits and tendencies, but which transcends them and in principle dominates them. This something is the intellect, and it is the intellect that normally provides us with the criteria which alone can shed light on the fluctuating and uncertain world of the *psyché*; this is obvious, but it nevertheless remains totally outside modern scientific and philosophical thinking.

It is important above all not to confuse intellect and reason: the latter is indeed the mental reflection of the transcendent intellect, but in practice it is only what one makes of it, by which we mean that, in the case of the modern sciences, its functioning is limited by the empirical method itself; at the level of the latter, reason is not so much a source of truth as a principle of coherence. For modern psychology it is even less than that, for if scientific rationalism lends a relatively stable framework to one's observation of the physical world, it reveals itself as en-

---

[1] C. G. Jung, *Psychology and Religion* (New Haven, CT: Yale University Press, 1938), p. 62.

[2] "I can find no reason to be surprised at seeing psychology exchange visits with philosophy, for is not the act of thinking, the foundation of all philosophy, a psychic activity which, as such, directly concerns psychology? Must not psychology embrace the soul in its total extension, which includes philosophy, theology, and countless other things? In the face of all the richly diversified religions, there rise up, as the supreme instance perhaps of truth or error, the immutable data of the human soul" (C. G. Jung, *L'Homme à la Découverte de son Ame*) [Paris, 1962], p. 238). This amounts to replacing truth by psychology; it is totally forgotten that there are no "immutable data" outside of that which is immutable by its own nature, namely, the intellect. In any case, if the "act of thinking" is no more than a "psychic activity", by what right does psychology set itself up as the "supreme instance", since it too is but one "psychic activity" amongst others?

tirely insufficient when it comes to describing the world of the soul; for surface psychic movements, those whose causes and aims are situated on the plane of current experience, can hardly be translated into rational terms. The whole chaos of lower—and mostly unconscious—psychic possibilities escapes both rationality and what transcends rationality, and this means that both the major part of the psychic world and the metaphysical realm will appear "irrational" according to this way of thinking. Hence a certain tendency, inherent in modern psychology, to relativize reason itself, a tendency that is self-contradictory, since psychology cannot dispense with rational methods. Psychology finds itself confronted with a domain which on all sides overflows the horizon of a science founded on empiricism and Cartesianism.

For this reason, the majority of modern psychologists ensconce themselves in a sort of pragmatism; it is in "committed" experience, together with a coldly clinical attitude, that they see some guarantee of "objectivity". In point of fact, the movements of the soul cannot be studied from the outside, as in the case of corporeal phenomena; to know what they mean, they have in a sense to be lived, and this involves the subject of the observer, as was justly pointed out by the psychologist at the outset. As for the mental faculty that "controls" the experiment, what is this but a more or less arbitrary "common sense", one inevitably colored by preconceived ideas? Thus the would-be objectivity of the psychic attitude changes nothing in regard to the uncertain nature of the experiment, and so, in the absence of a principle that is both inward and immutable, one returns to the dilemma of the psychic striving to grasp the psychic.

The soul, like every other domain of reality, can only be truly known by what transcends it. Moreover, this is spontaneously and implicitly admitted in people's recognition of the moral principle of justice, which demands that men should overcome their individual subjectivity. Now we could not overcome it, if the intelligence, which guides our will, were itself nothing but a psychic reality; and intelligence would not transcend the *psyché* if, in its essence, it did not transcend the plane of phenomena, both inward and outward. This observation suffices to prove the necessity and the existence of a psychology deriving in a sense from above and not claiming *a priori* an empirical character. But although this order of things is inscribed in our very nature, it will never be recognized by modern psychology; despite its own reactions against the rationalism of yesterday, it is no closer to metaphysics than any other empirical science—indeed quite the contrary, since its perspective, which assimilates the suprarational to the irrational, predisposes it to the worst of errors.

What modern psychology lacks entirely is criteria enabling it to situate the aspects or tendencies of the soul in their cosmic context. In traditional psychology, these criteria are provided according to two principal "dimensions": on the one hand, according to a cosmology that "situates" the soul and its modalities in the hierarchy of states of existence, and, on the other hand, according to a morality directed toward a spiritual end. The latter may provisionally espouse the individual horizon; it nonetheless keeps in view the universal principles attaching the soul to an order more vast than itself. Cosmology in a sense circumscribes the soul; spiritual morality sounds its depths. For just as a current of water reveals its force and direction only when it breaks against an object that resists it, so the soul can show its tendencies and fluctuations only in relation to an immutable principle; whoever wishes to know the nature of the *psyché* must resist it, and one truly resists it only when one places oneself at a point which corresponds, if not effectively then at least virtually or symbolically, to the Divine Self, or to the intellect which is like a ray that emanates from the latter.

Thus traditional psychology possesses both an impersonal and "static" dimension (namely, cosmology), and a personal and "operative" dimension (namely, morality or the science of the virtues), and it is necessarily so, because genuine knowledge of the soul results from knowledge of oneself. He who, by the eye of his essence, is able to "objectivize" his own psychic form, by that very fact knows all the possibilities of the psychic or subtle world; and this intellectual "vision" is both the outcome and, if need be, the guarantor of every sacred science of the soul.

For the majority of modern psychologists, traditional morality—which they readily confuse with a purely social or conventional morality—is nothing but a kind of psychic dam, useful on occasion but more often a hindrance or even harmful for the "normal" development of the individual. This opinion is propagated especially by Freudian psychoanalysis, which became widely applied in some countries, where it has practically usurped the function that elsewhere belongs to the sacrament of confession: the psychiatrist replaces the priest, and the bursting of complexes that had previously been repressed takes the place of absolution. In ritual confession the priest is but the impersonal representative—necessarily discreet—of the Truth that judges and pardons; the penitent, by admitting his sins, in a sense "objectivizes" the psychic tendencies that these sins manifest. By repenting, he detaches himself from them, and by receiving sacramental absolution, his soul is virtually reintegrated in its primitive equilibrium and centered on its divine essence. In the case of Freudian psychoanalysis,[3] on the other hand, man lays bare his psychic entrails, not before God, but to his fellow. He does not distance himself from the chaotic and obscure depths of his soul, which the analyst unveils or stirs up, but on the contrary, he accepts them as his own, for he must say to himself: "This is what I am like in reality." And if he does not overcome, with the help of some salutary instinct, this kind of disillusionment from below, he will retain from it something like an intimate sullying; in most cases it will be his self-abandonment to collective mediocrity that for him will play the part of absolution, for it is easier to endure one's own degradation when it is shared with others. Whatever may be the occasional or partial usefulness of such an analysis in certain cases, the state described above is its more usual result, its premises being what they are.[4]

If the medicine of the traditional civilizations knows nothing analogous to modern psychotherapy, this is because the psychic cannot be treated by the psychic. The *psyché* is the realm of indefinite actions and reactions. By its own specific nature, it is essentially unstable and deceptive, so that it can be cured only by resorting to something situated "outside" or "above" it. In some cases one will act favorably upon it by re-establishing the humoral balance of the body, commonly upset by psychic affections;[5] in other cases it is only by the use of spiritual means, such as exorcism,[6] prayer, or a sojourn in holy places, that the soul can be restored to health.

Everyone is aware of the fact that modern psychology tries to explain psychologically the

[3] The use of the adjective is to make it clear that it is indeed the method of Freud that we are discussing here, for in our own day some forms of psychoanalysis are more neutral and less pernicious, a fact which, from our point of view, is in no wise a justification.

[4] René Guénon has observed that the principle whereby every psychoanalyst requires to be psychoanalyzed himself before being empowered to analyze others, raises the troublesome question as to who occupied the first place in the queue.

[5] Usually a vicious circle ensues, with the psychic imbalance engendering a physical intoxication, which in its turn causes the psychic imbalance to worsen.

[6] Cases of diabolical possession, such as manifestly call for the application of the rites of exorcism, seem to have become rarer nowadays, doubtless because demonic influences are no longer "compressed" by the dam of tradition, but are able to spread more or less everywhere in forms that are in a fashion "diluted".

spiritual means just mentioned. In its eyes, the effect of a rite is one thing, and its theological or mystical interpretation is another. The effect of a rite, arbitrarily limited to the psychic and subjective domain alone, is attributed to psychic dispositions of ancestral origin, which the form of the rite is supposed to actualize. There is no hint of the timeless and superhuman meaning inherent in the rite or symbol—as if the soul could cure itself through believing in the illusory projection of its own preoccupations, whether individual or collective. There is nothing, however, in this supposition that would trouble modern psychology, since it is ready to go much further than this, when it asserts, for example, that the fundamental forms of thought, the laws of logic, merely represent a residue of ancestral habits.[7] This path is one that leads to the outright denial of intelligence and to its replacement by biological fatalities, if indeed psychology can go that far without encompassing its own ruin.

In order to be able to "situate" the soul in relation to other cosmic realities or realms, one must refer to the cosmological scheme that represents the degrees of existence in the form of concentric circles or spheres. This scheme, which makes symbolical use of the geocentric conception of the visible universe, symbolically identifies the corporeal world with our terrestrial surroundings; around this center extends the sphere—or spheres—of the subtle or psychic world, surrounded in turn by the sphere of the world of pure Spirit. This representation is naturally limited by its own spatial character, but it nevertheless expresses very well the relationship that exists between these various states. Each of the spheres, considered in itself, presents itself as a complete and perfectly homogeneous whole, whereas from the "point of view" of the sphere immediately above, it is but a content thereof. Thus the corporeal world, envisaged at its own level, does not know the subtle world, just as the latter does not know the supraformal world, precisely because it encloses only that which has a form. Furthermore, each of these worlds is known and dominated by that which exceeds and surrounds it. It is from the immutable and formless background of the Spirit that the subtle realities become detached as forms, and it is the soul which, through its sensory faculties, knows the corporeal.

This double relationship of things, which *a priori* is hidden from our individual vision, can be grasped in all its reality when one considers the very nature of sensible perception. On the one hand, this truly reaches the corporeal world, and no philosophical artifice will be able to convince us of the contrary; on the other hand, there is no doubt that all we perceive of the world are but those "images" of it that our mental faculty is able to keep hold of, and in this respect the whole fabric of impressions, memories, and anticipations—in short, everything that for us constitutes the sensible continuity and logical coherence of the world—is of a psychic or subtle nature. It is in vain that one will try to know what the world is "outside" this subtle continuity, since this "outside" does not exist: surrounded as it is by the subtle state, the corporeal world is but a content thereof, even though it appears, in the mirror of this state itself, as a materially autonomous order.[8]

It is obviously not the individual soul, but the entire subtle state that contains the physical world. The logical coherence of the latter presupposes the unity of the former, and this is manifested indirectly by the fact that the multiple individual visions of the sensible world, frag-

---

[7] They will say, for example, that logic is merely an expression of the physiological structure of our brain, and forget that, were it so, this statement would also be an expression of this same physiological fatality.

[8] Nothing is more absurd than attempts to explain the perception of the material world in material terms.

mentary though they be, substantially coincide and are integrated in one continuous whole. The individual soul participates in this unity both by the structure of its cognitive faculties, which is in conformity with the cosmic order, and also by its nature as subject, containing the physical world in its own way; in other words, the physical world is a "world" only in relation to the individual subject, by virtue of the cleaving of consciousness into object and subject, a cleaving that results precisely from the "egoic" polarization of the soul. By this same polarization, the soul is distinguished from the totality of the subtle state—the "total" or "universal soul" of Plotinus—without, however, being separated from it substantially. For if it were separated from it, our vision of the world would not be adequate to reality; but in fact it is so, in spite of the limitations and the relativity of all perception.

It is true that we ordinarily perceive only a fragment of the subtle world—the fragment that we "are", and that constitutes our "myself"—whereas the sensible world reveals itself to us in its macrocosmic continuity, as a whole that seems to include us. This is because the subtle world is the very field of individuation; in reality, we are plunged in the ocean of the subtle world as fishes are in water, and like them, we do not see that which constitutes our own element.

As for the opposition between the "inward" psychic world and the "outward" corporeal world, this is actualized only in relation to, and in function of, the latter. In itself, the subtle world is neither "inward" nor "outward"; it is at most "non-outward", whereas the corporeal world is outward as such, which furthermore proves that it does not enjoy an autonomous existence.

The corporeal state and the psychic state together constitute formal existence; in its total extension, the subtle state is none other than formal existence, but one calls it "subtle" inasmuch as it escapes the laws of corporeity. According to one of the most ancient and most natural symbolisms, the subtle state may be compared to the atmosphere surrounding the earth which pervades all porous bodies and is the vehicle of life.

A phenomenon can only be truly understood through its relations, both "horizontal" and "vertical", with total Reality. This truth applies particularly, and in a certain sense practically, to psychic phenomena. The same psychic "event" can simultaneously be the response to a sensory impulsion, the manifestation of a wish, the consequence of a previous action, the trace of the typical and ancestral form of the individual, the expression of his genius, and the reflection of a supra-individual reality. It is legitimate to consider the psychic phenomenon in question under one or other of these aspects, but it would be unwarranted to seek to explain the movements and purposes of the soul by one—or even by several—of these aspects exclusively. In this connection let us quote the words of a therapist who is aware of the limitations of contemporary psychology:

> There is an ancient Hindu maxim whose truth is incontestable: "What a man thinks, that he becomes". If one steadfastly thinks of good deeds, one will end by becoming a good man; if one always thinks of weakness, one will become weak; if one thinks of how to develop one's strength (bodily or mental), one will become strong. Similarly, if for years one is engaged almost daily in stirring up Hades,[9] in

---

[9] An allusion to the words of Virgil: *Flectere si nequeo superos, Acheronta movebo* ("If I cannot bend the Heavens, I shall stir up hell"), which Freud quoted at the beginning of his *Interpretation of Dreams*.

explaining systematically the higher in terms of the lower, and at the same time ignoring everything in man's cultural history which, despite lamentable errors and misdeeds, has been regarded as worthwhile, one can scarcely avoid the risk of losing all discernment, of leveling down the imagination (a source of our life), and of severely reducing one's mental horizon.[10]

Ordinary consciousness illuminates only a restricted portion of the individual soul, and the latter represents only a tiny part of the psychic world. Nevertheless, the soul is not cut off from the rest of this world; its situation is not that of a body rigorously limited by its own extension and separated from other bodies. What distinguishes the soul from the rest of the vast subtle world is uniquely its own particular tendencies, which define it—if one may employ a simplified image—as a spatial direction defines the ray of light that follows it. By these very tendencies, the soul is in communion with all the cosmic possibilities of analogous tendencies or qualities; it assimilates them and is assimilated by them. For this reason, the science of cosmic tendencies—the *gunas* of Hindu cosmology—is fundamental for the knowledge of the soul. In this connection, it is not the outward context of a psychic phenomenon—the accidental occasion for its manifestation—that matters essentially, but its connection with *sattva*, *rajas*, or *tamas*—the "upward", "expansive", and "downward" tendencies—which confers on it its rank in the hierarchy of inward values.

Since the motives of the soul are perceptible only through the forms that manifest them, it is on these forms or manifestations that a psychological assessment must needs be founded. Now, the part played by the *gunas* in any form whatsoever can be measured only in a purely qualitative manner, by means of precise and decisive—but in no wise quantitative—criteria, such as are entirely lacking in the wholly profane psychology of our time.

There are some psychic "events" whose repercussions traverse all the degrees of the subtle world "vertically", since they touch on the essences; others—these are ordinary psychic movements—only obey the "horizontal" coming and going of the *psyché*; and finally, there are those that come from the subhuman depths. The first mentioned are not capable of being expressed entirely—they comprise an element of mystery—and yet the forms which they may from time to time evoke in the imagination are clear and precise, like those that characterize authentic sacred arts. The last mentioned, namely demonic "inspirations", are unintelligible in their very forms; they "ape" the genuinely mysterious by the nebulous, obscure, and equivocal character of their formal manifestations; examples of this are readily to be found in contemporary art.

When studying the formal manifestation of the soul, one must, however, not forget that man's psycho-physical organism can display strange caesuras or discontinuities. Thus, for instance, in the case of the somewhat "anarchical" category of contemplatives known as "fools of God", the spiritual states do not manifest themselves harmoniously and normally and do not make use of the reason; inversely, an intrinsically pathological state—and as such dominated by infrahuman and chaotic tendencies—may incidentally and by accident comprise openings onto supra-terrestrial realities; this is but saying that the human soul is of an inexhaustible complexity.

---

[10] Hans Jacob, *Western Psychology and Hindu Sadhana* (London: Allen & Unwin, 1961). The author of this work is a former disciple of Jung, who later discovered the doctrine and method—immeasurably greater—of the Hindu *sadhana*, which enabled him to subject Western psychology to a just criticism.

Viewed as a whole, the subtle world is incomparably vaster and more varied than the corporeal world. Dante expresses this by making the entire hierarchy of planetary spheres correspond to the subtle world, whereas he makes only the terrestrial domain correspond to the corporeal world. The subterranean position of the hells, in his system, merely indicates that the states in question are situated below the normal human state; in reality, they are also part of the subtle state, and this is why some medieval cosmologists place the hells symbolically between heaven and earth.[11]

Experience of the subtle world is subjective—except in the case of certain sciences quite unknown to the moderns—because consciousness, in identifying itself with subtle forms, is affected by their tendencies, just as a ray of light is turned from its course by the form of a wave that it happens to traverse. The subtle world is made up of forms; in other words, it comprises diversity and contrast; but these forms do not possess, in themselves or outside of their projection in the sensible imagination,[12] spatial and defined contours as in the case of corporeal forms. They are entirely active or, to be more exact, dynamic, pure activity belonging only to the essential "forms" or archetypes that are to be found in the pure Spirit. Now the ego or individual soul is itself one of the forms of the subtle world, and the consciousness that espouses this form is necessarily dynamic and exclusive; it realizes other subtle forms only insofar as these become modalities of its own egoic form.

Thus it is that in the dream state individual consciousness, even though reabsorbed into the subtle world, nonetheless remains turned back on itself; all the forms that it experiences in this state present themselves as simple prolongations of the individual subject, or at least they appear so in retrospect and inasmuch as they verge on the waking state. For in itself, and despite this subjectivism, the consciousness of the dreamer is obviously not impermeable to influences coming from the most diverse "regions" of the subtle world, as is proved, for example, by premonitory or telepathic dreams, which many people have experienced.[13] Indeed, while the imagery of a dream is woven from the very "substance" of the subject—a "substance" that is none other than the progressive actualization of his own psychic form—it nonetheless manifests, incidentally and to different degrees, realities of a cosmic order.

The content of a dream can be considered in many different ways. If one analyzes the *materia* of which it is composed one will find that it is constituted by all sorts of memories, and in this respect the current psychological explanation, which makes the dream the expression of subconscious residues, is largely right. It is not, however, excluded that a dream may also comprise "matters" that in no wise proceed from the personal experience of the dreamer and that are like traces of a psychic transfusion from one individual to another. There is also the economy of the dream, and in this connection we can quote the following description by C. G. Jung, which is exact despite the radically false theses of the author:

> The dream, deriving from the activity of the unconscious, gives a representation
> of the contents that slumber there; not of all the contents that figure in it, but only

---

[11] In Islam, it is said that the throne of the devil is located between earth and heaven, a doctrine which also makes clear the temptations to which those who follow the "vertical" path are exposed.

[12] If some masters have compared the subtle world to the imagination, it is the imaginative activity, and not the images produced by the imagination, that they had in view.

[13] Empirical psychology no longer dares to deny this phenomenon.

of certain of them which, by way of association, are actualized, crystallized, and selected, in correlation with the momentary state of consciousness.[14]

As for the hermeneutics of dreams, this eludes modern psychology in spite of the latter's efforts in this direction, because one cannot validly interpret images reflected by the soul without knowing to which level of reality they refer.

The images one retains on waking from a dream generally represent only a shadow of the psychic forms experienced in the dream state itself. On passing into the waking state, a sort of decantation occurs—one can be aware of this—and something of the reality inherent in the dream evaporates more or less rapidly. There exists, nevertheless, a certain category of dreams, well-known to traditional oneirocrisy, the memory of which persists with an incisive clarity, and this can happen even if the profound content of these dreams appears to conceal itself. Such dreams, which mostly occur at dawn and continue until waking, are accompanied by an irrefutable feeling of objectivity; otherwise put, they comprise a more than merely mental certainty. But what characterizes them above all, and independently of their moral influence on the dreamer, is the high quality of their forms, disengaged from every turbid or chaotic residue. These are the dreams that come from the Angel; in other words, from the Essence that connects the soul to the supra-formal states of the being.

Since there are dreams of divine or angelic inspiration, their opposite must also exist, and these are dreams of satanic impulsion, containing palpable caricatures of sacred forms. The sensation accompanying them is not one of cool and serene lucidity, but of obsession and vertigo; it is the attraction of an abyss. The infernal influences sometimes ride the wave of a natural passion, which opens the way for them, so to speak. They are, however, distinguishable from the elementary character of passion by their prideful and negative tendency, accompanied either by bitterness or else by sadness. As Pascal said: "He who tries to play the angel will play the beast", and indeed nothing is so apt to provoke caricatures, both in dreams and out of them, as the unconsciously pretentious attitude of the man who mixes God with his own highly particularized ego—the classical cause of many of the psychoses studied by post-Freudian psychologism.[15]

It was starting from the analysis of dreams that C. G. Jung developed his famous theory about the "collective unconscious". His observation of the fact that a certain category of dream images could not be explained simply on the basis of their being residues of individual experiences led Jung to distinguish, within the unconscious domain whence dreams are fed, between a "personal" zone whose contents represent basically the other face of individual psychic life, and a "collective" zone made up of latent psychic dispositions of an impersonal character, such as never offer themselves to direct observation, but manifest themselves indirectly through "symbolic" dreams and "irrational" impulses. At first sight, this theory has nothing extravagant about it, except its use of the term "irrational" in connection with symbolism. It is easy to understand that the individual consciousness centered on the empirical ego leaves on the margin or even outside itself everything which, in the psychic order, is not effectively attached to that center, just as a light projected in a given direction decreases towards the surrounding

---

[14] *L'Homme à la Découverte de son Ame*, p. 205.

[15] In a general way, contemporary psychology delves into the observation of pathological cases, and views the soul only through this clinical perspective.

darkness. But this is not how Jung understands the matter. For him, the non-personal zone of the soul is unconscious as such; in other words, its contents can never become the direct object of the intelligence, whatever be its modality or however great its extension.

> Just as the human body displays a common anatomy, independently of racial differences, so also the *psyché* possesses, beyond all cultural and mental differences, a common *substratum*, which I have named the collective unconscious. This unconscious *psyché*, which is common to all men, is not made up of contents capable of becoming conscious, but solely of latent dispositions giving rise to certain reactions that are always identical.[16]

And the author goes on to insinuate that it is here a question of ancestral structures that have their origin in the physical order:

> The fact that this collective unconscious exists is simply the psychic expression of the identity of cerebral structures beyond all racial differences. . . . The different lines of psychic evolution start out from one and the same trunk, whose roots plunge through all the ages. It is here that the psychic parallel with the animal is situated.[17]

One notices the plainly Darwinian turn of this thesis, the disastrous consequences of which show themselves in the following passage: "It is this that explains the analogy, indeed the identity, of mythological motives and of symbols as means of human communication in general."[18] Myths and symbols would thus be the expression of an ancestral psychic fund that brings man near to the animal! They have no intellectual or spiritual foundation, since

> from the purely psychological point of view, it is a question of common instincts of imagining and acting. All conscious imagination and action have evolved on the basis of these unconscious prototypes and remain permanently attached to them, and this is especially so when consciousness has not yet attained a very high degree of lucidity, in other words, as long as it is still, in all its functions, more dependent on instinct than on conscious will, or more affective than rational.[19]

This quotation clearly indicates that, for Jung, the "collective unconscious" is situated "below", at the level of physiological instincts. It is important to bear this in mind, since the term "collective unconscious" in itself could carry a wider and in a fashion more spiritual meaning, as certain assimilations made by Jung seem to suggest, especially his use—or rather his usurpation—of the term "archetype" to signify the latent, and as such inaccessible, contents of the "collective unconscious". For though the archetypes do not belong to the psychic realm, but

---

[16] C. G. Jung, Introduction, *The Secret of the Golden Flower* (New York, 1931), Introduction.

[17] Ibid.

[18] Ibid.

[19] Ibid.

to the world of pure Spirit, they are nevertheless reflected at the psychic level—as virtualities of images in the first place—before becoming crystallized, according to the circumstances, in images properly so-called, so that a certain psychological application of the term "archetype" could at a pinch be justified. But Jung defines the "archetype" as an "innate complex"[20] and describes its action on the soul thus: "Possession by an archetype makes of a man a purely collective personage, a kind of mask, under which human nature can no longer develop, but degenerates progressively."[21] As if an archetype, which is an immediate and supra-formal determination of Being—and non-limitative by this very fact—could in some way cast a spell on and vampirize the soul! What is really in question in the more or less pathological case envisaged by Jung? Simply a dissociation of the possibilities inherent in the subtle form of a man, a form that includes multiple aspects, each of which has something unique and irreplaceable about it. In every non-degenerate human individual there is to be found in potency a man and a woman, a father and a mother, a child and an old man, as well as various qualities or "dignities" inseparable from the original and ontological position of man, such as priestly and royal qualities, those of a creative craftsman, of a servant, and so forth. Normally all these possibilities complete one another; here there is no irrational fund of the soul, for the coexistence of these diverse possibilities or aspects of the human form is perfectly intelligible in itself and can be hidden only from the eyes of a mentality or civilization that has become one-sided and false. Any genius-like development of one of these multiple possibilities or dispositions inherent in the human soul requires, moreover, the integration of the complementary possibilities; the true man of genius is a balanced being, for where there is no balance there is no greatness either. The opposite of such a development is a barren and pathological exaggeration of one of the soul's possibilities at the expense of the others, leading to that kind of moral caricature compared by Jung to a mask; and let it be added that it is the carnivalesque mask one must think of here, and not the sacred mask which, for its part, does indeed express a true archetype and therefore a possibility that does not bewitch the soul but on the contrary liberates it.[22]

Psychic dissociation always produces a fixation as well as a tearing apart between opposing poles, and this is rendered possible only by the clouding over of that which, in the soul, corresponds to the archetype. At the antipodes of this imbalance productive of hypertrophies, perfect virility, for example, in no wise excludes femininity, but on the contrary includes and adapts it, and the inverse is also true. Similarly, the genuine archetypes, which are not situated at the psychic level, do not mutually exclude but comprise and imply one another. According to the Platonic and hallowed meaning of the term, the archetypes are the source of being and knowledge and not, as Jung conceives them, unconscious dispositions to act and imagine. The fact that the archetypes cannot be grasped by discursive thought has no connection with the irrational and obscure character of the supposed "collective unconscious", whose contents are said to be known only indirectly through their "eruptions" on the surface. There is not only discursive thought, there is also intellectual intuition, and this attains to the archetypes from the starting-point of their symbols.

---

[20] See *L'Homme à la Découverte de son Ame*, p. 311.

[21] See *Two Essays on Analytical Psychology* (New York: Pantheon, 1966), p. 234.

[22] See the chapter "The Sacred Mask" in *Mirror of the Intellect Essays on Traditional Science and Sacred Art*, trans. and ed. William Stoddart (Albany, NY: SUNY, 1987), pp. 149-155.

No doubt the theory according to which ancestral structures constitute the "collective unconscious" imposes itself on modern thought all the more easily in that it seems to be in agreement with the evolutionist explanation of the instinct of animals. According to this view, instinct is the expression of the heredity of a species, of an accumulation of analogous experiences down the ages. This is how they explain, for example, the fact that a flock of sheep hastily gathers together around the lambs the moment it perceives the shadow of a bird of prey, or that a kitten while playing already employs all the tricks of a hunter, or that birds know how to build their nests. In fact, it is enough to watch animals to see that their instinct has nothing of an automatism about it. The formation of such a mechanism by a purely cumulative—and consequently vague and problematical—process is highly improbable, to say the least. Instinct is a non-reflective modality of the intelligence; it is determined, not by a series of automatic reflexes, but by the "form"—the qualitative determination—of the species. This form is like a filter through which the universal intelligence is manifested. Nor must it be forgotten that the subtle form of a being is incomparably more complex than its bodily form. The same is also true for man: his intelligence too is determined by the subtle form of his species. This form, however, includes the reflective faculty, which allows of a singularization of the individual such as does not exist among the animals. Man alone is able to objectivize himself. He can say: "I am this or that." He alone possesses this two-edged faculty. Man, by virtue of his own central position in the cosmos, is able to transcend his specific norm; he can also betray it, and sink lower; *corruptio optimi pessima.*[23] A normal animal remains true to the form and genius of its species; if its intelligence is not reflective and objectifying, but in some sort existential, it is nonetheless spontaneous; it is assuredly a form of the universal intelligence even if it is not recognized as such by men who, from prejudice or ignorance, identify intelligence with discursive thought exclusively.

As for Jung's thesis that certain dreams, which cannot be explained by personal reminiscences and which seem to arise from an unconscious fund common to all men, contain motives and forms that are also to be found in myths and in traditional symbolism, the thing is possible in principle; not that there is in the soul a repertory of types inherited from distant ancestors and bearing witness to a primitive vision of the world, but because true symbols are always "actual" inasmuch as they express non-temporal realities. In fact, under certain conditions, the soul is able to take on the function of a mirror that reflects, in a purely passive and imaginative manner, universal truths contained in the intellect. Nevertheless, "inspirations" of this nature remain fairly rare; they depend on circumstances that are, so to speak, providential, as in the case of dreams communicating truths or announcing future events, to which allusion has previously been made. Moreover, symbolic dreams are not clothed in just any traditional "style"; their formal language is normally determined by the tradition or religion to which the individual is effectively or virtually attached, for there is nothing arbitrary in this domain.

Now, if one examines examples of supposedly symbolical dreams quoted by Jung and other psychologists of his school, one notices that in most cases it is a matter of false symbolism, of the kind commonly met with in pseudo-spiritual circles. The soul is not only a sacred mirror; more often it is a magic mirror that deceives the one who views himself in it. Jung should have known this, since he himself speaks of the tricks of the *anima*, indicating by this term the femi-

---

[23] Editor's Note: "The corruption of the best is corruption at its worst."

nine aspect of the soul; and some of his own experiences, as described in his memoirs,[24] should have told him that an investigator of the unconscious depths of the *psyché* exposes himself, not merely to the wiles of the egocentric soul, but also to psychic influences coming from elsewhere, from unknown beings and entities, especially when the methods of analysis used derive from hypnosis or mediumship. In this context must be placed certain designs executed by sick patients of Jung and which the latter tries to palm off as genuine *mandalas*.[25]

Over and above all this, there exists a symbolism, very general in nature and inherent in language itself, as for instance when one compares truth to light and error to darkness, or progress to an ascent or moral danger to an abyss, or when one represents fidelity by a dog or craftiness by a fox. Now, to explain the occurrence of a similar symbolism in dreams, of which the language is naturally figurative and not discursive, there is no need to refer to a "collective unconscious"; it is enough to note that rational thought is not the whole of thought and that consciousness in the waking state does not cover the whole domain of mental activity. If the figurative language of dreams is not discursive, this does not necessarily make it irrational, and it is possible, as indeed Jung has properly observed, that a dreamer may be more intelligent in his dreams than in the waking state. It would even seem that this difference of level between the two states is fairly frequent among men of our own time, doubtless because the frameworks imposed by modern life are particularly unintelligent and incapable of vehicling in any normal manner the essential contents of human life.

This has obviously nothing to do with the role of purely symbolic or sacred dreams, whether these be spontaneous or evoked through rites; we are thinking here of the example of the Indians of North America, whose whole tradition, as well as their vital ambience, favors a kind of oneiric prophetism.

So as to neglect no aspect of this question, the following should also be said: in every collectivity that has become unfaithful to its own traditional form, to the sacred framework of its life, there occurs a collapse or a sort of mummification of the symbols it had received, and this process will be reflected in the psychic life of every individual belonging to that collectivity and participating in that infidelity. To every truth there corresponds a formal trace, and every spiritual form projects a psychic shadow; when these shadows are all that remains, they do in fact take on the character of ancestral phantoms that haunt the subconscious. The most pernicious of psychological errors is to reduce the meaning of symbolism to such phantoms.

As for the definition of "unconscious", it must never be forgotten that this is eminently relative and provisional. Consciousness is capable of gradation like light and is similarly refracted in contact with the media it meets. The ego is the form of individual consciousness, not its luminous source. The latter coincides with the source of the intelligence itself. In its universal nature, consciousness is in a sense an existential aspect of the intellect, and this amounts to saying that basically nothing is situated outside it.[26] Whence it follows that the "unconscious" of the psychologists is quite simply everything which, in the soul, lies outside ordinary conscious-

---

[24] The kind of introspection practiced by Jung by way of psychological investigation and of which he speaks in his memoirs, as well as certain parapsychological phenomena that he provoked by this method, takes one into a frankly spiritualistic ambience. The fact that the author proposed to study these phenomena "scientifically" changes nothing in regard to the influence they in fact had on his theory of "archetypes".

[25] See the Introduction to *The Secret of the Golden Flower*.

[26] Let us here recall the Vedantic ternary *Sat-chit-ananda* (Being, Consciousness, Bliss).

ness—that of the empirical "I" oriented towards the corporeal world—in other words, this "unconscious" is made to include both lower chaos and the higher states. The latter (which the Hindus compare to the bliss of deep sleep, the state of *prajna*) radiate from the luminous source of the Universal Spirit; the definition of the "unconscious" thus in no wise corresponds to a particular concrete modality of the soul. Many of the errors of "depth psychology", of which Jung is one of the chief protagonists, result from the fact that it operates with the "unconscious" as if it were a definite entity. One often hears it said that Jung's psychology has "re-established the autonomous reality of the soul". In truth, according to the perspective inherent in this psychology, the soul is neither independent of the body nor immortal; it is merely a sort of irrational fatality situated outside any intelligible cosmic order. If the moral and mental behavior of man were determined behind the scenes by some collection of ancestral "types" issuing from a fund that is completely unconscious and completely inaccessible to the intelligence, man would be as if suspended between two irreconcilable and divergent realities, namely that of things and that of the soul.

For all modern psychology, the luminous point of the soul, or its existential summit, is the consciousness of the "I", which only exists to the extent that it can disengage itself from the darkness of the "unconscious". Now, according to Jung, this darkness contains the vital roots of the individuality: the "collective unconscious" would then be endowed with a regulatory instinct, a kind of somnambulant wisdom, no doubt of a biological nature; from this fact, the conscious emancipation of the ego would comprise the danger of a vital uprooting. According to Jung, the ideal is a balance between the two poles—the conscious and the unconscious—a balance that can be realized only by the help of a third term, a sort of center of crystallization, which he calls the "self", a term borrowed from the doctrines of Hinduism. Here is what he has written on the subject:

> With the sensation of the self as an irrational and indefinable entity, to which the "I" is neither opposed nor subordinated, but to which it adheres and round which it moves in some sort, like the earth around the sun, the aim of individuation is attained. I use this term "sensation" to express the empirical character of the relationship between the "I" and the self. In this relationship there is nothing intelligible, for one can say nothing about the contents of the self. The "I" is the only content of the self that we know. The individualized "I" feels itself to be the object of a subject unknown and superior to itself. It seems to me that psychological observation here touches its extreme limit, for the idea of a self is in itself a transcendent postulate, which one can admittedly justify psychologically, but cannot prove scientifically. The step beyond science is an absolute requirement for the psychological evolution described here, for without the postulate in question I could not sufficiently formulate the psychic processes observed from experience. Because of this, the idea of a self at least possesses the value of a hypothesis like the theories about the structure of the atom. And if it be true that here too we are prisoners of an image, it is in any case a very living image, the interpretation of which exceeds my capacities. I scarcely doubt that it is a question of an image, but it is an image that contains us.[27]

---

[27] See *Two Essays on Analytical Psychology*, p. 240.

Despite a terminology too much bound up with current scientism, one might be tempted to grant full credit to the presentiments expressed in this passage and to find in it an approach to traditional metaphysical doctrines, if Jung, in a further passage, did not relativize the notion of the self by treating it this time, not as a transcendent principle, but as the outcome of a psychological process:

> One could define the self as a sort of compensation in reference to the contrast between inward and outward. Such a definition could well be applied to the self in so far as the latter possesses the character of a result, of an aim to reach, of a thing that has only been produced little by little and of which the experience has cost much travail. Thus, the self is also the aim of life, for it is the most complete expression of that combination of destiny we call an "individual", and not only of man in the singular but also of a whole group, where the one is the complement of the others with a view to a perfect image.[28]

There are some realms where dilettantism is unforgivable.

It is the balance to be realized between the unconscious and the conscious, or the integration, in the empirical "personality", of certain forces or impulsions emanating from the unconscious, that Jung paradoxically labels as "individuation", using a term by which was traditionally designated, not some psychological process or other, but the differentiation of individuals from the starting point of the species. But what Jung understands by this term is a kind of definitive pronunciation of the individuality which is taken as an end in itself. In such a perspective, the notion of "self" plainly loses all metaphysical meaning, but this is not the only traditional notion that Jung appropriates in order to debase it to a purely psychological and even clinical level; thus he compares psychoanalysis, which he uses precisely to promote this "individuation", to an initiation in the proper and sacred meaning of the term, and he even declares that psychoanalysis represents "the only form of initiation still valid in the modern age!"[29] Whence proceed a whole series of false assimilations, and intrusions into a realm where psychology is devoid of competence.[30]

---

[28] Ibid.

[29] See psychological commentary of the *Tibetan Book of the Dead.*

[30] Jung's psychological interpretation of alchemy has been expressly refuted in my book *Alchemy: Science of the Cosmos, Science of the Soul* (Shaftesbury, UK: Element Books, 1986). Frithjof Schuon, after reading the present chapter, sent me the following reflections in writing: "People generally see in Jungism, as compared with Freudism, a step towards reconciliation with the traditional spiritualities, but this is in no wise the case. From this point of view, the only difference is that, whereas Freud boasted of being an irreconcilable enemy of religion, Jung sympathizes with it while emptying it of its contents, which he replaces by collective psychism, that is to say by something infra-intellectual and therefore anti-spiritual. In this there is an immense danger for the ancient spiritualities, whose representatives, especially in the East, are too often lacking in critical sense with regard to the modern spirit, and this by reason of a complex of 'rehabilitation'; also it is not with much surprise, though with grave disquiet, that one has come across echoes of this kind from Japan, where the psychoanalyst's 'equilibrium' has been compared to the *satori* of Zen; and there is little doubt that it would be easy to meet with similar confusions in India and elsewhere. Be that as it may, the confusions in question are greatly favored by the almost universal refusal of people to see the devil and to call him by his name, in other words, by a kind of tacit convention compounded of optimism to order, tolerance that in reality hates truth, and compulsory alignment with scientism and official

Here it is not a case of the involuntary ignorance of some isolated seeker, for Jung carefully avoided all contact with the representatives of living tradition. During his visit to India, for example, he did not wish to see Sri Ramana Maharishi—alleging a motive of insolent frivolity[31]—doubtless because he feared instinctively and "unconsciously" (it is a case for saying it) a contact with a reality that would give the lie to his theories. For him, metaphysics was but a speculation in the void or, to be more exact, an illusory attempt by the psychic to reach beyond itself, comparable to the senseless gesture of a man who would pull himself out of a mudhole by his own hair. This conception is typical of modern psychologism, and this is why we mention it. To the absurd argument that metaphysics is only a production of the *psyché* one can immediately object that this judgment itself is but a similar production. Man lives by truth; to accept any truth, however relative it may be, is to accept that *intellectus adequatio rei*.[32] Merely to say "this is that" is automatically to affirm the very principle of adequation, and therefore the presence of the absolute in the relative.

Jung breached certain strictly materialistic frameworks of modern science, but this fact is of no use to anyone, to say the least—one wishes one could have rejoiced over it—because the influences that filter through this breach come from lower psychism and not from the Spirit, which alone is true and alone can save us.

Translated by William Stoddart

taste, without forgetting "culture", which swallows everything and commits one to nothing, except complicity in its neutralism; to which must be added a no less universal and quasi-official contempt for whatever is, we will not say intellectualist, but truly intellectual, and therefore tainted, in people's minds, with dogmatism, scholasticism, fanaticism, and prejudice. All this goes hand in hand with the psychologism of our time and is in large measure its result."

[31] See the preface to Heinrich Zimmer's book on Sri Ramana Maharishi.

[32] Editor's Note: "The intellect is adequate to reality."

Situating the Psyche[1]

William Stoddart

The Threefold Constitution of Man

"Psychology" means literally "the science of the soul". How, then, does one situate the "soul" metaphysically?

According to traditional metaphysics (be it Vedantic, Greek, Medieval, Islamic, or other), the constitution of man is threefold: namely Spirit (or Intellect), soul, and body.

The Intellect (the Spirit) is the faculty which enables man to conceive the Absolute. It is the source of his capacity for objectivity, and of his ability—in contradistinction from the animals—to free himself from imprisonment in subjectivity; it is the very definition of the human state. As Frithjof Schuon has said more than once: "The Intellect can know all that is knowable." This is because Heart-Knowledge or *gnosis* is innate, and fully present within us in a state of virtuality. This virtuality has to be realized and this process corresponds to the Platonic doctrine of "recollection" (*anamnesis*) which, in the last analysis, is one with the Christian practice of the "remembrance of God" (*memoria Dei*). "The Kingdom of Heaven is within you."

Intellect and Spirit are the two sides of the same coin, the former pertaining to the theoretical or intellectual, and the latter pertaining to the practical or spiritual. They pertain respectively to the objective (or discriminative) and the subjective (or contemplative) modes of knowing.

The three elements or "levels" in the constitution of man may be represented as follows:

English	Latin	Greek	Arabic
Spirit (Intellect)	*Spiritus* (*Intellectus*)	*Pneuma* (*Nous*)	*Ruh* (*'Aql*)
soul	*anima*	*psyche*	*nafs*
body	*corpus*	*soma*	*jism*

The Spirit or Intellect, with its two "faces", created and uncreated, is supra-formal or universal, and directly touched by the Divine; it is the only supra-individual, "archetypal", or objective element in man's constitution. The soul, on the other hand, is formal and individual. The Spirit is therefore the "measure" of the soul; the soul can never be the "measure" of the Spirit. The fundamental error of psychologists such as Jung is their failure to distinguish between soul and Spirit and consequently, in practice, their effective elimination of Spirit. At one stroke this abolishes the very basis of objectivity and, by the same token, of spirituality. The chaos and damage resulting from this fatal and anti-Platonic act of blindness are incalculable.[2] We are left stranded in a satanic kingdom where everything (truth, morality, art) is relative. Only the ancient philosophies—the traditional wisdom-systems—can oppose this error of modern psychology and of the new-age cults.[3]

---

[1] Many portions of this article are extracted from William Stoddart, "What is the Intellect?" in *Remembering in a World of Forgetting: Thoughts on Tradition and Postmodernism*, eds. Mateus Soares de Azevedo and Alberto Vasconcellos Queiroz (Bloomington, IN: World Wisdom, 2008), pp. 45-50.

[2] Jung, unlike Freud, is often considered to be friendly to religion! This is a classic case of "a wolf in sheep's clothing"!

[3] Editor's Note: There is a significant video clip with Dr. William Stoddart speaking about "New Age Thought"—

It must be understood that the term "Intellect" is here employed in the Eckhartian sense (*aliquid est in anima quod est increatum et increabile*: "there is something in the soul that is uncreated and uncreatable"). It should be said right away that there is no impenetrable barrier between the Intellect and the mind: the relationship of the former to the latter is like the relationship of the center of a circle to the circumference, or of the pinnacle of a cone to its circumferential base. Metaphorically speaking, the majority of philosophers since the end of the Middle Ages have concerned themselves solely with the circumference or periphery, with little or no transcendent input in their thought.[4] Henceforth the transcendent (previously known to be accessible either through revelation or intellection) has been regarded as mere "dogma" or "superstition". The result has been the tumultuous *dégringolade*—from Descartes, through Kant, to the narcissistic "philosophers" of the present day—known as the "history of philosophy"! One miraculous interruption of this cascading downwards was the Cambridge Platonists of the seventeenth century. Apart from such "miracles", the process seems irreversible; the words of Virgil were never more appropriate: *Facilis descensus Averno; sed revocare gradum, hic opus, hic labor est!* ("The descent to hell is easy; but, to turn in our tracks and go uphill, that is hard work!").

Unfortunately, slipshod modern parlance confuses "intellectual" with "mental" or "rational". In fact, unlike the Intellect which is "above" the soul, the mind or the reason is a content of the soul, as are the other human faculties such as: will, affect or sentiment, imagination, and memory. Thus:

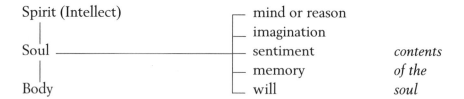

The Five Levels of Reality or the Five Divine Presences

"Ordinary" theology distinguishes between God and man, and within man, between soul and body. We thus immediately have three "levels": God, soul, and body. Mystical theology, on the other hand,[5] makes a distinction, within God Himself, between "Godhead" and "God", between "Divine Essence" and "God Creator-Helper-Judge", between "the Impersonal God" and "the Personal God", or between "Beyond-Being" and "Being". The Divine Essence and God the Creator constitute the first two of the five "levels"; each of these two elements is Divine and Uncreated. The soul and the body are the fourth and fifth levels; these two are human and created. There remains the third or intermediate level, and this is the Spirit or Intellect. The terms "creation" and "created" are synonymous with the terms "manifestation" and "manifested" respectively.[6]

online via World Wisdom's website: www.worldwisdom.com.

[4] This makes one think of the Zen saying: "When the finger points at the moon, the foolish man looks at the finger!"

[5] Including the universal metaphysics, as evidenced, for example, by Shankara in Hinduism, Meister Eckhart in Christianity, and Ibn 'Arabi in Islam.

[6] This exposition is taken from the writings of Frithjof Schuon. See, in particular Frithjof Schuon, *Esoterism as Principle and as Way*, trans. William Stoddart (London: Perennial Books, 1981).

These "Five Levels of Reality" or "Five Divine Presences", along with their meaning and relationships, are indicated in the following table:

The Five Levels of Reality

The Divine / EXISTENCE	Manifestation	subtle / gross	Level	UNCREATED / CREATED	ABSOLUTE / RELATIVE	ATMA / MAYA	DIVINE / HUMAN	HEAVEN / EARTH	IMMORTAL / MORTAL
The Divine — The Unmanifest, The Uncreated, The Metacosmic			(1) BEYOND-BEING (the Divine Essence, the Supra-Personal God)		ABSOLUTE	ATMA	DIVINE	HEAVEN	IMMORTAL
			(2) BEING (the Personal God, Creator, Judge; Divine Qualities)	UNCREATED LOGOS	RELATIVE				
EXISTENCE — The Manifest, The Created, The Cosmic	Universal or Supra-formal Manifestation		(3) Spirit, Intellect (Spiritual, Intellectual, or Angelic realm)	CREATED LOGOS	RELATIVE	MAYA	HUMAN		MORTAL
	individual or formal manifestation	subtle	(4) soul (animic or psychic realm)					EARTH	
		gross	(5) body (corporeal realm)					EARTH	MORTAL

The Doctrine of the Logos

Frithjof Schuon elucidates the doctrine of the Logos as follows:

The Divinity is absolute, creation is relative. Nevertheless, within the Absolute (or the Divine Essence), there is already a prefiguration of the relative, and this is the Personal God (or the Creator). This prefiguration of creation in the Uncreated is the "Uncreated Logos".

Furthermore, within creation, which is relative, there is a reflection of the Absolute, and this is the Spirit or Intellect. This reflection of the Absolute within the relative (or of the Uncreated within the created) shows itself in such things as Truth, Beauty, Virtue, Symbol, and Sacrament. It is also manifested as Prophet, Redeemer, *Tathagatha, Avatara*. This reflection of the Absolute in the relative is the "created Logos".

Without the Logos (and its two "Faces", created and uncreated), no contact between man and God would be possible. This seems to be the position of the Deists. Without the Logos, there would be a fundamental dualism, and not "Unity" (*ahadiya*) as the Sufis call it, or "Nondualism" (*advaita*) as the Vedantists call it. The doctrine and the role of the Logos can be expressed in diagrammatic form as follows:

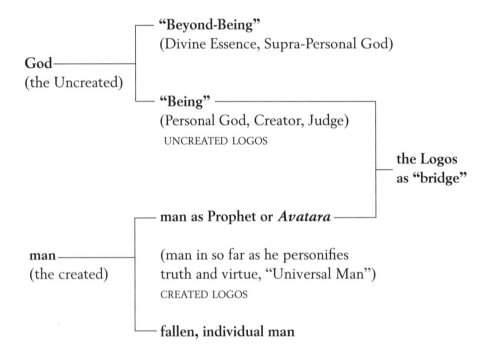

The spiritualities or mysticisms of all of the great religions teach that it is by uniting himself (in prayer and sacrament) with the "created Logos", that man attains to union with God.

The Science of Consciousness[1]

Philip Sherrard

On why a knowledge of the nature of consciousness does not lie within the competence of the modern scientist.

1. It is with my consciousness that I perceive whatever I do perceive.

2. Thus how something *appears* to me depends on the mode of my consciousness.

3. I can perceive only what I am capable of perceiving, observe only what I am capable of observing, understand only what I am capable of understanding.

4. Hence my understanding of the nature of something can only be according to the mode of consciousness that I possess; and this means that the true nature of what I perceive may be very different from that which I perceive it to be.

5. A higher mode of consciousness than mine will be capable of perceiving the true nature of something more clearly than I can perceive it; and so on, up to the highest mode of consciousness.

6. These same propositions apply also to a knowledge of the nature of consciousness itself; my understanding of the nature of consciousness can only be according to the mode of consciousness that I possess.

7. Nothing can be known except according to the mode of the knower.

8. A higher consciousness than mine will be capable of a higher understanding of the nature of consciousness than that of which I am capable.

9. Ultimately, to know what the nature of consciousness is in itself I must have attained the highest mode of consciousness that it is possible to attain, namely, that which is one with consciousness itself.

10. Only such a mode of consciousness can experience and in this way verify a knowledge of the nature of consciousness.

---

[1] Editor's Note: At the beginning of January 1992, an International Symposium organized by the Athenian Society for Science and Human Development was held at Athens, to discuss the theme, "Science of Consciousness." The participants were nearly all scientists of one kind or another; but a few non-scientists were invited. Among these was Dr. Philip Sherrard (1922-1995), author of *The Rape of Man and Nature* (1987) and *The Sacred in Life and Art* (1990). In the event, Dr. Sherrard decided not to attend the Symposium, and he explained his reasons for this in a statement which he sent to one of its organizers, this being followed, in response to a reply from the organizer, by a letter.

11. Only my experience of the nature of consciousness in itself can constitute knowledge of and evidence for it.

12. Short of that my understanding of the nature of consciousness can be but hypothetical, mere opinion tailored according to the limitations of my particular mode of consciousness, vitiated by the ignorance which these limitations impose, and totally inaccessible to verification through experience. In such circumstances, how consciousness *appears* to me will be very different from what it actually *is*.

13. The highest mode of consciousness, or consciousness in itself, is that in which there is no dualism between knower and what is to be known, observer and what is to be observed, consciousness and that of which consciousness is conscious.

14. This means that so long as there is in my own consciousness any dualism of this kind I can be sure that I have not attained the highest mode of consciousness that it is possible to attain. Hence my conception of the nature of consciousness can be but a hypothesis or opinion, distorted by the ignorance that pertains to any consciousness still in the thrall of the dualism in question. In the nature of things such hypothesis, or opinion, cannot constitute knowledge.

15. As the mode of consciousness effective for the modern scientist is one that is still in the thrall of such a dualism—for if this were not the case he could not be a modern scientist—it is only too clear that a knowledge of the nature of consciousness does not lie within his competence. His competence, in this respect as well as in other respects, is necessarily limited to hypothesis, opinion, speculation, and none of these can be said to constitute knowledge.

16. By definition, any attempt to understand the nature of consciousness that is not based on the experience and knowledge of those whose consciousness has transcended every form of dualism is doomed to futility. There is no point in wasting time on enterprises that *a priori* are doomed to futility.

17. Moreover, to proceed to an investigation of the nature of consciousness otherwise than through the study of the testimonials of those—divinely inspired metaphysicians, mystics, seers, prophets—who through direct experience have attained a knowledge of the nature of consciousness would be a manifestation of extreme arrogance, not to say sheer impudence; for to proceed otherwise than through such study would be to assume the possession of a degree of understanding and insight superior to those possessed by the finest intelligence known to the human race. It would in fact be an unexpected bonus to find at a conference such as the one proposed even a single scientist who has studied in depth—that is, with at least the same diligence and dedication as he has studied his own discipline—the writings of such people. Yet unless he has studied these writings in this way, what qualifications does he possess that entitle him to speak to any purpose on the theme under discussion? The blind cannot lead the blind.

18. And if in response to this last question it is claimed that the question itself is irrelevant because consciousness continually evolves and therefore our understanding of consciousness is in a continual state of evolution, what additional evidence is needed in order to demonstrate

both the bankruptcy of the mind that can make such a claim and the pointlessness of any further discussion?

Dear . . .[2]

I didn't mean to provoke such a response by sending you my short statement—though even that does rather illustrate my point, doesn't it, about the difficulty of having any fruitful discussion unless one has already resolved certain preliminary questions—questions which modern scientists on the whole don't ever take into account and are even completely unaware of. I suppose these questions might be called purely epistemological, in the sense that they are concerned with such matters as what conditions must be fulfilled before anyone can be said to know anything at all. I personally have never found such questions tackled by any scientist. And yet what is the point of trying to obtain a knowledge of something if you haven't first fulfilled the conditions which permit you to obtain it? My statement was simply meant to affirm that no modern scientist (so far as I am aware) has even begun to fulfill the conditions which would permit him or her to obtain a knowledge of the nature of consciousness.

I thought my statement did explain this clearly, but obviously it doesn't. I suspect that in any case there are at least two virtually insurmountable interrelated barriers to making it clear to scientists. The first is that very few, if any, scientists, even if they recognize supranatural realities, seem to realize that there are not two sciences, the one concerned with the material and outward aspect of things extended in time and space, and the other with their spiritual and eternal dimension, unextended in time and space. There is only one science. But what there are, on the other hand, are two dominant modes of consciousness in man: the first, what might be called his ego-consciousness, which is the lower mode of consciousness, corresponding as it does to what is most inhuman and satanic in him; and the second, his angelic or spiritual consciousness, which is his higher mode of consciousness.

The higher or spiritual consciousness perceives and experiences things as they are in themselves, inner and outer, spiritual and material, metaphysical and physical interpenetrating and forming a single unsundered and unsunderable reality. The profane or ego-consciousness cannot perceive and experience things as they are in this way. It can perceive and experience only what its own opacity permits it to perceive and experience, and this is merely the aspect of things extended in time and space, as though this aspect of things possessed existence and being, and even reality, in its own right. This kind of consciousness—the ego-consciousness—does not realize or understand that separated or sundered from its inner and spiritual dimension nothing belonging to the world of phenomena possess any reality at all, whether physical, material, or substantial, and that the notion that it does so is merely an illusion or distortion inherent as such in the viewpoint of the ego-consciousness.

In your letter, for instance, you say that a distinction must be made between consciousness and its formal expressions, and that while the scientist cannot study the former, he can study the latter. But this is precisely to posit that dualism in reality which is simply a selection of the fact that the ego-consciousness is sundered from the spiritual consciousness. And as such

---

[2] Editor's Note: Dr. Philip Sherrard thereafter prepared the following letter which further elaborates on his eighteen points listed above.

a dualism represents a totally illusory and distorted state of mind, and does not correspond to anything in reality itself, what "knowledge" of things not equally illusory and distorted can be gained by studying them as though it did correspond to something in reality—as though, that is to say, things do possess being and existence in their own right and apart from their inner and spiritual dimension?

I can put this another way: everything that possesses form is an expression of consciousness. How, then, can I possibly study the nature of a formal expression of consciousness if I am ignorant of the nature of the consciousness of which it is the expression, and in which its being and existence inhere?

To think that one can gain a knowledge of consciousness by studying its formal expressions is as dotty as thinking that one can gain a knowledge of the soul by analyzing, dissecting, quantifying etc. etc. the structure of the human body. Plato knew better: "If the soul wishes to know itself it must look into its own self." Exactly the same applies where a knowledge of consciousness is concerned: such knowledge can be gained only by consciousness "looking into" itself. No knowledge of it can be gained by studying its formal expressions. In fact, no knowledge of anything extended in time and space—on the "horizontal" plane—can be obtained without a prior knowledge of its spiritual and eternal dimension—its "vertical" dimension—unextended in time and space. There is absolutely no point in discussing the nature of consciousness at a conference unless this is understood.

That is the first point. And the second point, related to the first, is this: that it is extremely rare—so rare that one can say that it constitutes the exception that proves the rule—for anyone to attain the mode of the higher or spiritual consciousness without pursuing a path of spiritual discipline under the guidance, direct or indirect, of a qualified spiritual master. But even apart from this, to be in a position to discuss things as it were at second hand, after a study of the writings of such spiritual masters, or to be able to use the universal language of metaphysical discourse coherently, requires at least as long a training as it does to master the conventions of higher mathematics. And, as I said before, I have never come across a scientist who has learnt this language. When Einstein ventures into this sphere what he says is positively embarrassing in its naivety. And the few things I have read of people like [Niels] Bohr make it clear that they are little more than novices in these matters. The same goes for [Frithjof] Capra. In all cases those preliminary questions I spoke of at the beginning of this letter are simply ignored. So what dialogue can one have?

I hope this may have made it a bit clearer—or at least not have confused things more. The point to grasp, surely, is that the main determinant of knowledge—or of what we think is knowledge—is not the object about which we seek to obtain knowledge, but the mode of consciousness we possess when we seek to obtain it. If one can grasp that principle, the rest falls into place.

Yours,

Philip Sherrard

II

THEORIA

The Not-So-Close Encounters of Western Psychology and Eastern Spirituality

Harry Oldmeadow

The intellect does, in fact, harm the soul when it dares to possess itself of the heritage of the Spirit.

Carl Jung[1]

There is no place to seek the mind;
It is like the footprints of the birds in the sky.
The Zenrin[2]

A. Religion and Psychology

Western Psychology and Religion

No one needs reminding that the relations between modern psychology and traditional religions have not always been friendly. Freud struck the key note in his insistence that, to state the matter as briefly as possible, religious beliefs were a thinly camouflaged prolongation of childhood pathologies. He identified "three powers which may dispute the basic position of science": art, philosophy, and religion, of which, he said, "religion alone is to be taken seriously as an enemy." Philosophy, he suggested, is basically harmless because, despite its ambitious pretensions, it "has no direct influence on the great mass of mankind: it is of interest to only a small number even of top-layer intellectuals and is scarcely intelligible to anyone else." Art "is almost always harmless and beneficent; it does not seek to be anything but an illusion." This leaves religion as "an immense power" and an imposing obstacle to the scientific enlightenment of mankind, the project in which Freud understood himself to be engaged.

> The last contribution to the criticism of the religious *Weltanschauung*, he wrote, was effected by psychoanalysis, by showing how religion originated from the helplessness of children and by tracing its contents to the survival into maturity of the wishes and needs of childhood.[3]

This all sits somewhat uncomfortably with the fact that Freud himself made frequent reference to the insights of the art, philosophy, and religion of the past in his own inquiries, and found that they illuminated some of the darkest recesses of the human psyche. His most famous theoretical innovation, after all, took its name from Greek mythology. Perhaps we can defend Freud with the old adage that only small minds are consistent!

---

[1] C.G. Jung, "Commentary on *The Secret of the Golden Flower*" quoted in C. Ray, "Western Psychology and Buddhist Teachings: Convergences and Divergences," 27.

[2] *The Zenrin*, quoted in R. Sohl & A. Carr (eds), *The Gospel According to Zen*, 27.

[3] Freud quoted in W. Smith, *Cosmos and Transcendence*, 101-102.

Since Freud's time Western psychology has splintered into various schools and movements. At one end of the spectrum we have what might be called "objectivist," "behaviorist," and "empiricist" schools of thought which treat human consciousness as somehow epiphenomenal, or indeed, as irrelevant to the science of psychology. Recall the claim by one of the founders of behaviorist psychology, John Watson:

> Psychology, as the behaviorist views it, is a purely objective, experimental branch of natural science which needs consciousness as little as do the sciences of chemistry and physics.[4]

Here indeed is a science to clip an angel's wings! Of course, even within the domain of the so-called "hard sciences," the whole notion of an objective knowledge, anchored in empirical and verifiable experimentation and observation, has recently been called into the most serious question: one need only mention such developments as the Uncertainty Principle, Chaos Theory, and Quantum Physics to signal the tumult into which the tidy assumptions of Newtonian science have been thrown. We are now confronted with the sorry spectacle of the human and social "sciences" clinging to a borrowed epistemological paradigm which was never appropriate and which is now largely discredited by physicists and the like. Of course, we might want to take the same tack as B.F. Skinner. When it was pointed out to him that Heisenberg's Principle had undermined physical determinism and he was asked whether, in view of the fact that matter did not behave in a predictable fashion, was not psychological determinism rather problematic, he replied that "the muddle of physics" was physics' problem, not psychology's. Electrons might be unpredictable, but human beings, apparently, are not![5]

At the other end of the spectrum we have various humanistic, personalist, and existentialist schools which take the closest interest not in observable behavior but in human consciousness and in the inner world of the experiencing subject. Some psychologists of this kind would share John Welwood's view that

> Western psychology has so far failed to provide us with a satisfactory understanding of the full range of human experience. . . . It appears that we have largely overlooked the central fact of human psychology—our everyday mind, our very real, immediate awareness of being.[6]

The question arises: what is the nature of consciousness? What do we mean by this word? For my own part I would contend that consciousness, inextricably tied up with human subjectivity, is vital, complex, elusive, mysterious. As *The Zenrin* affirms, "There is no place to seek the mind: it is like the footprints of the birds in the sky." From another viewpoint we may share Stanislav Grof's contention, in accord with many ancient wisdoms, that "In its furthest reaches, the psyche of each of us is essentially commensurate with all of existence, and ulti-

---

[4] Watson quoted in F. Capra, *The Turning Point*, 177.

[5] See H. Smith, *Beyond the Post-Modern Mind*, 66fn.

[6] Welwood quoted in J.J. Clarke, *Oriental Enlightenment*, 150.

mately identical with the cosmic creative principle itself."[7] This is a matter for celebration, not a "problem" to be solved by a "science" with pretensions to explaining everything! To borrow a metaphor, trying to pin consciousness to the laboratory bench, or the computer screen for that matter, is like trying to capture the wind in a bag, or a river in a net. And thank goodness for that! Artists, theologians, philosophers, scientists, musicians, thinkers of all kinds have grappled with the mystery of consciousness since time immemorial. It is surely absurd to believe that we must now regard all these efforts as only the fumblings and gropings of unsophisticated minds, bereft of the benefits of modern science, and that it is only with the advent of a scientifically-constituted psychology that we can build a true knowledge of human consciousness and behavior. This is a staggering impertinence, but one altogether characteristic of the modern mentality. However, I share Grof's conviction that

> Many open minded scientists and mental health professionals have become aware of the abysmal gap between contemporary [mainstream] psychology, and the great ancient or Oriental spiritual traditions, such as the various forms of yoga, Kashmir Shaivism, Tibetan Vajrayana, Taoism, Zen Buddhism, Sufism, Kabbalah, or alchemy. The wealth of profound knowledge about the human psyche and consciousness accumulated within these systems over centuries and often over millennia, has not been adequately acknowledged, explored, and integrated by Western science.[8]

To return to the question: here's a rough working definition of "consciousness": all forms of human awareness, conscious, subconscious, or supraconscious, if one may be permitted such a term. This is to say that consciousness includes such modes as not only ratiocination, or what the Romantic poets called "cerebration" (by which they meant conscious mental operations of a more or less rational kind) but all those more subtle and enigmatic modes and states which we signal by such words as imagination, intuition, creativity, dream, fantasy, trance, reverie and the like. Recall these words from one of the nineteenth century's greatest psychologists, William James:

> Our normal waking consciousness . . . is but one special type of consciousness, whilst all about it, parted from it by the flimsiest of screens, there lie potential forms of consciousness entirely different. We may go through life without suspecting their existence; but apply the requisite stimulus, and at a touch they are there in all their completeness. . . . No account of the universe in its totality can be final which leaves these other forms of consciousness quite disregarded. How to regard them is the question. . . . At any rate, they forbid our premature closing of accounts with reality.[9]

---

[7] S. Grof, *Spiritual Emergency*, 21.

[8] S. Grof, *The Holotropic Mind*, 21. (We will forgive Grof's indiscretion in claiming Sufism, Kabbalah and alchemy for the Orient!)

[9] W. James, *The Varieties of Religious Experience*, 305.

There are, of course, those who believe that eventually we will be able to reduce all this to the material processes in the brain. To my mind this is ludicrous: it is a reductionism of the crudest and most damaging kind, what Blake called Single Vision. I can do no better than Kathleen Raine's characterization of reductionism as "that mentality which can see in the pearl nothing but the disease of the oyster."

Though modern science has doubtless revealed much material information that was previously unknown it has also supplanted a knowledge which infinitely outreaches it. We see the fruits of this tendency in the complacencies and condescensions of those scientists who like to suppose that we have "outgrown" the "superstitions" of our ancestors. Here is a random example from a prestigious contemporary scientist:

> I myself, like many scientists, believe that the soul is imaginary and that what we call our mind is simply a way of talking about the function of our brains. . . . Once one has become adjusted to the ideas that we are here because we have evolved from simple chemical compounds by a process of natural selection, it is remarkable how many of the problems of the modern world take on a completely new light.[10]

This kind of rampant materialism is presently "the reigning orthodoxy among philosophers of the mind."[11] Much academic psychology concerned with the mind has stumbled down the same blind alley.

Many contemporary psychologists are apparently oblivious to the fact that the ancient philosophers and artists of both Orient and Occident were profound psychologists. Indeed, one of the great historical religions might be seen primarily as a psychology, with the proviso that the inquiry is conducted within a religious rather than a profane and secular framework. The words of Christmas Humphreys remain as apposite today as they were in 1951:

> In the world of the mind, including that Cinderella of mental science, psychology, the West has more to learn from Buddhism than as yet it knows.[12]

Modern Western psychology exhibits both the strengths and weaknesses of a whole family of so-called sciences which crystallized sometime in the nineteenth century: we might mention such disciplines as anthropology, sociology, and what Carlyle properly called the "Dismal Science" of economics. The encounter of Western psychology and Eastern religion, limited though it has been, can help us to see more clearly what some of the limitations of modern psychology might be, and how these might be at least attenuated. With very broad brush strokes we shall portray the involvement of several modern psychological thinkers with the doctrines and techniques of Eastern spirituality. Later, after some passing remarks about several contemporary thinkers, a few reflections on what Western psychology might profitably derive from the East-

---

[10] F. Crick, *Molecules and Men*, quoted in T. Roszak, *Where the Wasteland Ends*, 188. For an almost identical profession by a scientific popularizer see Carl Sagan, *The Dragons of Eden*, 10.

[11] Daniel Dennett quoted in H. Smith, *Beyond the Post-Modern Mind*, 135-136.

[12] C. Humphreys, *Buddhism*, 223.

ern traditions. However, before that, we must take rather a lengthy detour through the critique of psychologism elaborated by traditionalists, and through their repudiation of some aspects of the work of the century's greatest East-West bridge builder in the psychological domain, Carl Jung.

A Traditionalist Perspective on Psychologism

From the perennialist perspective psychologism is a school of thought, a view of the human condition, built on the sands of a profane science, and as such, another symptom of modernism. Its intrusion into the religious realm has been attended by consequences no less disturbing than those coming in the train of evolutionism. As Coomaraswamy so neatly put it, "While nineteenth century materialism closed the mind of man to what is above him, twentieth century psychology opened it to what is below him."[13]

Psychologism can be described as the assumption that man's nature and behavior are to be explained by psychological mechanisms which can be laid bare by a scientific and empirical psychology. Before we proceed any further an extremely important distinction must be made between modern psychology and traditional pneumatologies with which it shares some superficial similarities. The latter derived from radically different principles, applied different therapies, and pursued different ends. Just as it is misleading to talk about modern European philosophy and traditional metaphysics in the same breath and under the same terms, so too with modern psychology and traditional pneumatology. A good deal of confusion would be averted if people would resist such terms as "Buddhist psychology" or "Zen psychotherapy." It would also help clarify the issues at stake if many of the dabblers in this field would abandon the extraordinary notion that the techniques of Western psychology can lead to the "liberation" spoken of in the Eastern traditions.[14] This is to confuse two quite different planes of experience.

Modern psychology can be censured against the backdrop of traditional doctrines in this fashion:

> Psychoanalysis doubly deserves to be called an imposture, firstly because it pretends to have discovered facts which have always been known . . . and secondly and chiefly because it attributes to itself functions that in reality are spiritual, and thus in practice puts itself in the place of religion.[15]

In this context we might take note of the fact that many of Freud's apparently revolutionary insights were perfectly well-known not only in the East but in the pre-modern West, and that many of Freud's ideas are actually prefigured in the Kabbalah. Indeed, David Bakan has adduced a good deal of evidence in favor of his claim that Freud's whole project can be read as the secularization of Jewish mysticism.[16]

---

[13] Coomaraswamy quoted in W. Perry, *Challenges to a Secular Society*, 13-14.

[14] On this issue see P. Novak, "C.G. Jung in the Light of Asian Philosophy" and J.M. Reynolds, *Self-Liberation Through Seeing with Naked Awareness*, Appendix 1.

[15] F. Schuon, "The Psychological Imposture," 98.

[16] See Perry's review of David Bakan's book *Sigmund Freud and the Jewish Mystical Tradition* in *Challenges to a Secular Society*, 17-38.

Psychology of the modern kind defines itself by its inability to distinguish between the psychic plane, the arena in which the more or less accidental subjectivities of the individual ego come into play in the depths of the subconscious, and the infinite realm of the spirit which, in terms of the human individual, is signaled by the capacity for the plenary experience and which is thus marked by an "inward" illimitation and transcendence. The muddling of the psychic realm of the subconscious with the mystical potentialities of the spirit and the boundless reaches of the Intellect has given birth to all manner of confusions. There is indeed a science which reveals the way in which the play of the psyche can communicate universal realities; this is one of the fields of traditional pneumatologies. But—the proviso is crucial—such a science cannot flourish outside a properly constituted metaphysic and cosmology. In this context the following passage from Burckhardt deserves the closest attention:

> The connection with the metaphysical order provides spiritual psychology with qualitative criteria such as are wholly lacking in profane psychology, which studies only the dynamic character of phenomena of the psyche and their proximate causes. When modern psychology makes pretensions to a sort of science of the hidden contents of the soul it is still for all that restricted to an individual perspective because it has no real means for distinguishing psychic forms which translate universal realities from forms which appear symbolical but are only vehicles for individual impulsions. Its "collective subconscious" has most assuredly nothing to do with the true source of symbols; at most it is a chaotic depository of psychic residues somewhat like the mud of the ocean bed which retains traces of past epochs.[17]

The confusion of the psychic and the spiritual, which in part stems from the artificial Cartesian dualism of "body" and "mind," was discussed by René Guénon at some length in *The Reign of Quantity*. The confusion, he said,

> appears in two contrary forms: in the first, the spiritual is brought down to the level of the psychic; in the second, the psychic is . . . mistaken for the spiritual; of this the most popular example is spiritualism.[18]

The first form of the confusion thus licenses a degrading reductionism and relativism, often as impertinent as it is inadequate. The "sinister originality" of psychologism lies in its "determination to attribute every reflex and disposition of the soul to mean causes and to exclude spiritual factors."[19] This tendency is often accomplice to a relativism whereby everything becomes

---

[17] T. Burckhardt, *An Introduction to Sufi Doctrine*, 37. See also S.H. Nasr, *Sufi Essays*, 46ff, and A.K. Coomaraswamy, "On the Indian and Traditional Psychology, or rather Pneumatology" in *Selected Papers 2*, 333-378. What Coomaraswamy said of the individual subconscious can be applied to the psychic realm as a whole: it is "a sink of psychic residues, a sort of garbage pit or compost heap, fitted only for the roots of 'plants,' and far removed from the light that erects them" (cited by Perry, *Treasury of Traditional Wisdom*, 437).

[18] R. Guénon, *The Reign of Quantity*, 286. See the chapters "The Misdeeds of Psychoanalysis" and "The Confusion of the Psychic and the Spiritual," 273-290.

[19] F. Schuon, "The Psychological Imposture," 99.

the fruit of a contingent elaboration: Revelation becomes poetry, the Religions are inventions, sages are "thinkers" . . . infallibility and inspiration do not exist, error becomes a quantitative and "interesting" contribution to "culture" . . . there is . . . a denial of every supernatural, or even suprasensory, cause, and by the same token of every principial truth.[20]

Like evolutionism, psychologism attempts to explain the greater in terms of the lesser and excludes all that goes beyond its own limits. In this sense, historicism, relativism, and psychologism are all cut from the same cloth:

> The mentality of today seeks to reduce everything to categories connected with time; a work of art, a thought, a truth have no value in themselves and independently of any historical classification. . . . Everything is considered as an expression of a "period" and not as having possibly a timeless and intrinsic value; and this is entirely in conformity with modern relativism, and with a psychologism . . . that destroys essential values. In order to "situate" the doctrine of a scholastic, or even a Prophet, a "psychoanalysis" is prepared—it is needless to emphasize the monstrous impudence implicit in such an attitude—and with wholly mechanical and perfectly unreal logic the "influences" to which this doctrine has been subject are laid bare. There is no hesitation in attributing to saints . . . all kind of artificial and even fraudulent conduct; but it is obviously forgotten . . . to apply the same principle to oneself, and to explain one's own supposedly "objective" position by psychological considerations: sages are treated as being sick men and one takes oneself for a god. . . . It is a case of expressing a maximum amount of absurdity with a maximum amount of subtlety.[21]

As Schuon remarks elsewhere, relativism goes about reducing every element of absoluteness to a relativity while making a quite illogical exception in favor of this reduction itself.[22]

Clearly these strictures do not apply with the same force to each and every attempt by scholars to detect and explain historical and psychological factors relating to particular religious phenomena. It is possible, for example, to take these kinds of considerations into account in a sympathetic and sensitive way without falling prey to a reductionist relativism. Nevertheless, Schuon's general point remains valid. It can hardly be denied that a kind of iconoclastic psychologism runs through a good deal of the scholarly literature on religion. A psychologism unrestrained by any values transcending those of a profane science can help to corrode religious forms by infiltrating the religious sphere itself. Schuon notes, by way of an example, the part psychologism has played in discrediting the cult of the Holy Virgin:

> Only a barbarous mentality that wants to be "adult" at all costs and no longer believes in anything but the trivial could be embarrassed by this cult. The answer to the reproach of "gynecolatry" or the "Oedipus complex" is that, like every other

---

[20] F. Schuon, *Dimensions of Islam*, 154-155.

[21] F. Schuon, *Light on the Ancient Worlds*, 32-33.

[22] F. Schuon, *Logic and Transcendence*, 7.

psychoanalytic argument, it by-passes the problem; for the real question is not one of knowing what the psychological factors conditioning an attitude may be but, something very different, namely, what are its results.[23]

The practice of dragging spiritual realities down to the psychological plane can everywhere be seen when religion is reduced to some kind of psychological regimen. Some of the neo-yogic, meditation, "self-realization," and New Age movements are of this kind.

> One of the most insidious and destructive illusions is the belief that depth-psychology . . . has the slightest connection with spiritual life, which these teachings persistently falsify by confusing inferior elements [psychic] with superior [spiritual]. We cannot be too wary of all these attempts to reduce the values vehicled by tradition to the level of phenomena supposed to be scientifically controllable. The spirit escapes the hold of profane science in an absolute fashion.

Similarly,

> It is not the positive results of experimental science that one is out to deny . . . but the absurd claim of science to cover everything possible, the whole of truth, the whole of the real; the quasi-religious claim of totality moreover proves the falseness of the point of departure.[24]

Of course the traditionalists are not alone in unmasking "the misdeeds of psychoanalysis." Thomas Merton, for instance:

> Nothing is more repellent than a pseudo-scientific definition of the contemplative experience. . . . He who attempts such a definition is tempted to proceed psychologically, and there is really no adequate "psychology" of contemplation. [25]

Lama Govinda, more alert to this danger than some of his colleagues, warns of the "shallow-mindedness" of those who teach a kind of "pseudo-scientific spirituality."[26] Mircea Eliade makes a more general point in writing,

> Psychoanalysis justifies its importance by asserting that it forces you to look at and accept reality. But what sort of reality? A reality conditioned by the materialistic and scientific ideology of psychoanalysis, that is, a historical product: we see a thing in which certain scholars and thinkers of the nineteenth century believed.[27]

---

[23] F. Schuon, "The Psychological Imposture," 101.

[24] F. Schuon, "No Activity Without Truth," 37. See also F. Schuon, *Stations of Wisdom*, 38, and *Light on the Ancient Worlds*, 34ff.

[25] T. Merton, *New Seeds of Contemplation*, 6-7.

[26] A. Govinda, *Creative Meditation and Multi-Dimensional Consciousness*, 70.

[27] M. Eliade, *No Souvenirs*, 269

Psychologistic reductionism has ramifications on both the practical and the theoretical level: on the one hand we have the notion that psychological techniques and therapies can take the place of authentic spiritual disciplines; on the other, the pretension that psychological science can "explain" religious phenomena. Both of these are related to the first form of the confusion of the psychic and the spiritual. Let us turn briefly to the obverse side, that of falsely elevating the psychic to the spiritual. There is a vast spiritual wasteland here which we cannot presently explore, but Whitall Perry identifies some of its inhabitants in writing of those occultist, psychic, spiritualistic and "esoteric" groups who concern themselves with

> spirits, elementals, materializations, etheric states, auric eggs, astral bodies, ids, ods, and egos, ectoplasmic apparitions, wraiths and visions, subliminal consciousness and collective unconsciousness, doublings, disassociations, functional disintegrations, communications, obsessions and possessions, psychasthenia, animal magnetism, hypnoidal therapeutics, vibrations, thought-forces, mind-waves and radiations, clairvoyances and audiences and levitations, telepathic dreams, premonitions, death lights, trance writings, Rochester knockings, Buddhic bodies, and sundry other emergences and extravagances of hideous nomenclature. [28]

—all the while imagining that these are the stuff of the spiritual life. Much of Guénon's work was directed to reasserting the proper distinctions between psychic phenomena and spiritual realities and to sounding a warning about the infernal forces to which the psychic occultists unwittingly expose themselves. As Schuon remarks, "modern occultism is by and large no more than the study of extrasensory phenomena, one of the most hazardous pursuits by reason of its wholly empirical character and its lack of any doctrinal basis."[29] Without the protective shield of traditional doctrines and disciplines, such as those which guarded the shamans, any forays into these realms are fraught with perils of the gravest kind. In a traditional discipline the psychic can be reintegrated with the spiritual but without the necessary metaphysical framework and religious supports psychism becomes wholly infra-intellectual and anti-spiritual. The traditionalists' critique of psychologism can be more sharply focused by a consideration of their response to the work of Carl Jung.

The Traditionalist Critique of Carl Jung

As we have already seen, Carl Jung was one of the century's most sympathetic commentators on Eastern doctrines and practices. He took a close interest in several key texts of the Chinese and Tibetan traditions. Despite some tension in his work between what might loosely be called the scientific and the mystical, Jung understood that the Eastern traditions enshrined an immense and richly variegated treasury of wisdom and was certainly not given to the preposterous dismissal of Eastern psycho-spiritual disciplines that we find amongst many Western psychologists. Nor did he display any of Freud's deep-seated animus to religion in the name of some kind of "objective" scientific knowledge. Jung's work, inevitably, was attacked from the scientific

---

[28] W. Perry, *Treasury of Traditional Wisdom*, 437.

[29] F. Schuon, *Logic and Transcendence*, 1. See also R. Guénon, "Explanation of Spiritist Phenomena," and S.H. Nasr, *Sufi Essays*, 40-41.

side as being "symbolistic," "mystical," "occultist" and the like. These kinds of criticisms are of no interest in the present context. Much more disturbing are the charges that have been pressed by exponents of the traditional religious outlook. There are four kinds of criticisms which deserve our attention here. They can be flagged by identifying their targets: pan-psychism; the denial of metaphysics; the tyranny of the ego; the subversion of traditional religion.

From a traditionalist perspective the first problem is that Jung's writings often seem to confound the psychic and the spiritual. In Jung's case it is a matter at times of reducing the spiritual to the level of the psychic, and at others of elevating the psychic to the level of the spiritual, or, to put the same point differently, of deifying the unconscious. In *Memories* Jung states that

> All comprehension and all that is comprehended is in itself psychic, and to that extent we are hopelessly cooped up in an exclusively psychic world.[30]

It is difficult to find in Jung's writings a completely unequivocal affirmation of the objective and supra-psychic reality of the *numen*, to borrow a term from Otto, a figure who significantly influenced both Jung and Eliade.[31] In the interview conducted by Mircea Eliade for *Combat*, Jung *does* say this:

> Religious experience is numinous, as Rudolf Otto calls it, and for me, as a psychologist, this experience differs from all others in the way *it transcends the ordinary categories of time, space and causality.*[32]

However, many of his formulations on this subject are ambivalent. It is also undoubtedly true that a great many people, including liberal Christian theologians, have used Jung's sometimes confusing ruminations as a theoretical platform for a wholesale psychologizing of religion—Don Cuppitt, to name but one popular exponent of the view that religion needs no metaphysical underpinnings.[33] This is to be guilty of the "psychological imposture," which Schuon castigates in these terms:

> The tendency to reduce everything to psychological factors and to call into question not only what is intellectual and spiritual . . . but also the human spirit as such, and therewith its capacity of adequation and still more evidently, its inward illimi-

---

[30] C.G. Jung, *Memories, Dreams, Reflections*, 385.

[31] The same kind of ambivalence is evident in most Jungian formulations concerning both the collective unconscious and archetypes. This, for instance, from Marie-Louise von Franz: "Really, it is a modern, scientific expression for an inner experience that has been known to mankind from time immemorial, the experience in which strange and unknown things from our own inner world happen to us, in which influences from within can suddenly alter us, in which we have dreams and ideas which we feel as if we are not doing ourselves, but which appear in us strangely and overwhelmingly. In earlier times these influences were attributed to a divine fluid (*mana*), or to a god, demon, or 'spirit,' a fitting expression of the feeling that this influence has an objective, quite foreign and autonomous existence, as well as the sense of its being something overpowering, which has the conscious ego at its mercy" (quoted in G. Wehr, *Jung: A Biography*, 170).

[32] C.G. Jung, *C.G Jung Speaking*, 230 (italics mine).

[33] See the glib commentary by Cuppitt on Jung's view of religion, quoted in S. Segaller & M. Berger, *Jung: The Wisdom of the Dream*, 179.

tation and transcendence. . . . Psychoanalysis is at once an endpoint and a cause, as is always the case with profane ideologies, like materialism and evolutionism, of which it is really a logical and fateful ramification and a natural ally.[34]

Schuon's reference to materialism and evolutionism alert us to these two bugbears (still very much with us, alas!) which occasionally raise their ugly heads in Jung's writings. Even in the autobiography written near the end of his life, Jung is capable of a kind of scientistic gobbledy-gook which betrays a failure to break free from the stultifying effects of these prejudices. Two examples: "Consciousness is phylogenetically and ontogenetically a secondary phenomenon."[35] (This is a variant on the absurd evolutionist inversion whereby the "flesh" becomes "word".) Likewise in his Introduction to *The Secret of the Golden Flower*, Jung descends into Darwinian hocus-pocus when he suggests that the analogical relationships of symbolic vocabularies and mythological motifs across many different cultures derives from "the identity of cerebral structures beyond all racial differences."[36] Here the psychic domain itself seems to have been reduced to nothing more than an epiphenomenon of a material substrate. This is Jung at his worst, surrendering to a materialistic scientism which he elsewhere deplores.

In *Psychology and Religion* Jung staked out his most characteristic position on metaphysics:

> Psychology treats . . . all metaphysical . . . assertions as mental phenomena, and regards them as statements about the mind and its structure that derive ultimately from certain unconscious dispositions. It does not consider them to be absolutely valid or even capable of establishing metaphysical truth. . . . Psychology therefore holds that the mind cannot establish or assert anything beyond itself.[37]

In similar vein, this:

> I am and remain a psychologist. I am not interested in anything that transcends the psychological content of human experience. I do not even ask myself whether such transcendence is possible.[38]

Jung, to his credit, was not always able to hold fast to this position. In 1946, for example, he was prepared to write that "archetypes . . . have a nature that cannot with certainty be desig-

---

[34] F. Schuon, *Survey of Metaphysics and Esoterism*, 195.

[35] C.G. Jung, *Memories, Dreams, Reflections*, 381.

[36] From Jung's Introduction to *The Secret of the Golden Flower*, quoted by Burckhardt in "Cosmology and Modern Science," 168. (Burckhardt's essay can also be found in his *Mirror of the Intellect*.) See also P. Sherrard, "An Introduction to the Religious Thought of C.J. Jung"; W. Smith, *Cosmos and Transcendence*, Ch. 6; and W. Perry, *The Widening Breach: Evolutionism in the Mirror of Cosmology*, 89. Sherrard argues that Jung's thought can best be understood as an agenda for the displacement of Christianity while Smith highlights some of the contradictions and the "dogmatic relativism" which betrays Jung's confusion of the spiritual with the psychic. Perry notes how Jung inverts the traditional doctrine of Archetypes. On Jung's psychologization of religion see also W. Hanegraaff, *New Age Religion and Western Culture*, 496-512.

[37] C. G. Jung, "Psychology and Religion," quoted in P. Novak, "C.G. Jung in the Light of Asian Philosophy," 68.

[38] Interview with Eliade for *Combat*, in *C.G. Jung Speaking*, 229.

nated as psychic," and that the archetype is a "metaphysical" entity not susceptible to any un-equivocal (i.e., "scientific") definition.[39] The status of archetypes is a critical issue, particularly if we take the following kind of claim seriously:

> The basis of analytical psychology's significance for the psychology of religion . . . lies in C.G. Jung's discovery of how archetypal images, events, and experiences, individually and in groups, are the *essential determinants* of the religious life in history and in the present.[40]

From a traditionalist point of view there are two problems: the first is the suggestion, not hard to find in Jung's writings, that the psychic domain contains and exhausts all of supra-material reality, a view we have designated pan-psychism. But even when Jung retreats from this position, he still insists that the psychic is the only supra-material reality that we can explore and *know*. From the viewpoint of traditional metaphysics this amounts to nothing less than a denial of the Intellect, that faculty by which Absolute Reality can be apprehended, and to which all traditional wisdoms testify.[41]

What of "God"? Jung's position, at least as Aniela Jaffé recalls it, is subtle but clear: "God" and "the unconscious" are inseparable from the point of view of the subject but not identical. One of Jung's most careful formulations on the subject goes like this:

> This is certainly not to say that what we call the unconscious is identical with God or set up in his place. It is simply the medium from which religious experience seems to flow.

The problem arises in what follows: "As to what the further cause of such experience may be, the answer to this lies beyond the range of human knowledge."[42] Elsewhere he affirmed that, "the transcendental reality . . . [beyond] the world inside and outside ourselves . . . is as certain as our own existence."[43] Nevertheless, it *necessarily* remains an unfathomable mystery. In denying the possibility of intellection and of absolute certitude concerning metaphysical realities Jung again falls foul of the traditionalists. Compare Jung's notion that we "are hopelessly cooped up in an exclusively psychic world" and that the cause of religious experience "lies beyond human knowledge" with this kind of claim from Frithjof Schuon (who is reaffirming a view that can be found in all traditional metaphysics—those of Plato, Eckhart, Nagajurna, and Sankara to cite several conspicuous examples):

> The distinctive mark of man is total intelligence, that is to say an intelligence which is objective and capable of conceiving the absolute. . . . This objectivity

---

[39] C.G. Jung, "On the Nature of the Psyche," quoted in A. Jaffé, *The Myth of Meaning*, 23.

[40] G. Wehr, *Jung: A Biography*, 291 (italics mine). On Jung and archetypes see E. Wasserstrom, *Religion after Religion*, 352, fn21.

[41] See P. Novak, "C.G. Jung in the Light of Asian Philosophy," 77. At other points Jung's philosophical position is also reminiscent of a kind of "existentialist" relativism. Thus, "the sole purpose of human existence is to kindle a light in the darkness of mere being" (*Memories, Dreams, Reflections*, 358).

[42] From "The Undiscovered Self," in *Civilization in Transition*, quoted in A. Jaffé, *The Myth of Meaning*, 40.

[43] From *Mysterium Coniunctionis*, quoted in A. Jaffé, *The Myth of Meaning*, 42.

. . . would lack any sufficient reason did it not have the capacity to conceive the absolute or infinite.[44]

Or, even more succinctly,

The prerogative of the human state is objectivity, the essential content of which is the Absolute. There is no knowledge without objectivity of the intelligence.[45]

Furthermore,

This capacity for objectivity and absoluteness is an anticipated and existential refutation of all the ideologies of doubt: if man is able to doubt, this is because certitude exists; likewise the very notion of illusion proves that man has access to reality.[46]

Another stumbling block for traditionalists concerns the relationship of the empirical ego and consciousness. Ananda Coomaraswamy signals the problem when he writes,

The health envisaged by empirical psychotherapy is a freedom from particular pathogenic conditions; that envisaged by sacred or traditional psychology is *freedom from all conditions and predicaments*. . . . Furthermore, the pursuit of the greater freedom necessarily entails the attainment of the lesser.[47]

In other words, Jung sought to rehabilitate the empirical ego rather than to dismantle it. From a traditionalist point of view Jung hoists himself on his own petard when he writes: "To us consciousness is inconceivable without an ego. . . . I cannot imagine a conscious mental state that does not relate to the ego."[48] Daniel Goleman elaborates the cardinal point:

The models of contemporary psychology . . . foreclose the acknowledgement or investigation of a mode of being which is the central premise and *summum bonum* of virtually every Eastern psycho-spiritual system. Called variously Enlightenment, Buddhahood . . . and so on, there is simply no fully equivalent category in contemporary psychology. The paradigms of traditional Asian psychologies, however, are capable of encompassing the major categories of contemporary psychology as well as this other mode of consciousness.[49]

---

[44] F. Schuon, "To be Man is to Know," 117-118.

[45] F. Schuon, *Esoterism as Principle and as Way*, 15ff.

[46] F. Schuon, *Logic and Transcendence*, 13.

[47] A.K. Coomaraswamy, "On the Indian and Traditional Psychology, or rather, Pneumatology," *Selected Papers 2*, 335 (italics mine). See also T. Burckhardt, "Cosmology and Modern Science," 174-175.

[48] From *Psychology and Religion*, quoted by P. Novak, "C.G. Jung in the Light of Asian Philosophy," 82.

[49] Quoted in P. Novak, "C.G. Jung in the Light of Asian Philosophy", 73. One again sees the problem in Jung's homologizing of the psychosis of the mental patient with the "mythopoeic imagination which has vanished from our rational age" (*Memories, Dreams, Reflections*, 213).

Fourthly, several traditionalists, most notably Phillip Sherrard, have argued that Jung's covert and perhaps not fully conscious agenda was nothing less than the dethronement of Christianity in all of its traditional and institutional forms, and its replacement by a kind of quasi-religious psychology for which Jung himself was a "prophetic" voice. A variant of this particular kind of argument has been elaborated by Philip Rieff and is adumbrated in the following passage:

> After the failure of the Reformation, and the further fragmentation of Christianity, the search was on for those more purely symbolical authorities to which an educated Christian could transfer his loyalty from the Church. Biblicism gave way to erudition, erudition to historical liberalism, and the latter to a variety of psychological conservatisms, of which Jung's is potentially the most attractive for those not entirely unchurched.[50]

This kind of argument would seem to have some cogency when we recall a few of Jung's many explanations of his own relationship to religion. Take this, for example, from a letter written in 1946:

> I practice science, not apologetics and not philosophy. . . . My interest is a scientific one. . . . I proceed from a positive Christianity that is as much Catholic as Protestant, and my concern is to point out in a scientifically responsible way those empirically tangible facts which would at least make plausible the legitimacy of Christian and especially Catholic dogma.[51]

The traditionalist response to this kind of claim is quite implacable. Thus Schuon: "Modern science . . . can neither add nor subtract anything in respect of the total truth or of mythological or other symbolism or in respect of the principles and experiences of the spiritual life."[52] In the light of these kinds of criticisms it is not hard to see why one traditionalist has suggested that "In the final analysis, what Jung has to offer is a religion for atheists,"[53] or why Rieff claims that Jung's thought amounts to "a religion for heretics."[54] In similar vein, Eric Wasserstrom has argued that not only Jung but the whole Eranos group were in search of "religion after religion." In a wonderfully ambiguous phrase, a Dominican admirer of Jung called him "a priest without a surplice."[55] It was meant as a compliment but if we take the lack of a surplice as signifying Jung's detachment from any religious tradition then the epithet carries a different freight. To make the same point differently, a priest without a surplice is no priest at all.

---

[50] P. Rieff, *The Triumph of the Therapeutic*, 110. See also R. Moacanin, *Jung's Psychology and Tibetan Buddhism*, 94.

[51] Quoted in G. Wehr, *Jung: A Biography*, 302.

[52] F. Schuon, "No Activity Without Truth," 36-37.

[53] W. Smith, *Cosmos and Transcendence*, 130.

[54] P. Rieff, *The Triumph of the Therapeutic*, 115.

[55] W. Smith, *Cosmos and Transcendence*, 130.

B. Eastern Spirituality and Western Psychology

Before proceeding to a consideration of the encounter of Western psychology and Eastern spirituality we must face the melancholy fact that Western psychology, taken as a whole but especially in its academic aspect, remains astonishingly ignorant of the psycho-spiritual traditions of the East. The exception is the rather small world of Jungian, existentialist and transpersonal psychology. Jung's contribution was to open the doors of an emergent late nineteenth century "science" to the wealth of psychological insight in the religious traditions of both East and West. As we have just seen, Jung's enterprise was fraught with all manner of ambiguities and anomalies. Nonetheless, it contrasts positively with all those modern schools of psychological thought which treat all religion as pathological and dismiss the whole spiritual dimension.

While Jung's somewhat ambivalent encounter with the East has been the most significant single avenue by which Eastern ideas and themes have flowed into Western psychology there are a good many other engagements of which we must take some note. Mention must be made of some of the pioneering figures in what can loosely be called the psychology of religious experience—William James, Rudolf Otto, Mircea Eliade. Here we shall dwell briefly on a few developments which signal some intellectual traffic between West and East: Erich Fromm's humanistic appropriation of Zen, existentialist interest in the East, the emergence of transpersonal psychology, and the somewhat curious phenomenon of biofeedback as it has been applied to various yogas.

Erich Fromm and Zen

After his interest in Zen Buddhism was sparked by a meeting with D.T. Suzuki, Erich Fromm participated, in 1957, in a conference on Buddhism and psychoanalysis; it led to a "considerable enlargement and revision" of his ideas, specifically with respect to "the problems of what constitutes the unconscious, of the transformation of the unconscious into consciousness, and of the goal of psychoanalytic therapy." Fromm was a humanistic psychologist who married his analytic work to larger social and moral concerns, and whose "emphasis on freedom, responsibility, and the quest for meaning, rather than on the unconscious, set him apart from Freudian orthodoxy."[56] Now, he wrote,

> the knowledge of Zen, and a concern with it, can have a most fertile and clarifying influence on the theory and technique of psychoanalysis. . . . Zen thought will deepen and widen the horizon of the psychoanalyst.[57]

Like Jung, Fromm believed that modern humankind was suffering from a deep spiritual malaise characterized by widespread ennui and alienation, the symptoms having been diagnosed by thinkers as diverse as Kierkegaard, Marx and Tillich—to whom we might add such exemplary nineteenth century figures as Nietzsche, Baudelaire, and Dostoevsky. For Fromm psychoanalysis was not so much a "cure" for an "illness" but a technique of self-knowledge and self-transformation, one with obvious affinities with Zen which he described as "the art of seeing into

---

[56] J.J. Clarke, *Oriental Enlightenment*, 156

[57] E. Fromm, "Psychoanalysis and Zen" in Erich Fromm, D.T. Suzuki & Richard De Martino, *Zen Buddhism and Psychoanalysis*, 140.

the nature of one's being; it is a way from bondage to freedom." Far from being a self-indulgent form of narcissistic navel-gazing, as detractors in the West often portrayed Eastern meditational practices, Zen demanded the most searching confrontation with one's immediate and present condition and "the realization of the relation of myself to the Universe," as Fromm put it.[58] Furthermore, he argued, the Zen path could help us transcend the limitations of rational thought by its emphasis on experiential knowledge, one wherein subject-object dualities are overcome.

Existentialism, Herman Hesse, Hubert Benoit

The reference to experiential knowledge provides us with a link to another school of European thought, much influenced by the emergence of modern Freudian psychology but also occasionally receptive to Eastern influences—existentialism. Here, as an example of the confluence of existentialism, Freudian psychology, and Eastern interests, we may cite the shadowy figure of Herman Hesse. Like many others who developed a serious interest in Eastern religion and philosophy, Hesse was the son of missionaries who had spent many years in the East; he grew up in a milieu saturated with mementoes of the Orient, some of them lovingly described in several of his autobiographical sketches. Hesse made several visits to the East (not entirely happy experiences) and retained throughout his life an abiding interest in Eastern spirituality and in a synthesis of religious ideas from East and West.[59] He was also deeply influenced, like so many European writers of his generation, by the ideas of Freud and Jung—consider, for instance, his fictional exploration of the fragile "self" and the idea of multiple personalities in *Steppenwolf* (1927), a novel in which the European sense of anxiety and cultural dislocation is dramatically rendered. Although Hesse was awarded the Nobel Prize for Literature, largely on the basis of his last novel, *The Glass Bead Game* (1943), the zenith of his acclamation was probably the counter-cultural enthusiasm for his novels *Siddhartha* (1922) and *Journey to the East* (1931) which became obligatory reading for the more serious-minded hippies of the late '60s. In *Siddhartha* Hesse attempted a distillation of what he had learned of Eastern spirituality mingled with what he found most valuable in his own pietistic Protestant background. Many literary histories tell us that *Siddhartha* recounts the life of the Buddha, an error which might be avoided by actually reading the book! Those who have read the novel will remember the charming portrait of the Buddha, but it is only a vignette in the story of the protagonist who shares one of the Awakened One's several names. Also central to Hesse's intellectual and creative projects was the attempt to affirm and demonstrate the underlying unity of all the branches of the human race.

In a psychological context one of the most interesting of those who attempted to weld together existentialist concerns and Eastern ideas was the French psychiatrist Hubert Benoit (1904-1992). His book *The Supreme Doctrine: Psychological Insights in Zen Thought*, published in 1955, drew attention to Buddhism's central concern with the sources of mental suffering. Zen, wrote Benoit, with its emphasis on spontaneity and the non-intellectual process of "emp-

---

[58] E. Fromm, "Psychoanalysis and Zen" in Erich Fromm, D.T. Suzuki & Richard De Martino, *Zen Buddhism and Psychoanalysis*, 135.

[59] See particularly "Childhood of the Magician" (1923) and "Life Story Briefly Told" (1925) in Herman Hesse, *Autobiographical Writings*. See also Ralph Freedman, *Herman Hesse: Pilgrim of Crisis*, 149-156, and Hesse's "Remembrance of India" (1916) in *Autobiographical Writings*.

tying out," could lead one into seeing one's own true nature.[60] At this point mention might be made of three other well-known psychologists who developed an interest in Eastern religion and spirituality sufficiently serious to impel extended visits to the sub-continent: the Swiss psychoanalyst Medard Boss, whose psychotherapy was also much influenced by Heidegger; Karen Horney, who spent some time in a Zen monastery in Japan; and the anti-psychiatrist R.D. Laing who practiced with Buddhist meditation teachers in Sri Lanka, Thailand, and Japan.[61]

Hans Jacobs on Western Psychotherapy and Hindu *Sadhana*

Hans Jacobs was a former pupil of Jung, and a practicing psychotherapist who traveled to India to study yoga and Hindu metaphysics under properly qualified teachers. He spent over a year there, lecturing for a time at Benares University, and studying and practicing yoga for several months at Kalimpong and Kedernath. In 1961 he produced one of the earliest and most thoughtful of what was to become a wave of works dealing with the relation of Western psychology to traditional psycho-spiritual disciplines and philosophy, *Western Psychotherapy and Hindu Sadhana*. Generally Jacobs managed to avoid the widespread and intensely irritating assumption that Western psychology was equipped to evaluate or to "confirm" the insights of Eastern traditions. (In much the same vein people are all too ready to talk of the ways in which modern physics "confirms" or "validates" ancient cosmological doctrines, as if these doctrines were hitherto suspect but have now been given the imprimatur of modern science. Rather, one might more properly speak in terms of some modern sciences, despite their limited epistemological base and their often highly flawed conceptual apparatus, becoming dimly and precariously aware of truths which were known to the ancients.) Among the many insights in Jacobs' book we find the following general remark:

> One may say, without much exaggeration, that the proper characteristic of Indian philosophy, a detailed exposition of the data and the possibilities of human consciousness, which alone gives man a status of his own ... has up till now been only rather inadequately faced in the Western world.[62]

Jacobs' book offers a judicious consideration of both Freudian and Jungian theory, identifying some of their innovations but also discussing the ways in which the Hindu tradition foreshadows their apparently new insights.

Humanistic and Transpersonal Psychology: Ken Wilber and Others

A group of psychologists sometimes loosely gathered under the canopy of "humanistic psychology," prominently Abraham Maslow, Rollo May, Carl Rogers, and Fritz Perls, reacted against the mechanistic models of behaviorist psychology and the medical orientation of psychoanalysis. We might characterize this school of thought as assigning more creative agency to the human individual than some other schools of contemporary psychology. Although none of these

---

[60] H. Benoit, *Zen and the Psychology of Transformation: The Supreme Doctrine*, rev. ed. (The title was changed for later editions.)

[61] J.J. Clarke, *Oriental Enlightenment*, 158.

[62] H. Jacobs, *Western Psychotherapy and Hindu Sadhana*, 18.

figures made a sustained study of Eastern doctrines and practices, "the whole flavor of their enterprise, with its emphasis on self-actualization and on the exploration and refinement of consciousness, has an Eastern tang to it."[63] One popular theme, for instance, taken up by both May and Maslow, was the need to overcome the Cartesian mind-body dualism so firmly entrenched in Western thought. Another was the interest in altered states of consciousness, evident in the Gestalt and Transpersonal Psychology of figures such as Claudio Naranjo, Stanislav Grof, Charles Tart, and Ken Wilber.[64] Roberto Assagioli's theory of "psycho-synthesis," best displayed perhaps in his late work *Transpersonal Development* (1991), belongs to the same general school. In its affinity with spiritual traditions of both East and West, transpersonal psychology parts company with mainstream psychology which has retained its nineteenth century hostility to all forms of religion and spirituality as primitive "superstition," "neurosis," or "delusion."

Over the last four decades we note the burgeoning literature on such subjects as near-death experiences, psychedelics, out-of-body experiences and the like, all familiar subjects in the religious literature of the East: one might think, for instance, of the vast mystical literature of the Tibetans of which *The Book of the Dead* is but only one text. As one commentator has observed, "thinkers with interest in transpersonal states of being have generally felt it necessary to look to Eastern thought as a source of conceptual language, theoretical models, and practical guidance."[65]

The leading contemporary figure in this field is Ken Wilber whose work is concerned with a synthesis of scientific and mystical understandings of consciousness, drawn from both East and West. Wilber accepts the perennialist view that at the core of all religious traditions is a single, unifying truth to which mystical experience gives access. To account for the empirical variety of mystical experiences Wilber posits a hierarchy of consciousness, a series of six levels, rising from the uroboric or oceanic consciousness up to the supreme consciousness, that of *Dharmakaya*, beyond all dualities. Different forms of spiritual and psychological practice mesh into different levels of consciousness: many Western psychological approaches, such as that of Freud, only tap into the lower levels of consciousness while the metaphysical and mystical traditions, particularly Vedanta, access the highest reaches.[66] Wilber's work is shot through with the notions of wholeness, integration, unity. He has attempted to integrate the findings and insights of a staggeringly diverse range of sources, ancient and modern, Eastern and Western, scientific and mythological. Admirers such as Tony Schwartz believe Wilber to be "the most comprehensive philosophical thinker of our times" but he has also drawn fire from a wide range of critics. One sympathizes with Jack Crittenden's view that "Most critics have taken umbrage at Wilber's

---

[63] J.J. Clarke, *Oriental Enlightenment*, 158-159. Likewise John Rowan in his history of humanistic psychology, in 1976: "Humanistic psychology today contains many things which came originally from the East" (quoted in J.J. Clarke, 159).

[64] As Frithjof Capra has remarked, "Transpersonal psychology is concerned, directly or indirectly, with the recognition, understanding, and realization of non-ordinary, mystical, or 'transpersonal' states of consciousness, and with the psychological conditions that represent barriers to such transpersonal realizations. Its concerns are thus very close to those of the spiritual traditions" (*The Turning Point*, 405).

[65] J.J. Clarke, *Oriental Enlightenment*, 159.

[66] For a sympathetic discussion of Wilber's basic schema see Bede Griffiths, *A New Vision of Reality*, chap. 2; for a critique of Wilber from a traditionalist perspective see J. Segura, "On Ken Wilber's Integration of Science and Religion," included in this volume.

attacks on their particular field, while they condone or concede the brilliance of his attacks on other fields."[67] Wilber cannot be pinned down in any disciplinary field: his work is perhaps best described as a creative synthesis of philosophy, comparative mysticism, transpersonal psychology, and the new physics. He emerged, in Crittenden's words, as something of a boy wonder, publishing his first book, *The Spectrum of Consciousness* at age twenty-three and turning out a steady stream of arresting and provocative works ever since. Perhaps the most troubling aspect of Wilber's work is his commitment to evolutionistic paradigms, always inappropriate in the spiritual domain. To subscribe to any form of spiritual evolutionism is to fall prey to the preposterous notion that the teachings of the Buddha, of Jesus, of the ancient *rishis*, can be improved upon, as if Truth itself were subject to the contingencies of time. All of this is simply of a piece with the pervasive historicism of the prevailing Western mentality, one which all too often afflicts thinkers who in other respects are quite traditional and orthodox.

One particular debate which impinges on our subject concerns "left-brain" and "right brain" modalities of consciousness, the general argument being that the West has privileged left-brain activities to the neglect of those of the right brain—which is to say that modern European thought has over-valued rationality and verbally-centered mental processes (often associated with "masculinity"), and devalued the intuitive, imaginative, holistic, and "feminine" modes and processes which, it is argued, are enhanced in Eastern meditation. The physicist Frithjof Capra states the matter in terms of the traditional Chinese polarities of *yin* and *yang*:

> Our society has consistently favored *yang*, or masculine values and attitudes, and neglected their complementary *yin*, or feminine counterparts. We have favored self assertion over integration, analysis over synthesis, rational knowledge over intuitive wisdom, science over religion, competition over cooperation, expansion over conservation.[68]

One of the leading figures in this field is Robert Ornstein, whose work has remained somewhat controversial since the appearance in 1977 of *The Psychology of Consciousness*, whilst other investigators include the Nobel laureate and neurosurgeon, Roger Sperry, and Betty Edwards, author of the best-selling *Drawing on the Right Side of the Brain* (1979).[69]

Throughout the West there are a growing number of psychotherapists, thoroughly trained in at least one of the branches of Western psychology, who have turned eastwards for both theoretical insights and practical therapeutic techniques. There is a mushrooming literature in this field. Jack Kornfield's books stand out but we might also mention the Australian John Tarrant, a Jungian psychotherapist who is also a Zen *roshi* and the author of the recent and widely-hailed book, *Inside the Dark*, David Brazier, an English psychotherapist, Zen Buddhist, and author of *Zen Therapy*, and Maura and Franklin Sills who teach Core-process Psychotherapy, firmly based on Buddhist principles, at the Karuna Institute in Devon. Akong Rinpoche of Samye Ling has also developed a five-stage system of therapeutic training.[70] We can also see many Oriental

---

[67] J. Crittenden in K. Wilber, *The Eye of the Spirit: An Integral Vision for a World Gone Slightly Mad*, viii.

[68] F. Capra, *The Tao of Physics*, 1991 edition, 15.

[69] See T. Schwartz, *What Really Matters*, 159-191, and B. Vinall, *The Resonance of Quality*.

[70] On Akong and Sills see S. Batchelor, *The Awakening of the West*, 364.

traces, often unacknowledged, in the works of pop psychologists such as Louise Hay, Wayne Dyer, and John Gray: various techniques of Eastern provenance, such as visualization exercises, the use of mandalas, breathing exercises, and yogic postures, have become stock-in-trade. We also find in the contemporary West a great many thinkers and practitioners who are seeking to blend the insights of modern psychology with some of the traditional modes of understanding to be found in the Western heritage—Thomas Moore, Clarissa Pinkola Estés, Robert Sardello, and Jean Shinoda Bolen among them.

Mystical Experience, Meditation, and Biofeedback

The study of mystical experience has been taken up in a variety of disciplines—anthropology (particularly through the study of shamanism and other "archaic techniques of ecstasy," to use Eliade's phrase), philosophy (the "cognitive status of the so-called mystical experience" is a staple of philosophy of religion courses), comparative religion, and psychology. The scope of the present work does not allow anything more than a passing glance at this vast and hazardous territory. A large part of the problem derives from the fact—already alluded to in the traditionalist critique of psychologism—that a purely psychological inquiry into mystical experience is doomed from the start as it is based on the false premise that the lesser (an empirical and quantitative psychology) can "explain" the greater (the plenary experience of the mystics). It is also a case of the conflation of the psychic and spiritual planes which constitutes one element of "the psychological imposture." The only psychology of mysticism likely to bear fruitful results is one which develops within the framework of a great religious tradition and which is guided by metaphysical principles—precisely what we find in the traditional "psychologies" and *sacra scientia* of the East (yoga, tantra, alchemy, the theory and practice of the mandala etc.), and precisely what we cannot find in Western psychology so long as it retains its pretensions as an autonomous and profane science—i.e., one which can proceed exclusively through empirical inquiry and analysis, and which is answerable to nothing outside itself.

Since the counter-culture of the '60s meditational practices of one sort and another have become increasingly popular in the West. In the psychological field, more narrowly defined, there has been a growing interest in the use of meditation to promote psychological well-being. Meditation itself has also come under stringent scientific investigation, in respect of both the physiological and "mental" changes it induces. Elmer and Alyce Green and Dale Walters, drawing on the work of Hans Berger and Joe Kamiya, were among the pioneers of the use of biofeedback to quantify changes in consciousness brought about by meditative states and to demonstrate the linkages between mind and body in the treatment of illness. Their work was based at the Menninger Clinic in Topeka, Kansas, but also included several months in India where they used biofeedback equipment to measure the self-regulatory abilities of Indian yogis. This research included the famous case of the Indian yogi who was buried underground for eight hours, without any air supply and who was apparently able to voluntarily enter a state of deep rest requiring the most minimal levels of oxygen.[71] Back at the Menninger Institute the Greens also conducted experiments and demonstrations with another Indian yogi, "Swami Rama of the Himalayas," about whom Doug Boyd (Alyce Green's son from an earlier marriage) wrote *Swami*.

---

[71] T. Schwartz, *What Really Matters*, 141. On the Greens and biofeedback see 117-154.

Biofeedback maps physiological changes in the subject—muscle tension, blood pressure, body temperature, brainwave activity. It also explores the way in which it is possible to bring various physiological processes under voluntary and conscious control and thereby change one's state of consciousness. Biofeedback, in Elmer Green's terms, "provides a bridge between the conscious and unconscious, voluntary and involuntary, cortex and subcortex, and even between reason and intuition."[72] Such work has had some beneficial clinical results (in the control of migraine headaches, the lowering of blood pressure, the alleviation of asthma and insomnia) and also tells us something of the physiological correlates of changes in consciousness. It has also promoted an acceptance of the fact that meditation can lower levels of stress, anxiety, depression, and neurosis, and promote feelings of self-worth and authenticity. However, as an "explanation" of meditative states and mystical experiences it remains drastically reductionist and one-dimensional.[73]

C. The Lessons of the East

Some of the figures under discussion have had a part to play in the "deprovincializing" of Western culture, that is to say, in overcoming the limits of our own restrictive Eurocentric assumptions and values at a time when, more than ever before, we need to be open to the lessons of other cultures. The most fertile connections between Eastern spirituality and Western psychology arise out of an interest in consciousness. Andrew Rawlinson usefully articulates four principles which inform most Oriental understandings of the human condition: 1. Human beings are best understood in terms of consciousness and its modifications; 2. Consciousness can be transformed by spiritual practices; 3. There are teachers and exemplars who have done this; and 4. They can help others to do the same through some form of transmission. One cannot maintain any vaguely serious interest in Eastern spirituality without being interested in consciousness and in the nature of the "self"—in short, in psychology. Alan Watts, rather recklessly, went so as far as to say this:

> If we look deeply into such ways of life as Buddhism and Taoism, Vedanta and Yoga, we do not find either philosophy or religion as these are understood in the West. We find something more nearly resembling psychotherapy. . . . The main resemblance between these Eastern ways . . . and Western psychotherapy is the concern of both with bringing about changes in consciousness, changes in our own ways of feeling our own existence and our relation to human society and the natural world.[74]

Looking at the large canvas, what might we discern as the theoretical and practical lessons of Eastern teachings? There is a great deal to be learned from Eastern traditions which have,

---

[72] T. Schwartz, *What Really Matters*, 119.

[73] Of the myriad books in this field one of the more sober and interesting is *Silent Music*, by William Johnston.

[74] A. Watts, *Psychotherapy East and West*, x. See also F. Capra, *The Turning Point*, 167-168. Recall, too, Jung's claim that "all religions, down to the forms of magical religion of the primitives, are psychotherapies, which treat and heal the sufferings of the soul, and those of the body that come from the soul" (C.G. Jung in a 1935 paper on psychotherapy, cited in G. Wehr, *Jung: A Biography*, 293).

for thousands of years, focused attention on the mysteries of human consciousness and on the problematic nature of the self. As Ramana Maharshi observed, there is one great philosophical, and we might say psychological, question which subsumes all others: "Who am I?" The principal lesson deriving from these traditions would seem to be that the "self" with which most of us identify ourselves, is a psycho-physical construct in a state of permanent change, itself without any permanence, and with no more than an evanescent or fugitive reality. Furthermore, the secret of human happiness, so such traditions teach, ultimately lies not in any rehabilitation or bolstering up of this egoic self, but in liberation from it, more particularly in detachment from what Chögyam Trungpa has called "the bureaucracy of the ego,"[75] a process Hubert Benoit calls "the integral devalorization of the egotistical life."[76] One Western psychologist has recently contrasted, in very general terms, the differing approaches of Western psychology and Buddhism to the problem of the self:

> Western psychology makes much . . . of the importance of a coherent self-image and of high self-esteem. It is healthy to have a clear sense of one's own identity and a feeling of autonomy, and to value oneself and one's achievements. Buddhism denies the existence of a self as a distinct entity. . . . The self is merely a construction, and yet it refers everything to itself and distorts experience. The goal is thus not to try further to enhance the self, but to undermine it.

She points out that Western models of psychological health often emphasize the importance of predictability and control while Buddhism encourages detachment and an openness where "the task is not to engineer positive outcomes and avoid negative ones, but to transcend all attachments and aversions."[77] Nothing could be further from the mechanistic theories of behaviorist psychology: one need only think of the title of one of the most influential, pernicious, and degrading works of our time, *Beyond Freedom and Dignity* by B.F. Skinner.

One might also suggest that at a time when the destructive consequences of Western dualisms, particularly that of subject and object, are becoming ever more apparent, not least in the so-called environmental crisis, there is a great deal to learn from Eastern teachings which "emphasize the basic unity of the universe" and in which

> The highest aim of their followers—whether they are Hindus, Buddhists, or Taoists—is to become aware of the unity and mutual interrelation of all things, to transcend the notion of an individual isolated self and to identify themselves with ultimate reality.[78]

Secondly, Eastern traditions, such as Tibetan Buddhism, can provide us with highly sophisticated maps of consciousness, and of states of being, which take account not only of what Freud termed the "subconscious" but also the "supra-conscious," a realm of experience acces-

---

[75] See Chögyam Trungpa, *Cutting Through Spiritual Materialism.*

[76] H. Benoit, *Zen and the Psychology of Transformation*, 26.

[77] C. Ray, "Western Psychology and Buddhist Teachings: Convergences and Divergences," 21.

[78] F. Capra, *The Tao of Physics*, 29.

sible through the individual psyche but by no means bound by it. To cite one example of such a map: the Buddhist Wheel of Life is not only a representation of various post-mortem states but is simultaneously a figuration of various states of consciousness and of the psychic mechanisms which bring them about. Such maps alert us to the limitations of materialistic and mechanistic accounts of consciousness in particular, and of the Cartesian and Newtonian paradigms of scientific inquiry in the West. As Frithjof Capra has observed,

> A science concerned only with quantity and based exclusively on measurement is inherently unable to deal with experience, quality, or values. It will therefore be inadequate for understanding the nature of consciousness, since consciousness is a central aspect of our inner world, and thus, first of all, an experience.... The more scientists insist on quantitative statements, the less they are able to describe the nature of consciousness.[79]

This last observation is critical. Unless we wish to surrender to materialist reductionisms of various ilk then we must accept the very far-reaching implications of Capra's claim that consciousness is simply not amenable to a quantitative analysis. Recall, too, Jung's admonition that, "Overvalued reason has this in common with political absolutism: under its dominion the individual is pauperized."[80]

In this context it must be observed that whilst Western psychology might learn a great deal from Buddhism as a psychological system, the teachings and practices of this tradition amount to something much more. In his autobiography Carl Jung said this: "The decisive question for man is: Is he related to something infinite or not? That is the telling question of his life."[81] One can only say that all Western attempts, especially by those with a tendentious agenda, to reduce Buddhism to one of its elements must be resisted, like all the manifold forms of an inveterate reductionism to which the modern scientific mentality is particularly vulnerable. We must always remember that Buddhism, like all religions, answers Jung's question in the affirmative. In so doing it parts company with all secular and humanistic "psychologies," including warm-and-fuzzy New Ageism which appropriates the term "spirituality" only to empty it of all meaning by wrenching it from its religious context.

On the practical level perhaps the most central lesson of the East is that various techniques of self-inquiry, such as meditation, are therapeutic in the broadest possible sense, which is to say that they are not meant only, or even primarily, for the "mentally ill" or the "maladjusted" individual, but for everyone. Indeed, from a certain perspective, we are *all* "mentally ill" and "maladjusted"! A Western professor of child psychology, asked recently why Westerners, and particularly psychologists, might profitably show some interest in Buddhism, wrote this:

> At its simplest level, the answer for the psychologist lies in the profound effect that Buddhism appears to have upon human behavior, an effect that many of us would accept is highly beneficial in that it promotes psychological health. That is,

---

[79] F. Capra, *The Turning Point*, 415.

[80] C.G. Jung, *Memories, Dreams, Reflections*, 333.

[81] C.G. Jung, *Memories, Dreams, Reflections*, 356-357.

if by psychological health we mean the ability to live in harmony with oneself and nature, to show tolerance and compassion to one's fellow human beings, to endure hardship and suffering without mental disintegration, to prize non-violence, to care for the welfare of all sentient beings, and to see a meaning and purpose in one's life that allows one to enter old age or to face death with serenity and without fear. . . . The most obvious reason for psychologists to interest themselves in Buddhism, therefore, is the issue of psychological health (their own as well as their clients'!)[82]

Similarly, Rawlinson writes of a spiritual psychology of the East which, far from being concerned only with some ethereal and "mystical" condition, touches on all aspects of life:

what it is to be alive, to be born, to have a body, to die; the nature of sickness and suffering, of happiness and love; what it is to be male, female. . . ; what it is to be a child, a parent; the nature of the family (and its alternatives. . .); how society should be organized and according to what principles; how one should eat, dress, and earn one's living; the proper form of the arts. . . ; the world and its origin; how consciousness works from the most mundane levels to the most rarefied.[83]

Huston Smith has usefully summarized eight psychological insights which have informed the Indian tradition for at least two millennia and to which the West is only now becoming sensitive. It is worth paraphrasing his catalogue (with a few minor modifications):

• Our consciousness is multi-layered, some levels being difficult of access to everyday awareness.
• The human being is a psycho-physical whole in which there is continuous and subtle interaction between these two aspects.
• In addition to the gross material body there exists a subtle body or sheath, still physical but subtle and invisible.
• With respect to the operations of the mind we must distinguish between rational, critical, analytical thought and deeper, more synthetic, symbolic and intuitive modes.
• The basic emotions are governed not by the superficial mind but by deeper forces.
• What we perceive is not a simple reflection of the external "objective" world "out there" but is, in part, a function of the perceiving organism.
• That life as we normally experience it is dislocated or out of joint (*dukkha*) and that the root cause of this is *tanha*, the drive to maintain a separate egoic existence.[84]

To imagine that we have nothing to learn from this vast body of experience and knowledge, in its myriad forms, is not only insufferably arrogant and provincial, but also, not to put too fine a point on it, obtuse in the extreme. Let us conclude with some hopeful words from the

---

[82] D. Fontana, "Mind, Senses and Self," 35.

[83] A. Rawlinson, *The Book of Enlightened Masters*, xvii-xviii.

[84] See H. Smith, *Essays on World Religion*, 10-11.

physicist and proponent of the Uncertainty Principle, Werner Heisenberg:

> It is probably true quite generally that in the history of human thinking the most fruitful developments frequently take place at those points where two different lines of thought meet. These lines may have their roots in quite different parts of human culture, in different times or different cultural environments or different religious traditions: hence, if they actually meet, that is, if they are at least so much related to each other that real interaction can take place, then one may hope that new and interesting developments may follow.[85]

---

[85] Heisenberg quoted in F. Capra, *The Tao of Physics*, 6.

The Impasse of Modern Psychology:
Behaviorism, Psychoanalysis, Humanistic, and Transpersonal Psychology in the Light of the Perennial Philosophy

Samuel Bendeck Sotillos

[T]he requirement imposed on anyone who wants to practice psychoanalysis as a profession of being first 'psychoanalyzed' himself . . . so from what source did the first psychoanalyst obtain the 'powers' that they communicate to their disciples, and by whom were they themselves 'psychoanalyzed' in the first place?[1]

The above quotation by René Guénon (1886-1951),[2] a pre-eminent exponent of the "Traditionalist" or "Perennialist" school of thought, has framed the most decisive question regarding the entire theme of psychology in relation to the perennial philosophy: from what source did modern psychology first originate? This question touches upon the very kernel of the issue raised in the title of this piece. The traditional or perennial method draws upon the universal principles underlying all modes of knowledge, from sensible perception of the contingent to the direct or non-dual perception of the Absolute via intellectual intuition (*noesis*).[3] These metaphysical principles, being eternal and immutable, provide the criteria for the discernment between "sacred science" and "profane science"—yet because they are for the most part absent from modern psychology, it is left in a precarious situation.[4] "[W]e have no clear exposition of

---

[1] René Guénon, "The Misdeeds of Psychoanalysis," in *The Reign of Quantity and the Signs of the Times*, trans. Lord Northbourne (Ghent, NY: Sophia Perennis, 2001), pp. 233-234.

[2] Sri Ramana Maharshi (1879-1950), a spiritual paragon of the twentieth-century, reverently referred to Guénon as "the great Sufi" (Roger Maridot, "Foreword," to René Guénon, *Miscellanea*, trans. Henry D. Fohr, Cecil Bethell, Patrick Moore and Hubert Schiff [Hillsdale, NY: Sophia Perennis, 2001], p. xviii); "He [René Guénon] probably did more than any other person to awaken Western intellectuals to their lost heritage by reminding them that there is a Goal and there are paths to the Goal" (Arthur Osborne, "Guidance and Orthodoxy," in *For Those with Little Dust: Selected Writings of Arthur Osborne* [Sarasota, FL: Ramana Publications, 1990], p. 76); "In my own education, no writer has been more helpful as an example of keen, spiritual discrimination than the French Sufi, René Guénon" (Theodore Roszak, "Introduction: Pico's Chameleon and the Consciousness Circuit," in *Unfinished Animal: The Aquarian Frontier and the Evolution of Consciousness* [New York: Harper & Row, 1975], p. 15); "Certainly no other writer [René Guénon] has so effectively communicated the absoluteness of truth" (Jacob Needleman (ed.), *The Sword of Gnosis: Metaphysics, Cosmology, Tradition, Symbolism* [London: Arkana, 1986], p. 12); see also Samuel Bendeck Sotillos, "Book Review: The Essential René Guénon," *Parabola: Myth, Tradition, and the Search for Meaning*, Vol. 35, No. 3 (Fall 2010), pp. 114-121.

[3] "[I]n civilizations of a traditional character, intellectual intuition lies at the root of everything" (René Guénon, "Sacred and Profane Science" in *The Crisis of the Modern World*, trans. Arthur Osborne, Marco Pallis and Richard C. Nicholson [Ghent, NY: Sophia Perennis et Universalis, 1996], p. 61).

[4] "Modern civilization, by its divorce from any principle, can be likened to a headless corpse of which the last motions are convulsive and insignificant" (Ananda K. Coomaraswamy, "Am I My Brother's Keeper?" in *The Bugbear of Literacy* [Bedfont, Middlesex: Perennial Books, 1979], p. 15).

guiding principles,"[5] says Carl Jung (1875-1961). This then leads us to the following dilemma: "What we call consciousness without an object, oneness, doesn't exist for modern psychology."[6]

No Psychology or Science of the Soul without Metaphysics

If it is the sacred or spiritual domain that, according to the perennial philosophy, not only situates the psycho-physical domain but balances and heals it, then an authentic and integral psychology needs *a priori* to be rooted in and intrinsically connected to a spiritual tradition in order to be effective. This is what allows for the *metanoia* or integral transformation known as *cura animarum*, or "cure of souls", the goal of what has been termed the "science of the soul" in the ancient sense.[7] While we acknowledge that each orthodox spiritual tradition contains a corresponding integral psychology, we are not suggesting that spirituality is psychology as such, for Spirit simultaneously supersedes the psyche and includes it. The reverse is not true for psychology, however, as the psyche is always subordinate to what is higher than it, namely the Spirit. We recall an illuminating point that speaks to the unanimity of all integral psychologies that correspond to their traditional spiritualities before the rupture of the modern world: "There is no science of the soul [psyche] without a metaphysical basis to it and without spiritual remedies at its disposal."[8]

Modern psychology for the most part has not only radically abandoned but negated its metaphysical origin.[9] It now seeks to cure the mind or cognition taken in isolation, rather than recognizing the separation of the soul from the spiritual domain as the root of the problem.[10] "The word 'mental' is often used to indicate the domain which has been explored by Western psychologists and which is often expressed by the word 'psyche,' so as to avoid metaphysical

---

[5] C.G. Jung, "Psychotherapy and a Philosophy of Life," in *Essays on Contemporary Events: The Psychology of Nazism*, trans. R.F.C. Hull (Princeton, NJ: Princeton University Press, 1989), p. 45. The same could be mentioned of William James's *The Principles of Psychology* (1890), considered by many to be a monumental work within modern psychology: "his *Principles* are not in any sense a system; but rather a collection of chapters that do not hang together" (Mortimer J. Adler, "The History of Psychology," in *What Man Has Made of Man: A Study of the Consequences of Platonism and Positivism in Psychology* [New York: Frederick Ungar Publishing, 1957], p. 86); "It is doubtful if any thinker can claim to have provided psychology with a fundamental set of concepts" (Robert Thomson, "The Achievements and Limitations of Psychology," in *The Pelican History of Psychology* [New York: Penguin Books, 1968], p. 426).

[6] Jean Klein, "London November 1982," in *The Ease of Being*, ed. Emma Edwards (Durham, NC: The Acorn Press, 1998), p. 68.

[7] Ananda K. Coomaraswamy, "On Being in One's Right Mind," in *What is Civilization? And Other Essays* (Ipswich, UK: Golgonooza Press, 1989), pp. 33-41, included in this anthology.

[8] Frithjof Schuon, "The Contradiction of Relativism," in *Logic and Transcendence*, trans. Peter N. Townsend (London: Perennial Books, 1984), p. 14.

[9] See Albert G. A. Balz, "The Metaphysical Infidelities of Modern Psychology," *Journal of Philosophy*, Vol. 33, No. 13 (June 1936), pp. 337-351.

[10] See James Hillman, *Re-Visioning Psychology* (New York: Harper & Row, 1975); Erich Fromm, "The Problem," in *Psychoanalysis and Religion* (New Haven, CT: Yale University Press, 1974), p. 6; Frederic Wiedemann, "Soul: The Mediator," in *Between Two Worlds: The Riddle of Wholeness* (Wheaton, IL: Quest Books, 1986), pp. 68-85; Georg Feuerstein, "The Changing Fortunes of the Soul: A Generation without Soul," in *Lucid Waking: Mindfulness and the Spiritual Potential of Humanity* (Rochester, VT: Inner Traditions, 1997), pp. 31-46; Edward S. Reed, *From Soul to Mind: The Emergence of Psychology, from Erasmus Darwin to William James* (New Haven, CT: Yale University Press, 1997).

and religious inferences suggested by the word 'soul'."[11] By distorting the original meaning of the term psyche or "soul," modern psychology has disabled itself and has only recently begun to realize this. In fact the entirety of modern psychology's enterprise could be astutely summarized in a few brief words underscored by one of its well-known proponents: "Psychology is the Science of Mental Life, both its phenomena and of their conditions."[12] The official beginnings of modern psychology—as an autonomous field of science separate from philosophy and physiology—is thought to have commenced in 1879 with Wilhelm Wundt's (1832-1920) establishment of the first experimental psychology laboratory at the University of Leipzig, Germany.[13] Some have suggested that modern psychology's inception began with John Locke (1632-1704), one of the most influential thinkers of the Enlightenment to whom was attributed, among other things, the formulation of the doctrine of empiricism.[14]

The complete disconnection of modern psychology and modern science from integral metaphysics, which has always brought order to the psycho-physical domain, has had catastrophic effects upon the world we live in; very few would argue against this. The origins of the perennial philosophy, quite to the contrary, are inseparably connected to the sapiential revelations. As René Guénon remarks:

> [W]hat is the origin of these traditional metaphysical doctrines from which we have borrowed all our fundamental ideas? The answer is very simple, although it risks raising objections from those who would prefer to consider everything from an historical point of view, and the answer is that there is no origin—by which we mean no human origin—that can be determined in time. In other words, the origin of tradition, if indeed the word "origin" has any place at all in such a case, is as "non-human" [supra-human or supra-individual] as is metaphysics itself. Metaphysical truth is eternal.[15]

Since modern psychology can trace neither its origins nor the continuity of its transmission[16] to what is sacred and transcendent—"[Modern] psychology, and indeed modern science itself, are historical products"[17]—it is undeniably at a profound impasse which it cannot go beyond

---

[11] Jean Klein, *Be Who You Are*, trans. Mary Mann (Salisbury, UK: Non-Duality Press, 2006), p. 94.

[12] William James, "The Scope of Psychology," in *The Principles of Psychology*, Vol. I (New York: Henry Holt & Company, 1913), p. 1.

[13] "Metaphysics should confessedly, as it does really, rest upon psychology instead of conversely" (Granville Stanley Hall, *The Founders of Modern Psychology* [New York: D. Appleton and Company, 1912], p. 320).

[14] ". . . Locke, the founder of modern psychology" (René Guénon, "The Postulates of Rationalism," in *The Reign of Quantity and the Signs of the Times*, p. 92).

[15] René Guénon, "Eastern Metaphysics," in *Studies in Hinduism*, trans. Henry D. Fohr, ed. Samuel D. Fohr (Ghent, NY: Sophia Perennis, 2001), p. 100.

[16] "[T]ransmission serves as a kind of 'quality control' to insure that a given teacher does not distort the teachings for his own personal gain" (John Welwood, "On Spiritual Authority: Genuine and Counterfeit," in *Spiritual Choices: The Problem of Recognizing Authentic Paths to Inner Transformation*, eds. Dick Anthony, Bruce Ecker and Ken Wilber [New York: Paragon House, 1987], p. 290).

[17] Rollo May, "Social Responsibilities of Psychologists," in *Psychology and the Human Dilemma* (New York: D. Van Nostrand, 1967), p. 207.

by its own efforts. In fact, the father of American psychology reached the following conclusion regarding the limitations of modern psychology: "[Psychology] a nasty little subject—all one cares to know lies outside."[18] The integral psychology of the perennial philosophy differs fundamentally from this perspective since it recognizes the sacred as infused into all domains of reality. This is underscored in the following passage from Whitall Perry (1920-2005), which speaks to what is designated by the term "Tradition" in this perspective:

> Tradition is the continuity of Revelation: an uninterrupted transmission, through innumerable generations, of the spiritual and cosmological principles, sciences, and laws resulting from a revealed religion: nothing is neglected, from the establishment of social orders and codes of conduct to the canons regulating the arts and architecture, ornamentation and dress; it includes the mathematical, physical, medical, and psychological sciences, encompassing moreover those deriving from celestial movements. What contrasts it totally with our modern learning, which is a closed system materially, is its reference of all things back to superior planes of being, and eventually to ultimate Principles; considerations entirely unknown to modern man.[19]

The Margins of the Human Psyche

The perennial philosophy insists that "the higher cannot emanate [proceed] from the lower,"[20] which is to say that the human psyche or the empirical ego cannot transcend itself—"the psychic cannot be treated by the psychic"[21]—without the agency and benediction of what is higher than itself. It is apropos of this that Sigmund Freud (1856-1939) described the empirical ego as "the true seat of anxiety,"[22] unconsciously highlighting its epistemological and ontological limitations—for only what is integrally spiritual can act as the true antidote for the modern and postmodern malaise, marked as it is by unequivocal relativism, the notion that *any opinion is as good as another.* It will thus be no surprise to find the following example of the relativism within which modern psychology is imprisoned: "The only reality I can possibly know is the world as *I* perceive and experience it at this moment. . . . And the only certainty is that those perceived realities are different. There are as many 'real worlds' as there are people!"[23]

---

[18] Henry James (ed.), *The Letters of William James*, Vol. II (Boston, MA: Atlantic Monthly, 1920), p. 2.

[19] Whitall N. Perry, "The Revival of Interest in Tradition," in *The Unanimous Tradition: Essays on the Essential Unity of All Religions*, ed. Ranjit Fernando (Colombo: Sri Lanka Institute of Traditional Studies, 1999), p. 4.

[20] René Guénon, "The Social Chaos," in *The Crisis of the Modern World*, p. 106.

[21] Titus Burckhardt, "Traditional Cosmology and Modern Science: Modern Psychology," in *Mirror of the Intellect: Essays on Traditional Science and Sacred Art*, trans. and ed. William Stoddart (Albany, NY: State University of New York Press, 1987), p. 50, included in this anthology.

[22] C.G. Jung, "Psychological Commentary," in W.Y. Evans-Wentz (ed.), *The Tibetan Book of the Dead* (Oxford, UK: Oxford University Press, 1968), p. xlvii; "ego is the real locus of anxiety" (Sigmund Freud, *The Problem of Anxiety*, trans. H.A. Bunker [New York: W.W. Norton & Company, 1963], p. 19).

[23] Carl R. Rogers, "Do We Need 'A' Reality?" in *A Way of Being* (New York: Houghton Mifflin Company, 1995), p. 102. This outlook is quite similar to the following, which is a prime example of flawed New Age thought: "you create your own reality" (Susan M. Watkins, "Togetherness in Space: Class Dreams and Co-Creations," in *Conversations with Seth: Book Two* [Needham, MA: Moment Point Press, 2006], p. 41).

No matter what theory or methodology the modern psychologist or therapist employs, although it might appear at first glance to be genuinely insightful or helpful, it is still bound to what is axiomatically relative and subjective because limited to the domain of individual interpretation, which consequently has nothing to do with intellectual intuition or the spiritual domain. Thus it can be affirmed that "We are in many ways the prisoners of a psychology based on Cartesian principles."[24]

Traditional Cosmological Perspectives on Health and Well-Being

Numerous individuals within varied disciplines have pointed out that the primordial norms of the past have cascaded into unprecedented disorder, establishing abnormality as a new norm. As Roberto Assagioli (1888-1974) has affirmed: "Humanity today is in a state of serious collective and individual crisis. . . . We could say that 'normal' people now live 'outside themselves' from a psychological or spiritual point of view—this expression, once used to refer to people who were mentally ill, is now quite an apt description of modern [and postmodern] humankind!"[25] Carl Jung (1875-1961) concurs when he says that "our age is afflicted with a blindness that has no parallel."[26]

What is altogether missing from the modern diagnosis and treatment of mental illness is the understanding of time and the human psyche in light of traditional cosmology.[27] The unfolding of time, contrary to contemporary schemas of "evolution" and "progress," was unanimously perceived in pre-modern times to be cyclical. Time begins with human individuals living in proximity to the sacred, but by its passing individuals become farther and farther removed from it; the psychological implication of this is that the human psyche, disconnected from Spirit, becomes farther and farther removed from its source *in divinis*. It is this distance from the spiritual domain that causes the human psyche to become deregulated, fragmented, and imbalanced. The present-day disequilibrium is firmly and unavoidably contextualized within what the Hindu tradition has termed the *Kali-Yuga* ("Dark Age"),[28] or what in the Buddhist tradition is known as *mappō* ("the decadent age of the *Dharma*").[29]

It is interesting to note that the *Diagnostic and Statistical Manual of Mental Disorders*, better known as the *DSM* (soon to be in its fifth edition), attempts to diagnose the very illness

---

[24] Rama P. Coomaraswamy, "The Problems that Result from Locating Spirituality in the Psyche," *Sacred Web: A Journal of Tradition and Modernity*, Vol. 9 (Summer 2002), p. 111.

[25] Roberto Assagioli, *Transpersonal Development: The Dimension Beyond Psychosynthesis* (Forres, UK: Smiling Wisdom, 2007), pp. 38, 82.

[26] C.G. Jung, "The Type Problem in Poetry," in *Psychological Types*, trans. R.F.C. Hull (Princeton, NJ: Princeton University Press, 1976), p. 185.

[27] See Titus Burckhardt, "Traditional Cosmology and Modern Science: Cosmologia Perennis," in *Mirror of the Intellect*, pp. 17-26.

[28] Traditional sources such as the *Vishnu-Purāna*, dating to the third century A.D., confirm the entropic trajectory of the present decline; see especially William Stoddart, "Progress or the '*Kali-Yuga*'?" in *Remembering in a World of Forgetting: Thoughts on Tradition and Postmodernism*, eds. Mateus Soares de Azevedo and Alberto Vasconcellos Queiroz (Bloomington, IN: World Wisdom, 2008), pp. 5-6; René Guénon, "The Dark Age," in *The Crisis of the Modern World*, pp. 10-30; and Martin Lings, *The Eleventh Hour: The Spiritual Crisis of the Modern World in the Light of Tradition and Prophecy* (Cambridge, UK: Archetype, 2002).

[29] See William Stoddart, "The Original Vow and the Pure Land School," in *Outline of Buddhism* (Oakton, VA: Foundation for Traditional Studies, 1998), p. 64.

that it itself is a byproduct of—the materialistic science of the eighteenth century Enlightenment, which gave birth to modern psychology. From this perspective the *DSM* could arguably be characterized as describing the many psychological disorders and pathologies that are part and parcel of the *Kali-Yuga*. If the spiritual domain is the only antidote for a human existence devoid of the sacred, then any true and authentic psychology requires that we recognize it and conform to it.

> Man can be truly human only when he is mindful of his theomorphic nature. When he ignores the divine in himself and in other existences he becomes sub-human. And when this happens not merely in the case of a single individual but in the case of society as a whole, then that society disintegrates through the sheer rootlessness of its own structure or through the proliferation of psychic maladies which it is powerless to heal because it has deprived itself of the one medicine capable of healing them.[30]

We cannot easily brush aside the fact that the *Kali-Yuga* has played a central role in diminishing the rightful place of religion or spirituality in today's secular milieu, which is marked by systematic dehumanization and chaos in all spheres of the human condition. In fact even the spiritual traditions themselves are not safe from the onslaught of these decadent times: "The *Kali Yuga* is not only the time when there is no longer anything but problems without solutions, nor the time when the sacred ceases to exist. It is the time when everything that fundamentally opposes the spiritual passes itself off as spiritual."[31] That psychology or therapy has blurred or even usurped the role of traditional spirituality—"it has been said that if science is the new religion, then psychotherapy is its place of worship"[32]—is a sure sign of the *Kali-Yuga*. "[P]sychoanalysis is one of those mass movements which are both a cause and consequence of spiritual decay."[33] The therapeutic age of today that endorses the empirical ego or self above all else has forgotten the crucial directive of one of its most celebrated figures, who unintentionally affirms tradition and thus the perennial philosophy: "Everything new must have its roots in what was before."[34] And the following statement is equally significant: "the history of psychol-

---

[30] Philip Sherrard, "The Desanctification of Nature," in *The Rape of Man and Nature: An Inquiry into the Origins and Consequences of Modern Science* (Ipswich, UK: Golgonooza Press, 1991), p. 100.

[31] Jean Biès, "Sacredness," in *Returning to the Essential: Selected Writings of Jean Biès*, trans. Deborah Weiss-Dutilh (Bloomington, IN: World Wisdom, 2004), pp. 136-137.

[32] Robert E. Mogar, "Psychedelic (LSD) Research: A Critical Review of Methods and Results," in *Challenges of Humanistic Psychology*, ed. James F.T. Bugental (New York: McGraw-Hill, 1967), p. 143; "[Modern] Psychology, in a certain sense, is a secular religion: It has its own belief system, its own practices, its own rituals. Psychologists do not speak of 'heresy'; they talk about 'pathology'" (Daniel Goleman, "The Impact of the New Religions on Psychology," in *Understanding the New Religions*, eds. Jacob Needleman and George Baker [New York: The Seabury Press, 1978], p. 113.

[33] Werner Kraft, quoted in Thomas Szasz, "Karl Kraus Today," in *Karl Kraus and the Soul-Doctors: A Pioneer Critic and his Criticism of Psychiatry and Psychoanalysis* (Baton Rouge, LA: Louisiana State University Press, 1976), p. 93.

[34] Sigmund Freud, "If Moses was an Egyptian. . . ," in *Moses and Monotheism*, trans. Katherine Jones (New York: Vintage Books, 1967), p. 22.

ogy is the history of forgetting."[35] What has been forgotten is that the human psyche has at all times and places been situated within the spiritual domain:

> The image of man presented to us by modern psychology is not only fragmentary, it is pitiable. In reality, man is as if suspended between animality and divinity; now modern thought—be it philosophical or scientific—admits only animality, practically speaking.
>
> We wish, on the contrary, to correct and perfect the image of man by insisting on his divinity; not that we wish to make a god of him, *quod absit*; we intend simply to take account of his true nature, which transcends the earthly, and lacking which he would have no reason for being.
>
> It is this that we believe we can call—in a symbolist language—the "transfiguration of man."[36]

The Critique of Modern Psychology

Though modern psychology is far from being homogeneous and most psychologists or therapists identify themselves as "eclectic" in their orientation, it can be divided into four general phases that are often described as "forces"—behaviorism, psychoanalysis, humanistic psychology, and transpersonal psychology, including their various schools. These "four forces" in modern psychology encompass a broad spectrum of approaches; most psychologists or therapists do not exclusively identify themselves with one of them, often availing themselves of more than one school within the "forces" themselves.[37]

The overarching traditionalist or perennialist critique of modern psychology has been termed *psychologism* by its exponents; however we would suggest that this critique also might include *scientism, evolutionism, syncretism,* and *New Age thought*. It is important to point out that all of these various ideologies of modernism, which extend into postmodernism, are not separate from one another; they often intersect and complement one another, while all of them share the error of *reductionism* or *relativism* which is inseparable from the loss of the sense of the sacred in the contemporary world:

> Relativism sets out to reduce every element of absoluteness to a relativity, while making a quite illogical exception in favor of this reduction itself. In effect, relativism consists in declaring it to be true that there is no such thing as truth, or in declaring it to be absolutely true that nothing but the relatively true exists. . . . In short, every idea is reduced to a relativity of some sort, whether psychological, historical, or social; but the assertion nullifies itself by the fact that it too presents

---

[35] Russell Jacoby, "Revisionism: The Repression of a Theory," in *Social Amnesia: A Critique of Conformist Psychology from Adler to Laing* (Boston, MA: Beacon Press, 1975), p. 44.

[36] Frithjof Schuon, "Foreword," *The Transfiguration of Man* (Bloomington, IN: World Wisdom Books, 1995), p. vii.

[37] Due to spacial constraints, we cannot delve into contemporary research in fields such as neurophysiology, biological psychiatry and neuroscience; however, it will suffice to point out that while they attempt to study consciousness or the complexity of the human psyche, they often do so by reducing it to the brain or its physical structures. In contrast, the traditional understanding of the psyche evades such attempts to limit it to the psycho-physical order and emphasizes that it cannot be properly understood unless it is situated in the spiritual domain. See Wolfgang Smith, "Neurons and Mind", *Sophia: The Journal of Traditional Studies*, Vol. 10, No. 2 (Winter 2004), pp. 15-41.

itself as a psychological, historical, or social relativity. . . . [I]ts initial absurdity lies in the implicit claim to be unique in escaping, as if by enchantment, from a relativity that is declared alone to be possible.[38]

This analysis encompasses a host of other reductions that have occurred and continue to perpetuate themselves in the modern and postmodern mindset, including the reduction of integral psychology to psychologism: "[P]sychologism attempts to explain the greater in terms of the lesser and excludes all that goes beyond its own limits."[39] These can be summarized as follows: the confusion of the Absolute with the relative, the Spirit with the psyche, the Intellect or *Intellectus* with reason or *ratio*, the Self with ego, and the Personality with individuality.[40] Modern psychology and the subject of the human psyche are by definition circumscribed by the relative or horizontal domain: "Psychological realities represent relative truth."[41] We might even say that in the contemporary era spiritual realization has been reduced to the attempt to attain mental health and well-being as "the practice of psychoanalysis . . . has come to replace religion in the lives of many people."[42] Of course we are not suggesting that there is something problematic in seeking psychological health and well-being, so long as it is not mistaken for spiritual realization; they are situated on two different levels. The higher spiritual includes the lower psycho-physical. Nonetheless, seeking *happiness for happiness' sake*, devoid of any deeper significance, is essentially pathological: "The soul, like every other domain of reality, can only be truly known by what transcends it."[43]

Psychologism: Hostage to the Empirical Ego

Psychologism is defined as the reduction of the spiritual to the psychological—the objective to the subjective—which is to say the psychologization of the spiritual domain. Within modern psychology itself psychologism has been defined as "An approach that reduces transcendental or spiritual events and experiences to the level of purely *psychological* explanation."[44] Without the inclusion of the spiritual domain the human individual must be defined or understood by the most superficial and whimsical criteria: "by their own theories of human nature psychologists have the power of elevating or degrading this same nature. Debasing assumptions debase

---

[38] Frithjof Schuon, "The Contradiction of Relativism," in *Logic and Transcendence*, trans. Peter N. Townsend (London: Perennial Books, 1984), p. 7.

[39] Harry Oldmeadow, "The Not-So-Close Encounters of Western Psychology and Eastern Spirituality," in *Journeys East: 20th Century Western Encounters with Eastern Traditions* (Bloomington, IN: World Wisdom, 2004), p. 314, included in this anthology.

[40] René Guénon, "Fundamental Distinction Between the 'Self' and the 'Ego,'" in *Man and His Becoming According to the Vedanta*, trans. Richard C. Nicholson (New York: The Noonday Press, 1958), p. 28; see also Martin Lings, "Intellect and Reason," in *Ancient Beliefs and Modern Superstitions* (Cambridge, UK: Archetype, 2001), pp. 51-60.

[41] John Welwood, "Realization and Embodiment: Psychological Work in the Service of Spiritual Development," *International Journal of Transpersonal Studies*, Vol. 18, No. 2 (1999), p. 177.

[42] Seyyed Hossein Nasr, "Modern Western Philosophy and Schools of Thought," in *A Young Muslim's Guide to the Modern World* (Chicago, IL: KAZI Publications, 1994), p. 174.

[43] Titus Burckhardt, "Traditional Cosmology and Modern Science: Modern Psychology," p. 47.

[44] Michael Daniels, "Glossary," in *Shadow, Self, Spirit: Essays in Transpersonal Psychology* (Exeter, UK: Imprint Academic, 2005), p. 304.

human beings; generous assumptions exalt them."[45] This underscores the implicit and operative unbridled subjectivity upon which modern psychology—whether behavioristic, psychoanalytical, humanistic, or transpersonal—is circumscribed. "Psychologism can be described as the assumption that man's nature and behavior are to be explained by psychological mechanisms which can be laid bare by a scientific and empirical psychology."[46] This reductionism cannot avoid confusing the spiritual with the psychic, denying what is higher than itself, and replacing it with the psychological. It must not be forgotten that Carl Gustav Jung, Freud's foremost disciple, considered to be seminal in the development of transpersonal psychology, unequivocally articulates the fundamentals of his own psychologism: "One cannot grasp anything metaphysically, but it can be done psychologically. Therefore I strip things of their metaphysical wrapping in order to make them objects of psychology."[47] The process of psychologizing can be so subtle that it sometimes occurs without the psychologist or therapist even being aware of it—"the real danger is that of mixing them [the spiritual domain and the psychological] without realizing it."[48] We need to emphasize, however, that there are also those within various schools of modern psychology who have challenged the phenomena of psychologism and what has been astutely identified as the "confusion of levels"[49]—the confusion of the psychic with the spiritual domain, the relative with the Absolute. "What I am protesting," says Rollo May (1909-1994), "is the confusion of religion and psychology which I believe does not do service to either."[50] We might add the often quoted passage: "Psychosynthesis [transpersonal psychology] does not aim nor attempt to give a metaphysical nor a theological explanation of the great Mystery—it leads to the door, but stops there."[51] A similar statement on "the decisive boundary" is mentioned by Viktor Frankl (1905-1997): "Logotherapy does not cross the boundary between psychotherapy and religion. But it leaves the door to religion open and it leaves it to the patient whether or not to pass the door."[52] With these cautions in place we still need to be mindful of the real boundaries that do indeed exist between the psychic and spiritual domains.

> [I]ts error consists in reducing the spiritual to the psychological and in believing there is nothing beyond the realm of psychology—in other words, that this very limited science can attain to all inner realities, which is absurd. This view would imply that psychology, or even psychoanalysis, could comprehend *Satori* or *Nirvāna*. Modern science, like modern civilization as a whole, is thoroughly pro-

[45] Gordon W. Allport, "The Fruits of Eclecticism: Bitter or Sweet," in *The Person in Psychology: Selected Essays* (Boston, MA: Beacon Press, 1968), pp. 3-27.

[46] Harry Oldmeadow, "The Not-So-Close Encounters of Western Psychology and Eastern Spirituality," p. 313.

[47] C.G. Jung, "Commentary," in *The Secret of the Golden Flower*, trans. Richard Wilhelm (New York: Harcourt, Brace & World, 1962), p. 129.

[48] Paul Tournier, "Psychology and Spirit," in *The Meaning of Persons* (New York: Harper & Row, 1973), p. 108.

[49] Roberto Assagioli, "Spiritual Development and Neuro-Psychological Disturbances," in *Transpersonal Development: The Dimension Beyond Psychosynthesis* (Forres, UK: Smiling Wisdom, 2007), p. 112.

[50] Rollo May, "Transpersonal or Transcendental?" *The Humanistic Psychologist*, Vol. 14, No. 2 (Summer 1986), p. 89.

[51] Roberto Assagioli, "Introduction," *Psychosynthesis* (New York: Penguin Books, 1976), pp. 6-7.

[52] Viktor E. Frankl, "Conclusion: Dimensions of Meaning," in *The Will to Meaning: Foundations and Applications of Logotherapy* (New York: Meridian, 1988), p. 143.

fane, having lost all sense of the sacred, reducing everything to merely individual and trivial dimensions.[53]

Scientism: Imprisonment in the Domain of the Five Senses

William Chittick underscores how predominant scientism is within the contemporary paradigm, even though many may be oblivious to its presence: "It is very difficult to characterize the modern worldview with a single label. One word that has often been suggested is 'scientism,' the belief that the scientific method and scientific findings are the sole criterion for truth."[54] And if we probe further into how this affects the human individual we arrive at the following: "The universe of scientism is a world devoid of consciousness and purposefulness."[55] Through deductive analysis of the above statements it is not difficult to discern their logical consequences, including the intrinsic relationship between scientism and psychologism, since they both seek to reduce reality and the psyche to their own measure: "The modern psychological and psychoanalytical point of view tries to reduce all the higher elements of man's being to the level of the psyche, and moreover to reduce the psyche itself to nothing more than that which can be studied through modern psychological and psychoanalytical methods."[56] Such methods of inquiry halt at the isthmus that divides the spiritual domain from the psychic and cannot delve further: "The metaphysics of scientism encourages man to stop his search for inwardness at the level of psychic contents."[57]

Scientism does not and cannot *ipso facto* affirm the existence of what is beyond the measurement of the five senses; it is thus cut off from what is sacred and transcendent: "As a science, [modern] psychology can neither prove nor disprove religion's claim to truth."[58] It will suffice to say that psychologism can be viewed as a prolongation of scientism; as Theodore Roszak (1933-2011) states: "Science is our religion because we cannot, most of us, with any living conviction *see around it.*"[59] The quintessence of the contradiction of scientism has been wonderfully summarized as follows: "the contention that there are no truths save those of [modern] science is not itself a scientific truth; in affirming it scientism contradicts itself."[60] Scientism's denial of and antagonism to the sacred science of the perennial philosophy explains why it is

[53] Frithjof Schuon, "Appendix," in *Light on the Ancient Worlds: A New Translation with Selected Letters*, trans. Deborah Casey, Mark Perry, Jean-Pierre Lafouge and James S. Cutsinger, ed. Deborah Casey (Bloomington, IN: World Wisdom, 2005), p. 136.

[54] William C. Chittick, "The Rehabilitation of Thought," in *Science of the Cosmos, Science of the Soul: The Pertinence of Islamic Cosmology in the Modern World* (Oxford, UK: Oneworld, 2009), p. 48.

[55] Jacob Needleman, "Magic and Sacred Psychology," in *A Sense of the Cosmos: The Encounter of Modern Science and Ancient Truth* (New York: E.P. Dutton & Company, 1976), p. 138.

[56] Seyyed Hossein Nasr, "The Western World and its Challenges to Islam," in *Islam and the Plight of Modern Man, Revised and Enlarged Edition* (Chicago, IL: ABC International Group, 2001), p. 215.

[57] Jacob Needleman, "A Brief Note on Jungianism," in *A Sense of the Cosmos*, p. 130.

[58] Gordon W. Allport, "The Religious Sentiment," in *Becoming: Basic Considerations for a Psychology of Personality* (New Haven, CT: Yale University Press, 1969), p. 98.

[59] Theodore Roszak, "Idolatry and Damnation," in *Where the Wasteland Ends: Politics and Transcendence in Postindustrial Society* (Garden City, NY: Doubleday & Company, 1972), pp. 134-135.

[60] Huston Smith, "The Way Things Are," in *Forgotten Truth: The Common Vision of the World's Religions* (New York: HarperCollins, 1992), p. 16.

incapable of providing an integral psychology, since it lacks the fundamental principles that are needed. And yet it is in a serious quandary due to the fact that all "four forces" of modern psychology rest on its foundations: "That is why modern psychology stands out among the sciences as a sort of strange disfigurement. The whole enterprise of modern, scientific psychology is rooted in an impossible contradiction: the attempt to subsume one level of reality under laws that govern a lower level."[61]

Evolutionism: The Greater Cannot Derive from the Lesser

We must not underestimate the contemporary mindset that attempts "to claim to derive the 'greater' from the 'lesser' . . . [which is] one of the most typical of modern aberrations."[62] It is important to note that evolutionary theory is deeply embedded in the theoretical outlook of all four "forces" of modern psychology.[63] As Charles Darwin (1809-1882) remarked: "[Modern] psychology will be based on a new foundation, that of the necessary acquirement of each mental power and capacity by gradation."[64] That man is said to be only an animal, and furthermore that he is seen as a product of accidental evolution, demonstrates Darwin's profound influence not only upon psychoanalysis but upon the whole of modern psychology, since these ideas are fixed *a priori* in its orientation. Transpersonal psychology, which along with humanistic psychology, acknowledges the spiritual domain, nonetheless still makes use of evolutionary doctrine. Evolutionary theory has been projected onto the spiritual domain via Sri Aurobindo (1872-1950), Teilhard de Chardin (1881-1955), Ken Wilber (b. 1949), Andrew Cohen (b. 1955), or even their forerunners such as Madame Blavatsky (1831-1891). Evolutionism, falsely coupled with spirituality, has put forward a suspicious hybridization that reaches its zenith in New Age spirituality—"evolutionary enlightenment"[65] or "evolutionary spirituality."[66] "[E]volutionism . . . pervades the New Age movement as a whole."[67] This is axiomatically in conflict with the perennial philosophy and all sapiential traditions. As René Guénon avers: "We do not believe in 'evolution' in the sense the moderns have given the word."[68] Evolutionism is part and parcel of scientism, of which it is a direct derivative; thus the perceptive reference to "the

---

[61] Jacob Needleman, "Magic and Sacred Psychology," in *A Sense of the Cosmos*, p. 138.

[62] René Guénon, "Materia Signata Quantitate," in *The Reign of Quantity and the Signs of the Times*, p. 20.

[63] "[T]he scientific basis of psychoanalysis was evolutionary biology" (Otto Rank, *Beyond Psychology* [New York: Dover, 1958], p. 28).

[64] Charles Darwin, *The Origin of Species* (London: John Murray, 1866), p. 576; "The implications of evolutionary theory for [modern] psychology have been profound" (L.S. Hearnshaw, *The Shaping of Modern Psychology* [London: Routledge, 1989], p. 115); see also James Rowland Angell, "The Influence of Darwin on Psychology", *Psychological Review*, Vol. 16, No. 3 (May 1909), pp. 152-169.

[65] See Andrew Cohen and Ken Wilber, "The Guru and the Pandit: The Evolution of Enlightenment," *What is Enlightenment?* Issue 21 (Spring/Summer 2002), pp. 38-49, 136-143; and Andrew Cohen, "Awakening to Evolution," *EnlightenNext: The Magazine for Evolutionaries*, Issue 42 (December 2008/February 2009), pp. 110, 112.

[66] Tom Huston, "A Brief History of Evolutionary Spirituality," *What is Enlightenment?* Issue 35 (January/March 2007), pp. 77-84.

[67] Wouter J. Hanegraaff, "The Evolutionary Perspective," in *New Age Religion and Western Culture: Esotericism in the Mirror of Secular Thought* (Albany, NY: State University of New York Press, 1998), p. 159.

[68] René Guénon, "Eastern Metaphysics," in *Studies in Hinduism*, p. 96.

great idol of scientism, *evolution.*"[69] The entire discussion could conclude with the concisely stated principle: "There is no spiritual evolution."[70] This is not to say that there is no spiritual development of the individual soul, as this is a definite possibility and an imperative; yet the spiritual evolution of the macrocosm is a fiction. The perennialist position differs greatly from the position of the creationists and they should not be confused with one another.[71]

Syncretism: The Parody of Synthesis

The confusion of "synthesis" with "syncretism" might at first appear to be irrelevant to the theme of modern psychology. When inquired into further, its significance becomes more apparent and its pervasive influence upon the modern and postmodern mindset irrefutable.

> "Syncretism" in its true sense is nothing more than a simple juxtaposition of elements of diverse provenance brought together "from the outside" so to speak, without any principle of a more profound order to unite them. . . . Modern counterfeits of tradition [or authentic spirituality] like occultism and Theosophy [i.e. the New Age Movement] are basically nothing else, fragmentary notions borrowed from different traditional [spiritual] forms, generally poorly understood and more or less deformed, are herein mixed with ideas belonging to philosophy and to profane science. . . . Whatever is truly inspired by traditional [or authentic spiritual] knowledge always proceeds from "within" and not from "without"; whoever is aware of the essential unity of all [spiritual] traditions [i.e. the perennial philosophy] can, according to the case, use different traditional forms to expound and interpret doctrine, if there happens to be some advantage in doing so, but this will never even remotely resemble any sort of syncretism.[72]

Again, we find ourselves confronting the isthmus that divides modern or profane science from the sacred science based upon metaphysical principles. The following definition by Ken Wilber illustrates the lack of discernment that often expresses itself as a confusion of syncretism with synthesis:

> *Integral*: the word means to integrate, to bring together, to join, to link, to embrace. Not in the sense of uniformity, and not in the sense of ironing out all the

---

[69] Charles Upton, "Religion, Evolution, and UFOs," in *Cracks in the Great Wall: The UFO Phenomenon and Traditional Metaphysics* (Hillsdale, NY: Sophia Perennis, 2005), p. 41.

[70] Jean Klein, "The Progressive and the Direct Approach," in *Who Am I?: The Sacred Quest*, ed. Emma Edwards (Salisbury, UK: Non-Duality Press, 2006), p. 136.

[71] "What both the Darwinians and most creationists have failed to grasp is that the corporeal universe in its entirety constitutes no more than the outer shell of the integral cosmos, and that the mystery of origins needs to be resolved, not at the periphery, but precisely at the center of the cosmic circle." (Wolfgang Smith, "Bell's Theorem and the Perennial Ontology," in *The Wisdom of Ancient Cosmology: Contemporary Science in Light of Tradition* [Oakton, VA: Foundation for Traditional Studies, 2003], p. 80); see also Frithjof Schuon, "The Message of the Human Body," in *From the Divine to the Human*, trans. Gustavo Polit and Deborah Lambert (Bloomington, IN: World Wisdom Books, 1982), p. 88.

[72] René Guénon, "Synthesis and Syncretism," in *Perspectives on Initiation*, trans. Henry D. Fohr, ed. Samuel D. Fohr (Ghent, NY: Sophia Perennis, 2001), pp. 38, 41.

wonderful differences, colors, zigs and zags of a rainbow-hued humanity, but in the sense of unity-in-diversity, shared commonalities along with our wonderful differences: replacing rancor with mutual recognition, hostility with respect, inviting everybody into the tent of mutual understanding.[73]

Syncretism—like its counterpart, New Age thought—often appears as a heterogeneous mixture of elements that are not genuinely reconcilable: "A truly integral psychology would embrace the enduring insights of premodern, modern, and postmodern sources."[74] Quintessential syncretism might initially appear to be harmless but over time erodes spiritual sensitivity: "One day, to open a seminar, I had two photographs which I'd juxtaposed. It was the head of Ramana Maharshi on the body of Frank Zane! I held it up in front of the group, and then I said, 'Well, this is what I want to talk about, folks.'"[75] Again the mixture of error with truth, however, cannot result in any true theory. In contrast to this example of syncretism we offer another insightful perspective on synthesis:

> Synthesis, on the contrary, will exist when one starts from unity itself and never loses sight of it throughout the multiplicity of its manifestations; this moreover implies an ability to see beyond forms, and an awareness of the principial truth which clothes itself in forms in order to express and communicate itself in the measure in which this is possible.[76]

While the syncretism present in behaviorism and psychoanalysis is more visible, Abraham Maslow (1908-1970), a key figure at the foundation of humanistic and transpersonal psychology illuminates the syncretism found within them: "It can be emphasized that the whole humanistic synthesis resembles a smorgasbord."[77] Some might not grant much importance to this disclosure and some might suggest that the establishment of both humanistic and transpersonal psychology could not have occurred without its essentially eclectic outlook; however, this does not remedy the difficulty at hand as the very definition of the "fourth force" in modern psychology is another example of syncretism. The dangers of syncretism should not be underestimated especially as they appear to be gaining tremendous traction: "The religion of mankind will be syncretistic."[78] However, we must not lose sight of the fact that "Syncretism is never something substantial: it is an assembling of heterogeneous elements into a false unity, that is, a unity without real synthesis."[79] And for those who mistake the perennial philosophy with this approach we offer

---

[73] Ken Wilber, *Boomeritis: A Novel That Will Set You Free* (Boston, MA: Shambhala, 2002), p. 15.

[74] Ken Wilber, *Integral Psychology: Consciousness, Spirit, Psychology, Therapy* (Boston, MA: Shambhala, 2000), p. 5.

[75] Andrew Cohen, "Integrating the Big Bang: An Interview with Michael Murphy," *What is Enlightenment?* Issue 15 (Spring/Summer 1999), p. 94.

[76] René Guénon, "Preface," *Symbolism of the Cross*, trans. Angus Macnab (Ghent, NY: Sophia Perennis et Universalis, 1996), p. xi.

[77] Abraham H. Maslow, "The Unnoticed Psychological Revolution," in *The Unpublished Papers of Abraham Maslow*, ed. Edward Hoffman (Thousand Oaks, CA: Sage Publications, 1996), p. 125.

[78] Gerald Heard, "The Future of Mankind's Religion," in *Vedanta for the Western World*, ed. Christopher Isherwood (New York: The Viking Press, 1966), p. 445.

[79] Frithjof Schuon, "The Universality and Timeliness of Monasticism," in *Light on the Ancient Worlds*, p. 104.

the following clarification: "[I]t is one thing to manufacture a doctrine by assembling scattered ideas as best one can and quite another to recognize, on the basis of what we willingly call the *Sophia Perennis*, the single Truth contained in various doctrines."[80]

New Age Thought: Counterfeit Spirituality

The New Age movement gives voice to the serpent's promise that "Ye shall be as gods" (Gen. 3:5); it fundamentally overlooks that "Though the Kingdom of God is within us, it is not *all* that is within us."[81] It is only by participating in one of the world's revealed traditions that the human individual can achieve wholeness *in divinis*. New Age thought, like its counterpart, the Human Potential Movement, is almost inseparable from humanistic and transpersonal psychology in that they both share a common origin, not to mention a shared social milieu from which they emerged. "From the germinal thoughts of humanistic psychology grew more developed perspectives, forming what is now called the human potential movement, a prime component of the New Age."[82] The reductionistic paradigm of New Age thought is summarized by Rama Coomaraswamy (1929-2006): "The new age movement has been well characterized as the secularization of religion and the spiritualization of psychology."[83] And, as Wouter Hanegraaff (b. 1961) remarks: "New Age [thought] shows a strong tendency towards a *psychologizing of religion combined with a sacralization of psychology*."[84] Theodore Roszak outlines a piercing and comprehensive critique of the various pitfalls within the humanistic and transpersonal approaches:

> The techniques and theories of Gestalt, Encounter, Transactional, Psychodrama, Transpersonal differ in many ways, but all the schools are united in asserting the essential health and innocence of human nature. They are the therapies of a narcissistic culture, and unapologetically so.[85]

At first glance, when presented with a behaviorism that eradicates the human psyche or soul and a psychoanalysis that pathologizes religion, the comparison with "New Age" thought does not necessarily appear fitting for the first two "forces" of modern psychology; yet if we look at some of the disciples these two "forces" have produced, we could make a case for the contrary. "Freudian renegades . . . have made a significant impact on the development of the New Age, in particular on that aspect known as the Human Potential Movement."[86] And the same is unfortunately not the case with the later two "forces" in modern psychology: "[T]he

---

[80] Frithjof Schuon, "Introduction," *Logic and Transcendence*, p. 2.

[81] Theodore Roszak, "Ethics and Ecstasy: Reflections on an Aphorism by Pathanjali," in *Unfinished Animal*, p. 222.

[82] Douglas R. Groothuis, "Exploring Human Potential in Psychology," in *Unmasking the New Age* (Downers Grove, IL: InterVarsity Press, 1986), p. 78.

[83] Rama P. Coomaraswamy, "Foreword," to Charles Upton, *The System of Antichrist: Truth and Falsehood in Postmodernism and the New Age* (Ghent, NY: Sophia Perennis, 2001), p. 30.

[84] Wouter J. Hanegraaff, "Meta-Empirical and Human Beings," in *New Age Religion and Western Culture*, pp. 196-197.

[85] Theodore Roszak, "Narcissism Revisited," in *The Voice of the Earth: An Exploration of Ecopsychology* (Grand Rapids, MI: Phanes Press, 2001), p. 275.

[86] Paul Heelas, "Developments," in *The New Age Movement* (Oxford, UK: Blackwell Publishers, 2003), p. 47.

primary psychological source for New Age was humanistic psychology, and most especially Abraham Maslow, clearly a key force in conceptualizing humanistic psychology [including transpersonal psychology]."[87] We can track the theoretical continuity between psychoanalysis and humanistic psychology and transpersonal psychology through the following illustration: "New Age belief has its background in psychoanalytic theories of repression and projection, adapted to a spiritual worldview."[88]

> Although humanistic psychology has contributed significantly to a more balanced and open-minded approach to psychic welfare, in its pioneering fervor it has succumbed to the error of advancing values and goals of human existence that properly belong to the realm of religion. Therapists have widely assumed roles once reserved for priests and religious counselors. Thus, the schools of the human potential movement have ended up as surrogate religions, without God, but with their own idiosyncratic doctrines and methods of "salvation." In this role they are now, arguably, slowing down the blossoming of genuine spirituality.[89]

Due to its lack of discernment and lack of commitment to both the inner and outer dimensions of religion, humanistic and transpersonal psychology have not been able to avoid the "New Age" label, "transpersonal worldview . . . qualifies as 'New Age'."[90] While humanistic and transpersonal approaches have strong reservations regarding religion as opposed to spirituality, there is also a misguided notion that tradition can be added to or created, which is a signature mark of pseudo-spirituality: "[T]he New Age approach seems to exemplify a phenomenon known as the 'invention of tradition'."[91]

Although there are myriad errors with the New Age movement, one core issue is that it holds modern science in high regard and strongly relies on it for its own validation, yet it paradoxically does not take account of the fact that modern science's origins are *de facto* reductionistic in essence. The attempt to establish a "new paradigm" upon this truncated foundation in order to escape the trappings of reductionism appears to be an impossible task.

The Noetic Function of the Intellect

From the traditional perspective modern or profane science cannot create *in vacuo* a psychology that facilitates the integration of the tripartite structure of the human microcosm: Spirit/Intellect, soul, and body.

---

[87] Paul C. Vitz, "Psychology and the New Age Movement," in *Psychology As Religion: The Cult of Self-Worship*, 2nd edition (Grand Rapids, MI: William B. Eerdmans Publishing, 2002), p. 117.

[88] Wouter J. Hanegraaff, "Matters of the Mind," in *New Age Religion and Western Culture*, p. 221.

[89] Georg Feuerstein, "The Humanistic Way of Self-Actualization," in *Holy Madness: The Shock Tactics and Radical Teachings of Crazy-Wise Adepts, Holy Fools, and Rascal Gurus* (New York: Paragon House, 1991), p. 192.

[90] Wouter J. Hanegraaff, "New Age Science," in *New Age Religion and Western Culture*, p. 70.

[91] Wouter J. Hanegraaff, "Historical Religions versus Universal Spirituality," in *New Age Religion and Western Culture*, p. 324.

English	Latin	Greek	Arabic
Spirit (Intellect)	*Spiritus (Intellectus)*	*Pneuma (Nous)*	*Rūh ('Aql)*
soul	*anima*	*psyché*	*nafs*
body	*corpus*	*soma (hylé)*	*jism*

It is only at the level of the transpersonal or the Absolute itself—what is above and higher and simultaneously at the center, both transcendent and immanent—that an authentic integration can be established.

Some might be curious and even challenge the definition of the Intellect as equivalent to the Spirit, but we need to stress that the Intellect in this context is not the discursive faculty of reason but what subsumes this lower faculty and transmutes it into a transcendent faculty. This spiritual organ, also known as the "Eye of the Heart" is illuminated by Hehaka Sapa or Black Elk (1863-1950), a remarkable sage of the Lakota Sioux:

> I am blind and do not see the things of this world; but when the Light comes from Above, it enlightens my heart and I can see, for the Eye of my heart (*Chante Ista*) sees everything. The heart is a sanctuary at the center of which there is a little space, wherein the Great Spirit dwells, and this is the Eye (*Ista*). This is the Eye of the Great Spirit by which He sees all things and through which we see Him. If the heart is not pure, the Great Spirit cannot be seen, and if you should die in this ignorance, your soul cannot return immediately to the Great Spirit, but it must be purified by wandering about in the world. In order to know the center of the heart where the Great Spirit dwells you must be pure and good, and live in the manner that the Great Spirit has taught us. The man who is thus pure contains the Universe in the pocket of his heart (*Chante Ognaka*).[92]

We can even see the faculty of the Intellect present within the anti-intellectual tradition of Zen, however hidden it may be to the superficial observer; consider the following *mondō* or Zen dialogue between Yakusan (Chinese: Yao Shan) and a visiting monk:

> Once Master Yakusan was sitting in deep meditation, when a monk came up to him and asked: "Solidly seated as a rock, what are you thinking?"
> Master answered: "Thinking of something which is absolutely unthinkable (*fu-shiryō*), 'not-to-be-thought-of'."
> The monk: "How can one think of anything which is absolutely unthinkable?"
> Master: "By the a-thinking thinking (*hi-shiryō*), 'thinking-which-is-non-thinking'."[93]

While some representatives of humanistic and transpersonal psychology have tried to affirm the role of the Intellect, the body, and the psyche, they usually do not have in mind the

---

[92] Frithjof Schuon, "The Sacred Pipe," in *The Feathered Sun: Plains Indians in Art and Philosophy* (Bloomington, IN: World Wisdom Books, 1990), p. 51.

[93] Toshihiko Izutsu, "The A-thinking Thinking," in *Toward a Philosophy of Zen Buddhism* (Boulder, CO: Prajñā Press, 1982), p. 158.

same transcendent function that the perennial philosophy designates by that term.[94] What these representatives of humanistic and transpersonal psychology appear to be acknowledging is reason or *ratio* not Intellect or *Intellectus*; the former has a horizontal function and the latter a vertical function. The horizontal function addresses the psycho-physical domain while the vertical function addresses the spiritual or transcendent domain.

> In fact, most of modern psychology, of which traditional [Freudian] psychotherapy is a part, denies the possibility of intuition in the strict sense: knowing by means other than the sensory pathways. Intuition in academic psychology means unconscious inference, not direct knowing. Yet the entire spiritual enterprise is based on the possibility of intuitive access to the transcendent.[95]

It is through the traditional spiritual practice—what is known as the "science of the soul"— that authentic integration of the psychic faculty can occur: "In a traditional discipline the psychic can be reintegrated with the spiritual but without the necessary metaphysical framework and religious supports psychism becomes wholly infra-intellectual and anti-spiritual."[96]

The "Four Forces" of Modern Psychology in the Light of the Perennial Philosophy

> Psychoanalysis and behaviorism thus laid the foundations of clinical and experimental psychology, which they dominated for most of the first half of the twentieth century, becoming known as the first and second forces of [modern] Western psychology.[97]

We cannot readily overlook the "psychologism with which Freud and his followers began"[98] nor the scientism of John Broadus Watson (1878-1958) and his followers, as it had a pervasive influence upon modern psychology as a whole. It is certain that what the perennialist school has termed *scientism* and *psychologism* apply to the first two "forces" within modern psychology: behaviorism and psychoanalysis. The first reduces the human individual to what is most external and outward: his behavior; the second reduces him to what is most superficial and base: his animalistic impulses.[99] And what can be said about the other two "forces" of modern psychology, the humanistic and the transpersonal? The preliminary thoughts of those familiar with both the works of the traditionalists or perennialists, and also with the writings of humanistic

---

[94] See John Rowan, "The Intellect," *Journal of Humanistic Psychology*, Vol. 31, No. 1 (Winter 1991), pp. 49-50.

[95] Arthur J. Deikman, "Spirituality Expands a Therapist's Horizons," *Yoga Journal*, Issue 88 (September/October 1989), p. 49.

[96] Harry Oldmeadow, "The Not-So-Close Encounters of Western Psychology and Eastern Spirituality," in *Journeys East*, p. 317, included in this volume.

[97] Roger N. Walsh and Frances Vaughan (eds.), "Introduction," to *Paths Beyond Ego: The Transpersonal Vision* (New York: Jeremy P. Tarcher/Putnam, 1993), pp. 1-2.

[98] Ira Progoff, "Sigmund Freud and the Foundations of Depth Psychology," in *The Death and Rebirth of Psychology: An Integrative Evaluation of Freud, Adler, Jung and Rank and the Impact of Their Insights on Modern Man* (New York: McGraw-Hill, 1969), p. 45.

[99] See Maurice Friedman, *Contemporary Psychology: Revealing and Obscuring the Human* (Pittsburgh, PA: Duquesne University Press, 1984).

and transpersonal psychology, might suggest that the latter two forces are extensions, although much less narrow in scope, of the same scientism and psychologism.[100] Former professor of psychology at Harvard University, Richard Alpert, known as Ram Dass (b. 1931) describes the inherent limitations of some representatives and pioneers of humanistic and transpersonal psychology:

> Psychotherapy, as defined and practiced by people like Erikson, Maslow, Perls, Rogers, the neo-Freudians, or the neo-Jungians does not in the ultimate sense transcend the nature of ego structure. They really seem to be focused on developing a functional ego structure with which you can cope effectively and adequately with the existing culture. . . . The psychological world is primarily interested in worldly adjustment, happiness and pleasure.[101]

The third and fourth "forces" are nonetheless marked by what in essence is a breach in the metaphysical principles of sacred science: "Humanistic and transpersonal psychologies try to include the concept of Essence or Being, plus the idea of inner development, in their formulations; however, as far as we can tell, the attempts are merely the addition of the spiritual perspective to the psychological one."[102] Yet the question still arises: does the perennialist critique of psychologism still apply to these more recent developments in modern psychology? Are humanistic and transpersonal psychology free of psychologism? Or is the very critique of psychologism itself outdated as some contemporary humanistic and transpersonal thinkers might suggest? Some peculiar attempts have been made to graft spirituality onto psychology, which is obvious in paradoxical terms such as "transpersonal behaviorism"[103] or the even more misleading "Zen Behaviorism"[104] that attempts to reconcile and fuse the first and the last "forces" of modern psychology—behaviorism and transpersonal psychology—with the transcendent domain. We could point out a similar example in the case of gestalt therapy, which is generally considered to be a humanistic psychology heavily influenced by Taoism and Buddhism, but which is interestingly termed "gestalt-transpersonal,"[105] when it is quite clear that Fritz Perls (1893-1970) was as hostile to orthodox spirituality as his seminal master Sigmund Freud.

---

[100] "Not Freud but Fromm, Maslow and Rollo May are the psychological gurus of the present day. And in certain respects their doctrine is very much opposed to the orthodox Freudian teaching which is not at all concerned with offering consolations. Nonetheless, it is clear that these later authorities are still following in the footsteps of the master, and that if it were not for the breach achieved by Freud, they could not have exerted any comparable influence upon society" (Wolfgang Smith, "The Ego and the Beast," in *Cosmos & Transcendence: Breaking Through the Barrier of Scientistic Belief* [Peru, IL: Sherwood Sugden & Company, 1990], p. 104).

[101] Jack Kornfield, Ram Dass (Richard Alpert), and Mokusen Miyuki, "Psychological Adjustment is not Liberation: A Symposium," in John Welwood (ed.), *Awakening the Heart: East/West Approaches to Psychotherapy and the Healing Relationship* (Boston, MA: New Science Library, 1985), pp. 34-35.

[102] A.H. Almaas, "Identity," in *The Pearl Beyond Price, Integration of Personality into Being: An Object Relations Approach* (Berkeley, CA: Diamond Books, 1998), p. 265.

[103] Charles T. Tart, "Science and the Sources of Value," *Phoenix: New Directions in the Study of Man*, Vol. 3, No. 1 (Summer 1979), pp. 25-29.

[104] Deane H. Shapiro, "Zen Behaviorism: When the Zen Master Meets the Grand Conditioner," in *Precision Nirvana* (Englewood Cliffs, NJ: Prentice-Hall, 1978), pp. 117-119.

[105] Lynn Williams, "Spirituality and Gestalt: A Gestalt-Transpersonal Perspective," *Gestalt Review*, Vol. 10, No. 1 (2006), pp. 6-21.

[Fritz] Perls was actually much closer to Freud than to Buddha (and Freud and Buddha had precious little in common). . . . [M]ost people, to this day, still don't realize that Perls was basically pop-Freud; brilliant pop-Freud, surely, but pop-Freud nonetheless. Perls's entire setup operated with introjection, projection, and retroflection (repression), reactivated in the client through group transference, manifested by resistance-avoidances, and countered by the therapist via working-through—all Freudian concepts, appropriately modified and streamlined for instant therapy.[106]

And when we turn to the transpersonal psychology of C.G. Jung, we must be highly suspicious of those portraying him as free of psychologism, even though it is recalled time and time again that "for Freud religion is a symptom of psychological disease, [whereas] for Jung the *absence* of religion is at the root of all adult psychological disease."[107] The transpersonal psychology of Jung is paradoxically a continuation of Freud's anti-spiritual psychoanalysis and other exponents within modern psychology: "I prefer to call my own approach 'analytical psychology.' I wish the term to stand for a general conception embracing both [Freudian] 'psychoanalysis' and [Adlerian] 'individual psychology,' as well as other efforts in this field."[108] Marco Pallis (1895-1989) frames the impasse of both Freudian and Jungian "depth psychology" in the light of the spiritual traditions:

> The latest and in many ways deadliest addition to this process of subversion is the psychological interpretation of religion, of which the Freudian and Jungian schools provide two representative forms, the one being avowedly materialistic and hostile, while the other affects a sympathetic attitude on the strength of a deftly nurtured system of equivocations, as between things of a spiritual and of a psychic order.[109]

Abraham Maslow, a pioneer of both humanistic and transpersonal psychology, remarked of Freud: "I consider him to be the greatest psychologist by far who ever lived, & I feel myself to be epi-Freudian (*not* Freudian) & to be carrying on the best of the tradition, but without being a loyalist."[110] Viktor Frankl could equally say of the founder of psychoanalysis: "[T]he greatest spirit in psychotherapy [is] Sigmund Freud. . . . Logotherapy in no way invalidates the sound and sober findings of such great pioneers as Freud, Adler, Pavlov, Watson, or Skinner."[111]

---

[106] Ken Wilber, "Odyssey: A Personal Inquiry into Humanistic and Transpersonal Psychology," *Journal of Humanistic Psychology*, Vol. 22, No. 1 (Winter 1982), p. 61.

[107] Victor White, "Freud, Jung and God," in *God and the Unconscious* (Chicago, IL: Henry Regnery Company, 1953), p. 47.

[108] C.G. Jung, "Problems of Modern Psychotherapy," in *Modern Man in Search of a Soul*, trans. W.S Dell and Cary F. Baynes (New York: Harcourt Brace Jovanovich, 1933), p. 28.

[109] Marco Pallis, "Considerations on the Tantric Alchemy," in *A Buddhist Spectrum: Contributions to Buddhist-Christian Dialogue* (Bloomington, IN: World Wisdom, 2003), p. 90.

[110] Abraham H. Maslow, *The Journals of Abraham Maslow*, ed. Richard J. Lowry, abridged Jonathan Freedman (Brattleboro, VT: The Lewis Publishing Company, 1982), p. 195.

[111] Viktor E. Frankl, "Preface," to *The Unheard Cry for Meaning: Psychotherapy and Humanism* (New York: Touchstone, 1978), pp. 14, 17.

In what has been regarded a standard work on transpersonal psychology we find the following statement: "However ambivalent most contemporary practitioners of transpersonal psychology may be about Freud, it is safe to say that there would be no transpersonal psychology as we know it without Freud's influence. Freud might be considered the grandfather of the entire movement."[112] It is then no surprise that within humanistic psychology, or the "third force" in modern psychology, the Freudian psychoanalytic identity of the human individual is accepted: "logically as well as psychologically we must go behind the ego-id-superego system and endeavor to understand the 'being' of whom these are different expressions."[113] Less zealous or more moderate apologists for psychologism might argue that "Freud's therapeutic formula is correct but incomplete."[114] Likewise a loyalist would voice the following with regard to behaviorism: "mechanistic science . . . which in [modern] psychology takes the form of behaviorism . . . [is] not incorrect but rather too narrow and limited to serve as a *general* or comprehensive philosophy."[115] The final result of this psychologism reaches its apex in this kind of statement: "[I]n broad terms, we want to integrate Freud and Buddha, we want to integrate lower 'depth psychology' with 'height psychology.'. . . If you don't befriend Freud, it will be harder to get to Buddha."[116] Finally, irrespective of the inherent contradictions within the reductionistic leanings of modern psychology, there appears to be an overwhelming appeal toward syncretism: "I have long supported all four forces of [modern] psychology, and I will continue to do so,"[117] says Ken Wilber. With this indiscriminate blending of truth and error one is left in a psychic wilderness devoid of any spiritual compass, a psychological no-man's-land if you will; this being the case, one can distort the world's spiritualities and the perennial philosophy and use them for one's own ends.

It will suffice to point out that:

> One of the most insidious and destructive illusions is the belief that depth psychology . . . has the slightest connection with spiritual life, whose teachings it persistently falsifies by confusing inferior elements with superior. We cannot be too wary of all these attempts to reduce the values vehicled by [spiritual] tradition to the level of phenomena supposed to be scientifically controllable. The spirit escapes the hold of profane science in an absolute fashion.[118]

[112] Mark Epstein, "Freud's Influence on Transpersonal Psychology," in *Textbook of Transpersonal Psychiatry and Psychology*, eds. Bruce W. Scotton, Allan B. Chinen and John R. Battista (New York: Basic Books, 1996), p. 29.

[113] Rollo May, "The Emergence of Existential Psychology," in Rollo May (ed.), *Existential Psychology*, 2nd edition (New York: Random House, 1969), p. 35.

[114] Wilhelm Reich, "Sexual Stasis: The Source of Energy of the Neurosis," in *The Function of the Orgasm*, trans. Theodore P. Wolfe (New York: The Noonday Press, 1970), p. 89.

[115] Abraham H. Maslow, "Mechanistic and Humanistic Science," in *The Psychology of Science: A Reconnaissance* (South Bend, IN: Gateway Editions, 1966), p. 5.

[116] Ken Wilber, "Freud and Buddha," in *A Brief History of Everything* (Boston, MA: Shambhala, 1996), p. 155.

[117] Ken Wilber, "Waves, Streams, States, and Self: A Summary of My Psychological Model (Or, Outline of An Integral Psychology)," in *The Eye of the Spirit: An Integral Vision for a World Gone Slightly Mad* (Boston, MA: Shambhala, 2001), p. 285.

[118] Frithjof Schuon, "No Activity Without Truth," in *The Betrayal of Tradition: Essays on the Spiritual Crisis of Modernity* (Bloomington, IN: World Wisdom, 2005), pp. 11-12.

In broadly reviewing the literature of both the third and fourth "forces" of modern psychology, we can point out that as long as a materialistic science is intricately embedded in its outlook, it is *ipso facto* marked by scientism and thus unavoidably limited in its efficacy:[119] "The perennial crisis of . . . [modern] psychology is due to the fact that it does not see that the problem lies in the meaning of science it adopted."[120] Modern psychology is embedded *in toto* in this materialist worldview, and though it adamantly proposes a "new" paradigm beyond the Cartesian-Newtonian outlook, it has not been able to establish one.[121] Even Jung is not free of the materialistic science of the Enlightenment, which is none other than scientism. As Josef Goldbrunner remarks:

> "What God is in Himself" is a question beyond the scope of psychology. This implies a positivistic, agnostic renunciation of all metaphysics. It is possible that metaphysical objects have their share of existence, but "we shall never be able to prove whether in the final analysis they are absolute truths or not." In saying this Jung clearly stands—as he himself admits—"on the extreme left wing in the Parliament of the Protestant spirit." One might therefore think of Jung as a positivist since in his view only the natural sciences lead to positive knowledge. But it must be added at once that he has penetrated and extended brutal positivism and fought for the "reality of the psyche." He has acquired a new province for empirical knowledge.[122]

The same certainly cannot be said for the integral and traditional psychology of the perennial philosophy; it does not belong to scientism but rather originates in *scientia sacra*, which "is none other than metaphysics if this term is understood correctly as the ultimate science of the Real."[123] We can therefore logically deduce that as both humanistic and transpersonal approaches are extensions of the Cartesian-Newtonian mechanistic worldview that endorses scientism and evolutionism, not to mention the fact that they often confuse the psychic and spiritual domains, they are still susceptible to the critique of psychologism. Frithjof Schuon (1907-1998), in his noteworthy essay titled "The Psychological Imposture," frames this theme with eloquent precision:

> Psychoanalysis [or modern psychology] doubly deserves to be classed as an imposture, firstly because it pretends to have discovered facts which have always been known and could never have been otherwise than known, and secondly and

---

[119] Rama P. Coomaraswamy, "Psychological Integration and the Religious Outlook," *Sacred Web: A Journal of Tradition and Modernity*, Vol. 3 (Summer 1999), pp. 37-48.

[120] Amedeo Giorgi, "The Crisis of Humanistic Psychology," *The Humanistic Psychologist*, Vol. 15, No. 1 (Spring 1997), p. 19.

[121] José Segura, "On Ken Wilber's Integration of Science and Religion," *Sacred Web: A Journal of Tradition and Modernity*, Vol. 5 (Summer 2005), pp. 71-83, included in this volume.

[122] Josef Goldbrunner, "Religion," in *Individuation: A Study of the Depth Psychology of Carl Gustav Jung*, trans. Stanley Godman (London: Hollis & Carter, 1955), pp. 161-162.

[123] Seyyed Hossein Nasr, "Scientia Sacra," in *Knowledge and the Sacred* (Albany, NY: State University of New York Press, 1989), p. 132.

chiefly because it arrogates to itself functions that in reality are spiritual, and thus poses practically as a religion.[124]

The truth of the Absolute is not awaiting empirical or observable proof that it exists, and this is what modern psychology, and the modern and by extension the postmodern outlook as a whole, entirely fails to comprehend. The integral psychologies of the perennial philosophy, being grounded in metaphysical principles, cannot be reduced *a priori* to empirical or statistical data, as they lie outside the psycho-physical domain which is verified by one of the earliest sapiential traditions of this temporal cycle, known as the *sanātana dharma*: "There is no empirical psychology in India. Indian psychology is based on metaphysics."[125]

> One could show, for instance, that psychology as it is understood to-day, that is to say the study of mental phenomena as such, is a natural product of . . . empiricism and of the attitude of mind of the eighteenth century, and that the point of view to which it corresponds was so negligible for the ancient world that even if it happened sometimes to be taken incidentally into consideration, no one would have dreamed of making a special science of it, since all that it might contain of any value was transformed and assimilated in higher points of view.[126]

Even if, by an unlikely chance, modern science were to arrive at similar conclusions as the ancient traditional sciences, it would be immaterial to the perennial philosophy because it and modern science belong to very different orders of reality that cannot be placed on equal terms. Both humanistic and transpersonal approaches to modern psychology continue to draw upon the spiritual domain, but in so doing they have blurred the essential distinctions between therapist and spiritual guide. That is *de facto* another facet of psychologism, not to mention a significant sign of the times:

> More and more therapists are reaching out to absorb methods and concepts from the ancient religious traditions of the Orient. As a result more and more troubled people no longer know whether they need spiritual or psychiatric help or both. In the personal crisis of my life, how far can psychotherapy take me? How far do I wish to be taken? Is there a line that separates the spiritual path from therapeutic progress? What will result from the current effort of Western psychotherapists to make use of teachings of the East—Buddhism, Hinduism, and Sufism? Can these efforts bring an expanded understanding of our human predicament, or will they result only in a reduction of the spiritual to the conventionally therapeutic? What

---

[124] Frithjof Schuon, "The Psychological Imposture," *Survey of Metaphysics and Esoterism*, trans. Gustavo Polit (Bloomington, IN: World Wisdom Books, 1986), p. 195.

[125] Jadunath Sinha, *Indian Psychology: Volume I Cognition* (Delhi: Motilal Banarsidass, 1986), p. xviii. "[I]n [the integral] metaphysics [of the perennial philosophy] there is no empiricism; principial knowledge cannot stem from any experience, even though experiences—scientific or other—can be the occasional causes of the intellect's intuitions" (Frithjof Schuon, "Preface" to *Roots of the Human Condition* [Bloomington, IN: World Wisdom Books, 1991], p. vii).

[126] René Guénon, "Sacred and Profane Science," in *The Crisis of the Modern World*, pp. 72-73.

actually takes place in [modern] psychotherapy when seen against the background of the vision of human nature offered by sacred tradition?[127]

The Decisive Boundary: The Confusion of the Psychic with the Spiritual

Modern psychology finds itself in a quandary arising out of its own *naïveté* with regards to what has been identified as "the decisive boundary"[128]—the separate domains of the spirit and soul—which either goes undetected or is altogether ignored. On the one hand, it appears that certain advances have been made in that the spiritual dimension is now acknowledged in both humanistic and transpersonal psychology, while on the other hand this development is impeded by a science that cannot fully implement its vision or substantiate its reality, not to mention a "spirituality" that is often blinded by New Age thought or a syncretistic fusion of one kind or another. We are reminded that the operative principles of the perennial philosophy are metaphysical in nature, and that metaphysics is *a priori* its own authority because it is higher than the psycho-physical domain; integral metaphysics is not limited to what is psychic, but the psychic is inherently limited and is thus fundamentally subordinate to the spiritual domain.

However, both humanistic and transpersonal psychology acknowledge the spiritual domain as an indispensable facet of human existence.[129] An unavoidable question then arises: for a psychology to participate in the transcendent sphere, is it enough to acknowledge the spiritual domain? And if the scientific paradigm itself has now changed, as has been suggested by some representatives of both humanistic and transpersonal psychology,[130] wouldn't this necessarily change the very scientific underpinnings of modern psychology as well? The following proposal is thus made:

> For western students of [modern] psychology and science, it is time to begin a new synthesis, to "translate" some of the concepts and ideas of the traditional psychologies into modern psychological terms, to regain a balance lost. To do this, we must first extend the boundaries of inquiry of modern science, *extend our concept of what is possible for man.*[131]

Although this approach is very appealing to contemporary minds, especially with all of the discussion generated by what has been termed the "new physics,"[132] all too often it is forgotten that while such a "synthesis" proposes to bridge the gap between traditional spirituality and

---

[127] Jacob Needleman and Dennis Lewis (eds.), "Preface," to *On the Way to Self Knowledge* (New York: Alfred A. Knopf, 1976), pp. x-xi.

[128] See Martin Lings, "The Decisive Boundary," in *Symbol & Archetype: A Study of the Meaning of Existence* (Cambridge, UK: Quinta Essentia, 1991), pp. 13-18.

[129] Samuel Bendeck Sotillos, "Humanistic or Transpersonal? *Homo Spiritualis* and the Perennial Philosophy," *AHP Perspective*, August/September 2010, pp. 7-11.

[130] John R. Battista, "Contemporary Physics and Transpersonal Psychiatry," in *Textbook of Transpersonal Psychiatry and Psychology*, eds. Bruce W. Scotton, Allan B. Chinen and John R. Battista (New York: Basic Books, 1996), pp. 195-206.

[131] Robert E. Ornstein, "The Traditional Esoteric Psychologies," in *The Psychology of Consciousness* (New York: The Viking Press, 1972), p. 99.

[132] See Wolfgang Smith, *The Quantum Enigma: Finding the Hidden Key* (Hillsdale, NY: Sophia Perennis, 2005).

modern science, it is quite obvious to the discerning mind where this must eventually lead—to the undermining of the sapiential traditions. If we wish to "extend the boundaries" of what man is in the light of what transcends him, we cannot turn a blind eye to the crucial lack of discernment between "synthesis" and "syncretism" which is all-too-evident in humanistic and transpersonal psychologies, and also for that matter in the "new physics." We can summarize this so-called more inclusive orientation within modern science as follows: "'new physics' is no more than the old physics in a new guise."[133] From the perspective of the perennial philosophy it is not enough to simply acknowledge the spiritual domain; the sacred science itself needs to be sanctioned through a revealed or orthodox spiritual tradition in order for the transcendent domain to be accessible. The Absolute provides grace (*baraka*) to what is below, yet the terrestrial cannot bypass the Absolute in order to make itself something other than what it is.

> . . . the power to tell the greater from the lesser reality, the sacred paradigm from its copies and secular counterfeits. . . . [W]ithout it, the consciousness circuit will surely become a lethal swamp of paranormal entertainments, facile therapeutic tricks, authoritarian guru trips, demonic subversions.[134]

Under the "new" scientific paradigm—which continues to be reductionistic, though more subtly so—the psyche is still left in a closed system, trapped in the cul-de-sac of its own subjectivity, due to its inability to realize what is higher than itself: "Profane man never attains the essence of things by the operations of his thought [*ratio* or ego]."[135] The fact that modern psychology is in a sense imprisoned within the landscape of the empirical ego is not a minor issue nor is it one that is easily corrected.

> All [modern] psychological therapies, psychoanalysis among them, are based on a point of view which, for *Vedanta*, is the very cause of what one might call a fundamental neurosis, a metaphysical neurosis, which is the arising of an ego believing itself to be separate.
> The aim of psychoanalysis is to restore health and balance to this separate ego which it considers as a justified reality. The psychoanalyzer wishes to restore a balanced and harmonious ego, an ego in harmony with its surroundings and with other creatures. This ideal appears on second thoughts to be entirely naïve. When we wish to be a balanced self we, in fact, wish to prolong an imbalance under the best possible conditions by appealing to energies which may reinforce, fix and establish an egotistic state which is really the basic imbalance, the source of all others. This is just as absurd as fighting the symptoms of an illness without applying oneself to the illness itself. The psychoanalytical cure is therefore not really a cure. It does not rid the sick man of his sickness, it helps him to live it, with the ego. His sickness is an imaginary one.[136]

---

[133] Philip Sherrard, "Modern Science and the Dehumanization of Man," in *The Rape of Man and Nature: An Inquiry into the Origins and Consequences of Modern Science* (Ipswich, UK: Golgonooza Press, 1991), p. 75.

[134] Theodore Roszak, "Introduction: Pico's Chameleon and the Consciousness Circuit," to *Unfinished Animal*, p. 13.

[135] Tage Lindbom, "Objectivity," in *The Tares and the Good Grain or the Kingdom of Man at the Hour of Reckoning*, trans. Alvin Moore, Jr. (Macon, GA: Mercer University Press, 1983), p. 51.

[136] Jean Klein, *Be Who You Are*, p. 46.

C.G. Jung makes a crucial confession exposing perhaps the quintessence of the traditionalist critique of psychologism in the following declaration, which in theory could perhaps alter or dispel the very notion that Jung was putting forth a complete spiritual psychology. This brings up many questions regarding transpersonal psychology as well, since he has been recognized as one of its pioneers:

> All conceivable statements are made by the psyche. . . . The psyche cannot leap beyond itself. It cannot set up any absolute truths, for its own polarity determines the relativity of its statements. . . . In saying this we are not expressing a value judgment, but only pointing out that the limit is very frequently overstepped. . . . In my effort to depict the limitations of the psyche I do not mean to imply that *only* the psyche exists. It is merely that, so far as perception and cognition are concerned, we cannot see beyond the psyche. . . . All comprehension and all that is comprehended is in itself psychic, and to that extent we are hopelessly cooped up in an exclusively psychic world.[137]

The question thus remains: is it possible for modern psychology to construct a *bona fide* spiritual psychology? And what benefit can come of utilizing spiritual practices outside an authentic spiritual tradition as has been the case with humanistic and transpersonal psychology?

> Another question that arises frequently is whether techniques from the domain of spiritual practice should be introduced into the psychotherapy situation. My own view is that they should not—unless the psychotherapist is also qualified as a spiritual teacher. Although a variety of procedures such as meditation, chanting, and visualization can be used to provide calmness and relaxation, the mystical literature indicates that such benefits are secondary. The sages who invented these techniques emphasized that they should be used as part of an integrated, individualized teaching system requiring the supervision of a [spiritual] teacher.[138]

And the same could be said with regards to offering "spiritual guidance" outside a traditional spiritual context.

> Both in theory and treatment [modern] psychology is replacing religion. Those who understand the ancient Guru-disciple tradition see that psychology is a truncated counterfeit of it. Just as physical science can attain only to Prakriti without Purusha, so psychology can only [attain] to the subconscious without the superconscious. Some psychologists are indeed coming to suspect and some even to admit openly that there is a superconscious, but that is not enough. What is needed is to have access to it, to have traversed it in oneself and to be able to guide the aspirant in doing so.[139]

---

[137] C.G. Jung, "Late Thoughts," in *Memories, Dreams, Reflections*, ed. Aniela Jaffé (New York: Vintage Books, 1965), pp. 350-352.

[138] Arthur J. Deikman, "Spirituality Expands a Therapist's Horizons," *Yoga Journal*, Issue 88 (September-October 1989), p. 49.

[139] Arthur Osborne, "Modern Idolatries," in *Be Still, It Is the Wind That Sings* (Tiruvannamalai: Sri Ramanasramam,

The Disunity within Modern Psychology

Another mark of psychologism that cannot be overlooked is the mass of disagreements and critiques within modern psychology and its numerous ever-growing schools that have not seen eye-to-eye on many key points vital to its integrity. As Frithjof Schuon remarks: "Relativism engenders the spirit of rebellion and is at the same time its fruit."[140] It could be argued, and rightfully so, that there are wide divergences within the religions; however, the *philosophia perennis* would suggest that these only reflect differences in points of view (*darshanas*), which do not fundamentally deny the "transcendent unity of religions"; in their widely differing ways, each religion recognizes the same Absolute Reality. Unfortunately the same cannot be said for modern psychology.

> Modern psychotherapy is plagued by an amazing lack of agreement among its different schools about the most fundamental questions concerning the function of the human psyche, nature and dynamics of symptoms, and the strategy and technique of psychotherapy. This does not apply only to the schools based on entirely different philosophical assumptions, such as behaviorism, psychoanalysis, and existential therapy, but also the various branches of depth psychology that evolved historically from the same source, the original work of Sigmund Freud (the Adlerian, Rankian, Jungian, Kleinian, Reichian, and Lacanian schools, ego psychology, and many others). The world of modern psychotherapy resembles a large busy marketplace, in which it is difficult to orient oneself. Each of the many schools offers different explanations for the same emotional and psychosomatic problems and a different therapeutic technique. In each case this will be accompanied with the assurance that this is the scientific way to treat this condition, or the "method of choice." It is difficult to envision a similar degree of disagreement in one of the hard sciences. Yet in psychology, we have somehow learned to live with this situation and do not usually even question it or consider it strange.[141]

This lack of agreement between the different schools and "forces" of modern psychology also makes one question the efficacy of such psychologies altogether.[142] It has been asserted that the particular orientation utilized is insignificant, which makes one wonder what need there is for so many different types of contemporary psychology, implying that this variety is not only perplexing to the layperson and professional alike, but actually unnecessary.

In summary, while both humanistic and transpersonal psychology were founded with good intention—and we are most grateful for their efforts to expand the scope of modern psychology as a whole and particularly for their attempt to transcend the reductionistic outlook of behav-

2003), p. 378.

[140] Frithjof Schuon, "The Contradiction of Relativism," in *Logic and Transcendence*, p. 16.

[141] Stanislav Grof, "Healing Potential of Non-ordinary States of Consciousness: Observations from Psychedelic Therapy and Holotropic Breathwork," in Seymour Boorstein (ed.), *Transpersonal Psychotherapy*, Second Edition (Albany, NY: State University of New York Press, 1996), p. 515.

[142] See Martin E.P. Seligman, "The Effectiveness of Psychotherapy: The Consumer Reports Study," *American Psychologist*, Vol. 50, No. 12 (December 1995), pp. 965-974.

iorism and psychoanalysis—they nonetheless unavoidably demonstrate a high level of *naïveté* due to the indiscriminate inclusion of behaviorism and psychoanalysis into their framework, which are irreconcilable with the spiritual dimension that they purport to affirm. The integral psychology of the perennial philosophy does not seek to purpose a new *theoria* or *praxis* outside what it itself is and has always been. The central need is to restore the psyche or soul to its rightful position, which has been known to traditional peoples of all times and places; it is only through the events of the so-called Enlightenment that the human psyche has become misplaced and dissociated from the spiritual domain.

Behaviorism was for the most part a reaction against psychoanalysis (especially introspectionism and mentalism); psychoanalysis was a reaction to the prevailing psychology of the time, yet it is more challenging to pinpoint because it is intimately allied with several other key revolts of historical import that in many ways catalyzed the modern world itself; humanistic psychology in turn was a response to both behaviorism and psychoanalysis, and while it recognized the noteworthy role of spirituality, its place was not always clear or agreed upon; transpersonal psychology however sought to definitively include the spiritual domain and by doing so, became the fulfillment of all three "forces," thus establishing itself as the "fourth force" in modern psychology. Yet the spiritual psychology of the perennial philosophy situates the human microcosm—Spirit/Intellect, soul, and body—*in divinis*, and does not need developmental phases nor an evolutionary trajectory for its completion; it was complete in principle and reflects its origin in what is transcendent and divine. This however, does not mean that the human individual does not go through developmental phases in life or on the spiritual path—recalling that in the premodern or traditional world the sacred was the center and origin of everything and human development along with spiritual development supported one another and were inseparable as they functioned for one and the same end: human completion—however spiritual psychology was complete upon its origin. As long as the discernment between the psychic and spiritual domains and presence of integral spiritual forms and their practice are missing from psychology in all of its "forces" and schools, the impasse of modern psychology will persist. "In conclusion, let us emphasize again that the perennial psychology is not a science for its own sake, and can be of no use to anybody who will not practice it."[143]

---

[143] Ananda K. Coomaraswamy, "On the Indian and Traditional Psychology, or Rather Pneumatology," in *Coomaraswamy, Vol. 2, Selected Papers: Metaphysics*, ed. Roger Lipsey (Princeton, NJ: Princeton University Press, 1978), p. 378.

The "Four Forces" of Modern Psychology and the Primordial Tradition[1]

Huston Smith

While Huston Smith (b. 1919) needs no introduction to the readership of *Studies in Comparative Religion*, few readers might be familiar with how closely involved he has been in the advancement of humanistic and transpersonal psychology. While he is not a psychologist or therapist by profession, he has become widely acknowledged as a specialist in the area of spirituality and psychology and one could maintain that he has served as a bridge-builder between both domains. He has known many influential psychologists and therapists of the twentieth century firsthand. He has also been invited to be a keynote speaker at numerous conferences relating to humanistic and transpersonal psychology and has received an honorary doctorate from the Institute of Transpersonal Psychology. Most recently, the Huston Smith Center (HSC), located in San Francisco, California, has emerged, which seeks to further inquiry into the relationship between spirituality and psychology. In addition, he is on the editorial board for both the *Journal of Humanistic Psychology* and the *Journal of Transpersonal Psychology*, including the *Journal of Consciousness Studies*. Professor Smith has published many articles and has also contributed essays to a variety of anthologies edited by key authors of these fields.[2]

It is through the lens of the Perennial Philosophy, or through what has been termed "spiritual anthropology," that Professor Huston Smith looks at modern psychology—in its behavioristic, psychoanalytic, humanistic, and transpersonal forms—in order to clarify various problem issues within the field.

Samuel Bendeck Sotillos: You are considered a doyen in the study of the world's religions, having reflected on their doctrines and methods for the greater part of your life. This has brought you into contact with unsurpassed spiritual luminaries of the twentieth century, principally Frithjof Schuon[3] and the other perennialist writers (i.e. Titus Burckhardt, Marco Pallis, Whitall

---

[1] Editor's Note: This interview was conducted at Professor Huston Smith's home in Berkeley, California on May 22 and June 19, 2010. The footnotes were compiled by the editor.

[2] See Huston Smith, "The Sacred Unconscious," in *Beyond Health and Normality: Explorations of Exceptional Psychological Well-Being*, eds. Roger Walsh and Deane H. Shapiro (New York: Van Nostrand Reinhold, 1983), pp. 265-271; also of interest are "Psychology, Science, and Spiritual Paths: Contemporary Issues," *Journal of Transpersonal Psychology*, Vol. 10, No. 2 (1978), pp. 93-111; "The Primordial Tradition," in *Thinking Allowed: Conversations on the Leading Edge of Knowledge with Jeffrey Mishlove* (Tulsa, OK: Council Oak Books, 1992), pp. 92-96; "Foreword," to Stanislav Grof, *The Ultimate Journey: Consciousness and the Mystery of Death* (Ben Lomond, CA: Multidisciplinary Association for Psychedelic Studies, 2006), pp. 11-12; "Foreword," to Charles T. Tart, *The End of Materialism: How Evidence of the Paranormal is Bringing Science and Spirit Together* (Oakland, CA: New Harbinger Publications, 2009), pp. ix-xi.

[3] "I discovered that he [Frithjof Schuon] situated the world's religious traditions in a framework that enabled me to honor their significant differences unreservedly while at the same time seeing them as expressions of a truth that, because it was single, I could absolutely affirm. In a single stroke, I was handed a way of honoring the world's diversity without falling prey to relativism, a resolution I had been seeking for more than thirty years" (David Ray Griffin and Huston Smith, *Primordial Truth and Postmodern Theology* [Albany, NY: State University of New

N. Perry, Martin Lings, Joseph Epes Brown, Seyyed Hossein Nasr,[4] William Stoddart, etc.). Could you please speak to the significance that the Perennial Philosophy—or the Great Chain of Being—plays upon your *oeuvre?*

Huston Smith: In answer to your first question, the Perennial Philosophy (alternatively the Great Chain of Being) is central to my entire thought. If I were to find myself deviating from it I would catch myself up short and say "No, Huston you are on the wrong track!" because the Perennial Philosophy is where the world's greatest thinkers speak in unison.

SBS: Modern psychology—behaviorism, psychoanalysis, humanistic psychology, and transpersonal psychology—is unable to deal adequately with the tripartite division of the human microcosm—Spirit/Intellect, soul, and body—which is not the case with the integral psychologies of the Perennial Philosophy. According to it, each spiritual tradition has a corresponding spiritual psychology. Could you please speak to the influence that the Perennial Philosophy has had upon modern psychology, most notably transpersonal psychology as well as humanistic psychology?

HS: I do not think of myself as a psychologist; I am a philosopher, but I will do what I can with your question. At the start of Western civilization these divisions among philosophy, psychology, and theology were not drawn. Take Plato's *Dialogues*—what is it? Is it philosophy? Of course! Is it psychology? Yes! Is it theology without using that word? Certainly, for it refers reverently to the Divine! And it even includes politics, for as we know, Plato titles his entire corpus the *Republic*. Divisions in the seamless web of thought come later, mostly through academic departments in universities.

I am a supporter of transpersonal psychology, which affirms that there is more to the mind than textbook psychology includes. Still, we have to work with the fact that the original union which overlaps philosophy, psychology, theology has broken down, and we have to work with its pieces. I continue to think that all authentic traditions include a transpersonal concept of the human psyche.

The traditionalist or perennialist thesis is that modern psychology does not go far enough in the direction of recognizing the sanctity of things which underlies their normal everyday appearance to us, not differentiating between the apparent and the Real—the ego from the Self.

SBS: The five principal confusions which affect all four branches of modern psychology are scientism, evolutionism, psychologism, syncretism, and New Age thought. All of these viewpoints are reductionistic, and their effect is to remove or abolish the theomorphic nature of the human individual. They do this in the following ways: by reducing man to the five senses (scientism), by alleging that the greater can derive from the lesser (evolutionism), by equating the spiritual with the psychic (psychologism), by mixing truth with error (syncretism), and by accepting teachers and/or teachings that do not originate either in a spiritual revelation or

York Press, 1989], p. 13). There are also three significant video clips with Professor Huston Smith speaking about Frithjof Schuon—"Who is Frithjof Schuon?" "Discovering Schuon," "Schuon's Historical Context"—online via World Wisdom's website: www.worldwisdom.com.

[4] See Seyyed Hossein Nasr, "Homage to Huston Smith," *Sophia: The Journal of Traditional Studies*, Vol. 5, No. 1 (Summer 1999), pp. 5-8.

an authentic chain of spiritual transmission (New Age thought). According to the Perennial Philosophy, all of these five prejudices or presuppositions are largely or totally false. In your view, what are the principal confusions (or reductionisms) that affect all four branches of modern psychology?

HS: I would agree that five great barriers to an authentic psychology are scientism[5]—which validates what is real only by what our physical senses report—evolutionism[6]—which only affirms the material order by what is horizontal, in essence excluding the archetypes or the transcendent, that *the greater derives from the lesser*—psychologism—which dissociates the human psyche from its origin in Spirit—syncretism—which parodies synthesis by attempting to fuse what is most superficial without the essential principles to unite them, and "New Age" thought—which identifies or confuses the Absolute and the relative, arguing that we are already in our everyday experience immersed in the Absolute. New Age is cut-flower psychology; it does not root back into the Great Tradition or the Perennial Philosophy. And as we know cut-flowers are short lived.

SBS: In recent years the Perennial Philosophy has undergone heavy critique by key representatives within transpersonal psychology (i.e. Ken Wilber and Jorge N. Ferrer), challenging its central role and importance as one of the core tenets of the "fourth force" in modern psychology. There have also been attempts to usurp the Perennial Philosophy under an updated guise of modernism or postmodernism—what has been dubiously been termed the "The Neo-Perennial Philosophy" or "Integral-Post Metaphysics." What are your thoughts on this curious development?

HS: That is their view, and I obviously disagree with it. With regards to Ken Wilber I just disagree with him; this may be close-minded of me but with all due respect to him, I do not think that he has the substance to stand up and critique the Perennial Philosophy.[7]

SBS: How do you envision the Perennial Philosophy assisting modern psychology and its two later currents—humanistic and transpersonal psychology—in bringing about an authentic psychology that addresses the fullness of the human individual—Spirit, soul, and body *in divinis*?

HS: In my book, *Tales of Wonder*, the Appendix contains "A Universal Grammar of Worldviews." I think of this Appendix as a synonym for the Perennial Philosophy. The thesis is that any adequate psychology needs (in whatever wording), to include these fourteen points [presented in summarized form].

---

[5] See Huston Smith, "Scientism: The Bedrock of the Modern Worldview," in *Science and the Myth of Progress*, ed. Mehrdad M. Zarandi (Bloomington, IN: World Wisdom, 2003), pp. 233-248; "The Tunnel's Floor: Scientism," in *Why Religion Matters: The Fate of the Human Spirit in an Age of Disbelief* (New York: HarperCollins, 2001), pp. 59-78.

[6] See Huston Smith, "Changing the Shibboleth of Evolution," *Sophia: The Journal of Traditional Studies*, Vol. 16, No. 1 (2010), pp. 7-8.

[7] Editor's Note: For a critique of Ken Wilber, see José Segura, "On Ken Wilber's Integration of Science and Religion" and John Herlihy's review of Wilber's *Integral Psychology* (both in this volume); for a critique of Jorge Ferrer, see Nahuel Sugobono's review of Ferrer's *Revisioning Transpersonal Theory* (in this volume).

1. Reality is infinite.
2. The Infinite includes the finite or we would be left with infinite-plus-finitude and the Infinite would not be what it claims to be.
3. The contents of finitude are hierarchically ordered.
4. Causation is from the top down, from the Infinite down through the descending degrees of reality.
5. In descending to the finite, the singularity of the Infinite splays out into multiplicity.
6. Reversing the drift of downward causation, as we look upward from our position on the causal chain we find that these virtues ascend the causal ladder, and as they ascend, their distinctions fade and they begin to merge.
7. When the virtues converge at the top of the pyramid, the inbuilt worldview makes its most staggering claim: absolute perfection reigns.
8. The Great Chain of Being, with its links that increase in worth as they ascend, needs to be qualified by the Hermetic Principle: "As above, so below." Everything "out there" is within us with the hierarchy inverted. When a mountain is reflected in a lake, its peak appears below its base.
9. Human beings cannot fully know the Infinite.
10. When articulated, as in the Bible, the Koran, the Upanishads, and the dialogues of Plato, the universal grammars have to be interpreted.
11. All these factors were taken for granted until the rise of twentieth-century fundamentalism with its obsession for taking language literally.
12. There are two distinct and complementary ways of knowing: the rational and the intuitive.
13. Walnuts have shells that house kernels, and religions likewise have outsides and insides.
14. Finally, what we know is ringed about with darkness.

All of the authentic enduring philosophies, psychologies, theologies have these fourteen points, so it is as if I have passed a strainer through the history of philosophy, psychology, theology and lifted out the common elements. I think that any psychology to be true— will have to coincide, include, incorporate these fourteen points. Now that is a very, very strong claim.

I am very happy that you are engaged in this project and I think that it can help to clear the atmosphere which is now very vague, confused, and cloudy. I honor and I am happy with the project.

SBS: Can modern psychology offer anything that is not already implicit within the perennial psychologies? If the question were put the other way around, one could suggest that not only do the perennial psychologies provide all that is necessary in a true psychology of the human individual but they are the only psychologies that are divinely sanctioned to provide a doctrine and method of transcending and integrating the empirical ego in what is higher than itself, which modern psychology is not and cannot be. One could also propose that if it were not for the phenomena of the Enlightenment in the West, there would have been no formation of modern psychology altogether as psychology would be part and parcel of religion or the spiritual domain as is the case with the Eastern spiritual traditions, not to mention the Shamanic traditions of the First Peoples. A follow up to this question, can therapy be of use to a sincere seeker that is committed and practicing an authentic spiritual tradition which addresses Spirit, soul, and body? And if so, how?

HS: I would start by confirming that modern psychology cannot offer anything authentically new to the perennial psychologies. Regarding the second part of your question, I would say yes. We get into glitches and we need assistance from professionals to help us understand and work our way through them. However it is important to note that psychology—or therapy—is not a replacement for the spiritual practices prescribed by the world's religions.

On Ken Wilber's Integration of Science and Religion

José Segura

Introduction

Ken Wilber has been much acclaimed by those who believe that he has constructed an ideological system in which science, religion, politics, and the arts are harmonized meaningfully for contemporary man. Seen through the lens of the "perennial philosophy," however, Wilber's system does not hold together since its material is the result of mixing traditional with secular knowledge. For obvious reasons, we cannot undertake a critical analysis of the totality of Wilber's system within the limits of an article. We have confined our task to show the false nature of the alleged integration of science and religion as articulated by Wilber, particularly in his book, *The Marriage of Sense and Soul* (henceforth *MSS*).

The Confusion of Categories

A preliminary problem arises when we consider the full title of *MSS*. It is titled: *The Marriage of Sense and Soul. Integrating Science and Religion*. If we turn to chapter 1, page 3, the heading reads: "The Challenge of our Times: Integrating Science and Religion." In that same page, though, "science" and "religion" have become "modern science" and "premodern religion." It is in fact on page 10 that Wilber first clearly sets forth his goal when he writes: "if we are to integrate both *premodern* religion and *modern* science, the truths of both parties must be brought to the union" (*emphasis added*).

We are now in a better position to define our task, for we have discovered that what Wilber really wants to integrate is "*premodern* religion" and "*modern* science." The reader must proceed with caution because the terms "science" and "religion" are distinguished by Wilber in a very limited and particular way—"premodern religion" is one thing; "modern science" quite another.

Wilber's real agenda—the integration of "premodern religion" and "modern science"—is from the traditional perspective a pseudo-integration in that it entails an impossible operation: the mixing of metaphysics-based traditional postulates with reason-founded secular knowledge. It is not so much then that science and religion are two different fields, but rather that the traditional doctrine in which premodern religion is located is incompatible with the secular premises of modern science. This is not integration, but aggregation. And it does not matter that Wilber divides and subdivides a great deal of fields and categories of being and cognition.

At this point, we can well imagine that a logical question has been put by the reader: on what ground do we suppose that Wilber's mixing of different fields is questionable? To properly answer that question we shall produce an illustration of Wilber's confusion of categories, an illustration which, without further delay, will place us in the very heart of our discussion. In dealing with the "Big Three," a fundamental notion of modernity which includes Morals, Science, and the Arts, Wilber states:

> Science—empirical science—deals with objects, with "its," with empirical patterns. Morals and ethics concern "we" and our intersubjective world. Art concerns the beauty in the eye of the beholder, the "I."

Such a statement, dealing with categories and classifications, is within the realm of the rationalist,[1] and in this sense we could say that it belongs to the sphere of secular knowledge. Things, however, start to be different when Wilber adds:

> And yes, this is essentially Plato's the Good (morals, the "we"), the True (in the sense of propositional truth, objective truths or "its"), and the Beautiful (the aesthetic dimension as perceived by each "I").
>
> The Big Three are also Sir Karl Popper's three worlds—objective (it), subjective (I), and cultural (we). And the Big Three are Habermas's three validity claims: objective truth, subjective sincerity, and intersubjective justness.[2]

The problem with such an addition is that in it Wilber has equated each element of the secular Big Three with their Platonic counterparts. But this is something that a traditionalist would never do, for he knows that "the Good," "the True," and "the Beautiful" in Plato are Ideas or principles in the metaphysical plane. In fact the Good is the Idea of the Ideas. This means that these three elements belong to metaphysics. Consequently to think, as Wilber does, that the normal sphere of the Good is morals or ethics; that the sphere of the True is "the sense of propositional truth, objective truths or 'its'"; and that the proper or immediate province of the Beautiful is "the aesthetic dimension as perceived by each 'I'" is the grossest distortion of Platonic metaphysics one can entertain; a distortion which is exactly the product of humanizing the divine, of ignoring that metaphysics is the proper realm of the Divinity.

Now the humanization of metaphysical things, which is one of the main characteristics of the rationalist, is a sign that the individual has misunderstood those things. That Wilber has an erroneous notion of "the Good, the True, and the Beautiful" is corroborated by the following statement he makes about them: "These terms were first introduced on a large scale by the Greeks, who were, in this regard, one of the precursors of modernity."[3]

The mechanics of the mistake made here by Wilber can be expressed in this sequence: having found it convenient to use something which pertains to a metaphysical system of the past, he decides now to view it as a precursor of the rationalistic deformation he has caused it to be. He has thus rendered his "source" rationalistic by implication. To portray the Greeks as the forerunners of modernity by citing their metaphysical designation of what Wilber terms the "Big Three" should be proof enough of his basic misunderstanding of metaphysics and of his confusion of categories.

With respect to the Platonic "Good," Wilber's mistake consists in equating it with the concept of ethical good; he thus declares: "The Good refers to morals, to justness, to ethics, to how you and I interact in a fair and decent fashion."[4] This is "the Good" reduced to the level of convention and common sense behavior. Wilber does not deem it necessary to found "justness"

---

[1] In the perennial philosophy a "rationalist" is an individual who does not recognize in actuality a faculty of cognition higher than human reason. In Wilber we observe that he includes such a higher faculty in his classifications, but he does not seem to apply it to grasp the substance of the "premodern religion" he wants to integrate with "modern science."

[2] Ken Wilber, *A Brief History of Everything* (Boston, MA: Shambhala, 1996), p. 122.

[3] Ken Wilber, *The Marriage of Sense and Soul* (New York: Random House, 1998), p. 49.

[4] Ken Wilber, *The Marriage of Sense and Soul*, p. 49.

on something suprahuman. For this reason his "justness" is a mere humanistic or rationalistic concept. If one refers to Plato, one finds that in his affirmation of "the Good" as the ultimate metaphysical foundation of everything, he comments:

> [T]he objects of knowledge [i.e. the Archetypes] not only receive from the presence of the Good their being known, but their very existence and essence is derived to them from it, though the Good itself is not essence but still transcends essence in dignity and surpassing power.[5]

The traditional view on morality, incidentally, is expressed by Frithjof Schuon in this compact formula: "Morality, in the widest sense of the term, is in its own order a reflection of true spirituality."[6]

With regard to "the True," Wilber's error is, from the traditional perspective, catastrophic, since he assumes that its field is secular science. We must remember that the sole science that in the Platonic system is related to "the True" is *episteme*, the knowledge of the realities of the metaphysical plane. The counterpart of *episteme* in the visible, impermanent sphere is an approximate knowledge of physical things, for "true" knowledge is only possible of that which is invisible and permanent. There is no *science* of the *physical* world in Platonism. There simply cannot be anything but "opinion." Which means that the real value of any secular science is similar to that which can be granted to a temporary sort of knowledge, one which must always be reshaped and corrected as more rational and empirical information regarding the physical plane becomes available. How can anyone, then, presume to equate "the True" with "modern science"!

As for "the Beautiful," which Wilber rashly consigns to subjective art, the reader is cautioned that there does not exist any Platonic conception of art as something which might or might not be found beautiful in accordance to the particular taste of the spectator. Beauty is not subjective, since it is not ultimately founded on the physical. The physical objects represented in the traditional work of art are to be taken symbolically. Art, *true* art, both in Plato and in any Tradition, is intellectual[7] and hence a transcendental reality. It might—and indeed it can—begin with the physical perception of the eye; yet that perception is to be used as a springboard for reaching the invisible beauty of archetypal reality. Beauty, as well as the True and the Good, is an attribute of God. Only as a result of its reflection in this world could we consider it to be present in our physical plane. In the theology of Dionysius the Areopagite, "the Beautiful" is "the Good";[8] in fact, we find that this metaphysical identification is already included in the traditional structure of the Greek language, for in Greek, *kalos* means both "beautiful" and "good." In the Christian revealed texts, we have confirmation that the ultimate Good is God in these words of Jesus: "Why do you call Me good? No one *is* good but One, *that is*, God."[9]

---

[5] Plato, *Republic,* Vol. II (London: Heinemann, 1980), p. 107.

[6] Frithjof Schuon, *The Transcendent Unity of Religions* (Wheaton, IL: Quest Books, 1984), p. 51.

[7] In the traditional vocabulary, the term "intellectual" refers to the "intellect," which is the faculty whereby the metaphysical principles are apprehend in an immediate fashion.

[8] Dionysius the Areopagite, *The Divine Names* (Surrey, UK: Shrine of Wisdom, 1957), p. 34.

[9] Matt. 19:17 (The New King James Version).

Before concluding this preliminary view of Wilber's use of concepts let us pause to enquire: what have we learned thus far? We have found that Wilber mixes some traditional concepts (the Platonic Good, the True, and the Beautiful) with secular ideas, a confusion that is rendered possible once he has secularized and humanized those particular traditional concepts. We might wonder why Wilber humanizes traditional things? Perhaps not because he intends to, but maybe because he assumes that all that is required to understand a traditional author is one's own mere rational faculty. To underscore this error we can refer to *MSS* where Wilber writes that Shakespeare's *Hamlet* is to be interpreted dialogically,[10] that is to say, by means of the "eye of mind." Wilber fails to see that because Shakespeare is a traditional author, his works will only be properly understood in their traditional sense by those who are familiar with the principles he employed to write them.

Wilber's Concept of Science

Wilber gives us a general definition of science in the following lines of *MSS*:

> Science is clearly one of the most profound methods that humans have yet devised for discovering *truth*.[11]

A few pages earlier he writes: "Truth, not wisdom or value or worth, is the province of science."[12] We do not have to resort to Tradition to know that, as R.G.H. Siu puts it:

> Despite its aspiration for truth, science is not organized around it. It is organized around concepts.

And Siu adds that the path of science does not necessarily lead to "reality" but to "utility."[13] This is a significant observation, since it points to a basic characteristic of modern science and underlines its close ties with technology, which, according to D.S.L. Cardwell, contributes to science as much as it draws from it.[14]

The fundamental point of modern sciences is that their validity must ultimately be found in a measurable or quantifiable proof; whereas traditional sciences obtain their validity from an all-encompassing science, which could thus be called "total science," and therefore coincides with metaphysics. This is why Titus Burckhardt can state: "[T]raditional science contemplates qualities independently of their quantitative associations."[15]

To be fair to Wilber, however, one has to take into account the fact that he is presenting a global system, which means that we have to include in his definitions the expanded view which

---

[10] Ken Wilber, *The Marriage of Sense and Soul*, pp. 159-160.

[11] Ken Wilber, *The Marriage of Sense and Soul*, p. 3.

[12] Ken Wilber, *The Marriage of Sense and Soul*, p. x.

[13] R.G.H. Siu, *The Tao of Science: An Essay on Western Knowledge and Eastern Wisdom* (Cambridge, MA: Massachusetts Institute of Technology Press, 1957), p. 23.

[14] D.S.L. Cardwell, *Turning Points in Western Technology: A Study of Technology, Science, and History* (New York: Neale Watson Academic Publications, 1974), p. ix.

[15] Titus Burckhardt, *Sacred Art in East and West*, trans. Lord Northbourne (Bedfont, Middlesex, UK: Perennial Books, 1976), p. 56.

later appears in a wider context. We learn more as Wilber unfolds his system. Let us then examine this unfolding as it relates to science.

A key—if not the key—for understanding Wilber is that he takes from the perennial philosophy what he considers its fundamental claim, namely, the Great Chain of Being, to which he adds epistemological pluralism[16] and its correlative fields: the sensorial, the mental, and the spiritual. Furthermore, from Weber and Habermas, Wilber takes what they consider to be the central achievement of modernity, namely the differentiation of the Big Three (Art, Morals, and Science; or their counterparts in a variety of domains: Self, Culture, and Nature/"I," "we," and "it," for example). The point being that, as these authors and Wilber believe in the "mythological worldview," the Big Three are not regarded as integrated but as "indiscriminately fused."[17]

Now, according to Wilber, the problem with the "indiscriminately fused" state in which the Big Three are found to exist in premodern societies lies in the interference of a domain in the free development of another. Thus he adduces the historical case of Galileo who, as a scientist, was unable to pursue his work on account of the limitations imposed on his research by religion. This unacceptable situation, Wilber insists, arises only because science and morals were not differentiated but fused or pre-differentiated; the same may be said of art, where artistic freedom could be regarded as hampered by the constraints of religion. In Wilber's system, differentiation is a prerequisite of integration.[18]

For Wilber, differentiation, introduced by the modernists of the sixteenth and seventeenth centuries, resulted in dissociation around the end of the eighteenth and the beginning of the nineteenth centuries. He calls dissociation (the malady of modernity) the separation of art, morals and science, which is followed by the invasion of the artistic and moral spheres by the scientific conception of things.[19] Wilber's main point of contention is that critics have only seen in modernity its negative aspect, namely, dissociation; and that they are unable to see that modernity is not negative if we permit differentiation to be the occasion for integration without falling into the trap of dissociation.

Now, let us emphasize this point in Wilber's system: integration is only possible by introducing into the differentiated state of the Big Three (Morals, Art, and Science) the basic worldview of religion (i.e., the Great Chain of Being coupled with epistemological pluralism and its three correlative fields of reality). What one achieves through integration, then, is a common threefold structure (sensorial, mental, and spiritual) of each of the three domains of Science, Morals, and Art. This common structure, according to Wilber, is what permits him to marry modern science to premodern religion.[20]

What could possibly be wrong in this apparently integrated view, in such a harmonious whole, the reader may ask. On the surface nothing; under the traditional lens everything. Let us substantiate our claim.

In the first part of his thesis Wilber commits the error of believing that, because in premodern societies religion interfered unwisely in matters of science and art, the three spheres had

---

[16] Wilber shortens the Great Chain to three modalities of being: body, mind, and spirit, to which he assigns their correlative levels of knowing: the eye of flesh, the eye of mind, and the eye of contemplation. See *MSS*, pp. 7-8, 35.

[17] See Ken Wilber, *A Brief History of Everything*, p. 124.

[18] Ken Wilber, *The Marriage of Sense and Soul*, pp. 48, 52.

[19] Ken Wilber, *The Marriage of Sense and Soul*, p. 55.

[20] Ken Wilber, *The Marriage of Sense and Soul*, pp. 24-25.

to be differentiated. The fact is that any given traditional system is a perfect living totality; it is man who makes it appear to be imperfect by failing to conform to it. We should not seek to replace Tradition by a secular doctrine merely because we might have discovered an imperfectly functioning traditional society.

The traditional concept of science as a totality was still taught by Enrique de Villena, a fifteenth-century Spanish traditionalist, who in this was following Walter Burley, a fourteenth-century English traditional author; "science," affirms Villena, "is the perfect order of immutable and true things."[21] What that definition shows is that Tradition conceives knowledge as a totality called properly *scientia* (Plato's *episteme*); and it is from this *totum* taken as a tree that each particular science branches out. Now, thus understood, *scientia* coincides with (traditional) metaphysics, so that each branch rests on a totality, which by definition embraces not only what we call "sciences" but religion, art, politics and every possible field of knowledge. The coherence of such a wholeness is remarked in the following definition of Tradition offered by Seyyed Hossein Nasr:

> . . . truths or principles of a divine origin revealed or unveiled to mankind and, in fact a whole cosmic sector through various figures envisaged as messengers, prophets, *avataras*, the Logos or other transmitting agencies, along with all the ramifications and applications of these principles in different realms including law and social structure, art, symbolism, the sciences, and embracing of course Supreme Knowledge along with the means for its attainment.[22]

We may suggest, then, that to say, as Wilber does, that (modern) science is a method to discover truth is to miss the real meaning of both (modern) *science* and (real) *truth*. We can see now how Wilber makes the mistake of attributing to science what in the eyes of Tradition belongs to religion, i.e. truth. Let us recall in conclusion the following assertion of Jesus: "I am the way, the truth, and the life."[23]

Wilber's Concept of Religion

On page 5 of *MSS*, Wilber declares: "Defining 'religion' is itself an almost impossible task," though he has already told us that "religion remains the single greatest force for generating *meaning*."[24]

Thus a definition was possible after all; it is, however, a startling definition, to say the least, since for a rationalist, for example, the only meaning he will recognize in religion is that which makes sense to his reason, implying that religious faith is subordinate to reason or its various substitutes such as modern psychology or modern science. The fact is that anyone who

---

[21] Enrique de Villena, *Arte de trovar*, in *Obras completas Vol. II* (Madrid: Turner, 1994), p. 359.

[22] Seyyed Hossein Nasr, *Knowledge and the Sacred* (Albany, NY: State University of New York Press, 1989), p. 68. On the subject of traditional science the reader will find in the works of Nasr the best all-around exposition available in the West. See also Titus Burckhardt's *Alchemy: Science of the Cosmos, Science of the Soul*, trans. William Stoddart (London: Stuart & Watkins, 1967).

[23] John 14:6, The New King James Version.

[24] Ken Wilber, *The Marriage of Sense and Soul*, p. 3.

approaches religion in the traditional way learns very soon that meaning in revealed matters is facilitated by understanding, which in turn is made possible by faith.

To better see the rationalist basis of Wilber's definition of religion we should examine it in light of the following definition found in the New Testament:

> Pure and undefiled religion before God and the Father is this: to visit orphans and widows in their trouble, *and* to keep oneself unspotted from the world.[25]

Now, keeping in mind that traditional texts are written in a special language, we shall approach the above passage mindful of the fact that the clarity of its literal meaning (which refers to the sphere of the *vita activa*) is a cover for its metaphysical (dark) content which relates to matters of the *vita contemplativa*. The darkness in question disappears when we understand the symbols involved. Thus if we analyze the words "orphans" and "widows" we can see that the former is an individual who has lost one of his parents or both; while "widow" is that person who has been bereft of her husband. If we now take the "orphan" as that part of the individual which has separated itself from its "worldly" parent or source, what we actually have is an articulation of the need to reconnect with one's rightful parent, in this case God. The loss of the "worldly" parent thus opens the possibility for being accepted again by God, our "spiritual" and true parent. In this sense, the act of visiting orphans translates into those actions which lead to the liberation of ourselves from any connection with the impure things of this "world." Such a liberation will prompt our heavenly father to look upon us as his deserving children. A similar analysis applies to the use of the term "widow," with the analogous symbolism of the husband and wife. In the context of this interpretation, the last portion of this verse carries the same meaning in a direct language to guide the interpreter and to make sure that the less fortunate minds may understand the essence of the revealed message.

Let us mention another instance where Wilber mishandles the topic of religion. In *MSS* he writes:

> By and large, classical religions *never* denied science—first, because science was not a threat [only with modernity does science become powerful enough to kill God]; and second, because science was always held to be one of several valid modes of knowing, subservient to spiritual modes but valid nonetheless, and hence there was no reason to deny its importance.[26]

The mishandling in these lines is fundamental. To state that "classical religions *never* denied science" because the latter posed no threat to the former amounts to an explanation of something by way of nothing. A traditionalist would rather say that in a traditional civilization religion has no reason to disagree with science simply because both are founded on the same principles. On the other hand, a rationalist can certainly state that in modernity science is strong enough to "kill God"—once he has accepted a rationalistic version of both science and God. For secular science can neither kill God nor traditional religion; it cannot even start doing those

---

[25] James 1:27 (The New King James Version).

[26] Ken Wilber, *The Marriage of Sense and Soul*, p. 16.

things, since rationalism is not qualified to judge what lies beyond its ken. There is nothing more groundless for the believer than the rationalist's attempt to "kill God."

In light of everything we have said about Wilber's misunderstanding of traditional matters, the second part of the above quotation is a sound statement in the hand of somebody who once more shows how it is possible to conflate wisdom and rationalism, once of course one has unknowingly humanized that wisdom.

Again, we can close this section by calling the reader's attention to the fact that Wilber refers to religion without making proper reference to its metaphysical foundation, suggesting that he regards it as a man-made rationalistic construct, and therefore valid for those who like to view religion as just another element within a system.

Some Characteristics of Wilber's Methodology

In order for the reader to better comprehend our traditional objections to Wilber's positions, it would not be out of order to give here some of his most salient methodological features. The first is his penchant for eclecticism, which is evidently connected with his tendency to mix traditional with secular ideas. In talking about the perennial philosophy Wilber declares:

> . . . it forms the esoteric core of Hinduism, Buddhism, Taoism, Sufism, and Christian mysticism, as well as being embraced, in whole or part by individual intellects ranging from Spinoza to Albert Einstein, Schopenhauer to Jung, William James to Plato.

And he goes on to say that the perennial philosophy, precisely because "in its purest form" it is not against science, has been accepted by scientists such as Isaac Newton, Einstein, Schrodinger, Eddington, David Bohm, and Sir James Jeans.[27] This is perhaps the statement which best illustrates the fact that Wilber does not actually understand the perennial philosophy, even though he sometimes appears to use it correctly. In this particular occasion, one simply has to ask: since when are those scientists well known for having accepted the perennial philosophy? Had these scientists embraced the basic traditional principles, we would today have a more traditional cultural environment.

The second relevant feature in Wilber is his belief that Jurgen Habermas is "the world's greatest living philosopher," a belief which leads him to draw "heavily, and gratefully, on Habermas' unending genius." This he does even though he admits that Habermas is "essentially a German rationalist" who "did not (and still does not) understand any God higher than Reason."[28]

A third feature in Wilber (which is directly related to his eclecticism) is to borrow from the best he finds in a variety of authors in order to construct a universal system which is apparently intended to satisfy as many people as possible. This is essential, since Wilber's integration of science and religion rests on such a method. We see that he draws liberally on ancients and moderns, Eastern and Western thinkers, without paying much attention to the fact that traditional wisdom is not something of the order of mere human reason.

[27] Ken Wilber, *Up from Eden: A Transpersonal View of Human Evolution* (Wheaton, IL: Quest Books, 1996), pp. 5-6.
[28] Ken Wilber, *The Eye of Spirit* (Boston, MA: Shambhala, 1998), p. 71.

The fourth and last feature in our list is the fact that Wilber has chosen the Great Chain of Being as the backbone of his presentation of the perennial philosophy, i.e., Tradition, for his eclectic system. This is an arbitrary choice, since Tradition is founded on the metaphysical unity of that which in the physical plane is diversified. In order to avoid arbitrariness in selecting the backbone of Tradition one would have to look for an all-inclusive definition of it, such as the one proposed by Nasr in the quotation previously used in this article. It is only within a concise global articulation of Tradition that one may emphasize its central core, namely that the essence of traditional religion—which is then an esoteric doctrine—is to lead humanity to union with its creator.

Conclusion

If we were now to point to the most obvious flaw in Wilber's proposed integration of science and religion, we would have to say that it lies in the contradiction inherent in his method: the mixing of traditional and secular knowledge. In his desire to marry modern science to pre-modern religion, Wilber has deemed it necessary to separate religion, science, and art so as to avoid a twofold dilemma: (a) the premodern tendency of religion to dictate its own rules for science and art; and (b) the modern tendency of science to rule over religion and art. Having thus separated these three elements so as to eliminate the interference of any usurper in the affairs of the others, what does Wilber do next? He colors, say, religion with the two modalities of being which characterize modern science, namely, the sensorial and the mental, producing thus a sensorial and a mental religion; he then proceeds to introduce into science and religion the third modality of being, the spiritual. Wilber calls this "integration"; we prefer to call it by another name: "regression," since he has reverted to the position he was so desperately trying to correct. He separates things in order to regroup them in his particular way. We can only wonder what is the advantage of having obtained by this *integration* a "spiritual science" and a "spiritual religion" when in fact both of them have always been united by Tradition from the very beginning, a union which has caused no internal theoretical problem. The problems are only caused by humanity's inadequacy in adhering to traditional systems and precepts; but its inadequacy does not warrant the correction or reshaping of Tradition.

To summarize: a preliminary traditional examination of the integration of modern science and traditional religion, as proposed by Wilber in *MSS*, shows that he is a secular author engaged in the construction of a secular solution for a problem created by his particular secular handling of some fragments of traditional knowledge, fragments which he goes on to insert in a wider rationalistic construct. The problem that Wilber seeks to resolve is the very one he creates as a result of misunderstanding the traditional material he employs in his misguided attempt to marry modern science to traditional religion, two mismatched elements which belong to totally different spheres and are therefore wholly incompatible, absent a proper metaphysical matrix.

The View of Selfhood in Buddhism and Modern Psychology

Donovan Roebert

1

From its inception as a science aiming at an understanding of the psyche-self, psychology in all its schools has admitted the tenuous, complex, and dynamic nature of selfhood, and this complexity has been described in a variety of ways. Yet, despite all attempts to assess the self in purely quantitative terms, the human psyche always spills, often messily, over the rim of the beaker in which it is being measured.

This is one of the reasons why, in its broader conception of selfhood, modern psychology, and especially the humanistic and transpersonal schools, have favored the Jamesian and Jungian over the Freudian view, the religio-mythological approach over the reductionism of the scientific method. This tendency goes to the heart of the matter. It is simply impossible, in spite of the bravest endeavors of theorists like Cattell and Skinner, to square the view of either the measurable or the irrelevant self with the vital experience of selfhood.

For one thing, the psyche-self, both experientially and under analysis, is always at one remove from itself. Selfhood is inextricably bound up with self-awareness and self-reflection. The unconscious self is beyond the reach of consciousness, and conscious experience and self-analysis depend on the degree and quality of individual awareness and reflection. This is true of all the processes that make up the personality, and also of its projection as outward persona in more or less authentic forms.

Those aspects of the total physico-mental organizational continuum which we call the human personal self are dependent for their perceived qualities on the acuity of self-awareness and reflection which interpret them, validate them, and sustain their presence in conscious being. This proposition works the other way round, too. A selfhood detached from the presence of the personality is not a recognizable self; it is only awareness of self-awareness (the state of "depersonalization").

Neurological findings concur with this view of self as a brain-centered awareness of "personality activities" occurring at various loci. It is this complex dynamic of "awareness of a self-aware selfhood," expressed in a dynamism of drives, mind-states, and functions, that is the object of psychological analysis and therapy.

This common notion of selfhood has been variously described and organized in the selfhood-models of the five main historical movements of psychological theory: the psychoanalytic, analytic-psychological, behaviorist, humanistic, and transpersonal.

Among these, Jung's school of analytic psychology has provided the least constrained and richest vein of religio-mythological theory. In doing so it could not but depart from the reductionist and mechanist views favored by theorists seeking to legitimize psychology as a pure science. Jung was concerned especially with the persistence in selfhood of collective archetypes whose roots lay in religious, magical, and mythological pre-figurations, and whose symbols stand for multiple aspects of vital mental experience. In terms of these symbols he attempted to sum up the total human experience of self, both collective and individual, in its development towards successful individuation-by-integration.

Humanistic psychology has drawn on the broader Jungian path, especially in its re-emphasis of Renaissance views on the centrality of full human experience and the essential "goodness" of the human condition. The broader humanistic school was founded with the intention to restore to human experience, and to the analysis of that experience, the irreducible qualitative factors avoided and even despised by the more "scientific" theorists; in other words, to restore to the model of human selfhood the subtler elements of the religious, artistic, intuitive, mystical, and spiritual. This was certainly a shift in the right direction, not only because it refused to draw artificial "scientific" boundaries around the fullness of human experience, but also because the psychologist, instead of playing the largely factitious role of "analyst" could return to being human in the presence of the patient, allowing for a more authentic interaction.

In transpersonal psychology the humanist approach (with its strong references to stoicism) has been taken beyond the mundane or quotidian experience of self to transcendence of the personal aspects of selfhood (mirroring, in this, the historical transformation of Roman stoicism through the teachings of the early Neoplatonists with their stress on final self-transcendence). What this essentially means is that selfhood is to be understood not only in its provisional manifestations but also in its possibilities for self-transcendence, and as allowing an experience of selfhood beyond the principles pertaining to a limited "awareness of self-aware selfhood" bound up only with the ordinary personality.

In doing so, transpersonal psychology has drawn heavily on the perennial wisdom, including the theory and practice of Indian spirituality, and more particularly on the paths of Hinduism and Buddhism. The perennial wisdom, while it arrives at apparently similar conclusions as to the final nature and destiny of the humanness of humanity, is drawn from a compendium of religious and philosophical sources, a closer study of whose doctrines reveals fundamental differences in certain views and practices.

The single most important of these differences lies in the varieties of interpretation of selfhood. Indeed, the particularities of these selfhood-models are the strongest determinants for the type of doctrine and practice, more or less efficient as paths to self-transcendence, which derive from them. Among these views, that of Buddhism has, of course, its own particularities expressed in a special technical language which has sometimes been misinterpreted, especially by western exponents. Dharmic concepts and reasonings regarding selfhood, often extremely subtle and complex, and couched in concept-specific jargon, have been especially prone to cognitive mistranslation.

It is therefore hard to say to what extent transpersonal psychology has absorbed and made use of the Buddhist theory of selfhood which has its roots in pre-Buddhist Vedantic thought, yet also departs from it in a radical shift of view summed up in the notion of *anatman* or *not-self*.

2

Whereas humanistic psychology in its analytical and therapeutic aims begins and ends with the study of human selfhood, and whereas transpersonal theory treats of personal transcendence with reference to the generality of metaphysics expressed in the perennial wisdom, the Buddhist approach makes the assertion that selfhood, inextricably bound up with the principle of *anatman*, cannot be fully understood unless it is studied in the full context of its total existential environment, whose essential nature is also *anatman* (not having ultimate selfhood).

Indeed, the dharmic doctrine of the "not-selfness" of all beings and phenomena in *Samsara* lies at the heart of the Buddhist view of their essential interdependence, to the extent of asserting that any being or thing possessing inherent selfhood would by that fact alone have to exist in utter independence of all else. The truly and inherently existing self would be *individual* in the ultimate sense of the word. By its methodology of incisive negations, the *Dharma* can find no inherently existing self that is improvable except insofar as its own provisionally existing mechanisms will allow self-development. In short, the very highest that selfhood can attain to must always fall short of the transcendent or spiritual.

In Buddhism, selfhood is seen as sharing the existential characteristics of all other sentient beings and all non-sentient phenomena in the reality of current experience, which it calls *Samsara*. The Buddha taught that everything that exists in *Samsara* is "suffering, transient and *not-self* (*anatman*)." These characteristics, shared by all beings and things, define the fundamental nature of their mode of existence.

The central question for Buddhism is not only how selfhood as an observable dynamism is constituted but, much more importantly, how it can be understood in its essential nature as a phenomenon simultaneously existing and not existing (being not-self, yet appearing as self).

The quest for a dharmic understanding of selfhood begins, therefore, not at the level of psychological investigation and analysis of the psyche-self, but in the deeper grounds of phenomenology. Psychological theorizing begins with the premise that there is an observable selfhood that is the self-evident object of psychological investigation, whereas Buddhism starts by asking the question whether the self can really be said to exist at all and, if so, what the mode of its existence might be.

From the point of view of dharmic counseling, it would be misguided and fruitless to approach the self (for purposes either of analysis or therapy) as though it were an entity existing only in the way it appears to exist. Such an approach, based on what is evident only to empirical experience, is likened to "mistaking a rope for a snake in the dark, and treating the rope as though it were really a snake." In terms of selfhood, and more particularly of the misperceived psyche-self, the theory holds that fundamental mistakes in therapeutic approaches are the inevitable consequence of a mistaken view of the mode in which the psyche-self exists and does not exist.

The dictum from the *Vajracheddika* or "Diamond Cutter" *Sutra* that "no self will ever be brought to enlightenment" is the key understanding here. Another way of putting it might be: "if the self is itself only a relative and provisional construct, how can it be treated as ultimately real, and how can it ever be brought into the state of ultimate reality?" Or, more pertinently: "how can the provisional construct of selfhood be brought to healthy functionality if its provisional nature is not understood from the outset?"

This view of the provisional and imputed nature of selfhood can best be understood by a closer examination of the doctrine of the three characteristics of all beings and phenomena existing in *Samsara*; that is, their suffering, their transience, and their quality of *anatman* or *not-self*.

3

The characteristic of the universal suffering of samsaric existence is the substance of the Buddha's First Noble Truth, that "all life is suffering." The Second Noble Truth describes the causes of suffering as "ignorance, attachment and aversion," the three afflictions which drive all personal activity in this world, which Buddhism calls the "desire realm."

The truth of suffering is divided into three categories, viz. "the suffering of suffering," "the suffering of change," and "the suffering of conditionality." The suffering of suffering refers to the many ordinary and necessary sufferings that inevitably occur in a relative realm of inescapable polarities: happiness and misery, health and disease, youth and old age, and, ultimately, living and dying. These are the kinds of suffering which afflict all sentient beings in the course of their samsaric lifespans, the obvious sufferings which no one can deny, and which everyone tries to avoid.

The suffering of change in the changeable samsaric domain is equally obvious, and is the source of profound insecurity and anxiety, and of entrapment in the hope-fear dynamic. Of course, changes for the better also take place, but even these remain subject to anxious clinging and the fear of loss or deterioration. At a more subtle level, the philosophy of the suffering of change is rooted in the understanding that all forms of samsaric pleasure or gratification eventually degenerate into forms of dissatisfaction. Sitting in the sun may be pleasurable for a while, but eventually becomes uncomfortable, and finally unbearable. In the same way, all forms of pleasurable activity inevitably eventuate in some sort of suffering. There is no form of provisional pleasure which continues indefinitely to render happiness. At the same time, there is no form of suffering that eventually transforms itself into happiness. Thus it is evident that the suffering of suffering and the suffering of change are inherent and existential qualities of sentient existence in *Samsara*.

These principles presuppose that the psyche-self cannot be brought to "genuine lasting happiness" or "adaptive functionality" while it seeks its happiness in provisional experiences, including even the most desirable of these, such as transactional love and other forms of provisional union. These, too, must eventually disappoint.

The suffering of conditionality is viewed as the most pervasive form of suffering. It arises from the karmic conditioning of the psyche-self. It imposes frustrating limitations on the insights and behavior of self, and predisposes the untranscended self to a repetitive round of conditioned reactions arising from a karmically acquired "attachment-aversion" syndrome. The karmically conditioned self is trapped in cycles of habitual reaction determined by attachment-aversion motifs current in the survivalist instinct. It is from this predisposing conditionality that Buddhist method, aiming at transcendence, works to free the suffering mind.

But these aspects of the truth of suffering do not refer only to the experience of the individual psyche-self. Suffering in all its forms is common to all sentient beings, and the suffering of all beings is inseparable from individual suffering. In the postmodern world of rapid and global information-sharing this truth is perhaps more obvious. The person of increased awareness knows that his or her suffering is bound up with that of all people and creatures in *Samsara*.

These dharmic insights into the existential significance of suffering are inextricably bound up with the Buddhist conception of selfhood. The unenlightened self is always a suffering self, even if certain individual selves do not yet realize this fact. Suffering, in the Buddhist view, is the product of ignorance; mistaking suffering for pleasure or contentment is evidence of an even deeper ignorance.

This view, then, constitutes the fundamental statement which Buddhism makes on the ordinary or "ignorant" experience of selfhood: that, as a skewed and false insight carried over into the way people live their lives, the ignorant interpretation of self and self-experience is the first, most severe and most universal form of common neurosis.

Whether or not the individual self realizes its entrapment in samsaric suffering, that same suffering is what underlies the fundamental neuroses manifested and acted out in the experience and behavior of the psyche-self in "thoughts, feelings, words, and deeds." It is the pressure of this suffering that draws the self towards one or another form of therapy or escapism.

Whereas the various escapist practices, ranging from substance abuse to neurotic religiosity, are obviously ineffective as paths to mental healing, any forms of therapy which ignore the fundamental truth of universal suffering will also prove ineffective in the long run. These include the kinds of "self-help" therapies promoted in modern "self-improvement" books and courses, which assume that suffering, so far from being an existential reality, is only a matter of inadequate ego strength. Such approaches are completely at variance with the Buddhist notion that any increase in ego strength is necessarily an increase in delusion about the essential nature of selfhood, and must result eventually in increased ignorance and even greater suffering.

In *Buddhadharma* (the full teaching of the Buddha), the only way out of the fact of existential suffering is by addressing its cause, which is existential ignorance manifested in an undue attachment to self and an undue aversion to all that is perceived as a threat to self. But this does not mean that Buddhist therapy aims at reduction of ego strength by one or another form of conditioning towards an "unselfish" attitude. Self-diminishment deriving from an anxious and uninsightful ego-discipline is considered not only harmful but useless. In fact, Buddhist therapy does not attempt to achieve a wholesome modification of self-expression and experience by a direct intervention into the behavioral mechanisms of selfhood. Its approach, rather, is to circumvent the self by working to establish "Right View": an accurate interpretation of selfhood in the context of the whole of samsaric experience. And the resultant interpretation is founded in phenomenological factors, through the gaining of insight into the mode in which the psyche-self exists and does not exist.

Only when the very basis of its existence is understood does the self become amenable to therapy, including self-therapy. This is because, in the Buddhist view, the self has no ultimate reality. Attempting to manipulate directly the dynamisms of self is therefore akin to granting factitious reality to something that is only a "show," a mere appearance. And it is only once the self is seen in its essence, as the mere appearance that it actually is, that it becomes fully amenable to transformation by transcendence. Only then, too, can the existential truth of suffering be transcended.

4

Transience as the second characteristic of samsaric existence is to be inferred not only at the level of the obvious. It is obvious that all beings and things in *Samsara* are impermanent, subject to change, decay and, finally, destruction. Nothing in the space-time-mind continuum endures forever, and the self itself is transient. It is transient because it shares with all other phenomena a provisional, relative, interdependent mode of existence. It partakes in their ultimate unreality, in their modes of simultaneous existing and not-existing.

But the principle of transience is to be understood also at deeper and more subtle levels, and in its dual aspects. In one aspect (the aspect arising from ignorance) it is the principle which reinforces entrapment in a flux of conditioned mind-states; in the other (the enlightened aspect) it provides the only proper means of escape from them.

The same dynamic of transience which keeps the ignorant self stuck in its cycles of cause and effect and habitual reaction, and in the larger cycle of living and dying, is also the principle which, when clearly understood, allows entry into the unconditioned realm, the realm beyond the appearances that hold the self in their cyclic thrall.

The key to understanding the opportunities for transcendent therapies inherent in the principle of transience lies in the dharmic view of the transitory and discontinuous nature of "moments" of mental activity-in-time. Here the view is that awareness-in-time does not occur along a single protracted continuum. Every moment of awareness-in-time is followed, binary fashion, by a non-moment; every moment of existence by an interlude of non-existence. These moments and non-moments occur in such rapid succession that our relatively sluggish perception interprets their binary interplay as an unbroken continuum of existence-awareness. It is this false interpretation that keeps the psyche-self in the grip of its single-continuum conditioned experience, in the apparently self-evident but ultimately false belief that awareness-in-time is a single continuous experience stretching from birth to death.

What the transience and discontinuity of existence-moments essentially means is that every moment of self-existence arising from the preceding non-moment is actually a new moment, a new self, a new experience of self, an entirely new moment of opportunity and potential. This is what is meant by the unconditioned "now." If every moment, arising from the preceding non-moment, is really a new moment, then the causal chain of prior conditioning is actually a fallacy, based on an empirical experience that is misinterpreting its existence as an unbroken continuum of cause and effect. It is to this delusion that Buddhism refers when speaking of "imprisonment in the cycle of karma."

Besides this important insight, there is the question of the nature of the non-moment itself. In the Buddhist view, the non-moment is the crucial "non-moment of transcendence." Just as the gap between the cessation of one thought and the arising of the next is the non-moment that is the essence of meditative practice—because true meditation is the practice of lengthening that gap—so the non-moment between one self-arising and the next is the gap in which, through practice, the ultimate non-reality of self can be understood and the transcendence of self attained.

The transience of self is therefore to be understood in the first place as the obliteration of self in every succeeding non-moment, and only in the second as the wider and more obvious pattern of birth, decay, and dying. Such an understanding leads, in the dharmic view, to a natural "letting go" of the habitual "grasping at a self," whereas the secondary understanding without the insight of the first might well result in a greater and even more neurotic self-attachment than is normal for human beings deceived by the false imperative of conditionality.

A profound grasp of the moment-by-moment principle of transience, strengthened by meditative practice and ongoing mindfulness, has also the result of lessening and finally eliminating attachment to other beings and things. And, in the Buddhist view, it is only when such transactional attachments are eliminated that authentic compassion (*karuna*) and love (*maitri*) can be generated spontaneously in the spacious mind that is no longer centered in the false notion of an abiding selfhood with its corollary of self-interested attachment to self.

5

The Buddhist concept of *anatman* or *not-self* is perhaps the most difficult of the characteristics to grasp. Its difficulty lies chiefly in the process of discerning what it is about selfhood that is to be negated. It is because of misinterpretation of this concept that Buddhism has sometimes been criticized as a "self-negating" philosophy. But, in fact, the dharmic view of the "*anatman* of selfhood" is, at bottom, a liberating and affirming doctrine, bringing balance and clear possibilities for therapy into the field of mental development and spiritual growth. It demonstrates, also, the inevitability of self-transcendence on the authentic path of human fulfillment.

The basic idea here is that selfhood, like all other relative and conditioned phenomena, has no inherent existence, or that it does not exist "from its own side." The crucial differentiation to be made is between "apparent or conventional existence" and "inherent existence." What is being negated in Buddhist psychology is the inherent existence of self. But this is not the same as the simple statement that the self does not exist at all. The self does exist, but it does not exist at an ontological level, as "a self arising from and established in its own selfness." The self arises from a number of causes and conditions other than itself.

In Buddhist theory the factors from which the self arises are the five aggregates or *skandhas*. They are: form, sentience, perception, mental formation, and consciousness. These are the called the "bases of the arising of an imputed self." None of these *skandhas* taken separately can be viewed as a self. Neither do they become an inherently existing self by acting in combination or as a confluence of processes, because an inherently existing self would have to arise from its own inherent selfness, and not from causes other than itself.

What occurs instead, through the operation of the *skandhas*, is a given set of mental processes (experienced as an immediate sense of self) to which the ordinary, conditioned, samsaric mind falsely imputes an inherently existent selfhood. Then, following on this mistaken imputation, and interpreting these processes at face value (by pure unreasoning experience), the samsaric mind labels them "I." (This is "I." It is what "I am." It is "all I am.")

As a samsarically "natural" consequence of this false imputation and labeling of "I," the survivalistically conditioned mind grasps self-defensively and self-servingly at its imputed selfhood. But what has really taken place, from the dharmic point of view, is the complete mistaking of a limited and misperceived set of physico-mental processes for an established and definite "I-ness." The classical analogy commonly used to demonstrate the false imputation to the sense of self of an ultimate "I-ness" (the mistaking of *ego essens* for *ego existans*) is that of the non-inherently existent chariot.

The "imputed chariot" arises from its parts (the causes) and from the recognizable assemblage of those parts (the conditions). When the correct parts have been assembled in a certain manner, in the manner that ensures both recognition and functionality, the phenomenon labeled "chariot" arises. But the chariot itself, as an inherently existing entity, has no ultimate existence outside of that which is imputed to it by the person perceiving and using it. Outside of the interdependent positions and functions of its parts, and outside of the person imputing existence to it, the "arising chariot" has no intrinsic existence from its own side.

This simplification of the reasoning of dependant origination (*pratitya samutpada*) is made clearer by a simple exercise in visualization:

1. The practitioner visualizes the parts (wheels, axle, base, walls etc.) of a chariot, spread out separately on the ground.

2. (S)he takes them one by one and puts them together in such a way that they form a recognizable, functional chariot.

3. (S)he takes the chariot apart and replaces the parts separately on the ground again.

4. The process of assembly, disassembly, and reassembly is repeatedly visualized until it arises spontaneously in the mind's eye.

5. Once this process becomes effortless, the meditator consciously removes the parts of the chariot and, while placing them separately on the ground beside the chariot, simultaneously holds in the mind's eye the complete form of the assembled chariot from which the parts have been removed.

6. Two sets of phenomena are now held in the mind's eye concurrently: (a) the vision of the chariot as it was before the parts were disassembled, and (b) the disassembled parts themselves spread out on the ground beside the visualized chariot.

7. The meditator inquires into the existential nature of the arising of the chariot phenomenon: How does it exist? Is its being the same as its existing? Can it be said to have existence from its own side? Where is the inherently existent, non-imputed chariot, apart from its causes and conditions, and apart from the mind which recognizes it? Etc.

In classical Buddhist language, the imputed chariot (a) is said to be *anatman* and *shunya* (void of inherent existence). If the parts (b) are studied and analyzed in the same way, their *anatman* and *shunya* nature is also recognized. But this does not mean that the chariot and the parts from which it arises have no existence whatsoever. They are not non-existent. But they do not exist in the way they are ordinarily perceived to exist. This is the reasoned pattern on which the dharmic negation of inherently existing selfhood is based.

6

The conventionally existent self, then, is, in its true nature, *not-self*. It is not "I" in any ultimate way, any more than the chariot arising from certain causes and conditions is ultimately a chariot. Self arises and becomes apparent on the same basis on which the "chariotness" of the chariot is imputed, and from "parts" that are themselves *shunya* and *anatman*.

This view of selfhood, and of the very "I-experience," goes to the root of the problem of self and its "acting out" manifestations in a variety of neurotic ways. Indeed, it demonstrates that the ignorant, ordinary self-view is essentially unbalanced and charged with an ultimate reality and centrality which, under closer analysis, it demonstrably does not possess. It is only when the self is authentically contextualized in this way that an accurate and efficacious therapy becomes possible. Because the contextualizing of self and the accurate recognition of its mode of existence immediately place the "I" within the realm of the boundless, spacious, total mental continuum that is the ultimate nature of "this." And it becomes apparent that even "this"—this infinitude of mental "space" in which the "I" is contextualized, also cannot be "I."

When these principles are clearly grasped and spontaneously recognized, the "I," brought fully into the light of its conventional, interdependent nature, becomes malleable, mutable, and void of unchanging "I-ness." Only at this point (which might be called the completion of the "essential therapy") can "I" be presented for "accidental therapy," the treatment of its acquired afflictions. The afflictions, too, are seen in their *shunya* nature, as arising from an inaccurately conditioned self-perception and the habitual responses which follow upon it. The total material under analysis and therapy, already brought into the context of the transcendent, is thus rendered more amenable to positive outcomes, the sum total of which Buddhism describes as "Right Understanding."

7

The full and profound recognition of the psyche-self as "suffering, transient, and not-self" is not easy to achieve, even after intellectual assent. The path to full realization is one of gradual de-conditioning, re-conditioning and, finally, transcendence of the conditioned "I." The two preparatory phases (de-conditioning and re-conditioning) are, of course, a matter of method, and Buddhist methodology is aimed at the removal of the "obscurations preventing Right View" and, as the final step before self-transcendence, the establishment of "Right View" as a spontaneously arising wisdom.

Method on this path (which might be termed a "path of existential therapy") is summed up in the method aspect of the Four Noble Truths, the Eightfold Path, whose components are: right conduct, right speech, right livelihood, right effort, right meditation, right mindfulness, right thinking, and right understanding. These are not to be thought of as a code of legalistic, self-regulating injunctions. Rather, they are a set of interdependent and mutually reinforcing techniques for sharpening awareness and insight. Their end is not self-improvement, but self-transcendence.

For this reason they are practiced, first and foremost, under the overarching imperative of *ahimsa* or non-harmfulness which by its nature includes ethical awareness of "the other." Combined with *ahimsa*, the practice of the Eightfold Path is also a method for deepening awareness of the interdependence of all beings and phenomena in *Samsara*. Thus, the Path is a simultaneous training in both wisdom and compassion, which are likened, in the Mahayana, to the two wings of a bird, both equally indispensable for flight.

In the assimilation of the Eightfold Path, meditation and mindfulness are the central reinforcing practices. Buddhist meditation is therefore goal-directed. While states of calm are inevitable by-products of meditative practice, these are not seen as an end in themselves. The goal of meditation is reinforcement of the intellectually apprehended principles of *ahimsa* and *shunyata*, so that they become transformed into a spontaneously arising fusion of wisdom-compassion; that is, a liberated, natural "seeing" of the real nature of selfhood in the total context of *Buddhadharma*. The end result, then, is the attainment of *moksha*, the cessation from suffering.

8

A criticism that has been leveled at the Buddhist view and treatment of selfhood is that they diminish the sense of self-actuation and functionality in the quotidian life; or that they leave the psyche-self vulnerable and deficient in the face of societal demands. (This criticism might be summed up in the words of Pope John-Paul II, who spoke of Buddhism as "a life denying philosophy.") In fact, Buddhist theory emphasizes the need for a strong sense of self, both as an internal experience and as an outward projection. But the same theory stresses that adequate and wholesome self-knowledge and expression can only occur once the self has been properly understood and located in existential or samsaric reality. And this accurate placement of self is not achieved by behavior-modifying coercion or manipulation of ego-mechanisms but by the prior establishment of an authentic insight. "Right Conduct" flows from a self-view authentically modified by wisdom.

The self thus grounded in its proper sphere and rooted in the understanding of its final mode of existence, becomes an efficient and confident tool for negotiating both the positive and negative experiences and challenges of samsaric life. Understood as a fractional aspect of the total mental continuum, sufficient for all the purposes and functions bound up with self-actuation or individuation, it is nevertheless liberated into the larger spaciousness of transcendent wisdom-being, rather than thrown onto its own limited and constricted (and increasingly neuroticized) resources.

One can see how such a placement of selfhood might be objectionable to those schools of psychology which posit self-actuation or individuation only in the development of the psyche-self, where the self itself is seen (as in the classical humanist model) as both the means and the end of all mental development.

The same can be said of religious paths that seek to bring the self itself to perfection. The crucial difference between these and the Buddhist view lies in the dharmic notion that the psyche-self, other than as a functional tool for negotiating *Samsara*, has no final relevance or ultimacy as "I." And the finality of this statement lies in the Buddhist conclusion that "I," when sought for under close analysis, is "nowhere to be found." It is in this paradox, in which selfhood is finally understood as neither existent nor non-existent, that the Buddhist practitioner attains to a liberation from the neurotic "I-imperative." This is a self-liberation that is neither self-denying nor self-affirming, because it sees through the appearance of self to the ground of its being, and recognizes that ground as "suchness," the middle ground between existence and non-existence.

In the only other available grounds, those of either non-existence or inherent existence (each of which Buddhism considers a false extreme), there is no possibility for true release. That which does not exist cannot be liberated because it does not exist. That which exists cannot be liberated because "it exists as that which it is." It is only on the middle ground, in the *shunya* nature of the existence of all beings and phenomena, that the potential for transcendence can be discovered. And, Buddhism asserts, so far from being only one among many possible views on the nature of self, this view on the middle ground represents "the way it is." It is only by coming into authentic harmony with this authentic view that self actuates itself by realizing its ultimate *not-self-ness*.

Profile of Unfinished Man:
Unveiling a Sacred Psychology of Humanity

John Herlihy

> Man has been truly termed a "microcosm," or little world in himself, and the structure of his body should be studied not only by those who wish to become doctors, but by those who wish to attain to a more intimate knowledge of God.
>
> *Al-Ghazzali*

Once upon a time (*in illo tempore*), in an era known as the Golden Age, a perfect being was created and placed within a paradisal garden to enjoy the wondrous cornucopia of nature, its majestic vistas, and the solemn outpouring of its inner harmony. Its fruits and pathways, forests and hidden sanctuaries were so transparent, the naked eye could actually see, and thus directly appreciate, the inner quality of spirit that hovered within the physical forms of nature. We are reluctant to refer to this primordial being as masculine in terms of its inner psychological profile as we understand it today, for what is male in isolation without its female counterpart as reflection and complement? We know from traditional sources, such as the Quran, that the form of this androgyne was created from the shadowy substances of earth and water by God Almighty, and thereafter was vivified into a living entity by the supreme "Breath of the Compassionate" (*nafas al-Rahman*). The Eternal Spirit fused into this beloved being a living and eternal soul, housed within a corporeal body that breathed fresh air as the terrestrial counterpart to the ethereal spirits of Heaven.

This soul, in the eternal pre-dawn of the creation, was asked by God to accept its place within the universal setting of the creation when the Supreme Being uttered the words, according to the Quranic account, "Am I not your Lord?" The newly created virgin soul responded in the affirmative: "Yes, we witness You,"[1] thus establishing, once and for all time, the principle of sacred trust that exists between God and His human creation. Adam,[2] for this is the revealed name of first man, enjoyed an original, unique, and pure nature that complemented the universal setting of what has come to be known as Mother Nature, uncorrupted, wild in its grandeur and beautiful, just as a field of lilies represents a perfection of beauty by being what it is within its true nature. As such, this soul, in the infancy of its eternal day, was ready to embark on the greatest journey that life could offer such a universal and perfected being, universal in that its consciousness was not bounded by the ages of time and the limitations of space, and perfect in that it reflected the qualities and attributes of its creator, namely the Supreme Being, the Just, the Loving, the Merciful, several of the 99 Names that are attributed to God in the Quran.

As documented within the revealed, sacred texts of the great world religions, we know what happened next in the ancient narrative of humanity. The story of human psychology is written within our minds and hearts as an irrefutable truth and within the Biblical and Quranic

---

[1] Quran 7:172.

[2] The Hebrew word adam has its root in the Hebrew word adamah, meaning soil, making the body of man an earth creation that gives Adam his name.

account of the creation and fall of the first couple that we cannot escape during the modern era, no matter how hard we try to believe in another, modern-day psychological myth, based on the suppositions of modern science and its accompanying worldview that suggests humanity emerged as an evolutionary process from ape to hominid to thinking humanity. The scriptures of the great world religions have given us an account of the fall from grace and the expulsion from the paradise that is our human legacy from the time of the Adamic first man. Even without these ignoble accounts of how the prototype human erred within his soul and betrayed the intimate trust that God had placed within His conscious and thinking creation, we know in our heart of hearts, within that deep cavern of consciousness that we all enjoy and that no one wishes to deny, that the fall of first man lies within us as a reprimand and challenge to our identity, a human condition that we cannot shake off like a piece of dust from the fabric of our well being and self-perception. With the fall from grace came not only the consciousness of ignorance and error, together with the responsibility of making moral choices; but also the expulsion from the paradisal garden signifies a much deeper dilemma we need to examine more closely, and which strikes at the very heart of the understanding of human psychology.

The unexpected leave-taking of the first couple from the Garden of Eden must have been desperate indeed. Adam and Eve entered a terrestrial world full of hardship and uncertainty that they had no precedent for in their experience of the primordial paradise. In addition, they had no nurturing support system to fall back upon to show them the way. Suddenly, they had a taste of what it meant to make a mistake, to take part in ignorance, and to be weak and imperfect, all as a result of a single choice to forget the immanence of God and to disobey His clear warning not to partake of the fruit of the Tree of Knowledge of Good and Evil. But that wasn't the worst of it. The beatitude that humanity lost in tasting the nectar of the apple far exceeded anything they could have anticipated in the primordial garden. After all, it was within its parameters that they were permitted to see through the solidity of the physical order with the transparency of the "third eye," an inner eye that enlivened everything they saw with the implicit meaning and spirit behind the pictorial symbols of the created universe. In the new terrestrial order of the universe, where everything cast a shadow and time moved laterally forward with the insistence of a metronome toward some unknown future, including themselves and the dark premonitions of their minds and hearts, they would have their first taste of what it truly meant to be a human being without the direct perception of the truth. They would enjoy the inner faculties of intuition, reason, imagination, and memory; they would enjoy the instruments of the senses that not only partake of the fruits of the physical world, but that also lead the soul inward to partake of the wisdom of the inner senses of seeing, hearing, smelling, tasting, and feeling; but they would no longer "see" God, and they would no longer walk with Him through the meadows of paradise. Outside the gates of paradise, the *real politik* of human psychology took its first steps with the emergence of Adam and Eve on the great savannahs of earth.

The primordial being, born with a pure and uncorrupted nature, who walked and talked with God and saw the physical creation as a transparent mirror of the spiritual world, had shed his cloak of transparency and perfection to become a terrestrial human being, with all the implications that humanity entails. The universal human prototype that partook of the qualities and attributes of the Supreme Being was now a relative earthling, subject to all the contingencies of the earthly condition. The perfected soul that breathed the Breath of the Compassionate and understood things according to their true nature, in commemoration of the Prophet's entreaty to "show me things as they truly are," was no longer perfect and needed to strive for that primordiality, universality, and perfection that was formerly a natural birthright; but that now must be earned through the experience of the human condition, on a journey of return to the peace and perfection that is the promise of unity (*tawhid* in Islamic terminology) with the Supreme Being. Something within the human soul had broken, but in breaking open had created an aperture for a new kind of knowledge, an essential knowledge based on revelation sent to humanity as the actual words of God throughout the course of history, to give shape and coloration to the human experience, and to provide guidance on how to escape from the human condition.

These revelations told of something that now remained hidden within humanity, lying in wait somewhere between the knowledge of the heart and the ground of the soul, a lost thing that hibernated within us in a kind of winter sleep that we could find again if we looked carefully, to awaken into the warm embrace of its redeeming knowledge; fragments on a parchment of an ancient knowledge that could never die, whose watermark was the calligraphic script of pure spirit, written with a feathered quill as a cryptic message within the human heart. Any return to the fold of the divine embrace through surrender and repentance would be accepted by the Divinity, so long as it was accompanied by sincere effort and purity of intention. Sincerity became the key to a golden door. Every good work, every concentrated effort, every sacrifice or smile performed with sincerity and love would reveal that secret treasure that lies within as the forgotten legacy of the primordial era. Everything we do becomes a symbol of return. Waiting, listening, and striving, seeking one's purest dreams, all things would lead to that great awakening where peace abides and perfection reigns.

Something within humanity remains unfinished and will come to completion and perfection through the path of return to God. This is the ultimate message of the great spiritual revelations; this is the lost secret of the human condition waiting to be whispered once again into the human heart. Between the Divine Disclosure poured like fresh milk into the soul through the verses of scripture, and the discovery of the lost secret that finds its own revelation in the living of one's life, the faithful soul may find its way back again to that primordial condition that marked the human being as a universal, true, and perfected soul during the primordial or Golden Era, wrapped in thrall within the Universal Spirit. These are the seeds of a sacred psychology that will identify for humanity their true nature and form the ground on the way of return.

* * *

With these initial themes gleaned from the Quranic revelation, an image of self-identity begins to emerge that has well-served humanity down through the ages, generations of people that, in principle, abided by a traditional point of view encased with a religious framework that placed them within a broader context of the life experience than what the modernist person presently enjoys with the narrow perceptions of evolution, progress, self-reliance, and the "infallibility" of the scientific method that seeks to expose the dark mysteries of Ultimate Reality to a gullible contemporary population on its own terms and conditions.

We are no longer perfected and complete beings in the Quranic sense of the *insan al-kamil* ("perfect man"); on the contrary, even the designation "human," when applied to the word "being," implies all the weaknesses and frailties that we are well familiar with as part of the human legacy and that we spend a lifetime coming to terms with. Infant children experience a period of grace when they fall out of the eternity of Heaven and take up residence here on earth as an infant soul in an undeveloped body. The English poet William Wordsworth saw the infant child trailing "clouds of glory" as it makes its way "from God, who is our home," while he adds in the spirit of simplicity that he espouses: "Heaven lies about us in our infancy."[3] While it has all the required instincts set in place to survive its encounter with the physical and sensorial world from the platform of a physical body, the infant mentality still enjoys the incredible sweetness of spirit that is the hallmark of the perfected and universal being, and still wears the sacred benevolence, grace, and unconditional love toward its immediate family of mother, father, and siblings that it surrounds itself with like a cloak of many colors, divine qualities of love and beauty that are virtually reflected within the delightful and spontaneous innocence of the toddler and young child and imprinted upon their timeless faces as well.

The narrative account of a sacred psychology of man has revealed an unfinished being that does not know its true self and has not fully reconciled its relationship with the world. It is in search of a quintessential knowledge that could resolve its inner doubt about the true nature of reality. Within the human framework, we are in search of a quintessential form of behavior that could bring about a transfiguration toward a perfected and complete entity, a potential that lies secreted within *Homo sapiens* as a promise awaiting fulfillment. It is a quest for meaning and certitude that leads from the kind of being that we know we are not and never were, such as the anthropoid, the hominid, and the ape, to the kind of being that we are in principle and hope to become, such as the "primordial man," the "true man," and the "perfect man" of the traditional world religions. It is a central quest that takes place within the distinctive domain of the human kingdom, rather than the broad expanse of the animal kingdom, a quest that partakes of a curious inner light of unknown origin that permits us to achieve our fullest potential during the course of life, to become something that no animal has ever been or ever will be.

The narrative account of the passage of humanity through time, and the mythic tale of its deliverance from itself, takes place primarily within the inner world of the mind and heart, contrary perhaps to the vivid and definitive experience of the physical, sensory, and phenomenal world of nature that serves as our external and natural habitat. It is an intuitive, emotional, and imaginal world that is fraught with sinister dangers because we are also called *Homo duplex*, a creature composed of body and soul and thus a being that manifests a split image of the self that is in search of a unity that would reconstitute humanity as a whole person with a spiritual identity that places its roots in the unity of God. We unevenly embody the elements of animal and saint, while our soul comprises impulses of both darkness and light. Because of the distinctive and pivotal nature of the human faculties and the condition of the inner cosmos that forms the framework of our active consciousness, our souls are able to walk readily from one world to the other without taking note of the boundaries that we pass through in the process. Because of the full range of our faculties, and because of the nature of the borderland they inhabit between outer and inner worlds, we are equally at home in the phenomenal world as we are in the world of the spirit, at least in principle.

To negotiate our way through the vicissitudes of life, we enjoy a number of inner faculties that entitle us to the name that not only distinguishes us from earlier forms within the genus *Homo*, but that have been adopted to characterize us during the historical era when the species

---

[3] *English Romantic Poetry*, ed. Stanley Appelbaum (Mineola, NY: Dover Publications, Inc., 1996), p. 53.

Homo sapiens emerged as a distinctive category within the genus *Homo.*[4] The human kingdom that we were destined to enter and fully inhabit came into existence and is characterized by the truly human faculties that make us what we are, not *Homo erectus* or *Homo habilis*, but *Homo sapiens:*[5] a wise human being whose intelligence is a light, whose consciousness is a mirror, whose imagination is a field, whose higher emotion is a flame, and whose virtue is a perfume, at least according to traditional symbolism.

The human kingdom that the primordial Adam and Eve entered and took possession of did not happen through the back door of a physical evolution so meticulously described by modern scientists, but through the creative and intelligent design of a Creator who has made possible the direct descent of the first generations of people, not through what some scientists have called the "rapid branching"[6] of a discontinuous process of evolution from primate to ape to hominid to *Homo erectus*, but rather as a human creation in principle and as such, with an inner nature (*al-fitrah*) that is unique to humanity. Although the primordial human archetype contained the seeds of becoming a revelatory oracle of mystery as well as an implicit promise of fulfillment and enlightenment, in this fallen condition as earthly wayfarers and seekers after truth, the earthly prototype in its historical manifestation is still an incomplete, unfinished being. This idea is later echoed in one of the essays of Emerson when he says that the mind of the human being reflects a higher power "that made him and has not done making him."

Unfinished man still has to undergo the completion and fulfillment of an individual destiny in order to return to that original, pristine nature that we inherited at the beginning of time and that we promised to fulfill as a human vocation through the sacred trust in God. To that end, we have an instrument called "mind" as opposed to "brain" that reacts to the stimulus of knowledge, the faculty of reason that analyzes cognitive thinking and follows the clear line of logic, a consciousness that brings a heightened awareness to every thought and action, an imagination that envisions alternative worlds and reacts to the impulses of the soul, and a heart that denotes the inner pulse of our moral actions and preserves their inner goodness within the inner sanctum of our truest desires. Still, this is not enough to qualify as the Taoist "true man" or the Islamic "perfect man," a living image of the Divinity and a hieroglyphic symbol of an enigmatic creature whose inner message contains a mystery that needs to be understood on its own, rather than human terms.

In order to explain the most fundamental of all the discontinuities in nature, we need something more than the "prebiotic soup" theory[7] of origins and the corporeal and cranial

---

[4] Technically speaking, humans are classified by scientists in the mammalian order of primates. Within this order, humans are placed alongside what are identified as "our nearest living relative," the apes in the family of *Hominidae*. The separate human line in the hominid family is distinguished by being placed in a sub-family, *Homininae*, whose members are then called hominines. It would all sound rather depressing, if not disquieting, if it were not for the fact that these speculations are actually modern-day figments of the purely secular imagination.

[5] Of course not everyone holds this view. John Gribbin, in his book *In Search of the Double Helix* (Baltimore, MD: Penguin, 1995), suggests that we put our "prejudices" aside by placing humanity, *Homo*, into a separate category on the evolutionary branch, to be called *Pan sapiens*, referring to a small still-living ape called *Pan paniscus*.

[6] On the transitional steps between the primates and humanity, Phillip Johnson writes in his compelling critique of Darwinism: "We have to imagine what Steven Stanley calls 'rapid branching,' a euphemism for mysterious leaps, which somehow produced the human mind and spirit from animal materials" (*Darwin on Trial* [Downers Grove, IL: InterVarsity Press, 2nd ed., 1993], p. 86).

[7] "'Warm little pond' was how Darwin described the pre-biotic environment in which 'life' might have originated from inanimate matter in an 1871 letter to a friend" (*The Creation Hypothesis: Scientific Evidence for an Intelligent*

resemblances—dissemblance may be a more appropriate word—to the representatives of the simian kingdom, to account for all that *Homo sapiens* finds within itself and in its relationship with the universe. Mortality is written into the very sinews and bones of our bodies and we cannot escape its logical conclusions, namely that when we die, so also dies the possibility to bring ourselves, within our given destiny, to the fulfillment and completion that we are destined for. There is a finite quality to everything within "this world"—colors fade, as does the light and the day. Wakefulness becomes sleep where we roam through dreams that have no accounting and are left behind upon awakening. So also, life becomes death which itself becomes a further awakening into another dimension altogether, where the soul reconstitutes itself back into its pure essence without the encumbrance of the human body.

The decisive factors within the human kingdom and the inner cosmos that form the foundation and ground of a sacred psychology are the discernment of the Real from the illusory and ultimately the possibility of union with that Reality. That is why human beings have inner faculties that will lead them through this wilderness and ultimately guide them across the borders of the mind and the horizon of the self. Human beings must express the knowledge they attain as internalized wisdom, and they must exhibit their behavior and actions as expressive virtue. In order to transcend the individual self for union with the Greater Self, we must transcend the limitations of our individual nature and go beyond the needs and desires of the individual self. We need to know *a priori* the source of our origin, the meaning of our life, and the true nature of our final end toward which all human effort is projected and against which all the wealth of this world is as nothing. To that end, we have a number of higher faculties that make our "little universe" a true reflection of the "great man" that is the macro-universe.

* * *

The human persona of man, through his body, his mind, and his very presence, inspires interrogatives about the true nature of human psychology: Who is man? What are the characteristics of his human nature? What lies at the core of his self-identity? Why does he exist and what is his purpose here on earth? Yet, beyond these perennial enigmas of origin, center, meaning, and final end lie the more profound and disturbing factors that strike at the heart of our conscious existence. Is the human being merely a physical being that is the accidental product of spontaneous and chance contingencies, a being who has evolved through a process that appears to be a straight line leading from nowhere and heading into oblivion? Is man the symbolic image of a primordial first man of the Edenic paradise who, through a slow process of spiritual evolution and the experience as fallen and traditional man, comes to rest full circle as the perfected being within a paradisal garden outside the envelope of time and space that we learn from revelation?

Modern psychology[8] represents the study of man from the purely human point of view rather than the spiritual and metaphysical point of view. It seeks solutions to the problems of

---

Designer, ed. J. P. Mooreland [Downers Grove, IL: Intervarsity Press, 1994], p. 175).

[8] Jung is considered the "father" of modern psychology and *the* major influence in its development. He is sometimes credited with drawing upon the themes of sacred psychology in the traditions, but he was perfectly capable of making statements, such as the following: "Psychology . . . treats all metaphysical claims and assertions as mental phenomena, and regards them as statements about the mind and its structure that derive ultimately from certain unconscious dispositions. It does not consider them to be absolutely valid or even capable of establishing a metaphysical truth" (C. G. Jung, *The Collected Works of C. G. Jung*, p. 481). To call metaphysical truths "unconscious dispositions" must represent a fundamental failure of "spiritual" intelligence on his part, to say the least.

modern man by an analysis of human nature and psychology through the humanities in general and through the sciences such as anthropology and sociology. In particular, modern-day psychology and the other social sciences are supposed to provide an insight into the very concept of man and his human "nature," without the authority of Heaven so to speak, and without the knowledge through revelation that the Divinity provides. The rebellion of man against Heaven that began during the Renaissance in the Western world has reached its logical conclusion during these times in modern-day individuals who have invested everything in the power of human reason alone to sift the data measured by the human senses in order to provide the definitive norm of what is real and what is not.

It seems that modern psychology represents the study of man through the reasoning and judgment of man himself and projects a conceptualization of the human being that excludes that which is most essential to the human condition, namely, the unifying principle of a Supreme Being and all that principle implies. A sacred psychology of man, on the other hand, represents the study of man based on knowledge of God that descends to humanity in the form of revelation and is made up of divine truths that are enduring and universal, rather than human theories that often fluctuate with the ideological fashion of the times. Traditional man, who understood himself to be basically a spiritual being, worshipped the Divine Being with a faith and a vigilance that implied an inward seeing with the "eye of the heart" (*'ayn al-qalb*), a direct and convincing vision that unites pure vision with pure emotion in order to produce a higher form of sacred psychology that fully engages the person and provides solutions to the quixotic character of life's ever-changing and unpredictable challenges, not to mention human weaknesses in the face of those challenges. In the present time cycle, however, we act *as if* we were purely psychological beings who define ourselves and find our meaning through human reasoning, memory, and imagination alone. In the contemporary view, the psychological aspect of a person's life is reflective of a purely mental process which is, in fact, an extension of physical energies rendered profoundly mental through machinations of neural phenomena interfacing somehow with the human psyche.

According to the major religious traditions, human nature identifies *Homo sapiens* as man "as such." In principle, the Muslim, the Buddhist, or the Christian is not contemporary man or psychological man, primitive man or modern man.[9] The traditional man is man in principle, a being that abides by the human nature he has been endowed with by the Supreme Intelligence. The faithful identify themselves according to an inward nature that is based upon the knowledge of God that has come to humanity through multiple revelations down through history. Because of the manner in which they identify themselves and who they understand themselves to be, they have the ability to transcend their earthly limitations and identify themselves as the Christian primordial man, the Taoist true man, the Buddhist universal man, and ultimately the perfected man (*al-insan al-kamil*) of the Islamic tradition. In other words, according to sacred psychology, we are "man as such,"[10] capable in essence of rising above our earthly and contingent selfhood in order to know the true nature of reality. Our nature reflects totality and is satisfied only with the Total. We are the mirror in which are reflected the names and attributes of God.

---

[9] Nor is he evolutionary man, Marxist man, or Freudian man.

[10] Man "as such" departs from the Creator and Source as an individual and unique soul creation. "Mankind! Fear and have reverence for your Lord, who created you from a single soul" (Quran 4:1).

A truly sacred psychology of man originates in the primordial time, in what some traditions refer to as the "Golden Age," in which humanity was understood according to its true "nature," with reference to a truly "human" nature. It is a human psychology that sinks its roots into a revelation from the divine Source of all essential knowledge and seeks to unlock the secrets that humanity contains within the very ground of the soul. "All is contained definitively in our own soul, whose lower ramifications are identified with the realm of the senses but whose root reaches up to pure being and the supreme essence, so that man grasps in himself the axis of the cosmos."[11] Needless to say, if the revelation refers systematically to the knowledge of God and to a knowledge of human "nature," then a sacred psychology of man must refer initially to that divine knowledge and its corresponding human behavior in order to fulfill its role as a tool in the exploration of the human mind; not, however, a fragmented human behavior that is incapable of revealing deeper aspects of human nature.

A highly respected traditional writer takes the thinking on human nature a step further: "The study of fragmented behavior without a vision of the human nature which is the cause of this behavior cannot itself lead to knowledge of human nature. It can go around the rim of the wheel indefinitely without ever entering upon the spoke to approach the proximity of the axis and the Center. But if the vision is already present, the gaining of knowledge of external human behavior can always be an occasion for recollection and return to the cause by means of the external effort."[12] The revelation offers an essential knowledge of who God is and who man is, including their respective natures. In addition, this knowledge clarifies man's position in relation to God and the other beings such as angels, devils, and jinn within the universe, so that humanity can understand its place within the great hierarchy of being. Islam, and more specifically the *Sunnah* and *Hadith* literature featuring the sayings of the Prophet, offers a behavioral knowledge that amounts to being a sacred psychology of man. It allows humans to be most truly themselves as they were intended to be, and provides a psychological basis through which human beings can transcend the limitations of both themselves and their own limited knowledge in order to achieve the perfection of soul and salvation of spirit in a paradisal reality that the human entity in principle is destined to achieve.

This is not to say that religion is *de facto* a sacred psychology, but it contains the elements of a psychology of man inasmuch as the religion reveals a concept of man that identifies his nature as primordial, permanent, universal, and complete. In the Islamic perspective, man is his own priest and therefore in a sense his own psychologist, permitting a sacerdotal role for every man that brings the sacred psychology of man into the routine of daily life, thereby uniting the individual with the universal even on the most mundane level of daily existence. In addition to a metaphysical doctrine, the Quran also offers the Muslims a spiritual identity. They understand that they come fully equipped as it were with an intellect and a free will to respond to the principial knowledge of the revelation.

The form of the religion contains the structural framework and offers a methodology of action with which humans can discipline themselves, come to know, and ultimately tran-

---

[11] J. Needleman (ed.), *The Sword of Gnosis*, p. 124. Although outwardly a small microcosm, man contains within him a reality that originates with the source of the cosmos itself. "Soon We shall show them Our signs on the horizons of the earth and within their own souls, until it becomes clear to them that this is the Truth" (Quran 41:53).

[12] S. H. Nasr, *Islam and the Plight of Modern Man* (London: Longman, 1975), p. 5.

scend the limitations of their personal consciousness without compromising the expansion of a heightened spiritual awareness. Once again, a famous saying of the prophet—"He who knows himself will know his Lord"—already emphasizes the truth that humanity must look within toward their own inner nature in order to understand both themselves and the Creator,[13] otherwise they would never advance along the path of a true spiritual evolution, nor could they achieve ultimate transcendence of their individual nature toward the universal truth, but rather would commence a spiral descent into the netherworld of psychological turmoil and spiritual darkness that is the genuine prelude to damnation of soul.

The question concerning the spiritual identity of man and his true inward nature—who is man?—is a question that modern psychology cannot rightly answer with any true certainty; whereas the spiritual perspective need not necessarily raise the question for the very reason that it so readily provides a coherent meaning for humanity and a corresponding spiritual identity that, while being individual, is also universal and complete. While the "supra-natural" nature of humanity is not as immediately apparent as are objects in the physical world that can be verified by the efficiency of scientific observation, it is perfectly comprehensible, unlike the purely physical world which in reality offers no fully comprehensive explanation. According to Frithjof Schuon, the "sacred sciences" such as revelation and symbolism need not adjust themselves to the modern scientific approach in the verification of objective knowledge. "The realm of revelation, of symbolism, of pure and direct intellection, stands in fact above both the physical and psychological realms, and consequently it lies beyond the scope of so called scientific methods. If we feel we cannot accept the language of traditional symbolism, because to us it seems fanciful and arbitrary, this shows we have not yet understood that language, and certainly not that we have advanced beyond it."[14]

Human nature is nothing short of a hidden disclosure that serves as an open door to the perception of man's true nature and thus leads to an understanding of the nature of reality itself. Based on the Quranic revelation, the word *fitrah*, in its Arabic root, can be understood to refer to the human "norm" from which, according to the Quran, humanity has fallen away. Having been fashioned from the creative "hand" of God, primordial man was innocent, pure, true to himself and free, virtuous, and understood his place in the great hierarchy of being. "So set thy face steadily and truly to religion, God's handiwork according to the nature on which He has created mankind. No change (let there be) in the work (wrought) by God: That is the standard religion, but most men know it not" (30:30). It reveals that the nature of man has been patterned on the nature of God (*fitrah Allah*) in terms of its original inception, and this of course cannot be altered in any respect.

Natural man, then, is already perfect man in principle, even if perfection does not come naturally to man because of the consequence of the fall from the paradisal garden. It is in this sense that we have identified ourselves here on earth as "unfinished beings." Before his fall from grace, Adam was considered primordial because he already enjoyed the perfection inherent

---

[13] Similarly, the *Tao Te Ching*, chap. 19 states: "Realize thy simple self. Embrace thy original nature. Goal of man, knowledge of self, and who he is in reality." And in another section of the *Tao Te Ching* (chap. 33), we read: "He who knows others is wise; He who knows himself is enlightened." Socrates likewise daringly proclaimed: "Know thyself," and to quote a medieval Western contemplative: "If the mind would fain ascent to the height of Science, let its first and principal study be to know itself" (Richard of St. Victor).

[14] Frithjof Schuon, "No Activity without Truth," *Studies in Comparative Religion*, Vol. 3, No. 4, Autumn 1969.

within man's nature and he saw and understood the world "from within." In other words, primordial man was the embodiment of a living spirituality.[15] Modern individuals can still claim a primordial nature in so far as they continue to enjoy the same inner nature that Adam exemplified in principle, once this nature is coupled with the aspiration to return to the original purity that people today are still capable of because of who they are in principle.

Beyond the concept of human primordiality lies the permanence of man's true nature, a nature which is unchanging in its basic construct since the beginning of the primordial era. Human nature partakes of permanence which began in the primordial era of the Edenic garden and which the soul takes on its journey of return to God. This idea also sharply contradicts the prevailing evolutionary concept that humanity has somehow "evolved," not only as a physical form but presumably also in the psychological and psychic capacity within his human nature, from a lower to a higher species. However, this runs counter to the spiritual perspective that admits only of a descent from higher to lower levels and not vice versa. In other words, the human norm is characterized by permanence. Thus, the goal of all human spirituality is to recognize and to return to that norm, to humanity's permanent and original nature, to the *fitrah* that lies within.

In addition, human nature is considered to be theomorphic because it originates in God and is distinguished by the qualities that God has placed within humanity. We can be a mirror of the divine attributes and qualities because of our theomorphic nature, which asks us to be and to behave in accordance with who we truly are. Our theomorphic nature requires us to be true to our "true" nature and requires us not to forget our "original" nature. We have been given a knowledge that the angels don't partake of. The Quran teaches us that Adam learned "the names of things" (2:31), so that he understood implicitly the inner nature and quality of things in their essence. Even though we try to float on the surface of our being, far from our own center, being made in the image of God reminds us that we are the theophany of God's names and qualities. This is a psychological reality that lies at the center of the human condition.

Finally, to say that our nature is universal means to imply that it is based on a prototype of humanity that transcends time and space and provides a holistic balance to the eternal aspect of the human soul. Universal man is both the true man of Taoism and the perfect man of Islam, true in so far as he reflects the qualities and attributes of the primordial man, and perfect in so far as he reflects the nature of the Prophet Muhammad and the nature of the Divine Being. Muslims imitate the Prophet both outwardly and inwardly, so that they can model and identify their own individual nature on the human nature of the Prophet. Thus, they have the potential of knowing themselves within their true nature and imitating the prototype of human nature as exemplified in the Prophet, who in the Islamic context is the perfect man. It is said that to enter into the mold of the Prophet's personality through the *Sunnah* and the *Hadith* is to enter into the very mold of the Quran, since his nature reflected the nature of the Quran.[16] In this way,

---

[15] Schuon emphasizes the importance of the primordial man within the modern man: "To realize the 'Ancient' or 'Primordial' man means to return to the origin which we bear within us; it means to return to eternal childhood, to rest in our archetype, in our primordial and normative form, or in our theomorphic substance" (*Understanding Islam*, trans. D. M. Matheson [London: Penguin Books, 1972], p. 102).

[16] It is part of the immense impact of the Quran that considering our "fallen nature," it "restores to us the condition of *fitrah*. It gives back to the intelligence its lost capacity to perceive and to comprehend supernatural truths, it gives back to the will its lost capacity to command the warring factions in the soul, and it gives back to sentiment

the nature of man can approximate the nature of God, through the revelation implicit within his own being, through the words and the example of the Prophet, and through the revealed knowledge of the Quran.

*   *   *

Human psychology is a spiritual wilderness of incredible possibility that we inhabit without the need for any formal borders. We move freely and easily between the two worlds of matter and spirit that shape our existence according to the physical impulses and spiritual instincts that drive us forward in life. It is within the borderland of the mind and spirit that we commence our search for the sounding cord of our being, a harmonious balance that has the power to return us to our primordial origins and recapture the perfection that we have lost, in order to become a "finished" person once again, complete and at one with God. In making these aspirations a part of our daily lives, tucked between the thinking that inspires our actions and the fulfillment and happiness that give direction to our thoughts, we can begin to realize the whole person that lies at the heart of our self-identity.

All of the spiritual traditions allude to something that has become hidden or lost as part of the legacy of Adamic man within the primordial tradition. We recall the *Soma* of the Hindus and the Persian *Haoma* that refers to the "draught of immortality" that confers on those who receive it the "sense of eternity." The origin and purpose of the Sphinx, whose wisdom is summarized in the noble head and whose strength is contained within the leonine body, is enclosed within the folds of some far-off epoch as an enduring mystery, a hint of something remote and a premonition of a secret that evanesces into thin air the moment we draw near. The Greeks recount the mythological tale of Jason in search of the Golden Fleece, while in Christianity there is the quest for the Holy Grail, revered as the sacred chalice that contained the blood of Christ and thus the "draught of immortality." The Jews highlight the symbolism of the word in which the true pronunciation of the divine Name has been lost because it could never be uttered. In this respect, we could also refer to the "lost word" of the Masons that symbolizes the hidden secrets of true initiation or the lost word of many of the former revelations whose original texts have disappeared with the lost civilizations of ancient history.

No one from former, more traditional times could have predicted the lost world of the self that is the clear condition of modern individuals who have abandoned their spiritual center and thus have lost their direct contact with the Supreme Center. In today's modern world, with all of its sophisticated achievements and technological wizardry, the central pin has been pulled from the axis of the cosmic universe. The vast world of the spirit that we cannot see, touch, or experience with the external senses is lost to us because we have closed the inner "eye" that once had the power, not to see directly, but could once "taste" the metaphysical reality as an inner, human revelation that complemented the Revelation and Divine Word of God.

The call of the world and the call of the spirit are the two halves of a single truth that cannot find their truest expression as isolated parts separated from the Whole. The open gate of the inner faculties, the feeling of expectation, of a hidden inner voice, of promises to be fulfilled and

---

its lost capacity to love God and to love everything that reminds us of Him" (Gai Eaton, *Islam and the Destiny of Man* [Cambridge, UK: Islamic Texts Society], p. 78).

hopes to be realized, are all there, in a well-preserved niche within our consciousness that we preserve as the expression of our inmost selves. It is the higher faculties of man that receive the essential knowledge of God and perceive the meaning of the one Reality, in order to create an external life that reflects the inner person who lives it. The passing of days, the change of seasons, the success of people, the construction of all the churches, temples, and mosques across the earth, the accumulation of friends, money, and fame are one and the same within the context of the world. They happen, they have their place, and then they crumble and are forgotten.

As unfinished beings, we as post-modern individuals need to transform ourselves once again into the spiritual beings that we are in principle and that we are destined to become in truth. Modern man lives now in the world as if he will live here forever, without realizing that the world he lives for will terminate and then forget him. What he needs to live for and defend is the world of the Spirit in which all things are possible and where all mystery is resolved in a unifying principle of knowledge that knows no limits. It is a world in which the intellect receives a higher knowledge of God and intelligence sends forth its light, a world in which reason casts a shadow and the human heart burns with the emotions of higher sentiment. The world of the spirit contains the source material for the broad range of higher conscious experience. It makes use of spiritual imagination that is the search instrument of the soul in its endeavor to expand the horizons of the mind and to internalize the essential knowledge of God.

When the time comes to take the last breath here on earth, it will not be in struggle and strife to hang on to the last vestige of this world as the dying breath of a lost soul. The last breath on earth will issue forth like a sigh of relief from another person entirely from the one who lay down to die. This will be a finished person, a finalized being and perfected soul, lifting away from itself an intolerable burden like an old suit of clothes, and rising into open, eternal space like a balloon into the air, free and unencumbered now by the laws of gravity and the burdens of terrestrial humanity.

Sometimes, when we wake up in the darkness of the night, a feeling floats by, as in a wakeful dream, of something we almost remember, before we slip back into the remoteness of sleep with a feeling of confusion and loss. In the same way when we awaken, we remember dreams that seem at first so real, but they quickly slip away over the horizon of the mind and cannot be recaptured. We are made in the image and substance of clay, the revelation tells us. Then we are shaped and molded by what we once were and what we will become. As the ultimate spiritual treasure, the spark of knowledge that inspired human faith becomes an internalized knowledge that will erase temporal history and return us intact to the primordial self. The wise man in *Homo sapiens* will finally realize that he is not alone, that there is meaning in holy intimacy, that he has lived according to the truth of his given nature, and that the truth he has always searched for and finally found has made itself felt as the experience of the one Reality.

Then we can safely say that the effort we have exerted all our lives to lift the veil separating truth from illusion has been worth it. Seeking knowledge that will bring us back together as a completed and finished being hasn't been a bad thing after all, a voice from somewhere else insists. Nor is the feeling of completeness and fulfillment that is its natural gift. The eternal knot that was loosened by the fall of humanity from the primordial garden, and that has been untied all our lives, will finally close in one sublime and never-ending embrace, as the soul of primordial man becomes united once again with the Spirit of God.

Drug-Induced Mysticism: The Mescalin Hypothesis

Whitall N. Perry

Flesh and blood cannot inherit the kingdom of God; neither doth corruption inherit incorruption.

I Cor. 15:50

Presumptuous are they, self-willed, they are not afraid to speak evil of dignities.

II Pet. 2:10

A persistent error which manifests both in Western thought and among certain Westernized orientals is the theory that spiritual development may be had apart from the question of personal qualifications and individual effort. Now it should be known that only the temple of God can receive God, namely, a soul predisposed by grace, grounded in doctrine, purified of sin, transformed in will, established in virtue—and all this with the aid of an adequate ritual or traditional affiliation. Every natural appetitive instinct of the fallen soul is fixed upon this world, and only the intervention of a major volitive effort under spiritual inspiration and direction can suffice to interrupt the centrifugal tendency towards dispersion and to reintegrate the soul in its primordial unity.

Nothing could be more erroneous than the belief that the magical operation of some external power on the psychic faculties could in itself effect a real and lasting transmutation of soul, especially apart from all question of suitability and preparation of the vehicle involved. As an extreme example, a drug through the violence of its poison can rupture the normal channels of consciousness so as to produce "openings" into extra-normal modalities of psychic experience, sometimes exalted, often exotic, but usually squalid if not actually deranged, and in any case never other than fragmentary in their positive content. But there can be no identification of the unregenerate subject with anything that may really have a transcendent character, owing to his lack of preparation and of ritual guidance; while inversely, this very lack, closely related in most cases to an impurity of intention stemming from inordinate desire, renders the subject peculiarly passive and unable to resist the solicitations of the drug from its poisonous and malefic side.

These considerations notwithstanding, the contrary thesis was developed in a radical manner by Aldous Huxley in *The Doors of Perception:*[1] "It had always seemed to me possible that, through hypnosis, for example, or auto-hypnosis, by means of systematic meditation, or else by taking the appropriate drug, I might so change my ordinary mode of consciousness as to be able to know, from the inside, what the visionary, the medium, even the mystic were talking about." With these words, he proceeds to tell his readers how he put his theory to the test: "I was . . . willing, indeed eager, to be a guinea-pig. Thus it came about that . . . I swallowed four-tenths of a gramme of mescalin dissolved in half a glass of water and sat down to wait for the results" (p. 7).

---

[1] London: Chatto & Windus, 1954.

Mr. Huxley conducted his experiment with the aid of his wife, an investigator, and a dictating machine. His findings reveal nothing startlingly new in the heavily-documented and dreary history of drug consumption and addiction; what is singular in his departure is that he presumes to identify the modifications of consciousness experienced with the spiritual states known to the saints and contemplatives of East and West. Most readers familiar with even the elementary tenets of theology should have little difficulty with the specious reasoning presented. On the other hand, precisely because the logic is specious, it has inevitably given rise to a neo-scientific fad, which makes it incumbent to answer some of the more salient points raised in the book.

At the very start he breaks abruptly and radically with Platonic teaching; for upon taking mescalin, he finds himself in the presence of "The Being of Platonic philosophy—except that Plato seems to have made the enormous, the grotesque mistake of separating Being from becoming, and identifying it with the mathematical abstraction of the Idea. He could never, poor fellow, have seen a bunch of flowers shining with their own inner light and all but quivering under the pressure of the significance with which they were charged . . . a perpetual perishing that was at the same time pure Being, a bundle of minute, unique particulars in which, by some unspeakable and yet self-evident paradox, was to be seen the divine source of all existence" (p. 12). In *Timaeus* (28 A), Plato distinguishes "that which always is and has no becoming" from "that which is always becoming and never is." "That which is apprehended by intelligence and reason," Plato continues, "is always in the same state; but that which is conceived by opinion *with the help of sensation and without reason,* is always in a process of becoming and perishing and never really is." To identify perpetual perishing with pure Being not only contradicts Plato . . . it also contradicts Meister Eckhart, St. Thomas Aquinas, William Law and all of the Western (and Eastern) contemplatives without exception from whose teachings Mr. Huxley claims to draw his own ideas. The error comes from confusing the Archetypal and principial realm of Platonic Ideas with the "mathematical abstractions" of modern philosophy, and is what René Guénon calls "a complete inversion of the relationship between Principle and manifestation.[2] Moreover, the author's use of the expression: "a bundle of minute, unique particulars" shows that it is with the quantitative and "atomist" view, or with the substantial pole of existence that he identifies his experience (which in fact was already evident in his earlier books[3] where he confuses the "Ground" with the "Godhead"), and this becomes even more evident if possible in what follows.

In the next paragraph the author speaks of "Grace," "Transfiguration," and "The Beatific Vision" which he associates with *Sat-Chit-Ananda,* although the latter properly refers to a more principial realm than the former. Now grace pertains to God, and is not under chemical control. The Beatific Vision is not within reach of the unregenerate soul, and neither, *a fortiori,* is *Sat-Chit-Ananda*—these expressions all connoting supra-individual states of formless manifestation, which completely transcend physical, sensorial, and psychic range. This he seems in a sense to understand, where he says (p. 58): "I am not so foolish as to equate what happens under the influence of mescalin . . . with the realization of the end and ultimate purpose of human life: Enlightenment, the Beatific Vision." But in the very next sentence he continues: "All I am suggesting is that the mescalin experience is what Catholic theologians call 'a gratuitous

---

[2] "Les idées éternelles," *Etudes Traditionnelles,* 1947, p. 223.
[3] See *The Perennial Philosophy* and *Time Must Have a Stop.*

grace,' not necessary to salvation but potentially helpful and to be accepted thankfully, if made available." But it should certainly be clear, at least to Catholic readers, that a "gratuitous grace" is not at the disposition of chemical agents. According to the *Catholic Encyclopedia Dictionary*,[4] gratuitous grace is "beyond the scope of man's attainment, outside the limits of human exigencies. It is wholly and entirely within God's power to dispense or withhold. Good works cannot merit it; the most persistent natural desires cannot obtain it."

The Void and the Godhead (p. 13) are metaphysical terms designating the Unmanifest, or ultimate Reality, and yet Mr. Huxley, with the help of mescalin, finds it "all as clear as day, as evident as Euclid." On p. 19 he implies that he has come as near "as a finite mind can ever come to 'perceiving everything that is happening everywhere in the universe.'" This frank disclosure of his spiritual condition reaches its zenith on p. 31, where he writes: "But now I knew contemplation at its height." On p. 56, he asks that we judge a tree by its fruits. One can apply this criterion, then, where he finds (p. 27) "Eternity in a flower" (where other contemplatives have found *infinity*), "Infinity in four chair legs" (which would more normally symbolize *eternity*), "and the Absolute in the folds of a pair of flannel trousers!" (The exclamation mark is his.)

Evolutionist Hypothesis

The basic fallacy of the book—the central error from which the others stem—is the "evolutionist" hypothesis, that would have the higher depend upon the lower, Pure Being upon becoming. His "Mind at Large" (p. 16) is evidently quantitative and not qualitative, equatable with the "cosmic consciousness" that belongs to the lower possibilities of the soul and the inferior states of the being. The confusion is between the psychic and spiritual planes of reality, where the unfamiliar, the strange, and the bizarre are mistaken for the transcendent, simply by the fact that they lie outside the ordinary modes of consciousness. He even identifies his thinking with Bergson, whose infra-rational intuitionism Guénon has dealt with in *The Reign of Quantity* (chap. XXXIII). For the rest, Mr. Huxley's experimental attitude is reminiscent of William James' *religious experience*. A transcendent state would not be at the mercy of physical vision (p. 34); and if the inner world of the contemplative possesses a "spiritually higher significance" than the outer, this is because the spiritual domain transcends the temporal, and not because "familiarity breeds contempt" (p. 36).

The book lacks a necessary modicum of consistency in many places—not least of all concerning the theory of evolution; for he writes: "I was seeing what Adam had seen on the morning of his creation—the miracle, moment by moment, of naked existence" (p. 11), an experience marked, it appears, by the heightening of intensity in colors; and yet this is followed by the strangely incongruous and "anachronistic" remark that "the heroes of the Trojan War hardly excelled the bees in their capacity to distinguish colors. In this respect, at least, mankind's advance has been prodigious" (p. 20).

It is not true, contrary to his thesis throughout the book, that symbols, languages, and art forms are hopelessly inadequate vehicles of communication—unless it really matters to "know what it feels like to be Sir John Falstaff or Joe Louis" (p. 9). Where the communication is of intellectual verities, and not of mere accidental and individual contingencies, each great tradition has had its *divinely-revealed* scripture or doctrine, its sacred canons of art forms, its iconography

---

[4] New York, 1941.

and symbolism and transmission of spiritual teaching with a "norm" or constant effectively continued through centuries as a fully adequate witness to the intelligibility of the forms involved to the people concerned. Traditional regularity is in fact a criterion of orthodoxy. To quote Eckhart: "Words derive their power from the original Word" (Evans, I.99). If at the close of his life St. Thomas Aquinas regarded his *Summa* as "no better than chaff or straw" (p. 63), then this was simply his testimony to the absolute transcendency of God over all human works, of the spiritual over the rational domain. But doctrine on the human level remains an adequate expression of the truth, and the *Summa* contains the legacy of a galaxy of saints and sages prior to the time of St. Thomas, whose *Summa* in turn has been an invaluable legacy to Roman Catholicism since his day. St. Thomas' gesture is a reminder that something more exists. If "systematic reasoning . . . tries, forever vainly, to comprehend" divine Mystery, it is not at the chair of St. Thomas that this charge can be laid. All spiritual authorities speak of transcending the realm of human reason and logic: none of them speak of contradicting it (p. 62). "Beauty has to do with cognition" (*Summa Theologica*, 1.5.4).

More surprising is his question, "What sort of pictures did Eckhart (and others) look at?" (p. 21) . . . "The questions are beyond my power to answer; but I strongly suspect that most of the great knowers of Suchness paid very little attention to art. . . . To a person whose transfigured and transfiguring mind can see the All in every *this*, the first-rateness or tenth-rateness of even a religious painting will be a matter of the most sovereign indifference" (p. 22). The answer to his question is that Meister Eckhart had the sacred iconography of the Middle Ages fresh before him; and that art was not of the most "sovereign indifference" to Eckhart is eloquently proven in Dr. Coomaraswamy's *The Transformation of Nature in Art*, chapter II: "Meister Eckhart's View of Art." There is not space here to resume the argument, but two citations from Eckhart should suffice: "Art amounts, in temporal things, to singling out the best" (Evans, I.461), and "All the works God does below he has first wrought on high. 'All form and likeness,' Dionysius says, 'he first took and sealed into the lowest angels by which means they are brought and sealed in creatures; just as an artist, inspired by his art, will carve in wood or paint on canvas or the wall, so the angels imprint God's light and consolation on the soul and the soul sees the heavens open and God leaning down'" (Evans, II.211). By way of comparison we have this to read in the book under discussion: "In the universe of art, over against Vermeer and the other painters of human still lives, over against the masters of Chinese and Japanese landscape painting, over against Constable and Turner, against Sisley and Seurat and Cézanne stands the all-inclusive art of Rembrandt" (pp. 32-33) . . . No explanation, no attempt at critical evaluation or justification is proffered the reader to help him follow the reasoning behind this incredible and unabashed opinion, so gratuitously dropped, as it were, into a void.

The Will

Returning more directly to the subject of mescalin, he reports, "The will suffers a profound change for the worse" (p. 18). Now William Law, whom Mr. Huxley frequently cites with approval, says of the will: "Nothing hath separated us from God but our own will, or rather our own will is our separation from God. . . . The fall of man brought forth the kingdom of this world; sin in all shapes is nothing else but the will of man driving on in a state of self-motion and self-government, following the workings of a nature broken off from its dependency upon, and union with, the divine will. All the evil and misery in the creation arises only and solely from this one cause."[5] "It is a question," asks Meister Eckhart, "what burns in hell? Doctors reply with one accord: 'self-will'" (I.48).

"Mescalin opens up the way of Mary," writes the author on p. 32, "but shuts the door on that of Martha. It gives access to contemplation—but to a contemplation that is incompatible with action and even with the will to action, the very thought of action." In reality, the way of Mary includes pre-eminently that of Martha (which the Gospel makes clear), implying as it does a spiritual and universal charity or "non-acting Action"—never an inability to act. The *arhat* does not have a "problem" (p. 32), for the simple reason that the center of his being by definition transcends the realm of contingencies, and contains principially all oppositions and contraries in harmonious equilibrium. Mr. Huxley is right in positing the necessity for charitable acts, but his opposition of *arhat* to *Bodhisattva* is based on an inadequate understanding of Buddhist terminology which leads to artificial and purely verbal distinctions—like his expression "Taoist naturalism" (p. 37). If "half at least of all morality is negative" (p. 33) (and by what yardstick does he measure?), certainly the other "half" is positive, since virtue is the unfolding on the human level of supra-human and metaphysical realities. Man is virtuous because God is Good.

One can readily endorse his estimation of the "personal subconscious" as a "mental world more squalid and more tightly closed than even the world of conscious personality" (p. 38); but when he suggests that the artist should, break through to "that Archetypal World, where men have always found the raw materials of myth and religion," one has every reason for supposing that it is not the Archetypes of Plato, rejected at the opening of the book, that are in question here, but rather—whatever his intention—the inverse reflection or counterpart from below, which is the equivalent in Jungian terminology of the *collective unconscious*, so called. For Jung as well speaks of "the chaotic sphere of the personal unconscious, which contains all that one would like to forget,"[6] but he stresses that it is "only a superficial layer, which rests on an entirely different foundation, which we call the *collective unconscious*," whose images "have a distinctly mythological character."[7] Titus Burckhardt writes: "The 'collective subconscious' insofar as it exists, has nothing of the character of a true cosmic principle, from the fact that a collectivity at best possesses but a vague and very relative unity. Moreover, if the lower confines of the soul are obscure and unintelligible, this does not make them 'profound'—quite the contrary. What is certain is that they have an eminently passive character, and are consequently open to all the currents of the collective psychism, which in addition makes them the instrument of innumerable duperies; for the rest, the fact that the collective psychism englobes certain seemingly 'folkloric' residues of true symbols goes strangely to solicit such confusions."[8] "While nineteenth century materialism closed the mind of man to what is above him," writes Coomaraswamy paraphrasing Guénon, "twentieth century psychology opened it to what is below him."[9]

The author rightly says that unregenerate souls cannot support "the burning brightness of unmitigated Reality" (p. 44), and yet he has told us that "there are certain mediums to whom

---

[5] *Selected Mystical Writings*, pp. 25, 30-31.

[6] *On the Psychology of Eastern Meditation: Art and Thought*, p. 177.

[7] Ibid., p. 178.

[8] *Etudes Traditionnelles*, 1949, p. 119.

[9] Ananda K. Coomaraswamy, *Hinduism and Buddhism*, p. 61.

the mescalin taker's brief revelation is a matter, during long periods, of daily and hourly experience" (p. 20). Are we, then, to believe that mediums have attained a degree of regeneration denied in this lifetime to the great majority of people practicing valid spiritual rites? On p. 45 he admits that "once embarked upon the downward, the infernal road, one would never be able to stop"; but his solution, "to remain undistracted" (p. 46), is hardly attainable through a drug which, by his own admission, has a deleterious effect on the will—the instrument of concentration, which alone can overcome distraction! His mental hospital with its "recorders, clock-controlled switches, public address systems, and pillow speakers" to remind the inmates of primordial facts is like a passage, out of his *Brave New World*—as is his insistence on "frequent chemical vacations from intolerable selfhood" (p. 51).

On p. 54 we are told that people should be able to find self-transcendence in religion, but that in practice they want alcohol as well as piety. "We see, then, that Christianity and alcohol do not and cannot mix" (p. 55). To this fantastic oversight regarding the rites of the Mass and Communion is added the equally fantastic statement: "Christianity and mescalin seem to be much more compatible." For evidence, we learn that "this has been demonstrated by many tribes of Indians, from Texas to as far north as Wisconsin." In the next sentence he speaks of "sacramental bread and wine," evidently this time having forgotten the incompatibility just stressed between Christianity and alcohol. Be that as it may, we are then told that "peyote-eating and the religion based upon it" have helped the Indian "to explain the universe by means of a coherent theology" (p. 57). No hint is given as to the tenets of this "theology."

The conclusions reached in the domain of education become frankly sinister, where, for example, the "intellectual" "would be urged and even, if necessary, compelled to take an occasional trip through some chemical Door in the Wall into the world of transcendental experience. If it terrified him, it would be unfortunate but probably salutary" (pp. 62-63).

* * *

The "mescalin-experience" as such is not under question in this article, any more than Mr. Huxley's insistence that the modern world is in urgent need of spiritual regeneration. Another matter is the line of reasoning pursued and the conclusions derived there from. Even were one to admit his fundamental hypothesis, still a scattering of peyote-eating Indians Christianized (more often simply "Protestantized") a generation or two ago, could hardly be adduced as weighty evidence for the benefic effects of a drug on Christian ritual. If the Indians can consume peyote without harmful results, the question of their own heritage—psychic and spiritual, and the concomitant ritual conditions are essential factors to be considered. But a footnote (p. 52) suggests that all has not gone peaceably with the drug on Indian reservations.

If drugs could change and transform consciousness, it is certain that this knowledge would have been incorporated into spiritual teachings from time immemorial. On the other hand, intoxicants and drugs have served universally as supports adjacent to ritual practices, even where the use is purely symbolic, as for example with wine in Islam, the outward use of which is proscribed even while the inner significance of spiritual inebriation has been retained as a great support in Sufic orders. It is only in the case of spiritual deviations and black magic that intoxicants, or drugs and narcotics—and sexual aberrations usurp the center of the rite; it is well documented, for example, that the Witches' Sabbath was copiously provided with unguents prepared from mandrake (allied to belladonna), aconite, opium, henbane, cicuta virosa, stramonium, and other poisons. Mr. Huxley seems to recognize this at one point (p. 49), but the remainder of the book stands as a denial; and in fact, the countless confusions and contradictions that exist throughout the treatise are one of its most disturbing features.

Another disturbing feature and "mark" of "inspiration" is an ever-present vulgarity ill befitting the spiritual realities discussed. Thus, one example from among countless: on p. 58, where he speaks of "the breech-clout of transcendental experience."

The phenomenon is one of psychic dissociation where he merges his "Not-self in the Not-self which was the chair" (p. 16); or again, where "my body seemed to have dissociated itself almost completely from my mind. . . . It was odd, of course, to feel that 'I' was not the same as these arms and legs 'out there'" (p. 40).

Frithjof Schuon stresses that "there is no possible spiritual way outside of the great orthodox traditional ways. A meditation or concentration practiced at random and outside of tradition will be inoperative, and even dangerous in more than one respect; the illusion of progress in the absence of real criteria is certainly not the least of these dangers."[10]

Mr. Huxley raises the question of schizophrenia on p. 42, in describing the "unspeakable beauty" experienced by a certain woman patient: "Alas, this paradise of cleansed perception, of pure, one-sided contemplation, was not to endure. The blissful intermissions became rarer, became briefer, until finally there were no more of them; there was only horror."

"One cannot be too distrustful," writes René Guénon, "of all that appeals to the 'subconscious,' to 'instinct,' infra-rational 'intuition,' or even a more or less badly-defined 'vital force'—in a word, to all these vague and obscure things which the new psychology and philosophy tend to exalt, and which lead more or less directly to contact with the lower states." He warns against being "confused or dissolved in a sort of 'cosmic consciousness' from which all transcendency is excluded. . . .

"Those who make this fatal error, forget or ignore quite simply the distinction of the 'Higher Waters' from the 'Lower Waters.' Instead of raising themselves to the Ocean above, they sink into the depths of the Ocean below; instead of concentrating all their powers in the end of directing them towards the formless world, which alone can be called 'spiritual,' they disperse them into the indefinitely changing and fleeting diversity of forms of the subtle manifestation (which corresponds as exactly as possible with the Bergsonian conception of 'reality'), and this without suspecting that what they take for a plenitude of 'life' is effectively but the kingdom of death and dissolution without return."[11]

---

[10] "Des stations de la Sagesse," *France-Asie*, 1953, p. 510.

[11] *The Reign of Quantity*, p. 240. This aspect of the question pertaining to the modalities of the subtle domain has been thoroughly documented in an excellent exposé entitled: "An Approach from India to Perception through Peyote," by Rishabhchand, being a reprint from *Bhavan's Journal*, Vol. VI, nos. 13-19, dated January-April, 1960.

Drug-Induced Mysticism Revisited[1]

Charles Upton

Charles Upton (b. 1948), poet, author, activist, and veteran of the counter-culture has voyaged and experienced firsthand the many facets of the New Age *cul-de-sac*, including its pitfalls which are all too often ignored. Since the 1960s, psychedelics[2] or hallucinogens, now termed entheogens,[3] have played a pivotal role in the modern and postmodern seeker's quest to circumvent the trappings of the empirical ego and attain self-realization. After a hiatus of nearly thirty years, psychedelic research has now made a revival, which should provoke much inquiry as to what underlies this phenomenon. It is interesting to note that the New Age Movement, the Human Potential Movement, Humanistic Psychology, and Transpersonal Psychology all emerged in a common setting; they do not only share many similarities but have also assisted in each other's development. For example, the English writer Aldous Huxley (1894-1963) could be said to be a single figure connecting all of the above movements via his popularizing of the perennial philosophy and his writings on psychedelics, both of which are acknowledged by the above movements and or disciplines. Huxley not only helped shape each of the above but provided an integrative theory in which they could take root. That said, while he popularized the perennial philosophy he is not considered to be a traditionalist or perennialist.

Where Charles Upton parts ways with his New Age and counter-culture comrades is that since his introduction to the works of the traditionalist or perennialist school—most significantly René Guénon (1886-1951), Frithjof Schuon (1907-1998), and Ananda Coomaraswamy (1887-1947)—he has affiliated himself with this orientation. Upton has written numerous books and articles on traditional metaphysics and the perennial philosophy, the most noteworthy of which are *The System of Antichrist: Truth and Falsehood in Postmodernism and the New Age* (2001), including its sequel, *Vectors of the Counter-Initiation: The Shape and Destiny of Inverted Spirituality* (2012). Although he has abandoned the practices of his early search in the New Age and counter-culture movements, he acquired an abundant knowledge and understanding of these pseudo-spiritualities and is in a position to inform and also caution contemporary seekers. The following interview offers a unique look at psychedelics in the light of the perennial philosophy by way of perennialist theory and also personal accounts of the author.

---

[1] Editor's Note: This interview was conducted electronically with Charles Upton between March and May of 2011. The footnotes were compiled by the editor.

[2] British psychiatrist Humphry Fortescue Osmond (1917-2004) coined the term "psychedelic" or "mind-manifesting" via his correspondence with Aldous Huxley. In responding to a letter that Dr. Osmond received from Huxley written on 30 March, 1956 he wrote in poetic reflection: "To fathom Hell or soar angelic, / Just take a pinch of psychedelic," thus giving birth to the term "psychedelic"; yet it was not known to the public at large or the scientific community until 1957 (Michael Horowitz and Cynthia Palmer (eds.), *Moksha: Aldous Huxley's Classic Writings on Psychedelics and the Visionary Experience* [Rochester, VT: Park Street Press, 1999], p. 107). It is also relevant to point out that it was Dr. Osmond who in May of 1953 first introduced Huxley to a synthesized form of mescaline, the psychoactive compound in peyote (among other psychedelic cacti) that in turn produced his work *The Doors of Perception* in 1954, which according to some launched the psychedelic revolution.

[3] "'Entheogen' means simply 'God generated within you!'" (Robert Forte, "A Conversation with R. Gordon Wasson," in *Entheogens and the Future of Religion*, ed. Robert Forte [San Francisco, CA: Council on Spiritual Practices, 1997], p. 69).

Samuel Bendeck Sotillos: Perhaps we could begin with the central perennialist critique with regards to what has been termed "consciousness expansion," "altered states of consciousness," "non-ordinary states of consciousness"—which distinguishes the psychic from the spiritual;[4] it is this critique that many readers outside the perennialist or traditionalist circles will not be familiar with, and yet it has created the greatest amount of confusion for contemporary seekers. Would you mind elaborating on this fundamental distinction which has profound implications with regard to recognizing authentic spirituality versus pseudo-spirituality or New Age spirituality?

Charles Upton: The psychic or intermediary plane is the world of subjectivity; the spiritual plane is objectivity itself. As the psychic world is higher than the material world and encompasses it, so the Spirit is higher than both psyche and matter, and encompasses them. The psychic world is made up of beliefs, perceptions, impressions, experiences; the spiritual world is composed of certainties—of things that are true even if we are not certain of them. When Beat Generation poet Lew Welch said, "I seek union with what goes on whether I look at it or not," he was positing the level of Spirit. The psychic plane is *relatively* objective in that it is not enclosed within the individual psyche; as Jung demonstrated, it also has a collective aspect. This collectivity is not limited to a mass human subjectivity or "collective unconscious," however; it is host as well to many classes of non-human beings, including those the Greeks called the *daimones*, the Northern Europeans the fairies, and the Arabs the *jinn*. It carries nothing less than the impressions of the experiences of all sentient beings.

The psychic plane is the (relatively) objective environment of the human psyche, just as the earth is the (relatively) objective environment of the human body. Our apparently individual subjectivity is co-extensive with innumerable other subjectivities, both human and non-human; as Huston Smith said, "the brain breathes thoughts like the lungs breathe air."

---

[4] For an interesting discussion on the distinctions between the subtle and nondual states of consciousness see the following two part video with Ken Wilber (b. 1949), a pioneer within transpersonal psychology, speaking about the uses of *Ayahuasca* or *Yajé* and psychedelics in general, highlighting the obstacles and dangers of their use to authentic spiritual growth: http://www.youtube.com/watch?v=0HPQgKbxIjk. After viewing the two video clips by Wilber, Charles Upton stated the following: "People do take psychedelics hoping for spiritual transformation, and a simple 'just say no to drugs' will not influence many of them; in view of this, Wilber did a good job of putting psychedelics in an insightful context when he said that their best use is to teach you that the most impressive visionary states and realized insights are not Absolute Reality since they all pass away; only the Atman, the Witness that witnesses them, is Absolute. This is something like the Sufi doctrine that spiritual states happen in relation to specific ego-attachments in order to burn out those attachments, after which the states in question do not return; the realized Sufi is beyond states. One difference between states based on drugs and states sent by God, however, is that drug-induced states can be psychologically habit-forming—largely because it is possible to pop the 'same' pill again and again, imagining you can repeat an earlier state—but it is not possible to induce God to send the same state again, seeing that 'Every day doth some new work employ Him' (Qur'an 55:29). A massive expansion of psychic experience is in no way an unmitigated good, since it can either wear away one's attachment to experience in favor of the Witness or veil the Witness by inflaming one's desire for more and more experience." With this said, Wilber should not be considered a "friend" of the perennial philosophy or the spiritual traditions themselves, nor a representative of the traditionalist or perennialist school for he has methodically undermined and attacked the integral metaphysics of the perennial philosophy, first as an insider by aligning himself with this universal orientation and then by attempting to usurp the traditions within the fold of his ever inclusive evolutionary and syncretic AQAL Model—all quadrants, all levels, all lines, all states, and all types.

But it remains essentially subjective for all that; it is the realm of experiences, not realities. An experience is an *impression* of an objective reality, either material or spiritual, as received by a limited subject, an impression that is edited by the inherent or acquired limitations of the subject experiencing it. It is *phenomenon*, not *noumenon*. Whatever relatively objective data can be accessed through psychic means (clairvoyance, precognition, etc.) always pertains to contingent entities immersed in one form or another of space and time, linear or multidimensional; eternal realities cannot be intuited by psychic means.

The spiritual plane, on the other hand, is purely objective. It is not composed of our impressions, but of things we have impressions *of*—of *noumena* that transcend sense experience and do not depend for their existence upon our awareness of them, just as—on the level of sense experience—the mountain outside our window is really there, whether or not we happen to be looking at it. The spiritual plane is the realm of the first intelligible manifestations or "names" of God—of metaphysical principles that are not simply abstract ideas, but living realities that have the power, under the proper conditions, to dominate, guide, purify, and conform our psyches to them—to "save our souls."

So spiritual realities transcend subjective experience. But if we never *experienced* them, they would not be effective to enlighten us and save us. Spiritual experiences, then—what the Sufis call the *ahwal* or spiritual states (which are necessary elements of the spiritual path) are psychic experiences grounded not in the psychic subjectivity of the one experiencing them but in objective realities that transcend the realm of sense—in the Names of God. To be subject to a spiritual state is to have a direct intellective intuition of an objective spiritual reality that transcends the state in question, one that the subjective state by which it is intuited will always both veil and reveal; and if spiritual realities partially transcend our subjective experience of them, God transcends our experience of Him absolutely. To experience God is to be called to immediately transcend that necessarily limited experience of Him, and come into naked existential contact with Him as He is in Himself, beyond all experience; as the Sufis put it, "the human being does not know God in His Absolute Essence; it is God who knows Himself within the human form." The Sufi practice of contemplating God in this manner is known as *fikr*, which might be defined as "the ongoing sacrifice of every conception of the Absolute, generated by the Absolute, in the face of the Absolute."

So we can say that spiritual realities are objective, and that God, the Source of all such realities, is the Absolute Object. But "object" here does not mean "whatever is perceived by a limited subject as other than itself"; taken in this sense, "object" is relative to that limited subject and so partakes of its subjectivity. God as Absolute Object is equally the indwelling Divine Subject, the Absolute Witness, what the Hindus name the *Atman*, what Frithjof Schuon calls "the absolute Subject of our contingent subjectivities." The Absolute Witness stands "behind" all psychic experience, impassively witnessing them, not identifying with them; here is the precise difference between the psyche and the Spirit.

We cannot reach God through the psyche, through experience; the essence of the spiritual path is to place ourselves in the presence of God, and let *Him* reach *us*. He may do this through experiences, through events, or through a secret action within the soul that we aren't even aware of. The function of spiritual experiences or states is not to "enrich the soul" with fascinating impressions of the Divine, but to *burn out* specific aspects of the ego, specific attachments and identifications; this is why the realized Sufi, the one who has transcended himself, died to himself, become objective to himself—or rather to the Absolute Witness within him—is beyond spiritual states entirely.

SBS: Following up with this point, what can you say about the assumption that the pursuit of expanding consciousness or achieving an altered state of consciousness is an end unto itself, as if it was a desirable human norm which contradicts perennial principles—"The goal is not altered states but altered traits."[5] This perilous approach often involves an *ad hoc* mixture of spiritual techniques rather than a persistent adherence to one orthodox spiritual form.[6] Could you please speak to this puzzling development?

CU: This is all a kind of council of desperation, as well as an indication that the breakdown of the traditional revealed religions, leading to a One-World Religion made up out of the resulting fragments—a development that will culminate in the regime of Antichrist—is proceeding right on schedule.[7]

As religion degenerates, the felt sense of the reality of God is progressively replaced by an obsession with morality for its own sake, and with religious fervor considered as an end in itself, both taken out of their own proper context. No longer is moral purity felt to be something we naturally owe to God in view of His love for us and of the fact that He created us, something that prevents us from falling into the ingratitude of worshipping the passions as idols in His place; now morality has become an idol in itself. By the same token, fervor has lost sight of the God who supposedly inspires it; it has become a substitute for His felt presence rather than a response to it. In a lot of contemporary Protestant hymns, for example—or rather contemporary "Christian pop" songs—the singer sings primarily about his or her own feelings, not about God. Likewise various "consciousness studies" programs now available in academia tend to concentrate on subjective states of consciousness, as well as the belief-systems that support them and the techniques by which they can sometimes be produced, rather than understanding spiritual states as reflections of an objective metaphysical order, and thus as instances of *knowledge* rather than simply experience. According to Sufi doctrine, spiritual states are not acquisitions but gifts of God. He sends them in order to "burn out" specific passions, attachments, and ego-knots; after the attachment in question is dissolved, that particular state does not return. For example, a habit of neurotic fear, burnt out by a state (*hal*) of ecstatic love, is transformed into a *station* (*maqam*) of courage and equanimity; a temporary "state" has resulted in an established "trait." And the fully-realized Sufi is said to be beyond both states and stations, since he no longer maintains any separative ego which could be the subject of them; he has attained objective metaphysical realization.

When traditional faith is strong, it is a source of security and certainty for the faithful; they feel that they are in the presence of sacred mysteries, mysteries that they can rely upon but need not pry into. But when traditional religions weaken, then certain people who would have

---

[5] Huston Smith, "Encountering God," in *The Way Things Are: Conversations with Huston Smith on the Spiritual Life*, ed. Phil Cousineau (Los Angeles, CA: University of California Press, 2003), p. 97.

[6] We recall the unequivocal words of Frithjof Schuon: "there is no possible spiritual way outside the great orthodox traditional ways. A meditation or concentration practiced at random and outside of tradition will be inoperative, and even dangerous in more than one respect; the illusion of progress in the absence of real criteria is certainly not the least of these dangers" (Quoted in Whitall N. Perry, "Drug-Induced Mysticism: The Mescalin Hypothesis," in *Challenges to a Secular Society* [Oakton, VA: The Foundation for Traditional Studies, 1996], pp. 15-16).

[7] See Lee Penn, *False Dawn: The United Religions Initiative, Globalism, and the Quest for a One-World Religion* (Hillsdale, NY: Sophia Perennis, 2004).

otherwise been spiritually satisfied simply to live within a sacred tradition and ambience, and who would have saved their souls thereby, conceive the desire for a direct mystical relationship with God so as to make up for what has been lost—a relationship that may not in fact be proper to them. They imagine that such a relationship could only result from some extravagant spiritual tour-de-force—and psychedelic drugs immediately appear as a plausible way of taking that tour. But the psychedelics, as well as various spiritual techniques such as secularized non-traditional yoga, are often approached on the basis of the very false and limiting context that people are seeking them in order to free themselves from: of the spiritual life as an exercise in self-will (as in the case of compulsive morality), and of God conceived as an experience rather than a Reality (as in the case of self-referential fervor; the New Age movement for example, which deifies experience, can be described as a kind of "non-Christian Pentecostalism"). In the absence of a felt sense of the Grace of God based upon *faith*, which St. Paul calls "the presence of things hoped for, the evidence of things not seen," nothing is possible in the spiritual life aside from the Promethean attempt to take heaven by storm and spiritual narcissism—two pathologies which are intimately related to each other and never appear apart. The will to cut off from the spiritual Intellect (which is always virtually in force wherever Faith and Grace are present) produces Prometheanism; the alienation of the affections from the Intellect produces narcissism.

It is highly interesting that psychedelic drugs burst upon the scene at precisely the same moment that the Second Vatican Council was abolishing traditional Roman Catholicism and deconstructing the sacramental order. It's as if the grace of the Roman Catholic sacraments, while they were still intact, overflowed their specifically Catholic context and maintained a certain level of elevation in the "collective unconscious" of the western world, an elevation which was rapidly lost when that grace was cut off. Faced with a sudden unconscious or half-conscious sense of spiritual loss, and the stifling sensation that always results when the psyche is cut off from the plane of the Spirit, the western collectivity became susceptible to the temptation of psychedelics, which at the very least can provide (though not without extremely negative consequences) a horizontal *psychic* expansiveness which appears to compensate for, and sometimes actually counterfeits, the loss of a vertical spiritual elevation, while at the same time concealing the fact that such a loss ever occurred. Psychedelics, in other words, were a kind of Luciferian "booby prize" offered as compensation for the fall of western Christendom.

SBS: Psychedelic advocates and researchers make the case that because psychoactive properties are naturally occurring in a number of plants (and are even endogenous to the human body)[8] that they have been used in sacred rituals throughout the world since time immemorial.[9] They suggest that

---

[8] "In 1965 a research team from Germany published a paper in the flagship British science journal *Nature* announcing that they had isolated DMT from human blood. In 1972 Nobel-prize winning scientist Julius Axelrod of the U.S. National Institutes of Health reported finding it in human brain tissue. Additional research showed that DMT could also be found in the human urine and the cerebrospinal fluid bathing the brain. It was not long before scientists discovered the pathways, similar to those in lower animals, by which the human body made DMT. DMT thus became the first *endogenous* human psychedelic" (Rick Strassman, "What DMT Is," in *DMT: The Spirit Molecule* [Rochester, VT: Park Street Press, 2001], p. 48.

[9] These include *Soma*, thought to be the Fly Agaric mushroom (*Amanita muscaria*), *Teonanácatl*—Náhuatl, language of the Aztecs: "God's flesh" or "flesh of the gods" (*Psilocybe mexicana*), Peyote cactus (*Lophophora wil-*

they could be the precursors to the foundation of religion itself.[10] These mind-altering plants have been suggested as the central components of the *Soma* of the Rig Veda or *Hoama* of the Avesta, identified as none other than the mushroom *Amanita muscaria*,[11] and the principal rite of the Eleusinian Mysteries (Plato, Aristotle, and Epictetus were said to have been initiates), utilizing *Kykeon*, purported to be the fungus ergot, which contains psychoactive alkaloids such as LSD (lysergic acid diethylamide);[12] it has also been asserted that that *Manna* of the Hebrew Bible was a psychedelic.[13] The use of psychoactive mushrooms have also been ascribed to the cult of Mithras,[14] and said to be used in ancient Egypt;[15] even the origins of Christianity and Christ himself are hypothesized to be the mushroom *Amanita muscaria*.[16] Could psychedelic drugs be the actual origin of any particular revealed religion? What are your thoughts on this important discussion?

liamsii), San Pedro cactus (*Trichocereus pachanoi*), Ololiuqui (*Turbina corymbosa*) and *Tlililtzin* (*Ipomoea violacea*) seeds of a Morning Glory, Ibogaine or Iboga (*Tabernanthe iboga*), Ayauasca or *Yajé* (*Banisteriopsis caapi*), *Kykeon* made with Ergot (*Claviceps paspali* and *Claviceps purpurea*), Henbane (*Hyoscyamus niger*), Belladonna (*Atropa belladonna*), Mandrake (*Mandragora officinarum*), *Datura*, *Brugmansia*, *Ska Pastora* (*Salvia divinorum*), *Pituri* (*Duboisia hopwoodii*), etc. The following provides a Traditionalist perspective regarding this point: "If drugs could change and transform consciousness, it is certain that this knowledge would have been incorporated into spiritual teachings from time immemorial. On the other hand, intoxicants and drugs have served universally as supports adjacent to ritual practices, even where the use is purely symbolic" (Whitall N. Perry, "Drug-Induced Mysticism: The Mescalin Hypothesis," in *Challenges to a Secular Society* [Oakton, VA: The Foundation for Traditional Studies, 1996], p. 15).

[10] "[*Question:*] So your view is that hallucinogens were involved in the origin of some religious traditions but not necessarily all?" "[Peter T. Furst:] No, I think that's also going too far. The use of the so-called 'hallucinogens' is a *function* of religion, not its origin" (Peter T. Furst, "Ancient Altered States," in Roger Walsh and Charles S. Grob (eds.) *Higher Wisdom: Eminent Elders Explore the Continuing Impact of Psychedelics* [Albany, NY: SUNY Press, 2005], p. 156).

[11] See R. Gordon Wasson, *Soma: Divine Mushroom of Immortality* (New York: Harcourt Brace Jovanovich, 1969). The Wasson hypothesis has been critiqued from within psychedelic circles: this from one of its most prominent voices, Terence McKenna: "The problem with this hypothesis is that *A. muscaria* is not a reliable visionary hallucinogen. It has proven difficult to obtain a consistently ecstatic intoxication from *Amanita muscaria*.... Wasson was on the right track, correctly recognizing the potential of *Amanita muscaria* to induce religious feeling and ecstasy, but he did not take into account the imagination and linguistic stimulation imparted by the input of African psilocybin-containing mushrooms into the evolution of Old World mycolatry" (Terence McKenna, "Mushrooms and Evolution," in *The Archaic Revival: Speculations on Psychedelic Mushrooms, the Amazon, Virtual Reality, UFOs, Evolution, Shamanism, the Rebirth of the Goddess, and the End of History* [New York: HarperCollins, 1991], p. 150).

[12] See R. Gordon Wasson, Albert Hofmann and Carl A.P. Ruck (eds.), *The Road to Eleusis: Unveiling the Secret of the Mysteries*, Twentieth Anniversary Edition (Los Angeles, CA: Hermes Press, 1998). Some researchers assert that both Kykeon and psychedelic mushrooms (*Amanita muscaria* and psilocybin) were used interchangeably in the rites of the Eleusinian Mysteries. See Carl A.P. Ruck, *Sacred Mushrooms of the Goddess: Secrets of Eleusis* (Oakland, CA: Ronin Publishing, 2006).

[13] See Dan Merkur, "Manna, the Showbread, and the Eucharist: Psychoactive Sacraments in the Bible," in *Psychoactive Sacramentals: Essays on Entheogens and Religion*, ed. Thomas B. Roberts (San Francisco, CA: Council on Spiritual Practices, 2001), pp. 139-144.

[14] See Carl A.P. Ruck, Mark Alwin Hoffman and José Alfredo González Celdrán, *Mushrooms, Myth and Mithras: The Drug Cult that Civilized Europe* (San Francisco, CA: City Lights Books, 2011).

[15] Andrija Puharich, *The Sacred Mushroom: Key to the Door of Eternity* (Garden City, NY: Doubleday and Company, Inc., 1959).

[16] See John Marco Allegro, *The Sacred Mushroom and the Cross: A Study of the Nature and Origins of Christianity Within the Fertility Cults of the Ancient Near East* (New York: Bantam Books, 1971).

CU: Since religions are founded by Divine action through prophets and avatars (Buddhism possibly excepted, yet Gautama Buddha is also considered to be the ninth avatar of Lord Vishnu within the Hindu tradition), to say that they have been initiated by psychedelics is to deny that God can act on His own initiative, and it is consequently to deny God. It is to make "religion" an entirely human affair, and thus to posit something that does not fit the definition of that word. No religious tradition claims to have been founded on the basis of psychedelic experience; such claims emanate from users of psychedelics who like to project their fantasies upon traditions they in no way intend to follow. Anyone who thinks that Moses met God on Sinai or Jesus became "Christ" after eating some mushroom, because how else could they have done it, has no sense of the sacred whatsoever. Within certain contexts and in certain *yugas* it *might* have been spiritually possible to open initiates to the graces of an already established spiritual way through the use of psychedelics, but such things are certainly not possible to us in our own time, except at great cost—and with what coin could we pay that cost, poor as we are? In any case it is certain that the establishment of a legitimate spiritual way through the use psychedelics has never been either possible or necessary.

SBS: While the perennial philosophy acknowledges the Shamanic traditions of the First Peoples, a central challenge to the notion that entheogens or psychedelics have been used since the earliest times is that the "beginning of time" or "pre-history" which some suggest to be around 5,000 BC,[17] when contextualized within cyclical time, is likely to be the *Kali-Yuga* or the Iron Age, the culmination of this temporal cycle or at best the *Dvapara Yuga* or Bronze Age, the phase preceding the final age.[18] Thus the use of sacred plants that have psychoactive properties occurred late in the cosmic cycle (*manvantara*) and not at its inception, the *Krita-Yuga* or *Satya-Yuga*, known as the Golden Age in Western cosmology. This would support prominent historian of religion, Mircea Eliade's (1907-1986) astute observation that "the use of intoxicants . . . is a recent innovation and points to a decadence in shamanic technique."[19] Could you please elaborate on the perennialist perspective with regards to this point?

---

[17] Peter T. Furst, "Ancient Altered States," in Roger Walsh and Charles S. Grob (eds.), *Higher Wisdom: Eminent Elders Explore the Continuing Impact of Psychedelics* (Albany, NY: SUNY Press, 2005), p. 153. Some psychedelic researchers regard the rock art found in the mountain range of Tassili n'Ajjer, in southeast Algeria, to be the most ancient verification of psychedelic use.

[18] Charles Upton, *Legends of the End: Prophecies of the End Times, Antichrist, Apocalypse, and Messiah from Eight Religious Traditions* (Hillsdale, NY: Sophia Perennis, 2004).

[19] Mircea Eliade, *Shamanism: Archaic Techniques of Ecstasy*, trans. Willard R. Trask (Princeton, NJ: Princeton University Press, 1974), p. 401. Anthropologist Peter Furst has claimed that Eliade shifted his position with regards to psychedelics at the end of his life: "[Entheogens] forced him to change his mind on this issue, and . . . to accept that there was no essential difference between ecstasy achieved by plant hallucinogens and that obtained by other archaic techniques" (Paul Devereux, *The Long Trip: A Prehistory of Psychedelia* [New York: Penguin Books, 1997], p. 108). We would still argue that his initial assessment makes an important point in light of cyclical time which all traditional societies throughout the world adhered to and still do to this day recognize. "In fact, there is reason to believe that much, not all, but much of this [psychedelic using] culture constitutes more of a degeneracy when compared with the possibility of what one will call golden age spirituality where a man was his own priest and carried Heaven's Law directly and naturally within himself and had access, through his intellect, to divine and earthly wisdom. Immanence of divine wisdom is the human norm" (Mark Perry, "The Forbidden Door," in *Every Branch in Me: Essays on the Meaning of Man*, ed. Barry McDonald [Bloomington, IN: World Wisdom, 2002], p. 271).

CU: I agree with Eliade's initial view of psychedelics; when a spiritual tradition degenerates there is no telling what people will try in order to regain what is felt to be lost. Perhaps, God willing, something can be partially regained through psychedelics under certain cosmic conditions—conditions we certainly do not enjoy today—but the very attempt to regain a former spiritual exaltation is evidence of a degeneration. The *Krita-yuga* was characterized by a "mass theophanic consciousness" in which psychedelics were not needed; in the words of Genesis, mankind "walked with God in the cool of the evening." In my view (and I am open to correction), shamanism came in with the *Treta-yuga* or Silver Age, when the cosmic environment was subject to imbalances due to demonic incursions that the shamans—as they themselves maintain, according to Eliade—were sent by God to correct. And as the shamans of our own time have asserted, also according to Eliade, their ancestors were immensely more powerful than they, and didn't need psychedelics; so the use of the psychedelic "crutch" undoubtedly came in later than the shamanic dispensation itself. Also of great interest is the fact that the Christian visionary and stigmatist Anne Catherine Emmerich [1774-1824], in her book *The Life of Christ and Biblical Revelations* [1979], based on her visions, mentions an early non-Biblical patriarch called *Hom*, who was either named after, or provided a name for, a particular plant he considered to be sacred. This plant, in my opinion, is the *Haoma* plant of the ancient Persians, equivalent to the Vedic *Soma*. According to Emmerich, the lineage that sprang from Hom, which included one Dsemschid (undoubtedly the legendary Persian king Jamshid), became polluted with satanic fantasies, though she apparently did not recognize the plant in question as an intoxicant. It is highly unlikely that Emmerich, a nearly illiterate Westphalian peasant, would have known anything about Persian history or Zoroastrian lore, much less about the effects of exotic psychedelics. So it may well be true that the use of such plants, at least beyond the cosmic era that might have allowed their use under certain conditions, represents a truly ancient deviation in humanity's relationship with God. (It must not be forgotten, however, that according to René Guénon and Ananda K. Coomaraswamy, *Soma* and *Haoma*, in their higher symbolic sense, are not psychoactive plants but the source of the "Draught of Immortality" which effects the return of the human form to its *fitra*, its primordial Edenic state before the Fall. In other words, they symbolize a particular stage of spiritual realization.)

As for Eliade's later notion that psychedelic ecstasy is identical to ecstasy produced by other means, I speculate that he said this only because he experienced psychedelics himself and had nothing else to compare them to. He was an incomparable scholar of religion, but he had no religious faith; he characterized religions, myths, and metaphysical beliefs as "artistic creations" referring to no objective reality; he placed them on the psychic plane, not the spiritual.

SBS: There is the notion that the use of peyote (*Lophophora williamsii*) via the syncretistic Native American Church (NAC) is compatible with other traditional shamanic rites which did not originally utilize this plant medicine. For example, there are some who suggest that the Sun Dance Religion is compatible with peyote use (some have even introduced *Ayauasca* or *Yajé* into this sacred ritual).[20] Yet traditional spiritual authorities within these communities, such as

---

[20] In this context we might also mention the controversial figure Bhagwan Shree Rajneesh or Osho (1931-1990), known as the "sex guru," a prototypical representative of all that constitutes "New Age" spirituality, who practiced a syncretism of everything under the sun. It is seldom mentioned that Rajneesh was said to be addicted to a certain mind-altering substance known as "laughing gas" or nitrous oxide (N2O). He is reported to have dic-

medicine man and Sun Dance chief, Thomas Yellowtail (1903-1993), suggest quite the opposite, that they are not compatible and that such syncretism or mixing of foreign elements such as peyote are in fact dangerous and could be spiritually harmful,[21] not to mention that they do not do justice to either spiritual way and end up watering each tradition down, ultimately leading to the demise of both. Do you have any thoughts on this?

CU: Yellowtail was right.

SBS: In conjunction with the amalgamation of the Native American Church (NAC) there is also the phenomenon of the psychoactive brew *Ayauasca* or *Yajé* from South America, which has been widely exported throughout the world made extensively available through the syncretic churches of Santo Daime, founded by Mestre Irineu or Raimundo Irineu Serra (1892-1971)[22] and União do Vegetal (Centro Espírita Beneficente União do Vegetal or UDV), founded by Mestre Gabriel or José Gabriel da Costa (1922-1971), combining Catholicism, Spiritism of Allan Kardec (1804-1869), African and South American shamanism.[23] In conjunction with this, we need to mention that the search for mystical experiences has also brought about the phenomenon of "spiritual tourism"[24] to remote parts of the Amazon basin that has its damaging effects on the traditional societies living in these areas, extending itself to all sapi-

---

tated three books—*Glimpses of a Golden Childhood* (1985), *Notes of a Madman* (1985), and *Books I have Loved* (1985)—under the influence of his very own dentist's chair; however there is one title that has not yet seen the light of day for obvious reasons: *Bhagwan: The First Buddha in the Dental Chair.*-

[21] Michael Oren Fitzgerald, "Rainbow" and "Notes," in *Yellowtail, Crow Medicine Man and Sun Dance Chief: An Autobiography* (Norman, OK: University of Oklahoma Press, 1994), pp. 56-57, 221; see also Fred W. Voget, *The Shoshoni-Crow Sun Dance* (Norman, OK: University of Oklahoma Press, 1984), p. 169. Frank Fools Crow (1890-1989), a Lakota (Sioux) spiritual leader, *yuwipi* medicine man, and the nephew of Black Elk or Hehaka Sapa (1863-1950), the Lakota Sioux sage, made the following declaration regarding the use of peyote: "I have not . . . used peyote like they do in the Native American Church. *Wakan-Tanka* can take me higher than any drug ever could" (Thomas E. Mails, "Little Hollow Bones," in *Fools Crow: Wisdom and Power* [San Francisco, CA: Council Oak Books, 2001], p. 40). Lame Deer (1903-1976), a Sioux medicine man, underscores the incompatibility of peyote use with the sacred rites of the Oglala Sioux: "I have my hands full just clinging to our old Sioux ways— singing the ancient songs correctly, conducting a sweat-lodge ceremony as it should be, making our old beliefs as pure, as clear and true as I possibly can, making them stay alive, saving them from extinction. This is a big enough task for an old man. So I cannot be a *yuwipi*, a true Lakota medicine man, and take peyote at the same time" (John (Fire) Lame Deer and Richard Erdoes, "Don't Hurt the Trees," in *Lame Deer, Seeker of Visions* [New York: Simon & Schuster, 1994], p. 228).

[22] With regards to Santo Daime, we need to mention another central figure, Sebastião Mota de Melo, better known as Padrinho Sebastião (1920-1990), one of the direct disciples of Mestre Irineu, who founded The Eclectic Center of the Fluent Universal Light of Raimundo Irineu Serra (CEFLURIS), the two communities Colônia Cinco Mil (Colony Five Thousand) and Céu do Mapiá; the second is considered to be the church's headquarters, yet both are located in Brazil. See Alex Polari de Alverga, *Forest of Visions: Ayahuasca, Amazonian Spirituality, and the Santo Dime Tradition*, trans. Rosana Workman, ed. Stephen Larsen (Rochester, VT: Park Street Press, 1999).-

[23] See Beatriz Caiuby Labate and Henrik Jungaberle (eds.), *The Internationalization of Ayahuasca* (Zürich: Lit Verlag, 2011); Beatriz Caiuby Labate, Isabel Santana de Rose and Rafael Guimaraes dos Santos, *Ayahuasca Religions: A Comprehensive Bibliography & Critical Essays*, trans. Matthew Meyer (Ben Lomond, CA: Multidisciplinary Association for Psychedelic Studies, 2008).

[24] Marlene Dobkin de Rios, "Drug Tourism in the Amazon," *Anthropology of Consciousness*, Vol. 5, No. 1 (1994), pp. 16-19.

ential traditions. Could you speak to these interesting phenomena, which are unquestionably a hallmark of New Age thought?

CU: To syncretize different forms of the sacred, assuming that they were originally true spiritual ways, not simply psychic "technologies," is to relativize and subjectivize them and thus drive everything down to the psychic level while sealing off access to the Spirit; and this is tantamount to demonic invocation. And even if the practices in question are fundamentally psychic to begin with, mixing them can only generate further chaos. Spiritual Unity is higher than psychic multiplicity and encompasses it, but once the Unity of the Spirit is veiled, the idea becomes: "You mean you only have *one* god? You are spiritually deprived! We have hundreds"—the "reign of quantity" with a vengeance! The problem with this approach is that no one of these many gods can be the Absolute Reality, or even a psychic symbol for it—given that, by definition, you can't have more than one Absolute. And the psychic chaos created by mixing African and South American shamanism with Catholicism and European spiritualism can only be compared to playing the music of Bach, the Moody Blues, Charlie Parker, and Inti Illimani all at the same time—a practice that could only destroy all presence of mind and unity of soul in the listener. Of course some people like that kind of thing; instead of transcending their individuality through spiritual ascent, they simply want to shatter it, and consequently sink below it, into the infra-psychic. It's called "postmodernism."

And spiritual tourism in places like the Amazon damages not only the indigenous cultures but the tourists too. (I recently saw a news item where one village prohibited such tourism; a villager characterized the North American strangers who'd visited them and immediately asked to be told all about the local sacred rituals and beliefs as, in effect, "creepy.") When well-heeled "Norteamericanos" and Europeans enter dirt-poor villages in the Amazon and elsewhere looking to satisfy their spiritual hunger, a hunger based on their abandonment and betrayal of their own spiritual tradition (usually Christianity), they tempt the village elders to what traditional Catholics call the sin of *simony*: selling sacred things for money. Spiritual tourists are by and large not pilgrims but thieves, vampires. In most cases they aren't looking for a spiritual path to dedicate their lives to, but simply picking up here and there whatever sacred art objects, or psychedelic experiences, or sacred rituals degraded to the level of mere spectacle, might suite their fancy—if, that is, they aren't actually sorcerers in search of "personal power." Very often their basic set is psychic rather than spiritual; like most tourists, they are looking for "experiences," not principles to live by. They leave behind them the destructive influences of their own profane postmodern attitudes, and return home polluted with the toxic psychic residues of the forms of the sacred they have plundered, so as to release them to do their damage within their own cultures.

SBS: Another important point to discuss is that while there are traditional shamanic societies who today still utilize psychoactive plants in their sacred rites—i.e. the Huichol, Tarahumara, Cora, Mazatec, Bwiti, Kayapó, Fang, Mitsogo, Jivaro, Yanomami, Koryak, etc.—this does not necessarily mean that those outside these racial and ethnic groups will also have the same spiritual and beneficial response with the use of these plants.[25] It is as if the different indigenous

---

[25] "If the Indians can consume peyote without harmful results, the question of their own heritage—psychic and

peoples were given different plant medicines particular to their human makeup and ecological context. Could you please speak to this sensitive theme as it is perhaps "politically incorrect"?

CU: This is undoubtedly true in many cases. If the invocation of the divine name *Allah* should not be expected to be spiritually fruitful for a Buddhist, then by the same token the use of certain psychoactive plants outside of their traditional cultural and ritual context is not likely to have the same effect as it would within those contexts, and will most likely have a much more negative one. Such psychic and cultural bleed-throughs may be accurately compared to the breakdown of discrete and self-contained ecosystems. Asian carp are fine in Asia; in the Great Lakes they are a disaster. And those who hope to benefit from the sacred worldviews of the Huichols, the Tarahumara, or the Native American Church should be willing to live under the same conditions of deprivation and oppression and social marginalization as the Huichols and the Tarahumara and the Native American Church. If you want the spirituality of the Reservation, accept the suffering of the Reservation.

Shamanism, even relatively degenerate shamanism,[26] has a certain practical justification under truly primitive conditions, since it represents a large portion of the *technological* heritage of the tribe. The shaman heals disease, finds and attracts game, carries on criminal investigations, influences the weather, protects the tribe in war, and guards it against psychological imbalances and/or demonic incursions. But under modern conditions, when at least some of these functions can be fulfilled by other means, shamanism loses a certain amount of its *raison d'être*. French poet and cinematographer Jean Cocteau [1889-1963] recounts the story of an anthropologist who was studying native folkways in Haiti, where trees are (or were) used for long-distance communication; when a woman's husband was away at market, she might send a message to him by speaking to a tree, and receive his answer by the same means. When the anthropologist asked the natives why they spoke to trees, their answer was: "Because we are poor. If we were rich we should have the telephone."

In my opinion, those persons of the postmodern West whose psychophysical nature is not already fully integrated into the Spirit, or at least fully submissive to It—a condition extremely rare in our time—should never touch the shamanism of the primal cultures, since westerners lack the protection provided by the basic spiritual set and character-formation of those cultures. The rare and exceptional case is that of the person who, by the grace of God, has found and been accepted not simply by a working traditional shaman or medicine man, but a true holy man of one of the primal spiritual ways—though how he or she could recognize such a holy man in the first place is hard to imagine.

---

spiritual, and the concomitant ritual conditions are essential factors to be considered" (Whitall N. Perry, "Drug-Induced Mysticism: The Mescalin Hypothesis," p. 15). "One might counter that there are cultures, the Amazonian Indian tribes notably, in which ritualized drug use is a normal mode of communion with the divine. However, this fact calls for two comments that should apply to similar cultures. First, because of destiny, the psychic homogeneity of such peoples combined with the consistency of their shamanic cosmology, cannot be compared with the porous psychic heterogeneity of Westerners. Thus, if under the guidance of a shaman, an Amazonian Indian can enter into communion in a predictably consistent manner with a spirit animal which will act as a teacher and a guide, the same result cannot be necessarily expected for a Westerner intent on duplicating the experience. Secondly, the prevalence of such ritualized psychism . . . does not constitute a superiority per se" (Mark Perry, "The Forbidden Door," pp. 270-271).

[26] René Guénon, "Shamanism and Sorcery," in *The Reign of Quantity and the Signs of the Times*, trans. Lord Northbourne (Ghent, NY: Sophia Perennis, 2001), pp. 177-184.

SBS: You have undertaken an in-depth study of UFO phenomenon in light of traditional metaphysics in your book *Cracks in the Great Wall* (2005).[27] There are numerous writers and researchers within the psychedelic world who claim that there is a connection between the psychedelic experience and UFO sightings and/or abductions, especially for those who use the substance DMT (dimethyltryptamine).[28] To many this might be the siren call or the advent of the New Age, but to the exponents of the perennial philosophy this has the characteristics of the *Kali-Yuga* written all over it. Could you please speak to this?

CU: As I see it, the UFO "aliens" are denizens of the intermediary or psychic plane, what Muslims call the *jinn*. So it is not surprising that the use of psychedelics could make one more vulnerable to incursions from that world. René Guénon, in *The Reign of Quantity and the Signs of the Times* [1945], spoke of "fissures" appearing in the "Great Wall" separating the material plane from the intermediary plane, fissures that open our world to "infra-psychic" forces; to me the UFO phenomenon is a perfect example of this process. These fissures appear due to cyclical degeneration and the approaching dissolution of our world, but they are further widened and exploited by human activity, sometimes unconscious, sometimes deliberate. I believe that such things as the spread of the electronic media, including the internet, the liberation of nuclear energy, the use of psychedelics, and the general fascination with psychic powers and the paranormal continue to widen the cracks in the Great Wall, which, since it acts as the border between the material and the psychic worlds, can be affected by both material and psychic means; the very fact that such powerful psychic experiences can be produced by a material substance like LSD undoubtedly furthers this process. And it is interesting in this context that, according to Timothy Leary [1920-1996], LSD was not "activated" as a psychedelic until the first atomic bomb was detonated in New Mexico. (On the material side, this border apparently has something to do with the electromagnetic spectrum, which is why automobile engines will often die and electronic equipment malfunction in close proximity to a UFO.) Furthermore, those people Guénon called "agents of the Counter-Initiation"[29] are working to widen the cracks in the Great Wall consciously and deliberately.

The case of pioneer rocket scientist Jack Parsons [1914-1952] comes immediately to mind. Parsons was a follower of black magician Aleister Crowley [1875-1947] and an associate of L. Ron Hubbard [1911-1986], another follower of Crowley, who founded the Church of Scientology and who also (according to my correspondence with Beat Generation writer William Burroughs [1914-1997] in the late 1960s, when Burroughs was in the process of breaking with Scientology) had a background in Naval Intelligence, something confirmed by Peter Levenda in his trilogy *Sinister Forces: A Grimoire of American Political Witchcraft*. Parsons, according to UFOlogist Jacques Vallée [b. 1939] in his book *Messengers of Deception* [1979], claimed to have

---

[27] Charles Upton, *Cracks in the Great Wall: The UFO Phenomenon and Traditional Metaphysics* (Hillsdale, NY: Sophia Perennis, 2005).

[28] See Terence McKenna, *The Archaic Revival: Speculations on Psychedelic Mushrooms, the Amazon, Virtual Reality, UFOs, Evolution, Shamanism, the Rebirth of the Goddess, and the End of History* (New York: HarperCollins, 1991); Rick Strassman, *DMT: The Spirit Molecule* (Rochester, VT: Park Street Press, 2001); Rick Strassman, Slawer Wojtowicz, Luis Eduardo Luna and Ede Frecska, *Inner Paths to Outer Space: Journeys to Alien Worlds through Psychedelics and Other Spiritual Technologies* (Rochester, VT: Park Street Press, 2008).

[29] See René Guénon, "Pseudo-Initiation," in *The Reign of Quantity and the Signs of the Times*, pp. 241-251.

met a "Venusian" in the Mojave Desert; according to Levenda he performed pagan rituals at his launchings. He went on to co-found both the Aerojet Corporation and the Jet Propulsion Laboratory; a crater was named after him on the dark side of the Moon. Parsons openly stated that he was working to open a "door" into another dimension; it was shortly after his Mojave Desert rituals that the first major post-WWII civilian sightings of UFOs occurred in North America, though of course there is no way of knowing if the two are related. (In the careers of Crowley, Parsons, and Hubbard we can see clear indications of the action of the Counter-Initiation.)[30] So conscious or unconscious "invocations" of the *jinn* appear to be a major factor in the breakdown of the energy-wall between the material and the intermediary plane; such invocations are undoubtedly inspired by the *jinn* themselves, specifically the *kafir* or unbelieving ones (the demons, that is; the Qur'an teaches that some of the *jinn* are unbelievers and some are Muslims). In other words, the *kafir jinn* are working to break down the Great Wall from their side as well. When the Wall finally crashes, our world will end.[31]

SBS: As you are a veteran of the counter-culture movement, I am wondering if you would not mind speaking about your own personal experiences with psychedelics. In doing so could you please describe the psychological and the environmental factors known in psychedelic circles as "set and setting," including what substance and quantity you ingested during any "positive" psychedelic experiences?

CU: My "set" was always: "I seek the Clear Light; I wish to open to higher consciousness; I hope to see God." And my setting was almost invariably a place of beauty in the natural world. Leaving aside my many more or less positive mescaline and peyote trips (though one was quite painful and rigorous—deliberately so), my two rather unpleasant experiences with psilocybin mushrooms, and my one extremely powerful trip on morning glory seeds (whose active ingredient is "organic acid," lysergic acid amide), the settings for my three LSD trip were 1) the valley below Alpine Dam on Mt. Tamalpias, Marin County, California; 2) the Rocky Mountains of British Columbia; 3) Joshua Tree National Monument in the deserts of Southern California. As for dosage, we who bought our acid "on the street" never really knew. Various microgram

---

[30] On a side note, we might mention here that Hubbard was a disciple of Crowley, and the fact that Hubbard influenced the field of transpersonal psychology, known in modern psychology as the "fourth force." This brings to light its unfortunate inclusion of New Age thought, which has not yet been sufficiently explored. "The crystallization and consolidation of the originally isolated tendencies into a new movement, or fourth force, in psychology was primarily the work of two men—Anthony Sutich and Abraham Maslow—both of whom had earlier played an important role in the history of humanistic psychology. Although transpersonal psychology was not established as a distinct discipline until the late 1960s, transpersonal trends in psychology had preceded it by several decades. The most important representatives of this orientation have been Carl Gustav Jung, Roberto Assagioli, and Abraham Maslow. Also the most interesting and controversial systems of dianetics and scientology developed by [L.] Ron Hubbard (1950) outside of the professional circles should be mentioned in this context" (Stanislav Grof, "Psychotherapies with Transpersonal Orientation," in *Beyond the Brain: Birth, Death, and Transcendence in Psychotherapy* [Albany, NY: SUNY Press, 1985], p. 187). It should also be noted that Timothy Leary was also an Aleister Crowley enthusiast and that Aldous Huxley is reported to have dined with Crowley in Berlin in the Fall of 1930. Some even suggest that it was Aleister Crowley rather than Humphry Osmond who introduced Huxley to mescaline.

[31] For a further discussion of this topic see, "UFOs, Mass Mind-Control, and the *Awliya al-Shaytan*" available online at: http://www.sophiaperennis.com/uncategorized/ufos-mass-mind-control-and-the-awliya-al-shaytan-by-charles-upton-an-update-of-cracks-in-the-great-wall-ufos-and-traditional-metaphysics-sophia-perennis-2005.

numbers were given or not given by our sources; many times we were just told "this is one hit" or "5 hits," or someone who had already ingested some of the batch in question might suggest how much we should take. The first trip came out of a blue pill, the second out of a "windowpane," and the third out of a "blotter." A windowpane was a tiny square of clear solid gelatin of the kind used for gelatin capsules; a blotter was a square of blotter-paper. Acid was sold in the latter two forms to demonstrate that it was most likely not adulterated, since you never knew what might be in a pill or capsule besides acid, or instead of acid.

SBS: Could you please describe in detail what transpired both inwardly and outwardly during this psychedelic session?

CU: *Session One*: essentially a "Second Bardo" trip, "the Bardo of Experiencing Reality" (or rather, as I would now say, "existence") according to the system developed by Timothy Leary and based on the *Tibetan Book of the Dead*.[32] Time slowed down immensely and became "specialized"; the landscape was transfigured into a scene of *unearthly* earthly beauty; matter was transformed into, or clearly recognized as, a coagulation of energy—if I squeezed a stone it would vibrate and sizzle in my hand; the celestial light of Heaven almost came down, or started to; wings almost sprouted on my shoulders; I looked at an acorn cap and thought I was seeing a newly-hatched baby snake still coiled up as he had been in his shell (later in Vancouver, British Columbia, after reading a poem based on that experience at a café, I was told by another of the performers, a traditional London "busker," that in that vision I had come upon a piece of Druid lore), etc. At one point a short, gnarled figure appeared whom I thought of as a "pirate"; he was disgruntled, irritated, as if to say "Hey you kids! Get off my property!" (I was tripping with a friend.) Later I realized that he was in fact a gnome, a spirit of the Earth element in the system of Paracelsus; I further realized that by dropping acid in that forested canyon by that clear stream of water we had done the equivalent of breaking into his house uninvited or even walking through his wall; no wonder he was angry! Here's the poem I wrote about that trip:

The Lightning's Kiss

I

the storm is directly above us:
boiling fog,
surf crashing on the shoreline
of the hills—
mingling elements
flashing white, blue
moil in a turbulence—
luminous webs
vapors streaming

[32] See Timothy Leary, Ralph Metzner and Richard Alpert, *The Psychedelic Experience: A Manual Based on the Tibetan Book of the Dead* (New York: Citadel Press, 1990).

and blotting the Sun
and revealing him again
in his course—

our external destinies
rush to crazy oblivion
in the sky above—

here below,
the Quiet:

grey, green, dark & almost white,
the treetrunks boil up to Heaven!
silver-muscled branches
light up like bleeding arteries;
slender arms and sinews of branches,
sparkling hieroglyphs of leaves,
architectural script of rock,
the gnarled old face of the vegetable Druid
frowning thunderous from the roots,
his countenance beating
like a human heart—

and the creek is filled
with men's voices
the single-minded, the inexorable
in one motion through time—
rare fluencies of speech,
sparkling emerald syntax
in the masculine sunlight,
illuminating the brilliance
of contention and declamation—

sounds of crickets, secrets,
goblets of Egyptian sound,
moving downstream—

the linked syllables of Karma
talking forever
in the direction of the
listening Sea—

and behind me, over my shoulder
the Tyger growls—
chewing the bones of his prey to splinters
in a keening, crying Wind.

II

and the wind in the leaves
is the voices of women
wailing in love
or lamentation—
coiling whispers around the treetrunks—
drawing long shimmering cadences
through the five-fingered strings of branches,
and making an anguish of visible pleasure
that moves through the forest
like the cries of living violins
as the bow draws over the nipples
releasing a wind of singing
that shivers in the branches
and through the branches of my flesh
like ripples through a
shaft of smoke.

(exotic poisons:
vitalities coursing
through rock & wood:
the war outside
by bomb, or dollar,
is ground through
wheels of Nature –
or Nature herself,
moaning
like this,
makes war outside
this canyon:
(the question
should be: not
Which is Origin, Man
or what he sees,
but:
Where can I work—
in these cool and
harpstringed elements,
or in the gut
of the machine
made of human hands
these elements see
in their Mirror?

If anyone thinks it is a "good" poem, this simply demonstrates the great gulf that exists between the aesthetic dimension and the spiritual dimension, though spiritual truth can certainly express itself by way of aesthetic beauty. The Qur'an calls the *jinn*-inspired poets of pre-Islamic Arabia those who *say that which they do not*, and Rumi, the greatest poet of Islam, had the following to say about his art:

> My disposition is such that I don't want anyone to suffer on my account. . . . I am loved by those who come to see me, and so I compose poetry to entertain them lest they grow weary. Otherwise, why on earth would I be spouting poetry? I am vexed by poetry. I don't think there is anything worse. It is like having to put one's hands into tripe to wash it for one's guests because they have an appetite for it. That is why I must do it.[33]

Session Two: a First Bardo trip, the Bardo of "the Clear Light of the Void," the "set" for which I had posited by reading the *Diamond Sutra* and the *Heart Sutra* right before ingestion: No hallucinations, no visual or auditory distortions, simply the obvious fact that experience could go along quite happily with no *experiencer* there at all; as the Beatles put it, "Life goes on within you and without you." And since "I" was empty of self-nature, essentially snuffed out, the world I saw—immense, beautiful, snow-capped mountains, viewed in pristine clarity—was equally empty. Nothing really there. This self-and-world annihilation only persisted, however, when I was alone; as soon as I approached another human being—a girl in this case—"I" began to come back into existence; from this I learned that relatedness, or polarity, is the principle of all manifestation—a truth that the Buddhists call "Indra's Net." As the *Heart Sutra* puts it: "Form is emptiness; emptiness is form." Precisely.

Session Three: probably a Third Bardo trip, "the Bardo of Seeking Rebirth," a condition in which ego-transcendence is blocked, and consequently the tripper (or the consciousness-principle after physical death) is experiencing the pain and suffering of chaos, leading him to attempt to escape from this chaos into some kind of stable form that isn't exploding in a million directions all the time. My "set" here may not have been as pure as that of Session Two, since I had already begun to read the books of "sorcerer" Carlos Castaneda [1925-1998],[34] whom I met on one occasion. I had a brief experience of the higher reaches of the Second Bardo when the world appeared as a "tree" whose fruit was a constellation of Buddha or Bodhisattva images as in a Tibetan *thanka* (sacred painting), but it didn't last; for the rest of the time I was just waiting to come down. When I closed my eyes the cactuses and thorny chaparral bushes of the desert around me were reproduced as writhing, thorn-studded whips or cables, like the ocotillo plant. I stared at my Toyota Land Cruiser and just couldn't make out *what it was*: it looked like an ever-shifting 17-dimensional arrangement of wheels, pulleys, and intersecting planes, like an M.C. Escher print. In this trip, like my two psilocybin trips, I was mostly just "doing time."

---

[33] Jalal al-Din Rumi, *Signs of the Unseen: The Discourses of Jelaluddin Rumi*, trans. W.M. Thackston, Jr. (Putney, VT: Threshold Books, 1994), p. 77.

[34] See Charles Upton, "The Postmodern Traveler: Don Carlos Castaneda," in *The System of Antichrist: Truth and Falsehood in Postmodernism and the New Age* (Ghent, NY: Sophia Perennis, 2001), pp. 201-221; Richard de Mille, *Castaneda's Journey: The Power and the Allegory* (Santa Barbara, CA: Capra Press, 1976); Amy Wallace, *Sorcerer's Apprentice: My Life with Carlos Castaneda* (Berkeley, CA: Frog, 2003).

SBS: From your own point of view, how would you consider these psychedelic experiences— "good trips" or "bad trips"—and what criteria could be used to asses this?

CU: To answer this question I need to define what "good trip" and "bad trip" usually meant to the hippies: a good trip was one that felt good, a bad trip, one that felt bad. Moral or intellectual or spiritual criteria were rarely applied; the most common standard of judgment was hedonistic—though some trippers were capable of realizing that the pain of certain psychedelic experiences might teach one something or work as a psychic catharsis. From that point of view, my first trip was mostly "good," my second trip "good," and my third trip mostly "bad"—though nowhere near as bad as a *real* bad trip, filled with paranoia and panic.

From the standpoint of spiritual insight, the second session was the only *real* "trip"—and it was the only one in which I wasn't going anywhere. It showed me the possibility and reality of ego-transcendence (though not how to attain it on any stable basis), and taught me, as I said above, that existence is fundamentally relational. The first session showed me the existence of another "world," specifically the "etheric plane," the layer of the intermediate or psychic plane where the elementals reside; that started me on a long series of excursions into the elf-world, probably because, without my knowing it, LSD had permanently breached the natural energy-barrier or "etheric wall" between my material and subtle (*not* spiritual) levels of consciousness—the microcosmic analogue of the "Great Wall" that René Guénon speaks of in *The Reign of Quantity and the Signs of the Times*. This left me with a lifelong over-sensitivity to psychic forces that has produced many experiences of great pain over the years, made it hard for me to meditate (too much psychic "static"), and caused me to be vulnerable to demonic attack. If any good came of this condition it was limited to an ability to "listen in," as it were, to the councils of the demons, and find out something about what they are up to on a collective level, so that I can avoid certain of their influences and warn others.

The third session was just sad; all I learned from that one was, "no more LSD."

SBS: Do you have any further reflections on these experiences in light of your present-day outlook on psychedelics? Did your use of psychedelics prompt you to enter a more sustaining spiritual path? And do you still use psychedelics in conjunction with your spiritual practice?

CU: Yes: the conclusion that, from the spiritual perspective, *no* trip is good—especially if one is actually able to access higher consciousness or "see God" by means of it (assuming, of course, that these experiences are not delusions, or so mixed with delusionary elements that the way to the valid experiences and insights they counterfeit is not in fact blocked forever). If you drop acid, see horrible hallucinations, and experience excruciating feelings of loneliness, degradation, and fear, you may actually be luckier than if you experience "ecstasy" and "profound insight" and "consciousness of God," if not (momentary) "liberation from the wheel of becoming." If you break your way into the Inner Chamber on your own initiative, you have committed sacrilege—how can you ever become obedient to and annihilated in God's will if you think you have the right to break into His house any time the fancy suits you? I am not saying that the higher consciousness that can on certain occasions be experienced through psychedelics may not sometimes have a positive effect on one's life and outlook—but at what cost?

Dr. Javad Nurbakhsh [1926-2008], my first Sufi shaykh, strictly prohibited the use of all drugs, including psychedelics. My 20 years under his guidance were mostly spent laboriously recollecting and healing the psyche I had blown to the four winds through the use of psychedelics, and also undoubtedly through the abuse of *kundalini yoga* practiced without benefit of a teacher and a tradition. If I had never entered the Sufi path, however, I might never have seen just how damaged I was; I might have tripped on from one psychic state to another and never realized that I was headed for destruction, if not in this world then certainly in the next. In the words of the Noble Qur'an, "God guides aright whom He will and leads astray whom He will. . . . God is the best of plotters." And as for whether or not psychedelics in some way prompted me to enter the Sufi path, that is hard to answer. I entered that path because God called me. Whether He called me through certain valid insights or salutary warnings provided by psychedelics is by and large irrelevant. If you find God after being disappointed in love or wounded in war, does this mean you can recommend such experiences to other people as a way of finding God? All these trappings of personal destiny are at best irrelevant, and at worst a case of idolatry. If you worship the occasion you will never find the Essence; if you worship the means you will never reach the End. It may be that psychedelics were part of the occasion for my entry into the spiritual path, but the occasion is not the cause. And I haven't used any psychedelic substance, including marijuana, for over 20 years.

SBS: In response to your comments about the implicit dangers of having a "good" trip versus a "bad" trip due to the nature of the experience, could not such an experience be a "door opener" to an authentic spiritual path, provided the attachment is dropped—"When you get the message, hang up the phone."?[35] All the more so in light of the many seekers that have had psychedelic experiences and have nonetheless formally affiliated themselves within a revealed tradition, most notably Huston Smith (b. 1919)?

CU: It could be; clearly it has been for some people. But its function as a door-opener is often overshadowed by the fact that psychedelic experience is so intense that all later spiritual experience and practice tend to pale by comparison; you keep judging them, consciously or unconsciously, as to whether they "measure up" to LSD. Huston Smith once complained to me that even after years of spiritual practice in a variety of traditions, notably Sufism, he was never able to "regain" the level of opening and insight provided by acid. That's the problem in a nutshell: to attempt to bring back the former glory of one's psychedelic days is to reject, often in total unconsciousness, what God is offering you *now*. God's will for you is always in the present, whereas, in the words of William Blake [1757-1827], "Memory is Eternal Death". In the Sufi view, the spiritual path is not the quest for higher consciousness but the purification of the soul from anything that would block the influx of higher consciousness. In light of this conception, experiences of rigor and abasement and contraction (*qabd*) are as important as experiences of spiritual expansion (*bast*); Ibn Ata'allah [d. 1309] even says that there is much more danger of violating spiritual courtesy (*adab*) with God in a state of *bast* than in a state of *qabd*—and to beg or demand that God bring back a past state as you remember it is certainly the height of discourtesy, besides being impossible. Furthermore, after LSD, it is very hard to overcome the illusion that God is an *experience*.

---

[35] Alan Watts, *The Joyous Cosmology: Adventures in the Chemistry of Consciousness* (New York: Vintage, 1965), p. 26. (This quote is not found in the original 1962 edition.)

SBS: The socio-historical context in which psychedelics first emerged onto the public domain is very interesting and there are probably many who even partook in the psychedelic experience without knowing the nefarious context in which their mass dissemination to the American public took place. Many individuals might be alarmed to know that the National Survey on Drug Use and Health (NSDUH) reported in 2007 that approximately 34.2 million Americans aged 12 and older (or 13.8% of the population) reported trying hallucinogens at least one time; some might argue that these numbers are quite low and underestimate the widespread use.

CU: And we also need not just to remember, but to grasp the full import of, the fact that LSD was first distributed in the United States by the CIA, partly in the context of the infamous MK-ULTRA mind-control program, which included experiments practiced upon unsuspecting American citizens that were worthy to stand beside those conducted in the Nazi death-camps (see the research of David McGowan, Henry Makow and Peter Levenda).[36] Timothy Leary was assigned to feed acid to the intelligentsia, Ken Kesey [1935-2001] to everybody else; the idea was to compare how it acted under "controlled conditions" with its effects in a totally free-wheeling, "party" atmosphere. And the hippies actually knew about this! They said, "SURE we were a CIA experiment, man—an experiment that GOT OUT OF CONTROL!"[37] But the

---

[36] Interestingly enough, James Fadiman (b. 1939), a pioneer within both humanistic and transpersonal psychology and cofounder of the Institute of Transpersonal Psychology (ITP), worked at the VA hospital in Palo Alto, California in a program that was administering psychedelics and researching their behavioral effects on veterans. In 1965 Fadiman completed his doctoral dissertation at Stanford University on this research, which was entitled: "Behavioral Change Following (LSD) Psychedelic Therapy." "In the shadows, the CIA had tried to use these [psychedelic] substances to confuse and terrify people. Through front organizations, the CIA also sponsored small conferences and publications where therapists and researchers shared their findings" (James Fadiman, "Therapeutic Effectiveness of Single Guided Sessions," in *The Psychedelic Explorer's Guide: Safe, Therapeutic, and Sacred Journeys* [Rochester, VT: Park Street Press, 2011], p. 104). In response to the above citation, Charles Upton notes: "The idea that the CIA wanted to use psychedelics to 'confuse and terrify' people is true as far as it goes, but they also apparently hoped that these substances could help their own agents gain magic powers: telepathy, remote viewing, etc. And they were entirely willing to confuse and *delight* people if that would serve their ends. The hippy myth that the CIA were a bunch of uptight straight people who 'couldn't hold their acid' and saw it only as a crazy-making pill needs to be permanently debunked. The Bohemian/magician/secret agent is a well-known type; both occultist John Dee (1527-1608/1609) (the original 007) and satanist Aleister Crowley worked for British Intelligence. The ultimate goal of the powers-that-be in terms of psychedelic research may be to create a type of 'spirituality' where even mystical experiences that are valid on a certain level will serve to establish their control. They want to own *everything*—even mysticism, even spiritual aspiration, even God."

[37] It is useful to recall that Adi Da or Franklin Albert Jones (1939-2008)—who Ken Wilber regarded as "the greatest living Realizer" (this being only one of a host of other extraordinary endorsements offered by Wilber in his praise)—considered himself to be the first and last seventh stage Adept above all other saints and sages of the perennial philosophy; interestingly enough, he was a scientologist before becoming the "first American Avatar." It is widely known that Adi Da has had a tremendous influence upon Wilber's work and that of quite a few others within the general humanistic and transpersonal orientation, many of whom prefer to be anonymous disciples from afar in order to escape the numerous controversies and criticism surrounding Adi Da. In light of this, it would be interesting to inquire into how many ideas Wilber has contributed to both humanistic and transpersonal psychology which are borrowed from Adi Da; one might even wonder if Wilber's Integral Movement itself is more or less a product of Adi Da's teaching. The following excerpt, taken from Adi Da's spiritual biography, which has subsequently gone through numerous revisions, provides much food for thought on the government's role in engineering elements of not only the counter-culture at large but New Age spirituality as well: "I voluntarily submitted to drug trials at the Veterans Administration hospital in Palo Alto, California. . . . At the VA hospital, I

fact is that LSD initiated a sort of "bardo" or revelatory decay of American culture; all the latent tendencies, good and bad, the dominant belief-systems, conscious or otherwise, were called up in a very short time, laid out for all to see—and much of the social and cultural potential of America and the Western world rapidly exhausted in the process. The family was largely destroyed (not by LSD alone of course); Christian morality (including the concept of human dignity) was undermined; political responsibility was seriously eroded. And the social engineers simply sat back and took notes. They noted the main trends, the major "cultural archetypes" operating in the "collective unconscious" of society, and devised various ways to appropriate, pervert, and control every one of them; in so doing they initiated the world we live in today. The hippies naively equated social control with a simplistic authoritarian repression; they rarely awoke to the fact that *real* control is based on co-optation, on the covert implantation of engineered beliefs and attitudes in the mass mind. The powers-that-be do not want heroes who courageously oppose them and die as martyrs; they would much rather find, or create, dupes who will obey their every command in the firm belief that they are following their own desires, their own creative expressions and "spiritual" intuitions, all in perfect freedom.

One other deleterious effect of psychedelics, which has clearly operated on the mass level (though not in every individual case), is that they broke down people's protection against the surrounding psychic environment; first you "open up" too much, and then compensate by "closing down" so as to protect yourself from the painful influences emanating from your surroundings, including other people. Excess empathy ends in paranoia; the artificial breaking down of what psychologist Wilhelm Reich [1897-1957] called "character armor" often results in a worse case of such armor later on. (Perennialist Titus Burckhardt [1908-1984], in his book *Alchemy: Science of the Cosmos, Science of the Soul* [1960], speaks of the close relationship between psycho-physical dissolution and psycho-physical petrification.) As Jesus put it, the demon we have exorcized wanders in waterless places until, returning to the soul from which he has been expelled and finding it swept and adorned, he brings with him seven demons more evil than himself. We probably could never have produced a society where millions spend hours a day alone before computer screens—while imagining that, via Twitter or whatever, they actually have thousands of "friends"!—if LSD hadn't softened us up first; the isolation and excess introversion produced in part by psychedelics has effectively broken down the kind of social solidarity we need if we are to maintain our political freedoms and human rights; we are all too happy in our cubicles, or at least afraid to leave them. A friend of mine once said to me, back in the 60s: "Acid would be great if you could have all that incredible imagery without those *feelings*." Bill Gates must have heard his plea; cyberspace reproduces in many ways the hallucinatory content of psychedelics without the accompanying insights.

And now government-sponsored psychedelic research is making a comeback. Anyone tempted to become involved with it should first do some in-depth research on exactly which

---

was given a dose of drugs one day per week. . . . I was told that I would be given mescalin, LSD, or psilocybin at three separate sessions, and, during a fourth session, some combination of these. . . . There were also various bizarre experiences and periods of anxiety. . . . I suffered mild anxiety attacks and occasional nervousness for perhaps of a year beyond the actual tests. . . . I had become conscious of the formal structure of the living human being, associated with . . . the 'chakra body.' The Kundalini Shakti was spontaneously aroused in me" (Adi Da Samraj, *The Knee of Listening: The Divine Ordeal of the Avataric Incarnation of Conscious Light* [Middletown, CA: The Dawn Horse Press, 2004], pp. 81-83).

individuals and institutions are sponsoring, publicizing, and funding such a move, as well as their background and connections (what is the Internet for, after all?). Looking back over the cultural and spiritual "scorched earth" of the psychedelic revolution in the years since the 60s, I shudder to think what they may have in store for us now. We should never forget that the CIA likely sponsored the *mass* dissemination of LSD as part of their MK-ULTRA mind control program. According to Peter Levenda, William Mellon Hitchcock, who was associated with CIA front organizations Castle Bank and Trust and Resorts International, as well as being Timothy Leary's landlord for his "psychedelic manor house" at Millbrook, paid a chemist by the name of Nicholas Sand [b. 1941] to produce *millions* of doses of acid.[38] Another figure from the psychedelic underground that should be mentioned along with Sand, is his collaborator chemist Robert "Tim" Scully [b. 1944]: together they produced enormous quantities of LSD known in these circles as "Orange Sunshine."

SBS: While you have elaborated on the psychic and spiritual dangers of using psychedelics, there are many individuals and researchers that affirm the healing potential of such substances.[39] After a three decade hiatus there is now renewed interest in psychedelic research and they are increasingly being studied as possible adjuncts to psychotherapy for various psycho-physical ailments: treatment-resistant anxiety disorders, post-traumatic stress disorder (PTSD), pain associated with terminal and end-stage cancer, cluster headaches, obsessive-compulsive disorder (OCD), alcohol,[40] cocaine and heroin dependency to name a few.[41] Could you please comment on this matter?

CU: The use of toxic pharmaceuticals and traumatic interventions is common and sometimes necessary in the practice of medicine, but these things have little or nothing to do with the spiritual path per se. Psychedelics—whose toxicity is by and large psychic, not physical—may have a therapeutic effect in cases of alcoholism, heroin addiction etc., but this doesn't mean

---

[38] Peter Levenda, *Sinister Forces—A Grimoire of American Political Witchcraft: A Warm Gun* (Waterville, OR: TrineDay, 2006), p. 317).-

[39] For some examples, see John C. Lilly, *The Scientist: A Novel Autobiography* (New York: J.B. Lippincott, 1978); Aleister Crowley, *Diary of a Drug Fiend* (York Beach, ME: Samuel Weiser, 1997); Tom Wolfe, *The Electric Kool-Aid Acid Test* (New York: Farrar, Straus and Giroux, 1968); Wade Davis, "The Red Hotel," in *One River: Explorations and Discoveries in the Amazon Rain Forest* (New York: Touchstone, 1997), pp. 151-152; Terence McKenna, *True Hallucinations: Being an Account of the Author's Extraordinary Adventures in the Devil's Paradise* (New York: HarperCollins, 1994); Terence McKenna and Dennis McKenna, "Psychological Reflections on La Chorrera," in *The Invisible Landscape: Mind, Hallucinogens, and the I Ching* (New York: HarperCollins, 1994), pp. 109-117; Laurent Weichberger (ed.), *A Mirage Will Never Quench Your Thirst: A Source of Wisdom About Drugs* (North Myrtle Beach, SC: Sheriar Foundation, 2003); Charles Hayes (ed.), *Tripping: An Anthology of True-Life Psychedelic Adventures* (New York: Penguin Books, 2000).

[40] William Griffith Wilson, more commonly known as Bill Wilson (1895-1971), the co-founder of Alcoholics Anonymous (A.A.) was convinced of the therapeutic potential of psychedelics, especially LSD with alcoholism. It is reported that in 1956 Gerald Heard (1889-1971), close friend and colleague of Aldous Huxley, guided Bill Wilson on an LSD session, which had a lasting impact on his life. It is interesting to note that, like Huxley, it was Dr. Osmond who first drew Wilson's attention to psychedelics. See also *"Pass It On": The Story of Bill Wilson and How the A.A. Message Reached the World* (New York: Alcoholics Anonymous World Services, 1984).

[41] Harris Friedman, "The Renewal of Psychedelic Research: Implications for Humanistic and Transpersonal Psychology," *The Humanistic Psychologist*, Vol. 34, No. 1 (2006), pp. 39-58.

that they create no problems of their own; it's a question of the lesser of two evils. And what may be a lesser evil in psychophysical terms may or may not be a lesser one in spiritual terms. Our post-Christian secular society obviously does not have the final end and eternal good of the human soul on its radar screen, nor does it hold a very clear idea of human dignity or the intrinsic value of the person; abortion, for example, is not even seen by many people as the taking of human life. Our society has no concept of suffering as spiritual purgation (by which I certainly don't mean to imply that all suffering is purifying simply because it hurts); its highest good seems to be *production*, consequently it tends to define healing in terms of making us "productive members of society." There are even muted but increasingly audible suggestions that non-productive citizens ought to be euthanized; Bill Gates recently stated that a certain degree of medical care ought to be denied the elderly and diverted to the maintenance of productive workers. And now, under the "war on terror," torture has become acceptable to us for the first time since the passage of the Bill of Rights. How can a society capable of such barbaric actions and sentiments be relied upon to accurately evaluate the effects of psychedelic drugs in either moral or spiritual terms?

Afterword

CU: Some time after granting this interview, I talked with a physician acquaintance of mine who had participated in the second round of psilocybin experiments within academia in the 1990s; I hadn't realized they had started up again that early. He investigated the source of the funding for the experiment he'd been part of at the University of New Mexico, and discovered that the money for the DMT research that led up to the experiments he had been involved in had been provided by the Scottish Rite Foundation for Schizophrenia Research—the Freemasons![42] In view of the fact that many traditional Catholics see the Second Vatican Council as a kind of Masonic coup within the Catholic Church, the apparent "coincidence" that psychedelic drugs became available to the masses at exactly the same time that traditional Roman Catholicism was being destroyed may in fact be much more than that; as René Guénon pointed out, though cyclical conditions may make the growth of the Counter-Initiation possible, the concrete manifestations of this counterfeit, Luciferian spirituality can only be brought about by actual human groups. Dr. Rama P. Coomaraswamy [1929-2006] in his essay "The Problem of Obedience," unpublished in hardcopy but available on the web, recounts the following:

---

[42] "A grant from a branch of the Masons, the Scottish Rite Foundation for Schizophrenia Research, helped establish the merit of my study a year before I actually began it. Why the Masons had an interest in schizophrenia in general, and DMT in particular, I do not know, but I believe that garnering such support enhanced the esteem of my study in the eyes of the relevant regulatory and funding agencies" (Rick Strassman, "DMT: The Brain's Own Psychedelic," in Rick Strassman, Slawer Wojtowicz, Luis Eduardo Luna and Ede Frecska, *Inner Paths to Outer Space: Journeys to Alien Worlds through Psychedelics and Other Spiritual Technologies* [Rochester, VT: Park Street Press, 2008], p. 48). "Curiously, another MKULTRA faction consisted of representatives of the Scottish Rite of Masonry, which had sponsored research into eugenics, psychiatry, and mind control since at least the 1930s. MKULTRA doctor Robert Hanna Felix (1904-1990) was director of psychiatric research for the Scottish Rite of Freemasonry, and the director of the National Institute of Mental Health. Felix was the immediate senior of Dr. Harris Isbell, already noted in relation to MKULTRA. Another prominent Freemason involved in MKULTRA was Dr. Paul Hoch (1902-1964), financed by the Army Chemical Center" (Jim Keith, "The CIA and Control," in *Mass Control: Engineering Human Consciousness* [Kempton, IL: Adventures Unlimited Press, 2003], p. 65).

A leading Freemason, Yves Marsoudon (State Master, Supreme Council of France, Scottish Rite) tells us: "The sense of universalism that is rampant in Rome these days is very close to our purpose of existence. . . . With all our hearts we support the 'Revolution of John XXIII'. . .". Not satisfied with this, Yves Marsoudon dedicated his book *Ecumenism as Seen by a Traditionalist Freemason* to the Pope in the following words: "To the Memory of Angelo Roncalli, Priest, Archbishop of Messembria, Apostolic Nuncio in Paris, Cardinal of the Roman Church, Patriarch of Venice, POPE under the name of John XXIII, WHO HAS DEIGNED TO GIVE US HIS BENEDICTION, HIS UNDERSTANDING AND HIS PROTECTION."[43]

And then, shortly after that conversation, I had a dream—a dream filled with flaming apocalyptic imagery which represented *the glory of God*. When I woke up, I realized that I was in fact being purified of the psychic residues of LSD, which I last ingested over 35 years ago. In light of this dream I began to understand in a much different light the tendency of all other spiritual states or practices to pale in comparison with the LSD experience. We may sincerely say, and believe, something on the order of: "I took LSD several times; later I practiced a Sufi *dhikr* for several years. Looking back on these experiences, I can now truthfully report that the LSD provided a more intense spiritual state and a greater depth of insight than did the *dhikr*." In making this judgment we assume of course that we are objectively comparing two experiences from a standpoint of detachment, that the scales we are using to weigh these experiences against each other are fundamentally sound. What almost never occurs to us is that LSD may have *imprinted* or *conditioned* a deeply-buried layer of our psyche such that all subsequent experiences of any psychic or spiritual depth are *filtered* through this conditioning, resulting in a biased evaluation. If it is possible to have LSD "flashbacks" years after the original experience, who is to say that a subtle "hangover," physically undetectable, or perhaps indicated by a potentially measurable "re-programming" of the brain due to the extreme intensity of psychedelic experience, may also remain in the deep psyche?

The fact that Richard Alpert, aka Ram Dass [b. 1931], was told by his Hindu yoga instructors, "You have a *kundalini*-blockage in your *vishuddha-chakra* [throat center] due to your past use of psychedelics," supports this hypothesis. It's as if LSD can act to breach the natural barrier between *Nous/Intellectus*, associated with the *ajña-chakra* or "third eye," and *dianoia/ratio*, associated with the *vishuddha-chakra*, thus flooding the lower rational mind with material from the higher Intellectual mind; the lower mind becomes overloaded with this higher material, now expressed on a lower level, and ends by counterfeiting the quality of the *Nous/Intellectus* and thus blocking access to it. Consequently, if spiritual methods practiced and spiritual states experienced after LSD seem in some sense to lie in the shadow of acid, this may simply mean that acid is still there, casting that shadow. The import of my dream was that the *glory of God* had arrived in order to burn out the residual psychic *glamor* left behind by psychedelics, and purify my soul of their ongoing influence; I attribute this event to the spiritual effect of my entry into my second Sufi order. It may in fact be the case that the use of LSD has the power to subtly damage the highest reflections of *Nous/Intellectus*, the "eye of the heart" ['*ayn al-qalb*],

---

[43] See Rama Coomaraswamy, "Catholic Writings" at the following website: www.the-pope.com/coomcawr.html.

in the individual psyche, just as the physical eye may be damaged by staring into the sun; the reason we almost never become aware of this damage is that it lies at a psycho-spiritual depth so great that we are rarely able to consciously return to it *without once more ingesting LSD*, thus compounding the damage. The use of powerful psychedelics may also produce in us a taste, or need, for deep spiritual experiences that we otherwise would never have sought out, and that may not really be proper to us, while at the same time preventing such experiences from translating us to the final station, where (in Sufi terminology) *fana*—spiritual annihilation—gives way to *baqa*—subsistence in God. Like Moses, we may be left standing on the mountain, looking down to where the Children of Israel are crossing over into the Promised Land, but eternally denied entrance into that land ourselves as punishment for the sin, while searching for water, of striking the rock twice instead of only once as our Lord commanded—in terms of spiritual realization, the sin of trying to force the hand of God. Furthermore, those who are brought so near to the *mysterium tremendum* while being denied the final consummation may be subject to Luciferian temptations that the rest of us will probably never encounter, chief among them being the temptation to embrace a Luciferian consummation in a counterfeit Absolute designed in the infernal regions. Anyone who succumbs to such a temptation (which will most likely be presented to him or her in the deep unconscious regions of the soul), or is even confronted with it—assuming that the victim is not able to allow God to heal the psycho-spiritual damage that makes him or her susceptible to it—may effectively be denied Union with Absolute Reality for the remainder of this life, and possibly also the next.

III

PRAXIS

On Being in One's Right Mind

Ananda K. Coomaraswamy

Repentance

Metanoia,[1] usually rendered by "repentance," is literally "change of mind," or intellectual meta-morphosis. Plato does not use the word, but certainly knows the thing: for example, in *Republic* 514f., the values of those who have seen the light are completely transformed, and, in *Laws* 803c-804a, we are told that those who have realized their true relation to, and actual depen-dence on, God will be "thinking (διανοέομαι) otherwise than they do now," and that "it be-hooves our fosterlings to be of that same (new) way of thinking"; cf. St. Augustine's *reformamini in novitate mentis* (*Confessions*, XIII.13). Further, Plato distinguishes "understanding" (συνιέναι) from "learning" (μανθάνειν) as knowledge from relative ignorance (*Euthydemus*, 278a); and the *Shepherd of Hermas* is certainly not misinterpreting the real meaning of μετάνοια when he says that "Repentance is a great understanding" (τό μετανοήσαι . . . σύνεσίς ἐστιν μεγάλη), and in fact, a transformation from the state of the fool (ἄφρων) to that of one possessed of intellect (νοῦς, *Mand.* IV.2.1, 2). In the same way Hermes, (*Lib.* I.18) opposes μετάνοια to ἄγνοια, this "ignorance" being, in *Lib.* XIII.7b, the first of the "irrational torments of matter," just as in the Buddhist *nidāna* series it is the primary source of all evils.[2]

It is, indeed, unfortunate that our word "repentance" translates μεταμέλεια rather than μετάνοια (*metanoia*); for the latter word imports far more than the merely moral meaning of regret for past error. The man who has really been "converted," i.e., turned round (τρέπω, στρέφω), will have no time to spend in punishing himself, and if he does impose hardships on himself it will not be by way of penance, but (1) as a discipline like that of an athlete in training and (2) in imitation of the divine poverty. On this level of reference there can be no room for remembrance of or sorrow for past errors, to which the words, "Let the dead bury their dead," are properly applicable, the "dead" being the "old man" who is now no more for those who can say with St. Paul, *vivo autem, jam non ego.*[3] "Such an one, verily, the thought does not torment, Why have I not done the right? Why have I done wrong?" (*Taittirīya Upanishad*, II.9.1). How, indeed, should one who has ceased to be anyone either recall or regret what "he" had done when he *was* someone? It is only when and if he returns from the unitive state to "himself" that he can again remember or regret.

τὸ μετανοήσαι = τὸ συνιέναι is, then, to come to an understanding *with*. We stress the word "with," because in order to grasp the problems involved it is essential to remember, what can easily be overlooked, that all words containing the prepositions co- or con-, *cum*, σύν, *sam*-, and all such terms as "self-control," "self-government," and "self-possession" (= com-posure), imply a relation between *two* things (cf. Plato, *Republic*, 431a, b, 436b), which two are, in the last analysis, respectively human and divine. For example, "When thou art rid of thy self,

---

[1] Cf. Hans Pohlmann, *Die Metanoia als Zentralbegriff der christlichen Frommigkeit* (Leipzig, 1938); also Fr. Tucker, *Syneidesis—Conscientia* (Jena, 1928).

[2] See references in PTS. *Pali Dictionary*, s.v. *paticca-samuppāda*.

[3] Editor's Note: This Latin quote is from the Bible, Galatians 2:20. It is translated "I live, yet not I" and is followed by the phrase "but Christ liveth in me."

then art thou Self-controlled (*dïnes selbes gewaltic* = ἐγκρατής ἑαυτοῦ = *svarājan*), and Self-controlled art Self-possessed (*dïnes selbes eigen*), and Self-possessed, possessed of God (*ist got dïn eigen*) and all that He has ever made" (Meister Eckhart, Pfeiffer, p. 598).[4] All this will apply to σύνεσις, σύνουσία, and σύννοια, to the verbs σύνειμι and σύνίημι, to "be together with" and "come together with," to Sanskrit *sam-ādhi*, "syn-thesis" or "com-posure" and the verbs *sambhū, sampad, samgam, sami*, etc., all implying congress and unification, a "becoming one" (*eko bhū*) in the erotic no less than in other senses. Cf. τελέω, to be perfected, to marry, or to die.

In other words, the "great understanding" is a kind of synthesis and agreement (Skr. *samdhi, samādhi, samjñāna*), by which our internal conflict is resolved, or as the Sanskrit texts also express it, in which "all the knots of the heart are loosed." If we ask, an agreement of what with what? the answer will be evident: unanimity (ὁμόνοια)[5] of the worse and better, human and divine parts of us, as to which should rule (Plato, *Republic*, 432); "assimilation of the knower with the to-be-known (τῷ κατανοουμένῳ τὸ κατανοοῦν ἐξομοίωσις), in accordance with the archetypal nature, and coming to be in this likeness" (Plato, *Timaeus*, 90d; cf. *Bhagavad Gītā*, XIII. 12-18, *jñeyam . . . anādimatparam brahma. . .*), "which likeness begins now again to be formed in us" (St. Augustine, *De spir. et lit.*, 37); *con-scientia* with our "divine part," when the two parts of the mortal soul have been calmed and the third part of the soul is so moved that we are "of one mind with our real Self" (σύεννοιαν αὐτός αὐτῷ ἀφικόμενος), thus obtaining the true knowledge in the stead of our opinion (*Republic*, 571, 572). In Indian terms this is also the marital agreement, or unanimity of the elemental self (*bhūtātman, śarīra ātman*) with the prescient solar *Spirit* (*prajñātman, aśarīra ātman*) in a union transcending the consciousness of a within or a without (*Brihadāranyaka Upanishad*, IV.3.21); in other words, the fusion of the Outer King with the Inner Sage, the *Regnum* with the *Sacerdotium*.

Metanoia is, then, a transformation of one's whole being; from human thinking to divine understanding. A transformation of our being, for as Parmenides said, "To be and to know are one and the same" (Diels, *Fr.*, 18:5), and "We come to be of just such stuff as that on which the mind is set" (*Maitri Upanishad*, VI.34.3). To repent is to become another and a new man. That this was St. Paul's understanding is clear from Ephesians 4:23, "Be ye renewed in the spirit of your mind" (ἀνανεοῦσθαι δὲ τῷ πνεύματι τοῦ νοὸς ὑμῶν).

On the "Two Minds"

God is "not a man that he should repent" (1 Sam. 15:29, cf. Ps. 110:4, and Ezek. 24:14). Metanoia is a "change of mind" differing only in its larger implication from the change of mind that has taken place when we repent of any intention. When we do this, it is because we feel ourselves to be now "better advised" and so able to act "advisedly," or as Plato would express it, κατὰ λόγον. Whose advice are we taking? Who gives counsel when we "take counsel with

---

[4] To bring out the meaning we distinguish "self" from "Self," as is commonly done in translation from Sanskrit to distinguish the mortal from its immortal Self; these two "selves" corresponding to Plato's mortal and immortal "soul," and to St. Paul's "soul" and "spirit," the former being that "soul" that we must "hate" if we would be Christ's disciples.

[5] "Ἃ γὰρ ὁ θεὸς διδάσκει, . . . αὐτῳ γίγνεται ὁμονοεῖν," Xenophon, *Occ*, XVII.3. For we then participate in his πρόνοια = Skr. *prajñāna*, Providence or Prescience.

ourselves"? On this point Socrates had no doubt, for he says, "When I was about to cross the stream, the daimonian sign that usually comes to me was given—it always holds me back from what I want to do—and I thought I heard a voice from it which forbade. . ." (*Phaedrus*, 242b).[6] Or, as Plato also says, "there is a something in the soul that bids men drink and a something that forbids, something other than that which bids," what draws us on being the passions and diseases, and that which holds us back the voice of Reason (*Republic*, 439). Everyone has had experience of this.

We hardly need to say that Plato speaks of the Leader (ἡγεμών) within us by many names, such as vocal Reason (λόγος), Mind (νοῦς), Genius (δαίμων), and most divine (θειότατος) and best or ruling (κράτιστος) and eternal (ἀειγενής) part of us, nor to be reminded that this Immortal Soul "is our real Self" (*Laws*, 959a) and that it is for "us" to be Its servant (ὑπηρέτης, *Laws*, 645a, *Timaeus*, 70d, etc.); how otherwise, indeed, should "Thy will be done on earth as it is in heaven"? This immanent divinity is likewise Philo's "Soul of the soul" (ψυχή ψυχῆς), Hermes' "Good Genius" (ὁ ἀγαθὸς δαίμων), and the "Shepherd" of Hermas. It is the Scholastic "Synteresis," Meister Eckhart's "*Funkelein*," and however attenuated, our own "Conscience"; but not by any means *our* "reason," or Bergson's "intuition." It is the Spirit that Scripture, as St. Paul points out, so sharply distinguishes from the soul, and his *jam non ego, sed Christus in me* (Heb. 4:12 and Gal. 2:20). It is the "Self of the self, called the 'Immortal Leader'" (*ātmano'tmā netāmrtākhyah*, *Maitri Up.*, VI.7), the "Inner Controller" (*antaryāmin, Brhadāranyaka Up.*, III.7.1, etc), "Self (or Spirit) and King of all beings," or "of all that is in motion or at rest" (*Brhadāranyaka Up.*, I.4.16, II.1.2; *Rgveda*, I.115.1, etc), the immanent Genius (*yaksa*) of *Atharva Veda*, X.8.43 and *Jaiminīya Upanishad Br.*, IV.24, and the impassible "immortal, incorporeal Self" of *Chandogyā Up.*, VIII.12.1, the "That" of the famous dictum "That art thou."[7] And, just as for Plato, so in the Vedic books this deathless impassible Inner Man and very Self "dwells together with" the human, mortal, passible self in the "house" or "city" of the body for so long as "we" are alive. It is this (Holy) "Ghost" that we "give up" when we die; and the poignant question arises, "In whom, when I go forth, shall I be going forth?" (*Praśna Up.*, VI.3), the answer, according to which we shall be "saved" or "lost" depending upon whether before the end we have known "Who we are" (*Jaiminīya Upanishad Br.*, IV.19.4, 5; *Brhadāranyaka Up.*, IV.4.14; *Bhagavad Gītā*, IV.40, etc).

We still make use of such expressions as to be "double minded," "strong or weak minded," "in two minds" (about a purpose) and "not to know one's own mind"; we also "make up our minds,"[8] and only when this has been done do we really know what we are really "minded to

---

[6] It is rather strange that in one context Socrates supposes that "the daimonian sign has come to few or none before me" (*Rep.*, 496c) but this is contradicted elsewhere, notably in *Timaeus*, 90d and *Phaedo*, 107d; and cf. *Odyssey*, III.26.

[7] This implies a con-sent of the two wills involved.

[8] That "We (I) have the mind of Christ" (I Cor. 2:16) is but another way of saying the same thing, and it will be seen that the new mind and the new man are one, or in other words that to know one's real mind is the same as to know or love one's real Self (φιλήσας δὲ σεαυτόν νοῦν ἕξεις, Hermes, *Lib.*, IV.6b), the Self of all beings. To have that Mind is to be "blest with a good genius" (εὐδαίμων), but sole dependence on our own unstable mind is to be "cursed with a bad genius" (χαχοδαίμων, Philo, I.37, 38). Our "free will" does not consist in doing what we like (i.e., what we must, by a "natural" compulsion) but in a choice of guides, a choice between the good and evil Genii, "the good Daimon" and the Evil, whose name is Legion.

do." We use these expressions (like so many other inherited phrases) without a full consciousness of their meaning, just as we speak of "self-government" or "self-control" without realizing that "the same thing will never do or suffer opposite things in the same context and in relation to the same thing and at the same time. So that if we ever find these contradictions in the functions of the mind we shall know that it was not the same thing functioning" (*Republic*, 436b, cf. 431 a, b; and *Parmenides* 138b).[9] Actually, all these expressions derive their meaning from the age-old doctrine of the duality of human nature,[10] stated in terms of a duality or bivalence of mind (νοῦς, Skr. *manas*). It is this doctrine which Professor Goodenough seems to find so strange in Philo:[11] and yet, without it, the notion of repentance would be unintelligible. To know one's own mind is the same as to "know oneself" or "love oneself" in the superior sense of Aristotle (*Nich. Eth.*, IX.8), Hermes (*Lib.*, IV.6b), St. Thomas Aquinas (*Sum. Theol.*, II-II.26.4), and the Upanishads (BU., II.4, etc.). Philo says that "There are two minds, that of all (beings),[12] and the individual mind: he that flees from his own mind flees for refuge to the mind of all in common." The one is ungenerated and immortal, the other generated and mortal (I.93). The soul being "dead" when it is entombed in the passions and vices (I.65, and as for St. Paul) he points out that "That which dies is not the ruling part of us, but the subject laity, and for so long as the latter will not repent (μέχρις ἄν μετανοία χρησάμενον) and acknowledge its perversion (τροπή), so long will it be held by death" (I.80). The individual mind is the same thing as our "sensibility" (I.131);[13] "the easy-going man sinks down into his own incoherent mind" (I.94, cf. *Bhagavad Gītā*, II.67 and VI.34),[14] i.e., "estimative knowledge" in terms of "hunger and thirst."

It amounts to the same thing to deny the name of "mind" to the estimative faculties of the sensitive soul, governed by its wants. Thus in Hermes, *Lib.*, I.22, it is asked, "Have not all men mind?" and answered, "Mind comes only to those that are devout and good and pure" (καθαρός = *śuddha*). In Platonic terms, the soul is mindless (ἄνους) at birth and may still be unconscious (ἀνόητος) at death (*Timaeus*, 44a, c); the unchanging Mind that is contrasted with opinion subject to persuasion is to be found only in the Gods and a small number of men (*Timaeus*, 51e). If, however, we intend by "mind" merely the human instrument of discursive

[9] Philo I.94 seems to contradict, but is at fault; for it is not the same man who "rubs himself" and is also rubbed; it is, say, a finger that rubs and a leg that is rubbed, and these are not the same man but two parts of the same man. Subjectively, it may be the better part that wills to rub, and the worse that needs rubbing; or the worse part that wants to be titillated and the better part that yields.

[10] Plato, *Republic*, 604 b, etc; II Cor. 4:16; St. Thomas Aquinas, *Sum. Theol.*, II.11.25.4; Upanishads, *passim*.

[11] E.R. Goodenough, *By Light, Light*, pp. 382-86.

[12] The plural ὅλων cannot mean "the universe," and ought not to be rendered thus, as it is by Colson and Whitaker in the Loeb Library edition. The "mind of all in common" (συμπάντων) is that of the "Self of all beings" in Plato, *Phaedo*, 83b: "Philosophy exhorts the soul to trow in nothing but her Self, that she may know her Self itself, the very Self of all beings" (αὐτὸ τῶν ὄντων = Skr. *sarvabhūtānām ātmā*). Xenophon remarks that "When the God is our teacher, we all come to think alike" (ὁμονοεῖν, *Occ.*, XVII.3). It is when we "think for ourselves," knowing only too well what we think, that we disagree.

[13] "The carnal mind is enmity against God" (Rom. 8:7).

[14] We ought then to "pour out as a libation the blood of the soul and sacrifice our whole mind to God" (Philo, I.76). Eckhart says "the mind must be demented of itself"; that implies by no means the modern anti-intellectualism (in favor of instinctive behavior) but Plato's "divine madness," for "The men whom He dements He uses as His servants . . . it is God himself who speaks through them" (*Ion*, 534d).

thought, then to participate in the divine manner of knowing will be, humanly speaking, to be "out of one's mind"; so, of the Prophet through whom God speaks, Plato says that "his mind is not in him" (*Ion*, 534), a state of "mania" that must not be confused with insanity (*Phaedrus*, 244, 265): "the wisdom of this world is foolishness with God" (I Cor. 3:19).

We have now seen that the notion of a "change of mind" presupposes that there are two in us: two natures, the one humanly opinionated and the other divinely scientific; to be distinguished either as individual from universal mind, or as sensibility from mind, and as non-mind from mind or as mind from "madness"; the former terms corresponding to the empirical ego, and the latter to our real Self, the object of the injunction "Know thyself." We shall conclude by briefly noticing the equivalents of these formulations in the Indian sources.

The formulation in terms of two minds is explicit in Manu I.14: "From himself the Self-existent drew forth the mind, whose nature is the real and the unreal" (*sadasad-ātmakam*);[15] the mind, that is, with which one thinks "both good and evil" (*punyam ca . . . pāpam ca, Jaiminīya Upanishad Br.*, I.60.1) and which is, therefore, a means "either of bondage or liberation" (*Maitri Up.*, VI.34.11). "The mind is said to be twofold, pure and impure (*śuddhāśuddham*): impure, by connection with desire, pure by separation from desire.[16] . . . Indescribable his bliss who abides in the Self, his mind's defilement washed away by Self-composure"[17] (*samādhi-nirdhauta-malasya niveśitasya ātmani, Maitri Up.*, VI.34.6, 9).

The distinction of Mind from sensibility (νοῦς from αἴσθησις) is analogous to that of *Manas* from *Vāc* (Skr. the "Voice" or "Speech"), the power or faculty of expression. Mind becomes a name or hypostasis of God,[18] than whom there is no other intelligizer (*nānyad ato'timantr, Brhadāranyaka Up.*, III.8.11). *Manas* is the sacerdotal principle that knows and wills, *Vāc* the power of action without whom nothing would be effected. It is her function to "imitate" (*anukr*) him[19] and to act as his follower and messenger, "for she is by far the lesser and he the superior" (*Taittirīya Samhitā*, II.5; *Śatapatha Brāhmana*, I.4.4.7 and 5.11). But though Victory depends upon her co-operation, she may be reluctant to fulfill her office (*Śatapatha Brāhmana*, I.4.4.12; *Taittirīya Samhitā*, II.5.11, etc); she is easily seduced from her allegiance to Mind and Truth to the service of what she likes to think, and then merely babbles (*ŚB*, III.2.4.11, etc., cf. Philo, I.94).

In the Indian texts we also meet with the notion of a meliorative dementation as noted above. For when "mind" is thought of only as part of the psychic organism, then to be "mindless" and "unconscious" is the superior, and conscious mental operation the inferior condition.

[15] *Sat* and *asat* are primarily being, reality, truth and their contraries. In the Supreme Identity (*tad ekam*), without otherness (*advaitam*), these are no longer contraries; but considered apart, where *ens et bonum convertuntur*, *asat* as "non-being" is "evil" by the same token that English "naught-y" is "bad."

[16] As in Hermes, X.16, νοῦς, καθαρὸς . . . των ἐνδυμάτων. The "purification" enjoined (*cittam . . . śodhayet, Maitri Up.*, VI.34.3) is precisely the Platonic Katharsis, "a separation of the 'soul' from the 'body,' as far as that is possible," the kind of "death" that is practiced by philosophers (*Phaedo*, 67c-e, cf. *Sophist*, 227d); for Plato, purification and liberation are coincidental (*Phaedo*, 82) just as in the *Maitri Up.*, VI.34.11 the mind detached from sensible objects (*nirvisayam*) is liberation (*moksa*).

[17] *Samādhi* (literally synthesis, composure) is the consummation of *yoga*, and what is meant by Plato when he exhorts the soul to "collect and concentrate itself in its Self" (αὐτὴν δὲ εἰς αὐτὴν, *Phaedo*, 83a).

[18] *Taittirīya Samhitā*, II.5.11.5, VI.6.10.1; *Śatapatha Br.*, X.5.2.1; *Brhadāranyaka Up.*, V.5.6, etc.

[19] Cf. Hermes, *Lib.*, XII. 1.13a, ὁ οὖν λόγος ἐστὶν εἰκων τοῦ νοῦ, καὶ ὁ νοῦς τοῦ θεοῦ.

Thus, "When the mind has been immolated in its own source for the love of Truth, then the false controls of actions done when it was deluded by sensibilia likewise pass away" (*Maitri Up.*, VI.34.1, 2); "None whose mind has not been immolated can attain to Him" (*Katha Up.*, II.24); viz., the Person, who being devoid of all limiting attributes is necessarily "mindless," though the source of mind (*Mundaka Up.*, II.1.2, 3). God does not think and does not know in our imperfect way of knowing in terms of subject and object; we may say that he thinks, but there is no second thing other than himself of which he might think (*Brhadāranyaka Up.*, IV.3.28, etc.).[20] In this sense, then, it is said that "when one attains to the state of dementation (*amanībhāva*), that is the last step" (*Maitri Up.*, VI.34.7), and we recognize the like doctrine in St. Thomas Aquinas, *cum vero intellectus jam ad formam veritatis pertingit, non cogitat, sed perfecte veritatem contemplatur* (*Sum. Theol.*, I .34.1, *ad* 2). We must only be careful not to confuse this superior mindlessness of the supra-rational and super-conscious with the mindlessness of the Titans who are still irrational and subconscious, just as we distinguish the non-being of the divine super-essentiality from the non-being of what has not yet come into being or could not be.

To resume: in the first part of this article our intention was to show that what "repentance" really means is a "change of mind," and the birth of a "new man" who, so far from being overwhelmed by the weight of past errors, is no longer the man who committed them; and in the second part, to outline the doctrine of the duality of mind on which the possibility of a "change of mind" depends, and to demonstrate its universality; to point out, in other words, that the notion and necessity of a *metanoia* are inseparably bound up with the formulations of the *Philosophia Perennis* wherever we find them.

---

[20] Cf. Witelo, *Intelligentia semper intelligit . . .* (*sed*) *se ipsam cognoscendo non cognoscit alia* (*Liber de intelligentiis* XXIV, XXVII), the Commentary adding (*id est*) *perceptionem non intelligit, sicut anima.* (Editor's Note: The sense of this quote is that the intelligence can comprehend everything, but it can only understand itself through looking within its own [spiritual] nature, not through external objects.)

Being Oneself

Lord Northbourne

If the observations in this chapter are addressed to the reader in person, it is because the question dealt with concerns only the individual as such, as it were in his relationship to himself. It is not abstract, theoretical, and remote, but immediate and personal. It arises out of the advice, so lavishly bestowed on us all in these days, to the effect that, since pretence and hypocrisy are odious, it is above all necessary to "be oneself." This advice seems simple enough until one begins to wonder exactly how to apply it to one's own case. For you, the reader, "one's own case" is your own case, and nobody else's.

What in fact are you, essentially and not accidentally? What are you "in yourself," and not as butcher, baker, or candlestick-maker? You cannot profitably try to be yourself unless you are sure that you know the answer to that question.

Are you a being created by God in His own image, appointed by him as his representative on earth and accordingly given dominion over it, and equipped for the fulfillment of that function with a relative freedom of choice in both thought and action? Do you have freedom, which reflects the total absence of constraint attributable to God alone, but at the same time makes you liable to err? Are you essentially that, and only accidentally anything else?

Or, alternatively, are you essentially a specimen of the most advanced product so far known of a continuous and progressive evolution, starting from the fortuitous stringing together of a protein molecule in some warm primeval mud, that mud itself being a rare and more or less fortuitous product of the evolution of the galaxies from a starting point about which the physicists have not yet quite made up their minds?

If you choose the first, the mystical or religious alternative, you do not necessarily exclude *a priori* any plausible description of your physical situation in the Universe. You do however exclude absolutely both the primacy and the finality of any such description. It can never be more than a description, and as such not an explanation, even if it is as complete and as correct as man can make it. So, if you accept the mystical alternative, you must refuse to accept any mere description as an adequate explanation of what you are.

If you choose the second, the physical alternative (and the word "physical" is here more or less equated to the word "natural," so that it includes the mind as well as the body) you thereby exclude the first. You then regard your body, your thoughts, and your feelings as comprising all that you are, so that whatever may be called "mystical" or "religious" can only be explained as a product of these three. If you choose this physical alternative, to "be yourself" means simply to give free rein to your bodily desires, your thoughts, and your feelings. That, in effect, seems to be what you and I, and especially our children, are being advised to do. The consequent disorder often excites our surprise and disapproval. Incidentally, if you do give free rein to these three things, you are playing straight into the hands of anyone who knows how to manipulate them for his own ends. With the aid of modern psychology, that manipulation has become a science.

And yet how right the advice offered to us is! If we are indeed "made in the image of God," all we need to do is to "be ourselves."

If with that end in view you try to find out what you are by looking at yourself, what you appear to yourself to be will be what you are accidentally and not what you are essentially. When you look at yourself, or think that you are doing so, there is one who looks and there is something he sees. They cannot be the same. If they were the same they would be one and not two, so that no relationship, either of "looking at" or of any other kind could arise. That is why, when you look at yourself, the essential "you" is really looking only at the accidental "you." In other words, you are looking at what would nowadays be called your "personality."

Yet you are one person and not two. You are that same one person whatever may happen to you; you remain yourself under all the vicissitudes that may effect your body or your mind, at least as long as you are sane. Your mind and your body together constitute what is sometimes called your "psycho-physical complex." That complex is never the same for two minutes together, either materially or psychically; but your identity remains constant whether you are young or old, fat or thin, happy or miserable, awake or asleep. If that were not so, there would be no continuity in your existence, no individuality, and no awareness of change. There is a "you" that is the invariable point of reference, or center, and there are the changeable things of which it is conscious. The former is not identifiable with the latter. Those changeable things include everything you can perceive and know distinctively, and they are environmental, peripheral, or external with respect to the conscious center that is the real "you." Your whole psycho-physical complex, insofar as you can perceive and know it distinctively, is evidently among these external and changeable things. It belongs to you, but it is not the "you" to which it belongs. It is the "personality" which you may seek to develop, but it is not the "you" that seeks to develop it.

Therefore, if you want to know what you really are, in order that you may know what it means to "be yourself," you must direct your attention inwards and not outwards; that is to say, away from all objects of the senses, including your own body, mind, and feelings, towards the non-distinguishable central point of your being. This inwardly directed attention must evidently be aimed in a direction opposite to that of outward attention. Outward attention is, precisely, what we call observation. We are all taught nowadays that the only way to ascertain the truth is by way of the intensification and refinement of observation. For most of us therefore inward attention involves something we may never have consciously attempted, or perhaps even considered.

It is true that we cannot live without observation, our senses having no other function. Nevertheless, if what has been said is true, any approach to truth that relies on observation and on nothing else excludes the realization of the most important truth of all, the truth on which all other truths hang, namely, the truth about what we ourselves really are. If we are misled concerning what we are, and therefore concerning what anything else is, and what the purpose of our life is, and what our destiny is, it is not much use knowing anything else, because the chances are that we shall then misapply our knowledge, probably to our own hurt. Is not that obvious? And does it not suggest rather alarmingly exactly what seems to be happening?

You will no doubt already have realized that this other approach to truth, this inward attention or "concentration" which is as it were the opposite, or the complement to the approach of observation, can be nothing other than the way of contemplation, the way followed by wise and holy men of all ages and peoples. Since its goal cannot be perceived distinctively, this way cannot be mapped out. Those who have followed it, and they alone, can teach it. If you are not one of those to whom the scientific approach alone is valid, all this will not seem to you mere empty sophistry. It may therefore be worthwhile to try to carry the matter a little farther.

You have probably noticed that to say "your" essential being may suggest that it belongs to you; that it is even to some extent at your disposal or subject to your influence, as if it were your property. Of course it is not so. Nothing that you can do affects in any way the fact that you are what you are. As we have seen, your essential being remains what it is while the current of changeable and perishable forms flows past it. There is therefore no particular reason to suppose that it is perishable, and moreover, for a believer, there is every reason to suppose that it is not. But your essential being must not be confused with the accidental accretions that are so closely associated with it during its sojourn on earth, including of course your observable psycho-physical complex itself. That is where so many believers get into a muddle when they are considering the posthumous states of the essential being, which are sometimes called "heaven," "purgatory," and "hell."

One more point. If your "accidentality" alone is distinguishable while your essentiality is not, the same applies to your neighbor. That suggests that you and he are essentially one and only accidentally two. If you saw the situation in that way you would naturally love him "as yourself"; but you can only see the situation in that way insofar as you have realized what you yourself are. This realization involves bypassing the ever-changing multiplicity of your terrestrial accidentality and seeking with all your heart and mind and strength the changeless Unity that is the central and essential reality of yourself, of your neighbor and of all beings. And you can only hope to find it where it is to be found, and that is "within you."

You do see, don't you, that the words "being oneself" can be interpreted in two critically different ways?

The Integration of the Soul

Seyyed Hossein Nasr

What do we mean by integration? Not only do I want to pose this question from the point of view of Sufi metaphysics, but also of other forms of metaphysics as well. Oneness in its absoluteness belongs to the Absolute alone. It is only the One who is ultimately one. This is not a pleonasm, not simply a repeating of terms. It is the reassertion of a truth which we are easily apt to forget while we are seeking the One in Its reflections on lower levels of reality and on the plane of multiplicity. We must always remember this metaphysical truth: that oneness in its highest and absolute sense belongs only to God as the Absolute, to Brahman, Allah, the Godhead, the Highest Reality, the Ultimate Reality. Precisely because of this truth, no benefit could be gained in our search for unity by being immersed only in multiplicity. In fact, without the One, multiplicity itself could not exist. It would be nonexistent, because multiplicity always issues from the One, always issues from the Supreme Principle. If we remember this truth, we shall then be able to understand what is truly meant by integration.

Nearly everybody is in favor of integration these days, without bothering to search fully for its meaning. In the modern world attempts are often made to achieve integration by seeking to bring forces and elements together on a single plane of reality without recourse to the Transcendent Principle or a principle transcending the level in question. But this is metaphysically impossible. It is only a higher principle that can integrate various elements on a lower level of reality. This truth is repeated throughout all of the levels of the hierarchy of the universe. Throughout the universe it is ultimately only the Divine Principle—God—who either by Himself, or possibly through His agents, makes possible the integration of a particular level of reality and the integration of that level itself into the whole of existence. On all levels, from the *deva*s of the Brahmic world or the archangels or whatever corresponding language you wish to use, to the lower angelic world, to the psychological world, and finally to the physical world, it is always by means of a higher principle that the elements and forces involved on lower levels of reality are integrated. Let us give a concrete example.

Take the human state. It is composed of body, soul, and spirit. There is no way one can integrate the body without the presence of the soul. That is why when the soul departs, the body falls apart. Furthermore, the remarkable, integrated functioning of various parts of our body is one of the greatest miracles, to which we usually pay little attention. By accepting Descartes' reductionist conception of the body as a machine, we have fallen into the crisis concerning the relation between body and soul that we now face. The body is not a machine at all. If we look at the body, we see that it has this remarkable integrative function. But the moment the soul departs, the principle of integration departs and the body begins gradually to decompose. The same truth holds *mutatis mutandis* for the soul. Our souls and minds are scattered, like particles dispersing from a center—we usually live in a scattered world. The common everyday English usage of the term "scatter-brain" reflects the fact that in a sense the mind is scattered. There is absolutely no way to integrate the soul and the mind without the presence of the spirit and intellect, which are ultimately the same reality. It is only the spirit that is able to integrate the psyche, and the intellect the mind. The vital power of integration is not only related to God as the Supreme Reality, but also involves higher principles in relation to every level of reality down to the physical world in which we live; although of course the power of integration on all levels of reality comes ultimately from the Supreme Principle, which is One.

To speak seriously about integration, we must accept the vertical dimension of reality. The reason that we have such difficulty to integrate anything in the present-day world is the eclipse of knowledge of that vertical dimension. We are always trying to integrate and bring together various realities in a united and harmonious manner. We talk about how people should be friends, society should become integrated, races should seek harmony, religions should be in accord and not in conflict. But of course that is only for the most part wishful thinking, as we can observe from what is going on in our world. The most fundamental unit of our society, the family, is going the other way; it is breaking up to an ever greater degree, because there are so few people who possess an integrated inner being. The reason for this state of affairs is that we refuse to accept a principle above the individual order, we have forgotten the vertical dimension of existence and have fallen into a state of dementia.

Now, it is in light of these metaphysical truths that I wish to discuss Sufism and its relationship to the integration of man, first inwardly and then outwardly. Sufism is the esoteric or inward dimension of Islam, as you have heard mentioned many times. Islamic esoterism is, however, not exhausted by Sufism. It has certain manifestations within Twelve-Imam Shi'ism and Isma'ilism in its classical forms, but the main manifestation and the most important and central crystallization of Islamic esoterism is to be found in Sufism. Let us now ask what is meant by esoterism. It is a somewhat dangerous word to use in the modern world if not well defined, because it is confused often with occultism, or with the simply obscure and incomprehensible. It should be noted, however, that it is only in the modern West that the phenomenon that we know as occultism arose. There was no occultism in classical Hindu, Islamic, or Buddhist civilizations or in the Christian West when esoterism was fully present and accessible. So, by esoteric, I do not mean occult and certainly not obscure, although of course for those who do not possess the necessary intellectual and spiritual qualifications, it might appear as obscure and inaccessible, as would higher mathematics for someone who is not mathematically inclined. But in neither case is the subject obscure in itself for those qualified to know it. In any case, by esoterism I mean the inner dimension of both religion and reality itself—of manifested reality.

Everything in this world issues from the hidden to the state of manifestation. We ourselves are born from the wombs of our mothers. We come from darkness into light, to the manifest or external world. As you know, the water of life in all mythologies flows from a dark cave where its source and fountain are to be found. This darkness is not, however, simply emptiness or nothingness; rather, it symbolizes the hidden or non-manifested level of being. Everything in this world that we are able to experience or study (even in the field of quantum mechanics), issues in a sense from the unmanifested to the manifested, or from the hidden to the apparent. Furthermore, metaphysically the hidden or inward refers to a transcending reality which is also immanent as, symbolically speaking, the esoteric also means that which transcends appearances as well as being immanent to them. Of course, as far as religion is concerned, the exoteric dimension does not issue from the esoteric but, like the esoteric, comes from God. But the esoteric represents both the inner reality of the exoteric and that which lies on a higher level of reality, and in this sense transcends it. This is how these dimensions are experienced as one marches on the way to that Truth which is the Transcendent, as well as the Immanent as such. In any case, instead of using the image "from inside, out," we can also use "from up, down," which is more familiar to those who come from an Abrahamic background. (For Hinduism, especially of the school of the Vedanta, of course it would be the other way around.) Let us for the moment just keep to the vertical hierarchy of existence.

In the Islamic context there is first of all God, the One (*al-Aḥad*), one of whose Names is *al-Ḥaqq*, the Truth, to which Christ also referred in the Gospels. As for truth, when one refers to the truth of this or that matter, this is called *al-Ḥaqīqah* in Arabic, which also means reality. The two terms *al-Ḥaqīqah* and *al-Ḥaqq* are related etymologically and on the higher level refer to the same Reality. The term *Ḥaqīqah* means truth as it is grasped and lived at all different levels, while *al-Ḥaqq* is the Name of God, who is Truth in the most exalted meaning of the term. So, *Ḥaqīqah* at its highest level of meaning also refers to the Divine Truth, which lies at the heart and center of the Islamic religion and is, from the Islamic point of view, the ultimate goal of human life. Then there is the level of the path or *Ṭarīqah*, the spiritual path leading to *Ḥaqīqah*, the path which is associated with Sufism. The phrase *al-ṭarīq ila'Llāh*, that is, the path towards God in Arabic, is practically synonymous with Sufism, although in its early history, up to the end of the eleventh Christian century, Sufism had not as yet been ordered and crystallized into what we call *ṭarīqah*s or Sufi orders today. After the period in question, *ṭarīqah*s came into being bearing the names of their founders such as the Rifāʿiyyah, Qādiriyyah, Shādhiliyyah, Niʿmatullāhiyyah, Naqshbandiyyah, and the Chishtiyyah orders, the latter being so widespread in India. Nevertheless, the idea of a *ṭarīqah* or *ṭarīq ila'Llāh* goes back to a *ḥadīth* of the Prophet of Islam himself in which he said, "The number of paths (*ṭuruq*, pl. of *ṭarīqah*) to God is equal to the number of children of Adam." That is, it is the path, the *Ṭarīqah* that connects each of us to God, and before each human being there stands a path to Him as long as he or she follows the Divine Law or *Sharīʿah* by virtue of which that person stands on the circumference of a circle every point of which is connected by a radius (*Ṭarīqah*) to the Center (*Ḥaqīqah*). That does not mean of course that there are 5.5 billion individual *ṭarīqah*s, but that there are many possible paths which have become crystallized over time, as far as Islam is concerned, into the various orders, each of which leads us to God.

The actual named orders came somewhat later, but the reality of Sufism begins with the inner dimension of the Quran and the *Sunnah* and the spiritual power of the Prophet of Islam and originates everywhere from these sources. At the foundation of Islamic religious life there stands the *Sharīʿah*, the Divine Law, which defines Islamicity on the external plane of life. So you have a vertical hierarchy, of the *Sharīʿah*, the *Ṭarīqah*, and the *Ḥaqīqah* on the human plane, corresponding to the macrocosmic hierarchy. Furthermore, in the case of the *Sharīʿah*, *Ṭarīqah*, and *Ḥaqīqah*, it is also the higher principle that integrates that which belongs to a lower-level order on the hierarchy of human existence.

The goal of all levels and domains of Islamic reality is of course *tawḥīd*, which means both unity and integration. This word in Arabic also exists in all other Islamic languages, including many of the languages of India, such as Gujarati, Punjabi, and Bengali. This term possesses several shades and levels of meaning in the original Arabic and is really untranslatable into a single term in European languages. It is a noun implying a state while at the same time implying action. It is both a noun meaning oneness or unity and it implies the act and process of integration, of bringing into unity, the act of making into one. One therefore needs to use more than one term in English to bring out its full meaning. It is important to bear this point in mind when trying to understand what Sufism means by integration.

In the Islamic perspective then integration means to achieve *tawḥīd*, to become embellished with a quality which on the highest level belongs only to God, for God alone is One. One should never forget that supreme *tawḥīd* belongs to God alone. We can never achieve complete unity unless we realize that ultimately we are nothing and God is everything. It is through *fanā'*, the awareness of our nothingness before God, that the Sufis believe we can achieve that supreme unity. In the Hindu tradition this corresponds very much to "That art Thou"—that is, "Thou art the Supreme Reality," which cannot but be one. Every aspect of life bears the imprint of that unity whether we are aware of it or not, and everything that we do should direct us more and more towards *tawḥīd*. This begins at the level of the *Sharīʿah*, the Divine Law, with which I will not deal here in detail, but I just want to add the following by way of a parenthesis.

There are too many imponderables in the world of chaotic multiplicity in which we live for our unaided intelligence to impose order and integration upon the chaos of this world; especially this modern world, which is itself the result of man seeking to live as if he no longer had any need of God's laws. The chaotic nature of this age is mentioned not only in traditional Islamic sources, but also in the classical texts of Hinduism concerning the Kali Yuga in which we live. This is an age in which many flaunt the Divine Law, the Hindu *dharma*, something that would have been unimaginable in days of old. The situation is not the same today as when classical Sufi authors invited men to journey beyond the outward teachings of the *Sharīʿah*—which were taken for granted—to the Divine Truth. There are of course some pseudo-Sufis today who make the call to cast aside the *Sharīʿah* in order to reach the Divine, while misusing some of the sayings of certain Sufis of old. These days it is much easier to cast away the *Sharīʿah* than before without, however, reaching the Divine at all, in fact falling below forms rather than transcending them. Contrary to what many pseudo-Sufis claim, by abandoning the *Sharīʿah*, one is in danger of falling easily into the bottom of the well rather than being able to reach the Empyrean. The reason the books of certain so-called Sufi teachers sell well in the West is that they claim that one can disregard and flaunt the *Sharīʿah*, and yet reach the *Ḥaqīqah*; that one does not need to do the hard work that serious spiritual effort requires. They claim that it is enough just to read the poetry of Rūmī and so forth in order to achieve integration. But that is not possible, least of all in the chaotic, modern world in which we live, where the need for the order given by God's laws is greater than ever before. Seeking inner integration seriously can only bear fruit if it is based on following God's laws on the outward plane, whichever religious universe one happens to be living in.

As for Islam specifically, to achieve inner integration requires that one must first of all accept and practice the *Sharīʿah* as the norm which integrates our everyday life and provides a cadre that prevents the soul from falling into various pitfalls. By disciplining the soul horizontally, divine laws prepare the soul to journey vertically, and there is no possibility of the vertical journey without certain boundaries and limitations on the horizontal plane. He who seeks to achieve freedom merely horizontally will never achieve true freedom. The history of the modern and post-modern worlds has demonstrated that truth sufficiently.

At the first stage in integration, it is on the basis of accepting and practicing the *Sharīʿah* that the teachings of Sufism become operative. Now, according to the *Sharīʿah* in its ordinary understanding, God judges us by the actions that we perform. If one has the intention of murdering someone, but does not do so, then that person is not punished by the Law. Sufism starts from this basic, external position, but then takes a further step internally. It is interested most of all in our *niyyah*, our intention, in performing an act. According to a *ḥadīth* of the Prophet, "Actions (*al-aʿmāl*) are judged [by God] according to our inner intentions (*niyyāt*)." It is essential to follow the *Sharīʿah*, but more than that, one must seek to integrate the soul and purify intentions through the inner practices and methods of the *Ṭarīqah*.

It is even more difficult to integrate the soul than the body, much of whose organic and integrating functions are beyond our control. How many of us are healthy physically but are psychologically dispersed; often the body is doing a much better job of integration than our psyche. One of the maladies of modern human beings is to live in a state of scatteredness and dispersion, rather than being integrated within the psyche while at least temporarily being physically healthy, even though the health of the body and the psyche are interrelated and the two react often upon each other in many ways. Sufism enters into human life to heal the psyche and make it whole; which means to integrate it. But even this laudable goal is not the ultimate end. The final goal of Sufism is not the health of the psyche of the adept (as with modern psychiatry or psychology, which is really a parody of traditional psychology), and spiritual teachings like Sufism are not there to provide us with only physical health. The end of Sufism is *tawḥīd*, that is, union or unity, and preparation of the soul for proximity to God, who is One.

Sufism turns to the higher levels of the human microcosm without neglecting the outward physical domain. It tries to integrate the psyche both within itself and through its wedding to the spirit, and in a sense also includes the body in this process of integration. But how does it go about achieving this process of integration? First of all, it always emphasizes the effect that the body has upon the psyche and vice versa. Sufism never deals with the psyche as an abstraction, as a dismembered mind floating in the air. Every aspect of the action of the body is of some importance. One's postures, the way one sits and walks, the traditional courtesy or comportment (*adab*, which again is a very difficult word to translate)—all of these elements play a role in the life of the soul as well as the body. Does the body play a role in the final integration of the human state? The answer is yes, for one cannot just be indifferent to the body. Not only actions, which are to be governed by the Divine Law, but also the way people dress, the way they display certain gestures, the way they act with the body, all have an effect on the soul. This cause and effect is to be found in spiritual climes everywhere, as can be seen in the traditional teachings of Hindu and Buddhist spirituality, as in other religions.

The body, however, has a dual purpose in the spiritual life. Sometimes it has a negative role to play and becomes an impediment to the integration of the soul, and sometimes it has a positive role. There are all kinds of possibilities in Sufism's training of the soul, which aims at integrating the soul into its center, whilst not divorcing it from the body. As Rūmī says, the body is the horse, the steed on which we ride in this life. And there is a profound relationship between the nature of the steed and the ultimate goal toward which body and soul together transport us. The body also has a positive role in this journey. But at the moment of death, we have to leave the steed behind. There are, therefore, certain spiritual exercises and practices in this life which lead to spiritual death and the soul distancing itself from the physical body, while refining and strengthening the subtle body, which accompanies the soul after physical death.

In addition to doctrine, Sufism is based on the practice of certain forms of prayer, accompanied on the higher levels with meditation, as well as the cultivation of virtues, which lie at the very heart of the effort towards integration. Putting doctrine aside, which is actually a metaphysical elaboration of the supreme formula of unity in Islam, that is, *lā ilāha illa'Llāh* ("There is no divinity but God"), I want to mention the last two elements briefly. First of all prayer. All devout Muslims pray five times a day. That is in itself a miraculous occurrence, to have so many hundreds of millions of people systematically breaking their daily routine of life—we call it life but it is really daydreaming—five times a day to stand before the Absolute, before the One. Those canonical prayers are the foundation of all other forms of prayer. But the soul can fall into forgetfulness, even if it turns five times a day to God. So the Sufis try to expand the experience of prayer to what can be called, in its highest form, the prayer of the heart, whose practice, ideally, is to fill all times of the day and even the night when one is asleep, in perpetual prayer. The final goal, however, is not only to pray at all moments, but to become prayer. The very substance of the soul must become prayer. It must become totally identified with prayer. That is why the Quran mentions so often the word *dhikr Allāh, dhikr* meaning remembrance and also invocation or quintessential prayer. To become fully integrated, one must remember God at the center of one's heart, where God Himself resides, where He is always present, even if we forget because we no longer live at our own center and are absent from our deeper self. It is we who have forgotten God because we have forgotten the center of our own being, having become scattered at the periphery of the circle of existence. I always like to recall a passage from Rūmī's *Mathnawī* where, referring to perfect prayer, which embraces all levels of one's being, even the most outward, he says (in paraphrase): "Go sit cross-legged in a corner, take a rosary into your hand and invoke the Name of God; say '*Allāh, Allāh*' until your very toe is invoking God's Name, for it is not sufficient that your tongue invoke it."

In Sufism prayer is essentially the remembrance of God, and the remembrance of God is quintessential and supreme prayer. It is impossible to pray without remembering God, and it is impossible to remember God without praying in one way or another. Sufism, like yoga, has extraordinary methods and spiritual techniques for making possible the penetration of prayer into all levels of human existence, from the physical body (of which I have just given an ex-ample) and the tongue (which is part of our body), to the air that comes out of our lungs, which represents the more subtle state of manifestation (like the Sanskrit *prana*), to the mind, and finally to the heart. The final goal of Sufism in prayer is that every time the heart beats it should repeat the Name of God. Every time we breathe we should invoke God. We take our breathing so much for granted, but every time we breathe in, we do not know if that breath will come out. We never know which breath will be our last, therefore we must always be mindful of the preciousness of every moment of life (what Buddhism calls "right mindfulness"). Every breath we inhale should be identified with the remembrance of God, and every breath that we exhale should likewise be identified with the remembrance of Him. In the present cyclic condition, there is no greater and more efficacious means to integrate man than prayer, which ultimately penetrates into the whole of one's being and unifies the human state.

To individual practices that actualize the integration of the soul are added communal prac-tices; invocation by groups, combined (sometimes) with beautiful music and poetry. All these elements help the soul to pay attention to its center and to become integrated. All these dif-ferent means are used, because the fallen soul loves to do anything except pay attention to the "one thing necessary," to remember its own Origin and End. That is what makes continuous prayer with concentration difficult and also makes a second element, that is, meditation, neces-sary.

We are not only soul and body, but also spirit. As for the soul, there is a part of it which is like a mirror that reflects the intellect, but it is not the intellect itself. The intellect is not simply reason in the modern sense of this English word. According to a *ḥadīth, Awwalu mā khalaqa'Llāhu al-ʿaql* and also *Awwalu mā khalaqa'Llāhu al-rūḥ*, that is, "The first thing that God created was the Intellect" and "The first thing God created was the Spirit." These sayings refer ultimately to the same reality. Intellect resides at the center of our heart (*qalb*) at a point that is transcendent with respect to what is called the individual subject. It is reflected upon the mirror of the soul, what in modern thought is called the mind. It is interesting to note that, in French, the word for spirit and mind is the same, *l'esprit*. In German also the word *Geist* means both. In English we are in one sense fortunate in that we can make a distinction between spirit and mind, but this situation also makes it possible to forget the relation between the two. In any case we are not just minds, but we possess a mind which, as usually understood, refers to that part of our inner being where concepts are present, in which ideas arise, often in a manner that is beyond our control, and where the process of rational thinking takes place.

We also have another faculty in our soul which does not deal with concepts and ideas, but with forms and images. This faculty is the imagination, which can have both a negative and a positive function. The late Henry Corbin, basing himself mostly on major philosophical and mystical teachings of the great Andalusian Sufi Ibn ʿArabī and other Islamic masters such as Suhrawardī and Mullā Ṣadrā, has made the ontological status and spiritual and artistic significance of imagination known again to the modern West. What he calls the *mundus imaginalis*, the imaginal world, embraces the total imaginative function in all its positive and negative aspects. But we are not the masters of that world, any more than we are masters of concepts that flow into our mind this very minute. All of you sitting here are trying hard to follow what I am saying. My humble words may be of interest to you, but even so it is easy for your concentration to go astray after a few moments, so that you have to bring your mind back again and again to concentrate in order to follow what I am saying. It is extremely difficult to control the ever-flowing forms that the imagination creates, and the concepts and ideas that come into the mind. Again, to quote Rūmī, "You think you are the master of your mind but it is your mind that is the master of you, not you of it." So we have this very difficult problem of how to concentrate. All of these techniques you have heard about in Yoga, Zen, and Taoist practices, as well as the spiritual techniques of Sufism and Christianity especially as found in the great Hesychastic tradition, which is still alive on Mount Athos and elsewhere in the Orthodox world, are there to enable the disciple to concentrate.

Sufism, too, has very elaborate methods of meditation to make possible concentration, which must accompany inner prayer if that prayer is to become efficacious in being able to integrate our being. But in contrast to certain other traditions, such as Hinduism and Buddhism, little has been written in Sufism about this subject, its teachings having been passed down mostly through oral tradition, with each Sufi order having its own types of meditation. The goal of these various forms of meditation is, however, always the same. It is to control and integrate both aspects of the soul; what we call the mind, concerned with concepts and ideas, and what is known as imagination, dealing with forms and images. The methods of meditation within Sufism are too diverse for me to deal with here, but it is essential to remember their role in the integration of our inner being. Meditation (*fikr*) grows from and accompanies invocation (*dhikr*) and finally is reintegrated with it.

Then there is the question of embellishing the soul with virtues. The cultivation of virtues is so central that the early books of Sufism seem to be for the most part no more than books on virtue. Many people in the West who have fled from a kind of unintelligible moralism are put off by works that deal with virtue. They are attracted more to works on Oriental teachings that speak primarily about metaphysical and cosmological matters. But it is not possible to realize metaphysical truths without the possession of virtues. Truth belongs to God; it does not belong to us. What we have to ask is the question of how we can participate in the Truth. We can do so only by attaining virtue, although according to Sufism, virtues also come ultimately from God and belong to Him and it is He who has made it possible for us to attain them through the channel of His messengers and prophets. In the Islamic universe the virtues were embodied in the most palpable way in the character of the Prophet of Islam. For a Christian, all virtues belong to Christ and there is no virtue that a Christian can possess which was not possessed by Christ. It would be absurd and blasphemous to claim otherwise. Such is also the case in Islam. There is no virtue that any Muslim has possessed or will possess, anywhere from the southern Philippines to the Canary Islands, that was not possessed by the Prophet. This might seem astounding to many of you, because of the negative image of the Prophet that has been presented in the West via inaccurate biographies. The lack of an authentic account of the life of the Prophet in English was finally corrected by the wonderful biography of him by Dr. Martin Lings, my dear friend, published in England some years ago. Yet even now the inner, esoteric virtues of the Prophet are not well known to Western audiences. There is still a need for an "esoteric" biography of the Prophet in Western languages, such as exists in Arabic and Persian poetry, like the famous *Burdah* song of al-Būṣīrī in Arabic and its equivalents in Persian, Turkish, and other Islamic languages.

Now, how do we cultivate these inner, spiritual virtues and be successful in emulating the Prophet? That is a very difficult task indeed. It is easy to talk about virtues, but very difficult to attain them and cultivate them. God can give certain people the intelligence to understand doctrinally, that is, metaphysically. Such an understanding is already a gift from Heaven; it is a sacred science. But between the mental knowledge of metaphysics and its actualization in our being there is a great distance. I always compare the situation to seeing a mountain and climbing that mountain. If you come to the foot of the Himalayas, you can see the beautiful mountains before you. If, by the grace of God, you behold their majesty, that is a great gift and blessing. But how much more difficult it is to climb the mountains and to reach their exalted peaks. That is the difference between the mental understanding of doctrine, including the doctrine pertaining to virtue, and the realization of metaphysical truth, which means also the realization of the virtues with our whole being.

This third important element of Sufism is the one that makes possible the realization of Sufi doctrine and renders our prayers and meditations completely efficacious so as to transform the chaos of the soul into order and bring about unity within it, or, in other words, to integrate it. Once that is achieved, then the spirit (which is the only part of our being which is already integrated, being God's viceroy in us, as well as being identified with the heart/intellect) becomes wed to our soul, and the chaotic life of the soul becomes transmuted into that gold in which all the elements are integrated in perfect harmony. Inner integration enables that viceroy, the inner king, to rule within us, so that all of the chaos of the psyche and the various functions of the body, which we usually identify falsely as ourselves, become integrated into a center which is at once their center while itself belonging to a higher level of reality. Through the rule of this inner king each part of the soul is put into its proper place and made to function according to its proper nature, with the result that harmony and integration become established in the inner kingdom, and then by extension to the outer world.

Some Thoughts on Soliciting and Imparting
Spiritual Counsel[1]

Marco Pallis

The function of *upaguru* or "occasional instructor," to which René Guénon devoted an article,[2] is one that cannot be defined in terms of any special qualification: any man, thanks to a particular conjunction of circumstances, may some day be called upon to exercise it, and it may even happen that the office in question will devolve, outside the circle of human relationships, upon an animal, plant, or even an "inanimate" object that becomes, at that moment, a substitute for the human instructor in bringing enlightenment to someone in need of it—here the word "enlightenment" is used in a relative sense, this goes without saying; but provided the knowledge thus gained really counts spiritually, being thus related in greater or lesser degree to the gaining of Enlightenment in the full sense, then the use of the self-same word is justified. Naturally the function itself is exercisable, in the case of a human being, in more or less active mode, that is to say with greater or lesser awareness of what is involved; in the most favorable case the agent of instruction will accept the responsibility that has come to him as being part of his own *karma*, a by-product of anterior causes, that is to say in a spirit of submission to the universal law of causality or to that Divine Will which translates it in personal terms; but at the same time he will regard it as a spiritual opportunity, an episode of his own vocation or *dharma*, to be welcomed accordingly.

This experience is one which must have been shared by many of those who, inspired by Guénon's example, have themselves come to publish books or essays treating of the traditional doctrines: speaking from his own experience, the author of these notes has in fact repeatedly found himself in the position of being consulted by people anxiously seeking spiritual advice with a view to giving effect, in the face of the modern world and under its pressure, to that which, thanks to their own reading of Guénon or other works imbued with the traditional spirit, had become for them a matter of pressing necessity.

These inquiries, however, though animated by a common motive, have in fact taken on many different and sometimes most unexpected forms, calling for answers no less variable: it is nevertheless possible, looking back, to recognize some features of common occurrence that may allow of a few profitable generalizations touching the way in which a man should prepare himself to meet an opportunity of this kind. It must however be clearly understood that any suggestions offered here, even if they commend themselves, are intended to be carried out, whenever the occasion presents itself, in a resourceful spirit and with the greatest flexibility, lest by faulty handling on one's own part the person most concerned be driven back prematurely on his defenses, as can so easily happen with temperaments either passionately or else timidly inclined. Ability or willingness to discuss a vital matter in a spirit of detachment, as experience has shown again and again, can but rarely be taken for granted in anyone; a certain failure in this respect at the outset must not cause the other person to be written off

---

[1] To one who provided the occasional cause for this essay.

[2] *Études Traditionnelles*, January 1948.

as "uninteresting," as a result of a summary estimate of his character and motives; in handling such matters a remembrance of one's own limitations can be of great service as a corrective to impatience or complacency.

At the same time, neither is it necessary to wrap up every statement or avoid every straight issue for fear of causing pain, and if some question productive of an answer from oneself couched in rigorous terms happens to awaken an unexpectedly strong sentimental reaction in one's interlocutor this too must be accepted patiently and without surprise; the cause of such hitches may well lie in the fact that anyone with a mind seriously divided about spiritual questions will necessarily be living under some degree of strain and this state of acute doubt may well give rise in season to symptoms of irritability. On the other hand it also sometimes happens that an inquirer, professedly asking for counsel, has already made up his mind, if unconsciously, and all he is really seeking is a peg on which to hang a decision prejudged on the strength of secret desires; in such a case a straight answer, that brings matters sharply to a head, may be the only way left open to one. Nevertheless, these cases are comparatively rare, and the greater number of consultations of the kind here referred to are more likely to follow a line of gradual and also of fluctuating approach.

For the sake of those who, either from natural diffidence or for any other reason, might feel dismayed at the possibility of having some day to impart spiritual counsel to another, and possibly even to one who, at the mental level, is more highly equipped than themselves, it should be repeated that the function here under discussion, that of *upaguru*, is not one that depends on the possession of any kind of transcendent qualification, though within the very wide limits defining the field of its possible exercise all manner of degrees are to be found. If it be argued, rightly as it happens, that the function of instructor, even in its most relative sense, will always carry with it some implication of superiority over the person instructed, the answer in this case will be that the mere fact that the latter has come to one seeking spiritual advice itself constitutes recognition of a certain superiority, however temporary and however limited in scope. To accept this fact in no wise runs counter to true humility; for in fact no human instrument as such is ever adequate to a divinely imparted vocation at any degree, therefore also his own unworthiness can never rule a man out altogether. One can take comfort in the fact that the very disproportion of the two terms involved serves to illustrate the transcendence of the one and the dependence of the other: paradoxically, it is the "good man's" personal luster which might, in the eyes of the world, seem to mask the seemingly distant source of its own illumination, but this can hardly be said of the sinner's!

Incidentally this same principle contains an answer to the classical attack of the man of "protestant" turn of mind on various sacred offices because of the occasional, or even frequent, moral deficiencies of those traditionally entrusted with their exercise. The function itself remains objectively what it was at the origins; neither can the saintliness of one holder validate it further, nor the corruption of another invalidate it, be the facts what they will. If reform be needed, it must rest on this principle, otherwise it is more likely to become a wrecking, the displacement of a relatively normal evil by one wholly out of control.

So much for the call to upaguruhood: when it comes to the case of a spiritual master, however, *guru* in the full sense, his superiority rests on the twin poles of initiatic status, which is not a personal attribute, and of spiritual realization which likewise confers an objective quality that once gained cannot afterwards be forfeited; in that sense the *guru* can be called infallible, and a mouthpiece of the Self. Should it happen, however, that the disciple becomes equal in knowledge to his master, then, if he wants further guidance he will have to go elsewhere, as indeed sometimes occurs in the initiatic life; there are even cases on record when a master, recognizing the fact that a disciple has surpassed him, has exchanged places with him, descending willingly from the instructor's seat to sit at his feet, an example both of the highest humility and also of the purest realism. With the occasional office of *upaguru* the case is different, as already pointed out: apart from the temporary superiority conferred by the occasion, an adviser may well be, on balance, inferior by comparison with the person who has consulted him, though the reverse can just as well be true; in either case this question is irrelevant.

If, however, the questions as addressed by the inquirer are felt to be beyond one's powers of adequate handling it is always open to one—this hardly needs saying—to send him elsewhere to someone better equipped for the purpose; which is not the same as simply wanting to get rid of him, in a spirit of indifference lacking charity.

Cases may also occur which are of a very doubtful character, calling for an attitude of reserve on one's own part; besides which there are all sorts of inquiries having an obviously superficial bearing, when all that is needed is to refer the other person to suitable books which, if read attentively, might at least serve to awaken some understanding as to what the spiritual life really entails and this in its turn might produce consequences of an incalculable kind. The present comments, however, are only meant to cover the case of the more or less serious seeker, without trying to extend the discussion to borderline cases. Having been compiled under the impulse of a recent experience, they have an almost entirely practical bearing, and in any case there has been no intention of treating the subject exhaustively.

A. For the Guidance of the Person Consulted

(1) Speaking generally, it is usually good policy to start off by dealing with whatever question one's would-be client has chosen for a gambit, and this holds good even when one suspects that there may be other and deeper-seated perplexities still unavowed. Very often one's own first contribution will consist in framing the question itself correctly: half the unanswerable questions in the world remain so because they are already vitiated by the intrusion of special pleading (in other words, of passion) or because they harbor some undetected confusion between different orders of reality with consequent false comparisons—the history of religious controversy abounds in such examples, which does not mean, however, that it consists of nothing but that, as professed enemies of dogma would like to argue. Given that the case is such, however, once a question has been accurately and fairly rephrased, it will already be half way to begetting its own right answer, which can then be left to the inquirer himself to elicit far better than if one tries to supply it for him. It often happens, however, that the questions addressed to one are of a very general kind, amounting, that is to say, to an inquiry how to find a spiritual way unaccompanied by any pointer indicating a particular line of approach, and in that case it will be advisable to begin by investigating those spiritual possibilities that appear to be most accessible to the person concerned and least beset by practical obstacles, while being careful to leave the door open to other and seemingly more remote possibilities. At the same time there should be a conscious attempt to prevent the scales from being hastily weighted, by either party, in favor of or against a particular solution (unless the form of the question as put is such as to admit of only one answer, which will not happen very often), because the considerations governing any eventual choice of a path are necessarily complex and include not only practical factors of time and place and personal associations, but also factors of psychic affinity or incompatibility which cannot be assessed at a first glance.

(2) One should deliberately frame one's comments and answers on the basis of the traditional norms, with the minimum intrusion of one's personal opinions or preferences: it must all along be borne in mind that one is not called upon to substitute one's personal will for that of the other party, who must on the contrary be encouraged to take proper responsibility for any decisions taken, whether in a provisional or in a more far-reaching sense. One is there, in a situation not of one's own seeking, as the temporary spokesman of tradition itself, across its every form, and this requires an attitude of calculated detachment, which must not for a moment be abandoned under whatever provocation from the other party or because of some sentimental attachment of one's own. It is neither by getting involved in a debate nor by any one-sided advocacy of this or that but rather by consistently holding the mirror of pure metaphysical knowledge in the face of the other person's aspirations and difficulties that one will best succeed in dispelling the confusions and contradictions that beset the entrance to the Way: these are likely to be more than usually troublesome if the inquirer happens to be an "intellectual" (in the modern sense), one whose mind, that is to say, is haunted by a throng of abstract concepts, besides laboring under the mass of factual information which a man of retentive brain can hardly escape being burdened with under present circumstances.

(3) Sentimental prejudices, if they happen to reveal themselves, should be shown up for what they are; but in doing so, firmness should be duly tempered with courtesy and sympathy, since the realm of the feelings is one where, by definition, violent reactions are in the order of things and once these have been evoked it is not easy for anyone to return to a state of impartial consideration; he must be given time to regain his balance.

(4) One must abstain from engaging in an attempted psychological analysis of the other person: the less one delves into his or her private life, antecedents, etc., the better, and questions of this kind should only be put where some fact or other appears quite indispensable for the purpose of rendering a spiritual problem more "concrete." Once again, it is well to remind oneself that for someone to be seeking advice of this nature does in itself argue a degree, and often an acute degree, of "spiritual distress" that deserves all one's sympathy. It should be added that in trying to probe the nature of another's spiritual need, small, apparently irrelevant signs will often tell one more than any rationalized explanations, since the latter, even when honestly advanced, are almost bound to take on an apologetic and forensic character, affecting their usefulness as evidence to a greater or lesser extent.

B. Concerning the Need for a Traditional Framework

In the case of one who is already attached to an authentic traditional form, the positive possibilities of that form must first be taken into account, if only for the reason that the individual concerned will already have been molded psychically according to that form, at least in part, and will understand its language without special effort.

As for one who is "unattached" traditionally, the primary necessity of a traditional basis for a spiritual life must, as Guénon has done repeatedly, be stressed in unequivocal terms; an esoterism *in vacuo* is not to be thought of, if only from the fact that man is not pure Intellect, but is also both mind and body the several faculties of which, because they are relatively external themselves, require correspondingly external means for their ordering. This insistence on the "discipline of form" is a great stumbling-block to the modernist mentality, and not least so when that mentality is imbued with pseudo-esoteric pretensions. Therefore it provides, over and above its own correctness, one of the earliest means for testing the true character of a man's aspiration, even to the point of bringing about an immediate "discrimination of spirits": only here again one must beware of making a system of this test, since it has become such a commonplace, on the part of modern writers on spiritual subjects, to decry the value of forms that a person not already forearmed can be pardoned, at least in some cases, for having developed a similar distaste in the sincere belief that he is merely escaping from the servitude of the letter in the direction of "pure spirit"; whereas all he is doing is to substitute mental abstractions for concrete symbols, and human opinions for the traditional wisdom and the laws that express it outwardly. Nevertheless, in the long run, a persistent unwillingness to accept any traditional formation for oneself, on the common plea that there is no form but has exhibited imperfections in greater or lesser degree in the course of its history, must be reckoned as evidence of spiritual disqualification. Form necessarily implies limitation and this in its turn implies the possibility of corruption; it would be futile to wish things otherwise. This fact however does not invalidate the efficacy of a formal disposition for those elements in the individuality that belong themselves to the formal order, of which thought is one. For this reason one must not allow oneself to weaken in regard to the principle of traditional conformity, which does not mean, however, that one should try to ignore incontestable facts concerning various manifestations of human corruptibility that have occurred in the traditional civilizations, especially in more recent times, from some of which, moreover, the modern profanity itself can be traced in lineal descent.

C. What Attachment to a Traditional Form Implies

Attachment to a revealed form which, to meet its corresponding necessity, must be an effective and not merely "ideal" attachment, will imply, as an indispensable condition: (a) The taking up of an *active* attitude towards the world, in opposition to the attitude of passive acceptance that has become so general in these latter days, and it also implies a symbolical but still relatively passive participation in the mysteries, firstly through faith and secondly through general conformity to the traditional institutions. This relatively (though not wholly) passive participation is in fact the distinguishing "note" of an attitude properly qualifiable as "exoteric," in contrast to an "esoteric" attitude (b) which, for its part, implies, over and above, an active, truly "intellectual" participation in the mysteries with a view to their effective realization, sooner or later, in the heart of the devotee. In the latter case the more external side of the tradition, with all its component elements, instead of appearing to fill the entire spiritual horizon, will rather be thought of as offering two advantages, namely (i) as imposing the indispensable discipline of form upon the psycho-physical faculties of the being, the rational faculty included, so that they may all serve, and never obstruct, the activity of the central organ or spiritual heart and, (ii) as providing teacher (when found) and disciple alike with appropriate "supports," symbolic or other, wherewith the more inward activities can be steadied in the course of development, and more particularly in the earlier stages.

These supports if they are to be utilizable in an effective sense, as instruments of a spiritual method, must be formally consistent (hence the objection, voiced by Guénon, against any arbitrary "mingling of forms"); otherwise all kinds of psychological dissonances are likely to arise. The modern mind, with its habit of conceiving progress in terms of an indefinite amassing of things regarded as beyond question beneficial and not so merely under a given set of conditions, finds it especially hard to admit that two elements, each advantageous in its own place, can nevertheless be mutually exclusive and capable, when brought into association, of producing far more harm than good. Behind this reluctance there lies in fact a serious metaphysical fallacy, due to a radical inability to grasp the true nature of forms which, to be such, must each display aspects of inclusion and exclusion, both.

D. Concerning the Nature of Tradition

For any human being, his "traditional attachment" can be regarded as a minimum condition defining him as human, at least in intention, and this, regardless of the greater or lesser extent of that being's spiritual horizon: in this sense, tradition will appear as the chief compensating factor for man's fall from grace, and as a means for regaining a lost state of equilibrium. In a sense, it is untrue to speak of a man's attachment to tradition; it would be more accurate to say that by tradition man is connected with the source of Knowledge and Grace, as by an Ariadne's clue, one that gives him his direction as well as the hope and promise of safety, if he will but use the opportunity it offers him. For every man, his tradition will be evocative of certain spiritual "values," besides providing the ritual and formal supports (as explained before) which are the carriers and catalysts of celestial influences, at all degrees of receptiveness and participation. The tradition will dedicate that man or woman in principle to the Way and it will unlock the door to all the possibilities of realization. Likewise it will serve to "regulate" all the more external aspects of human activity and it will, under normal conditions, suffuse its characteristic "color" or "flavor" over all the elements of daily life.

For an esoterist the same holds good, with the difference that the whole conception of the Way will be raised, as it were, to a higher power, its finality being transposed beyond individual and indeed beyond all formal limits.

E. Digression on Orthodoxy

Faith has been defined as confident acceptance of a revealed truth, orthodoxy marking a parallel conformity of thought and expression to this same revealed truth. It is not our purpose here to attempt a detailed study of this important aspect of traditional participation, the one that imparts to spiritual life its formal consistency. There is however one aspect of the subject which must find a place here because in practice it often plays its part in the difficulties surrounding the early stages of spiritual quest: it is the distinction, not always apparent to everybody, between an expression of traditional orthodoxy in the strict sense and a private opinion which happens to coincide with the orthodox teaching. From the point of view of its objective content, such an opinion can be accepted at its face value since, as St. Ambrose pointed out, truth by whomsoever expressed is always "of the Holy Ghost." Subjectively judged, however, the correctness of an opinion so held, though creditable to its author and in any case welcome, still remains "accidental" and therefore precarious; the traditional guarantees are not in themselves replaceable thanks to any purely human initiative, carried out, that is to say, outside that spiritual current whence the doctrine in question itself emanates.

The same question might also be presented in another way: it might be asked, which is preferable, that a man be regularly attached to an orthodox tradition while holding some erroneous opinions or that he hold correct views while remaining outside any actual traditional framework? To such a question the answer must be, unequivocally, that regular attachment is in itself worth more than any individual opinion for the simple reason that thoughts, whether sound or mistaken, belong "to the side of man" whereas a traditional doctrine, as deriving from a revelation, belongs "to the side of God"—this without mentioning the "means of Grace" which accompany the doctrine with a view to its realization and for which there exists no human counterpart whatsoever. Between the two positions the distance is incommensurable and once this is seen the original question loses all its point. It was necessary to touch on it, however, because the pretension to share in the things of tradition "ideally," that is, without paying the price, is one to which many people are addicted from a somewhat clumsy wish to safeguard a non-existent freedom—non-existent because still waiting to be gained through knowledge.

F. Concerning the Structure of a Tradition

Every complete tradition implies three elements, utilizable by all concerned and at all degrees of knowledge though in differing proportions. These elements are: (a) a form of doctrine, expressed in the appropriate "spiritual dialect" (which, to some extent at least, will exclude other dialects), the vehicle of that doctrine being not only the spoken or written word, but also arts, manners, and indeed everything great or small forming part of the tradition in question: and (b) certain "means of Grace," whether transmitted from the origins or else revealed at some subsequent time, these being the specific supports of the spiritual influences animating that tradition: and (c) a traditional law regulating the scope of action, positively and negatively, in various ways.

For an exoterist (a), the doctrine, will largely be a field for faith in its more ordinary sense, which represents a relatively passive aspect of knowledge, whereas that same doctrine will, for an esoterist, be treated from the point of view of full awareness through "ontological realization," that is to say from the point of view of knowledge in its active mode. The Christian dialect may still continue to apply the word "faith" to the latter case also, but it must then be taken in the sense of "seeing is believing" and mountains are able to be moved in virtue of it. Similarly, in the case of the sacramental element (b), it will be accepted by the exoterist as a mystery which will often amount, for him, to little more than the implanting of a germ, one which, however, watered by faith and warmed by the other virtues, is bound to bring forth fruit in season.

An esoterist, for his part, will share in the rites with the conscious intention of actualizing their fruits in the fullest degree; his attitude is active by definition—if the latter term can be applied to an intention which accepts no limits whatsoever. As for (c), legislative conformity whether ritual or moral, this is required of exoterist and esoterist alike so long as any of the components of a human individuality still remain unordered and uncentered. The final term of this condition of being "under the law" is a converting of one's human status, which since "the Fall," as variously pictured in the different traditions, has been merely virtual, into an irreversible actuality, by a return to the human norm symbolized by the axis passing through the center of all the "worlds" or degrees of existence, that axis being in fact identical with the path by which the Intelligible Light descends from its source in order to illuminate the darkness of ignorance, thus also indicating the direction of escape along the same road.

G. Concerning "Solitaries"

A passing allusion must be made to those rare beings, the *afrad* of Islamic tradition, known also to other traditions, for whom initiation in the supreme knowledge comes, so to speak, directly from Heaven, if only to show that the Spirit bloweth where it listeth. These, the spontaneously illuminate, owe nothing to any living master, nor have they any reason to be attached to a visible traditional form, though they might so belong accidentally. The formless Truth is their only country and their language is but the Inexpressible.

Given that their existence does represent a possibility, if a remote one, it is expedient to mention it here: all that need be said on the subject, however, is that any suggestion that such and such a person belongs to this rare category could only begin to be considered on the strength of quite overwhelming evidence; and even then only those who were themselves endowed with the insight born of profound knowledge would be in a position to hold an opinion on the subject, let alone to claim certitude. As for a person who made such a claim on his own behalf, this would under all ordinary circumstances amount to an evident disproof of the claim, a case of "outer darkness" being mistaken for "solitude" in its higher sense. A genuine state of *fard* (= solitude, whence the derivative *afrad*), like "spiritual silence," "voidness" and other such terms, corresponding, as it does, to a possibility of non-manifestation, would seem to preclude any definable sign of its possession or any organized expression in action.

The true solitaries are in fact but "the exception that proves the rule" and their occasional appearance in the world, necessary in order to affirm the Divine Playfulness, as the Hindus have eloquently called it, does not in any way affect the need for a tradition, as far as the overwhelming majority of human beings is concerned, a need which is moreover attested, if further evidence is needed, by the fact that most if not all spiritual masters known to have existed in our time or in former times have spoken in the name of a tradition and have used its appropriate modes of expression when instructing their disciples: whereas it is almost a commonplace for self-appointed teachers to repudiate the traditional norms and to encourage a similar attitude in others, hoping thus to attract the unwary by playing upon their naïve self-esteem as persons who supposedly stand beyond the need of outmoded formal disciplines. This is, moreover, an habitual stumbling-block for the Western "intellectual," as also for his westernized Eastern counterpart, being not the least among his accumulated spiritual disabilities.

H. Concerning the Viability of Forms

For a tradition to fulfill its purpose in any given case, it must be "viable" in relation to the circumstances of the person concerned, that is to say it must be sufficiently accessible in time and space, as well as assimilable in itself, to render participation "operative." It would, for instance, be useless to try and attach oneself to an extinct form such as the Pythagorean tradition; and even with a still extant form such as Taoism, it would be practically impossible to establish contact with it, save by rare exception, because of the immense physical and psychic obstacles standing in the way of any Occidental who wished to resort to a Taoist master—always supposing that such is still to be found hidden in some remote corner of the Chinese world, which today is not easy to prove or disprove.

By pursuing this line of argument it will be seen that the range of choice is not actually very wide and that even within that range a distinction has to be made, in the case of a European, between traditions existing in his immediate vicinity, and those which, if assimilation is to become a practical proposition, can only be approached through travel to more distant regions; and even if this be possible, the question of maintaining contact subsequently is not without pertinence, given the small probability, in any average case, that a high degree of contemplative concentration will have been attained soon enough to reduce the formal aspects of the tradition to relative unimportance.

It must not be thought, however, because of the emphasis laid on accessibility, that this condition is to be treated as a completely overriding one or applied systematically to all cases alike. Though it is reasonable to give preliminary consideration to what seems to be the nearest solution, its apparent advantages may, despite all the extra difficulties consequent upon a more remote choice, have to yield before some alternative solution, one governed by considerations of natural affinity, for instance, or by some other factor not perceivable at the outset. It is in fact always good to bear in mind the oft-heard statement that in the end it is the tradition that chooses the man, rather than the reverse. All that human reasoning can do is to prepare the way for the final discrimination prior to which he can only preserve an attitude of "prayerful expectancy."

In the case of an Occidental it is evident, however, that his mental conformation, whether he likes it or not, will have been powerfully affected by Christian ways of thinking and acting and that the very words he uses are charged with inherited implications bearing a Christian tinge: this is as true of those who have cast off (or so they would have it) their traditional yoke as of those who still remain attached to some branch of the Christian Church, at least in name. Such being the case, it would seem most prudent to consider the possibilities offered by the Christian path first of all, provided one does so with a mind unbiased by irrelevancies, whether in a positive or negative direction: this last remark applies equally to both parties in the discussion. As to the question of what criteria may be applied when investigating the spiritual possibilities presently offered by any particular traditional form, this will be reserved for a section to follow.

I. A Few Remarks about Existing Forms

Besides the two Christian traditional forms—their differences need not be stressed in the present instance—which between them cover the European world together with its American and other prolongations, there are also certain Eastern traditions, including the Islamic, which come within the bounds of practicability for Occidentals, at least in exceptional cases; this is especially true of the last-named, which both by reason of a certain kinship with the Christian form and still more by reason of its own structure is particularly fitted to meet the needs of men in the latter days of the cycle, a fact which is not generally recognized in the West, where ignorance on the subject of Islam and consequent prejudice is still rather general. Howbeit, it is in the direction of one or two of the Oriental traditions that those souls who, for any reason, find themselves out of tune with their dechristianized environment usually turn. Whoever does so ought not, however, to underrate the practical difficulties of an Oriental attachment on the part of one who intends to continue living a life which, in all other ways, will conform to the Occidental pattern. Whereas this is a very real drawback, it is not an altogether insurmountable one, though it does mean that rather exceptional qualities are required to overcome it, chief of which is a markedly contemplative turn of mind. Prudence demands that these obstacles should be faced from the start in a spirit of realism, otherwise a revulsion of feeling may wreck the whole enterprise after the first enthusiasm has begun to cool. On the other hand it does not do to be too cautious either, where spiritual matters are concerned; a readiness to plunge boldly for the prize is also a quality of the spirit. The Way is beset with dangers, and to follow it at all is inseparable from certain oft-repeated discomforts, which have to be accepted for what they are, as part of the price to be paid by one who would fain walk with the Spirit. It is well to recognize that the very existence, for so many, of an apparent problem of choice is in itself an abnormal happening, due to the chaotic circumstances of the times. The alternative to solving it effectively is a relapse into indifference, a virtual atheism.

J. Of Attraction and Aversion

Wherever a person spiritually intent and not already in a tradition evinces a disproportionately violent aversion for a particular form (whatever arguments may be advanced in justification of the dislike) this feeling can be ascribed, roughly speaking, to one of two possible causes: the aversion may be due to the presence, in that person's psychic make-up, of elements which do not harmonize with some of the formal elements of the tradition in question and in that case the feeling of repulsion, though never insurmountable in itself, must be regarded as a negative sign affecting the choice of a form in a manner worth heeding: or else the aversion may be due to an inverted attraction for a form that really, in essentials, agrees with that person's psychic constitution, the apparent hostility then being due either to purely accidental causes such as inherited historical or racial oppositions or else to some deep-seated desire to remain in the profane world which, by covert means, is trying to hinder a positive decision of any kind. The passionate symptoms, in the first case, can be counted as of relatively small importance, froth upon the surface of an otherwise genuine aspiration; but in the second case passion betrays diabolical instigation and means must be found to allay it before judgment on the main issue becomes even possible. Discernment in these matters is never easy for either party to the conversation and the most one can say on the subject, in the early stages at least, is that attraction and aversion are twins, born of one mother, and that the intellect, by referring them both back to their common principle, should be able to effect an eventual discrimination between them. To hate a thing one may actually be very near that thing oneself, though this is not necessarily the case (two causes being possible as mentioned above); that is why one must not be too ready to take expressions of dislike at their face value, where spiritual problems are concerned, but must rather do all one can to restore a state of dispassion, after which difficulties of the kind described are likely to clear up of their own accord.

K. Concerning Criteria

Among factors allowing one to distinguish between form and form there will assuredly be some partaking of a subjective character, such as for example the way in which the art belonging to a certain tradition may have been instrumental in giving impulse to one's own spiritual yearnings, while others again will have a more objective bearing, such as the degree of corruption by which one or other form is presently affected, and still more the nature of that corruption, as well as the type of collective psychism prevailing in each of the traditional forms under consideration—a most important element in any attempted judgment. Nevertheless these factors, though they cannot but affect the question, must still count as accessory, if only for the reason that none of them is such as to outweigh all others by its presence or absence alone. The essential criterion still remains to be applied, and till this has happened some degree of doubt will adhere to any choice one may have in mind.

The essential question to be asked is whether the traditional form one is thinking about does or does not, under present circumstances, actually provide the means for taking a man all the way in the spiritual life or not? In other words, are the formal limits such as to leave an open window looking towards the formless Truth, thus allowing room for the possibility of its immediate or ultimate realization? If the answer is in the affirmative then that form, however degenerate it may have become, must still be admitted to be adequate as regards the essential, which is all that, rigorously speaking, matters; if on the other hand that form, however pure it may have remained as regards its more peripheric aspects, does in fact fail to pass the essential test, then there is nothing further to be said in its favor.

When applying this criterion, moreover, important corroborative evidence can be drawn, in support of a positive decision, from the knowledge that some people at least, however few in number, have succeeded at this time, while attached to such and such a form and using the means of grace it provides, in cultivating their spiritual possibilities to the full in the face of whatever local difficulties have been created for them by the traditional environment in question. All the great traditions are necessarily affected at the human and historical level by corruption in larger or lesser measure and even those sanctuaries that hitherto had been most immune, even Tibet, are now feeling the pressure of the modern profanity, over and above all the harm suffered as a result of petrifaction or dilution, which are the two types of natural corruption in a form. In such a changing situation there are many temporary distinctions to be made: sometimes evils which seem most blatant may turn out to have been relatively superficial while others, though less noticeable, may go nearer the essence and it is this last factor that will tell us, ultimately, whether the disease has reached the mortal stage or not.

One thing however is certain in all this, namely that at the level of forms anything like a watertight determination does not exist: for though under the most favorable conditions a given form may be conveniently described as perfect this can only be taken in a relative and therefore transient sense, since the very phrase "perfect form," strictly speaking, is a contradiction in terms. In adhering to the support of a form, therefore, one must never ask to be relieved of every cause of dissatisfaction of body or mind, for that is impossible at the level of the world even under the most favorable circumstances: in those ages which, to us, seem to have come closest to the ideal, the saints of the time were denouncing errors and vices and calling on men to abjure and repent—which does not mean we are wrong in our view of those ages, on the strength of the positive evidence. What it does mean is that every world is by definition a place of contrasts and this will always necessitate an accepting of the rough with the smooth, even when leading the religious life at its best. As a Sufi master once said to the writer: "There is always something unpleasing about any spiritual way."

Actually, the kind of impediment that takes the form of saying, "I would so gladly adhere to such and such a religion which attracts me, if only just this one feature in it could be different," is a very common one, especially among persons of apparent goodwill who are second to none in decrying the modern world and its materialism but who, when it comes to their taking any positive step, will invariably find yet another gnat to strain at. Repeated experience has shown that this is one of the most difficult obstacles to surmount from the very fact that the hard core of resistance to the call lies concealed behind such an evident show of theoretical understanding coupled with sympathy for sacred things. To such the answer can only be that revealed religion, like everything else in manifestation, will have its crosses as well as its consolations: to approach the Way with a mind full of inflated expectations of a pleasurable kind, or else with one charged with puritanical gloom, is quite unrealistic. What one needs is to keep a firm hold on essentials, on metaphysical truth, and, for the rest, to view the doings in the world with some sense of proportion though never without discernment, while getting on with the task in hand.

Defects apparent in a form, the inevitable abuses, the relativity of the formal order itself, negative factors though these be from one point of view, have at least one positive compensation inasmuch as by their presence they proclaim the fact that a form, however hallowed, is not God and therefore also the fact of their own ultimate non-entity in the face of His transcendence. It is not the image nor even the mirror that counts, but the Light which reflector and reflection alike veil and reveal.

L. Further Notes on Discrimination

Both the facts and causes of worldwide corruption not being contestable by anyone who rejects the profane view of things, there is but little profit in dwelling on this subject except for occasional and chiefly practical reasons, otherwise one might soon be reduced to despair. When however a cause does arise for so doing, the need for a nicely balanced discernment will be relatively greater or less according to the nature of one's own natural vocation or, as the Hindus would put it, of one's "caste."

For the man of action, since his focus of attention is external by definition, a more or less dualistic outlook, spelling inherent oppositions, is normal; though an attitude of non-attachment to the fruits of action can also lead him beyond the point where those oppositions have power to bind him. Again, for the *bhakta*, the man of devotional temperament, his whole spiritual field will properly be suffused with an emotional tinge (which does not mean "sentimental" in the sense of inhibiting intellectuality in the way that applies to certain forms of "mysticism" but not to true *bhakti*). In the first of these two human types judgment concerning forms other than one's own may be biased by loyalties, just as in the second case it may be blurred by a loving fervor that has no use for discernment; but in either case an occasional exaggeration on the lines described is of relatively small importance, because the feeling which prompts it, though not exactly desirable, goes with a temperament into the composition of which feeling largely enters as an integrating factor.

Not so, however, with the *jnani*, the man whose vocation is predominantly "intellectual" and for whom, consequently, the intellectual virtues of dispassion and discrimination are essential, and not accessory, constituents of his spirituality. For that man, a just appraisal of "foreign" forms will have positive importance and the reverse also applies inasmuch as criticism that goes beyond its brief, as a result of a passionate intrusion, is liable to have subtle repercussions which, unless neutralized, may seriously affect that person's chances of rendering all forms (including his own) transparent and thus acceding to the formless Knowledge. That is why, if such a thing should occur with an inquirer of markedly jnanic type, the person consulted should, even at the risk of incurring a certain suspicion of favoring a particular form, do his best to discourage criticisms which, though partly justified, exceed the limits of accurately balanced discernment, based as this must be on traditional and not on arbitrary criteria. Over this matter of criticism none has been more severe than Guénon, and if he was ready to accept certain forms as being still orthodox, despite admitted corruptions, it would certainly be wrong to attribute this fact to leniency on his part, or to think of outdoing him in rigor.

Mention has been made occasionally by Coomaraswamy and others of certain Occidentals living in fairly recent times, of whom the poet-painter Blake provides an oft-quoted example, who in their works displayed a power of metaphysical insight that seems, when viewed against the background of their time, to be explainable in terms of a hidden traditional connection or even, as some have maintained, of a quasi-prophetic gift. It would be difficult for a stranger to this field of study to offer an opinion upon the spiritual qualification, or otherwise, of these rather enigmatical figures, of whom a number made their appearance here and there during the centuries following the rupture of the Middle Ages. However, even where someone has special reason for devoting attention to this problem, it is yet well to remember that for purposes of spiritual precedent there is little to be gained by searching among the anomalies of that twilight period in the West, when the traditional doctrine at its most rigorous and spirituality at its most normal are so much more plainly observable at other times and places. Whatever the intellectual antecedents of these exceptional exponents may be, one has no right to refer to them as "traditional authorities"; the fact that they showed that wisdom was still able to manifest itself sporadically in an age when the forces of materialism and rationalism seemed to be carrying all before them is already much to their credit and one must not try and add to this in the absence of conclusive evidence.

What does however emerge from the foregoing discussion is that there is a distinction to be made between a man of greater or lesser "metaphysical genius" and the normally quali-fied spokesman of a traditional teaching—though the two things may, of course, coincide in one person, as in the case of Sri Shankaracharya, for instance. The principle of discrimination between the two states just mentioned is this: in the metaphysical genius his human mind will play an essential part, hence the often amazing powers of doctrinal expression displayed; whereas in the traditional teacher, whose mental powers will not necessarily be much above average, the intellect may manifest its presence more or less unsupplemented by special tal-ent—the latter "incarnates" rather than "thinks out" the truths he communicates. It can also be said that the first-named in fact exemplifies the highest possible use of human reason, or in other words the use of reason placed at the service of intellect, while the second primarily ex-emplifies an effacement of the human individuality (reason included) before the spiritual order and before the tradition that conveys its influence in the world.

Above all, it must be recognized that true metaphysical insight, in any degree, is only pos-sible for one whose mind remains "open" to the things above, otherwise its activities must needs degenerate into philosophizing, whether speciously brilliant or merely dull. It is by apply-ing this criterion that one is able to distinguish without fail between the mind of a Coomaras-wamy or a Guénon and that of a ratiocinative or manipulative *virtuoso* of the kind that occurs so commonly today and astonishes by its feats in various departments of the scientific field. The former, thanks to its intellectual non-limitation, is able to reach and therefore to communicate truths of the principial order; whereas the latter can reach no further than the general which, when cut off from the universal, can be a most fruitful source of errors.

It is on the basis of these distinctions that any eventual judgment must rest.

M. On Finding the *Guru*

The question of how a man is to find his spiritual way in the midst of this labyrinth of a modern world is often accompanied by another, closely bound up with the first, which takes the form of asking where, if anywhere, a spiritual master or *guru* is to be found; in any case this second question is always more or less implicit in the first one, unless one is dealing with a person whose horizon does not for the time being extend further than the individual realm and for whom a religious attachment, in its more external sense, will provide all that is needed to regu-late his life and quicken his fervor. It should be added that whereas access to tradition is every man's right as well as his duty, the same does not apply to the initiatic path, which is selective by its own nature so that access to a master, even if his whereabouts be known, will always imply some degree of qualification in a would-be disciple before he is accepted. It is moreover evident that spiritual masters are not common anywhere today and that those who do exist are mostly to be found in the East, though obviously this is not a necessary condition. Nor is search for a master made any easier by the existence, in all directions, of bogus masters, usually persons of abnormal psychic development who, unlike the true kind, lose no opportunity of advertising their presence in an endeavor to attract disciples to their side.

In a normal civilization the urge to find a *guru* would arise naturally in a mind already conditioned by a whole tradition and likewise the channel of approach to the *guru* would pass through that same tradition. Passage would, in any typical case, be from peripheric aspects, gradually, towards the center, as represented by that innermost knowledge which it is the object of an initiatic teaching to awaken. But under the extremely anomalous conditions of our time the need for the most inward things will often strike on the consciousness of a person situated outside any tradition, as a result of reading or from some other accidental cause. In that case an aspiration already pointing, at least in principle, towards the center has, as it were, to be "underpinned" by means of a traditional attachment of appropriate form, and the acceptance of things pertaining to the more peripheric orders would, in that case, have to be aroused *a posteriori* for the sake of the higher prize and not just as a matter of course or simply as forming part of the spiritual nationality into which one has been born and the language of which one both speaks and listens to continually. To follow an unusual process is perfectly reasonable in the circumstances.

From the above it follows that once having found his master, a hitherto unattached aspirant would adhere to that master's traditional form, and not to another, for obvious reasons. This would apply both in the case of someone who found his *guru* close at hand or who was compelled to travel far afield for this purpose, for example to some Asiatic country. It is perhaps well to point out, however, that there have been exceptions to this rule, especially in India where the number of Hindus resorting to Muslim masters or vice versa has been quite considerable. Where an ability to contemplate the metaphysical principle underlying all formal variety is common, the latter element largely ceases to oppose a barrier. But even nearer home there have been exceptional cases of this kind so that it would be a mistake to exclude this possibility altogether, even while recognizing that it answers to very special conditions, personal or other, in the absence of which the argument of normality and convenience holds good.

There is one case, however, that still remains to be considered, namely the case of one who, though already seeking a spiritual teacher, has not been able to find one up to the moment of speaking. Is that person to remain idle hoping that something will turn up or can he be doing something already which will favor the purpose in view? Here the lesson offered by the Parable of the Talents applies: to sit back blaming one's bad luck because others have found their teachers or been born in the right country or the right century while one has been able to get no farther oneself than mere aspiration is an unworthy attitude and the passivity it expresses is in itself a sign of disqualification. The initiatic path is active by definition and therefore an active attitude, in the face of difficulties that might even outlast a lifetime, is the proper prelude to entering that path—herein is to be seen the difference between hope, in the theological sense, and mere desire. The true seeker does not only wait for Grace to descend upon him but he also goes out to meet it, he knocks continually at the door, while at the same time he accepts delays not of his own making in a spirit of submissiveness towards the Divine Will, whether this shows itself in bestowing or withholding.

It is in this situation that a man's traditional connections will count more than ever: for then he can reason to himself thus and say: "Though at present the mysterious gate appears closed, I can at least use the resources of the existing exoterism, not in a perfunctory way nor for the sake of a minimum of conformity, but generously, by pushing out as far as its very farthest frontier, to the point where the realm of my hope begins. Let me then take advantage of every rite and every traditional rule, and at the same time let me do all I can to fit myself for the reception of the initiatic grace, if ever it comes, both by study of Scriptures and of the more rigorous commentaries ('browsing' is to be avoided, even among traditional things) and also by the daily practice of the virtues and above all by assiduous attention to the smallest details—and who shall say what is small and what great under such circumstances?" An attitude of this kind (the writer had an actual example in mind) is well calculated, if one may so express it, "to attract the grace of the *guru*" when the moment is ripe for such a thing: besides which, twin terms like "exoteric" and "esoteric," convenient though they may be, are meaningless apart from one another, and likewise the supposed line of demarcation between their respective realms is but a point of reference, so that one who has realized the full possibilities of the one realm will, as it were, already have got one foot across the barrier into the other; also that barrier will grow more tenuous and transparent in proportion as the heart of the aspirant, pursuing this form of self-discipline, unhardens itself until one day (God willing) the barrier will simply cease to be—and on that day the *Guru* also surely will appear.

*   *   *

A friend to whom the above notes were shown made this comment:

> . . . after all, persons who approach us supposedly do so because they have understood the doctrine expressed in the books (of Guénon and Schuon); that is to say, essentially, they have understood pure metaphysic, which is supra-dogmatic and universal, and likewise the validity of orthodox traditional forms which, for their part, vehicle that metaphysic while adding to it secondary perspectives and spiritual means of varying importance. Even if one does not feel a particularly marked affinity for such and such a religious form, one must know that it is valid, and this by reason of its own criteria, intrinsic on the one hand and extrinsic on the other; the intrinsic criteria derive in fact from metaphysic, while the extrinsic criteria are of the phenomenal order: for example, there are all kinds of historical, psychological, and other criteria of this kind which prove in their own way that Islam cannot but be an orthodox tradition and the same would apply in all comparable cases.
>
> . . . Prejudices cannot stand in the face of those ideas which are supposed to be at the very basis of the search; at most there may be question of a "climatic" preference, such as is legitimate wherever choice is possible, and on condition that the elements governing choice are sufficiently known . . . if such difficulties were to arise in the mind even of a comparatively informed inquirer, in dealing with him there would be no reason to embarrass oneself with too much psychology; it is enough that the inquirer should be "recalled to order" by referring him to the Doctrine.

Love

Tage Lindbom

Secularization is a fish in troubled waters. It in no way signifies, as its spokesmen like to suggest, that men would turn aside from religious "superstition" in order to find light and perspicuity in rationalism. Secularization, on the contrary, implies the loss by man of his capacity of objectivation, of his power to distinguish illusion from reality, falsehood from truth, the relative from the absolute. The deepest objective of secularism is precisely to "liberate" man from the order by which he is submissive to his Creator, to "emancipate" him from his existential source, to "change" the system of truth in which he lives into a factual and mental relativity. Thus an inevitable consequence is, not an accrued perspicuity in the imaginative life of man, but on the contrary an ever growing opacity.

Love is one of the first victims of the growing confusion provoked by secularization. It is not a system or an article of faith which could be integrated and defended in the cadre of orthodoxy. Nor is it a doctrine to thrust forward in opposition to other theories. This is why it is more vulnerable and more exposed to alternations and falsifications than anything else in the world of spiritual concepts. Just as crustaceans, at the time of shedding their shells, are easy prey to rapacious animals of the sea, love is a choice booty for the falsifiers serving the cause of secularization. In the first place, this falsification consists in passing under silence and in effacing from human consciousness the essence and source of love.

All creation, all production is a gift. Love is such a gift. As all that is created and produced is, in the final analysis, traced back to its divine source, it is God who is the source of all love. God is love, and this is true in relation to His creation. Love is an "aspect" of the divine reality. God "becomes" love by his manifestation, for in the created work He manifests and objectivizes Himself. The creation is simultaneously expression and object of His love.

The creation is a gift, but also a possession. It is an incessant flux coming from the Creator Himself, but also a community in that God in His omnipotence includes all His created work. Love in its divine origin has a double scope as it is at the same time both gift and possession. But this does not imply duality. This latter is to be found only on the terrestrial level of love. God's love is one and indivisible and therefore cannot be divided into a duality. If we say that it is double, that must be understood in the sense that God, for the one part, manifests Himself in creation; and for the other, He "is" in the created work as universal spirituality. Loving Father, He always watches over His work and over his children on earth. He possesses, keeps, and protects the created work in order to restore to the source of love, when the times will have been accomplished, that which love has created. This cyclic aspect of creation is thus tied to love, which finds there its perspective of eternity even in terrestrial manifestation: love "changes not" even from the terrestrial point of view.

The created work is a cosmos, an order. As love is an essential element in creation, it cannot therefore be outside this order. On the contrary, it is integrated in it and this is why it is possible for us to live it in an objective fashion. Love is not some sort of pseudo-metaphysical "fire," nor some current of sentimental energy passing through the world. Nor, certainly, is it a "natural force" which "liberates" man and gives him the subjective right to elevate himself above all legal order. Even less is it a legislative power permitting man to say that "love is always right." It does not justify a pretended liberty to "suppress frontiers." It does not legitimize chaos. It is a part of the created order; it is in defense of this order, not in its destruction, that love is realized.

The love of the Creator is one and indivisible, but, on the terrestrial plane of reflection, we find duality, that precisely which differentiates the Heavens from the earth. Certainly there exists a "love of self" of which the young Narcissus is the prototype in Greek mythology, but something is morbid there which is already figured in the legend: Narcissus, lovingly contemplating his own image, languishes and dies. The ultra romantic and always tragically vain efforts to reinterpret the myth by making of narcissism an "experience of oneself" confirm the truth that love is participation.

In this regard terrestrial love is faithful to its celestial model, being at once gift and possession. But it is a duality, a tension between two poles which persists the more, not only in that they unite, but in that they preserve their independence. Love thus becomes simultaneously community and experience of oneself, union and polarized tension.

The primordial manifestation of all terrestrial love is procreation. In nature as in the human species, there goes on without ceasing this process founded on the duality man-woman, these two beings who are endlessly drawn the one to the other, meeting and uniting without, however, the element of tension which separates them being abolished. When Goethe speaks of the eternal feminine which attracts us, he expresses his opinion that love pertains to the being of creation, that the feminine and the masculine are archetypal forces which condition the perpetuation of the created work and from which flows constantly a new production of life.

We encounter divine as well as terrestrial love, and this on two levels of manifestation. To the procreative love between man and woman is added the love of parents for the fruits of their procreation. This latter is hierarchic encounter between the superior and the inferior while procreative love is encounter between equals. The hierarchical aspect is the form of love linking Heaven and earth. Such is the divine love which descends into creation and is reflected in the relationships of parents with their children. But in the created work, production follows a horizontal course; it is the encounter between man and woman, or in the Vedantic terms, between *Purusha* and *Prakriti*.

Can we then speak of superior and inferior love, carnal and immaterial, of Eros and Agapé? Is it advisable to establish such categories? First, it is necessary to remember that the love of God is universal and includes all. It penetrates all, even earthly love under its most sensual and sexual forms, for the divine love also comprises archetypes which are the models of earthly love and of the masculine and feminine principles. Thus terrestrial love, even in its most carnal form is prefigured in the divine order. The organic world, vegetables and animals and humans, accomplish on the terrestrial plane the work of divine creation, and it is in the same manner that we continue this work by our toil.

The struggle against the "flesh" is not an expression of a duality of love. Love experienced on earth does not suffer from a tragic and irremediable division between Eros and Agapé. Certainly one rightly speaks of a more or less elevated quality of love—it is a question then of the hierarchic and vertical order—just as one designates it with just as much reason as platonic or physical. But it is not there that the differences in principle reside. All is united in the energy of the divine creation, just as the Christian cross is the reunion of two branches, the one vertical and the other horizontal. If not thus, how would family life be possible? How could the "carnal" union of spouses combine with the "disincarnated" love of parents for their children?

The important fact is that divine love penetrates all earthly love, even in its most carnal manifestations. This is why the combat against the flesh is not the expression of some irreducible dualism of love. On the contrary, it is destined precisely to oppose itself to such a dualism, and to hinder the creature from withdrawing from its Author, to impede earthly love being "liberated" from its celestial source. The love of God encompasses all, such is the final response to the question. Even the apostle Paul, so wroth against the flesh, proclaims that this latter is ennobled by the Spirit. "What! know ye not that your body is the temple of the Holy Spirit which is in you, which ye have of God, and that ye are not your own?" (1 Cor. 6:10).

Love is one, but its forms of manifestation are multiple. It is manifested under aspects and forms of the most varied kinds. The "pleasures of the flesh" are not a tragic and culpable destiny which hangs over humanity. The most sensual enjoyment of love does not in itself comport a shadow of sin and of guilt. On the contrary, it is in holding that there are two essential forms of love—tragic division realized especially by the Calvinist sects—that one removes the possibilities of "ennobling the flesh" spiritually.

Certainly love is not egotistical. Nevertheless one cannot say that the object of love would be "lacking in interest" or unworthy of being sought. For love tends at the same time to give itself and to possess. Union and relationship are not renunciation of oneself nor the effacement of him who loves. God does not efface Himself in his uninterrupted creation, any more than man and woman lose the characteristics of their sex when they unite with one another physically and corporeally. On the contrary, the inclination to possession can merge into a force that apparently carries the marks of egotism and disorder. But its object is situated outside self, and this object is union. The fusion of the self in a relationship with the other, of possession and gift, is something that is designated, not without reason, as the mystery of love: as in an alchemical process, the apparently contrary elements are blended into a creative union.

Every created being has a beginning and must have an end. If a created thing had to endure eternally, that would signify that it would escape from the omnipotence of God to establish its own order, independent of the absolute character of eternity. The divine omnipotence would be traduced. When we recognize this omnipotence we recognize at the same time that the created is found in a cyclic process, with a continual return to its source. The human relation with the Creator then assumes a double aspect: on the one part, we thank Him for the life we have received and for all that is given in our terrestrial life; and for the other part we aspire to communion, to the rediscovery which definitively constitutes the termination of the cycle.

This is why the philosophy of Plato sees in the human aspiration for the Supreme Good not an empty speculation, but a wisdom drawn, as he himself informs us, from more ancient sources. It is on the basis of the same wisdom and with the same certitude that Aristotle founded his doctrine of natural process: there is an immovable center that puts all into movement, in the same manner that the beloved object sets into motion him who loves; it is to this which philosophy has given the famous appellation *kinei hos eremenon*.[1] This fundamental idea is found with Plato, with St. Augustine, as well as with the mystics and theologians of the Middle Ages: man tends towards a goal which is divine and with which he aspires to be united. It is not the man who "wills," it is the goal which elicits the aspiration.

There is in our terrestrial life a place where these multiple aspects of love converge as in the focus of a lens; that is to say, the family. It is the point where the love between man and woman meets that which exists between parents and children. It is the nucleus whence germinates all

---

[1] The Greek *kinei hos eremenon* signifies, in the words of Aristotle (*Metaphysics* 12.7 [1072b]): "The final cause, then, produces motion as being loved, but all other things move by being moved."—Translator.

the life of love; and in that love it becomes the sanctuary where the child, for the first time, encounters the love of Heaven as well as that of the earth, which surrounds his education. It is a microcosmic circle which reflects the macrocosmic totality. On the level of terrestrial manifestation it is the point of crystallization of divine love.

Even if the family is infinitely more than a simple bourgeois institution, its social importance is none the less for being so. Thanks to education within its cadre, the new generation acquires on the personal level a consciousness of identity and on the social level a consciousness of community. The family is also a school for life in society and through the family the child learns to protect the weak and the disabled, to assume responsibilities, to show respect, as well as to practice solidarity and mutual aid. It is the place where the younger generation encounters paternity and fraternity which it experiences not as literary phenomena nor as clichés on posters at public meetings or in the texts of resolutions, but as realities of the familial community.[2]

There is, in the Kingdom of Man, much uncertainty and even confusion on the subject of man's situation vis-à-vis love. It has been pretended for generations that humanity was going to become a single great fraternal community. Liberty and equality must open the way to fraternity. But it has never been shown convincingly where the spiritual force was coming from that would permit the race to surmount the egoism of profane and sensual men, and thus prepare the advent of universal human love. Nevertheless, the idea that a humanity deprived of paternity might even so reach a universal community of love has not ceased to engender hope as men anticipate the great projects for the establishment of a world of security, well-being, equality, and justice.

Institutional revolutions and radical reforms, as well as the education which is inspired by them, apparently, are supposed to be the royal way leading to this fraternity full of love. But another way to reach this goal is also proposed. And it is here that Sigmund Freud intervenes as principal guide with the libido relationship between men and women. The source of all love is not God, but the carnal nature of man himself. Freud suppresses the hierarchic relationship even in the terrestrial sense. His work contains no allusion to the love between parents and children. On the contrary, one of his fundamental notions is the alleged Oedipus complex: the mother becomes a "sexual object" for her son and the father a "rival" with respect to this "object." Thus the parents, reduced to the same level, become objects for the libidinous inclinations of the new generation of children. Love then becomes "unidimensional." King Eros exercises an absolute sovereignty on all levels. King Oedipus has shown us the line to follow: that which we desire is to kill our fathers. King Marx has shown us the way to collective parricide, which is revolution. His spiritual cousin, Sigmund Freud, would teach us individual parricide.

Even if the Oedipus doctrine must naturally be interpreted in a symbolic sense, it nevertheless gives expression to the ungoverned satisfaction of libidinous inclinations. Is humanity,

---

[2] A beautiful description of the traditional Chinese family was published almost a century ago by Tcheng-Ki-Tong, military attaché of China then posted at Paris, in an article in the *Revue des Deux Mondes*. The Chinese family, he says, develops into a community, a great family comprising hundreds of members, a "sort of religious order subject to fixed rules." Under the authority of the oldest, all resources are gathered together to be divided equitably and if a member of the family falls ill or is out of work, the others intervene. The family obeys an order of equality and fraternity, "great words which are inscribed in the hearts and not on walls" (Tcheng-Ki-Tong, "La Chine et les chinois," *Revue des Deux Mondes* 63 (15 May 1884): 278ff.

therefore, to be given up to a sexual war without mercy? In no way. The prophets of sexual liberation have quite different aims. He who finds a libidinous partner in love goes beyond the narrow limits of his selfhood when he is sexually united with another creature, or so it is pretended. This union is an act of peace and fraternity, of human reconciliation. Eros becomes the divinity of peace and fraternity. Divine love, and that of earthly parents, have no business in this context. Orthodoxy, dogmas, rules of morality are only obstacles provoking neurotic troubles. Freud proclaims, contrariwise, that the free libidinous experience of free individuals contains the germs of a relaxed, peaceful, and harmonious social life. This is the gospel of sexual democracy and sexual pacifism.[3]

The views of Freud on the problems of human life in common are in no way simple. He often expresses, and in a surprising manner, an accentuated pessimism. But his fixation on carnal love, the libido, is and remains central. In his suite have come generations of enthusiastic combatants for sexual democracy, doctrine of the free practice of the instinctive life between equal humans which, we are assured, is the way leading to the great community of men. Just as Marxism had declared that the final object of communism was work in free association, sexual radicalism proclaims that free libidinous association is the way to human harmony.

Whether one chooses the one or the other of these ways, that of institutional revolution in combination with a strictly egalitarian education, or that of the god of Eros, both are confronted with the same dilemma. It is believed possible to "create" love, and awaken to life something that is not found in the sensory life where one lives. Love exists, but not there where the moderns seek it. It is in its divine source, and in the world he finds it who knows how to draw from that source his strength and inspiration.

If one chooses the way of revolution, one places oneself at the point of view of collective egoism. If one gives oneself to the revolution or to the sexual life, the point of departure can be only that of the man egotistically bound to his sensory desires. No love, and no community animated by love, can be born from this egoism, for love exists already, as well as community, and that because we are all children of the same Father. This community does not become a reality except when we find this paternity and acknowledge it.

The Kingdom of Man is a social order without love. It is obliged to have recourse to growing numbers of laws and ordinances, to threats and reprisals, in order to maintain the cohesion of its troops when all the seductions of the all providential State no longer suffice. One cannot avoid noting the disappearance of all true fraternity, as well as the simple and daily sentiment of solidarity, of helpfulness and of solicitude. Let us not embellish the past. The history of humanity overflows with familiar conflicts and fratricidal struggles. Where can one find the community, the family, responding perfectly to ideal desiderata? Even if the family is presently decadent one has no reason to forecast a future for human relations envisaging, not only that the family is placed in question as an institution but that it is openly menaced with annihilation. For where there is no longer love nor charity, the door is open to brutality. Such is human nature.

Again, let us look at a form of life that is totally different from that which love wants to realize on the level of human relations. Let us look at its extreme opposite, ascetic isolation. Is not asceticism in conflict with love and with love's plenary fulfillment? Cannot one compare the ascetic with a sick man, a voluntary invalid? In appearance, he cuts himself off from the expres-

[3] See particularly, Sigmund Freud, *Massenpsychologie und Ich-Analyse*, Gesammelte Werke 12, pp. 112ff.

sion of love which, from the terrestrial point of view, is the most engaging and generous—the family. He remains apart from paternity and from a common life with the other sex. Thus love does not enter his life, neither under its hierarchic aspect, nor under its egalitarian aspect in the union of man and woman. Is the ascetic, therefore, the negator of all love?

These questions are the more significant in that asceticism is always presented with the pretention of representing an elevated terrestrial form of divine love. Asceticism is encountered in worship, in sacerdotal life, and in charitable activities exercised in the name of religion. No one can deny that it is a question here of ascetical forms of love on this earth. That must lead us to ask ourselves if love manifested here below does not have a dimension other than those that are expressed under the hierarchic and egalitarian aspects.

Asceticism is the third aspect. It is neither gift nor possession, but abstention from the expression of love through the flesh. It is submission to the divine love and at the same time aspiration to communicate this love on the terrestrial level without undergoing the influence of the flesh. It is not negation of carnal love, nor of any element of earthly life as such. Asceticism does not proceed from a dualist conception that envisages a superior existence "without sin" and an inferior world consisting of "sinners." The ascetic holds himself apart from the "world," but he does not deny it. The world is no more sinful for him than it is for others who live in it and enjoy terrestrial love to the full. The ascetic attitude is a confirmation—even if in negative terms—of earthly love, and not its negation. It is a fundamental error to see in asceticism a comportment that is hostile to material life, an error which constantly leads to the confusion of asceticism with puritanism.

Human love is participation. Divine love is also participation in the sense that God loves His created work; but divine love is, in its essence, a totality. It is eternal, immutable, absolute, having nothing relative in it. God "is" love. It is this absolute, eternal, and immutable love that the ascetic, in his imperfection, seeks to manifest on earth. It is of less importance to know if this takes the form of eremitic or cenobitic isolation, or of charitable action.

Cannot one say, finally, that all love bears a mark of asceticism? All profound and authentic love, whether it is in the flesh or not, is an "engagement" which is prolonged far beyond one's own person. Love is "blind," it is said, and that indicates that the "engagement" is combined with an abandonment of one's own interests, a devotedness, a sacrifice, a gift, all qualities of disinterestedness. An animal satisfaction of his instincts in promiscuity becomes insupportable to man in the long run. Love in its biological and fleshly form is joined to the spiritual, which not only "ennobles the flesh" but even abstains from the satisfaction of its immediate instinctive impulses. In that abstention, in that ennoblement, man acquires the possibility of raising his attention towards this love which reunites the fleshly and the immaterial in the source from which come all things and to which all must return.

Translated by Alvin Moore, Jr.

BOOK REVIEWS

The Power of Now:
A Guide to Spiritual Enlightenment

By Eckhart Tolle

Novato, CA: Namaste Publishing & New World Library, 2004

Jettison the ego, still the incessant chatter of the mind, abandon the mind-created "pain body," live in the present moment, be a channel for the Divine. What do I need? Well, for starters, a copy of Eckhart Tolle's *The Power of Now*,[1] the book which, with a little help from Oprah, inaugurated Tolle's career as "spiritual teacher" and has since taken up permanent residence in the best-seller charts, along with the more recent *A New Earth* (2005). Tolle is now a hugely popular speaker on the "spirituality" lecture/seminar/workshop/retreat circuit. Business has never been better!

Many readers will be familiar with the outer facts of the Eckhart Tolle phenomenon. He was born Ulrich Tolle in Germany in 1948. He spent some time as a youth in Spain and studied literature, languages, and philosophy at London and Cambridge universities, enrolling in but never completing doctoral studies. Until his thirtieth year, Tolle tells us, he lived in a state of "continuous anxiety" and suffered from "suicidal depression" (p. 3). His life was altered by a "profoundly significant" transformative experience which awakened him to his real nature as "the ever-present *I am*." Later, he writes, he learned to enter "that inner timeless and deathless realm" and to dwell in states of "indescribable bliss and sacredness." After his "epiphany" he finds himself with "no relationships, no job, no home, no socially defined identity," but with a sense of "intense joy" (p. 5). He spends a lot of time in parks. Somewhere along the line he takes on the name of the great medieval mystic. In the mid-90s he meets Ms. Constance Kellough, a marketing executive, management consultant, and "wellness expert" who soon publishes *The Power of Now* on her start-up imprint, Namaste. Sales remain modest until 2002 when Oprah Winfrey's acclamation of *The Power of Now* as "one of the most important books of our times" lifts Tolle out of the general ruck of New Age teachers and, virtually overnight, turns his books into chart-toppers. *The Power of Now* has since been translated into upwards of thirty languages, and sold over five million copies. Tolle lives in Vancouver with his business partner, Kim Eng, now also a teacher of sorts. Beyond this sketchy biographical outline further details are remarkably scarce. (Tolle: "I have little use for the past and rarely think about it" [p. 3].)

Tolle's books, five in number, have been variously described as "New Age mystical texts," "self-help manuals," "spiritual classics," and the like. He belongs with those many contemporary "spiritual teachers" without any firm commitment to a particular religious tradition—Deepak Chopra and Shakti Gawain might serve as examples. He also shares some ground with those "self-help" teachers who draw on psychotherapy and transpersonal psychology, and sometimes on successful business and advertising techniques. (One may mention such figures as Dale Carnegie, Norman Vincent Peale, Wayne Dyer, Louise Hay, and Richard Carlson.)

---

[1] Eckhart Tolle, *The Power of Now: A Guide to Spiritual Enlightenment* (Novato, CA: Namaste Publishing & New World Library, 2004). All intertextual citations are to this work.

Tolle writes in a simple and often quite engaging style, and weaves together teachings from and allusions to the world's great religious traditions. Among his favorite sources we find the spiritual classics of Taoism and Zen Buddhism, Rumi, the New Testament, and *A Course in Miracles*. One can find reverberations of traditional teachings throughout his writing and much of what he says is quite unexceptional, often nicely put. He has also acknowledged a considerable debt to the teachings of Barry Long (1926-2003), the Australian journalist and self-styled "tantric master." Asked in an interview about the influences on his work, Eckhart Tolle identified the great Advaitin sage of Arunachala, Ramana Maharshi, and the Indian iconoclast and counter-culture "guru," Jiddu Krishnamurti (also a formative influence on Long, and on Deepak Chopra). His own work, Tolle claims, is a synthesis of these two influences—a case of mixing gold and clay! The fact that Tolle registers no sense of dissonance here, that he can apparently situate these two figures on the same level, just as he can without embarrassment juxtapose *A Course in Miracles* and the teachings of Jesus and the Buddha, alerts us to one of the most troubling aspects of his work—not only the conspicuous failure to discern between the authentic and the spurious but also the lack of any sense of the different levels at which such figures and their teachings might be situated, a lack of any sense of proportion. One might say the same of his treatment of "the mind" in which he fails to differentiate its many functions or to understand that all manner of modes and processes might come under this term; for Tolle the mind seems to be no more than a rather mechanical accomplice to the ego. Moreover, the ego-mind is the root of all our troubles. Now, of course, there is an echo of traditional teachings here—but in Tolle's hands, the idea is robbed of all nuance and qualification, and his writing on the subject often degenerates into rhetorical sleight-of-hand. "Being" is another word bandied about in cavalier fashion.

Tolle's general philosophical position as modern-day magus can be summed up this way: non-dualistic, a-religious, vaguely "Eastern" but with pretensions to universality, tinged with "spiritual evolutionism" (one of the calling cards of New Age teachers), and directed towards an inner transformation bringing peace and joy. He promotes a "new consciousness" to liberate us from the fetters of the analytical and ratiocinative mind which is the principal instrument of the ego. Associated with the ego-mind is the "pain body" in which reside all manner of negativities (hatred, jealousy, rage, bitterness, guilt, and so on—some echoes of Wilhelm Reich here). Both our individual and collective ills derive from the false but tyrannical constructions of the ego-mind and its associated "pain-bodies." We must break out of "inherited collective mind-patterns that have kept humans in bondage to suffering for eons" (p. 6). Readers familiar with the genre will readily understand the kind of fare on offer through the most cursory glance at Tolle's chapter headings: "You Are Not Your Mind," "Consciousness: The Way Out of Pain," "Moving Deeply into the Now," "Mind Strategies for Avoiding the Now," etc. Tolle's central message is signaled by the title of the book under review. Here is a characteristic passage:

> Realize deeply that the present moment is all you ever have. Make the Now the primary focus of your life. Whereas before you dwelt in time and paid brief visits to the Now, have your dwelling place in the Now and pay brief visits to past and future when required to deal with the practical aspects of your life situation. Always say "yes" to the present moment (p. 35).

This theme was popularized in counter-cultural "spirituality" by books such as Douglas Harding's *On Having No Head* (1961), Alan Watts' *The Book on the Taboo Against Knowing Who You Are* (1966), and Ram Das' *Be Here Now* (1971). Of course, it has many antecedents, both in orthodox religious teachings, particularly Buddhist, and in their modern dilutions and counterfeits.

There is no doubt that Tolle, and others like him, answer—or seem to answer—to a widespread spiritual hunger in the contemporary Western world. There is also no gainsaying the fact that Tolle is a writer of considerable intelligence and charm, and some insight—his ruminations on the tyrannical regime of "time," for instance, are not without interest (see Chapter 3). Nor, as far as I can see, is there reason to suspect Tolle of being a charlatan who shamelessly fleeces his followers in the manner of a Rajneesh or a Jim Bakker; this is not to ignore the fact that his writings are finely calibrated to an affluent Western market with an apparently insatiable appetite for the quick "spiritual" fix, especially of the "self-help" and "you can have it all now" variety.

In the early 1970s Whitall Perry examined various "prophets" of "new consciousness," among them Gerald Heard, Aurobindo, Gopi Krishna, Alan Watts, and Krishnamurti. Among the characteristics he discerned in their teachings, in varying degree, were the following (here enumerated for easy reference):

> I. a patent individualism, II. a scientific and moralistic humanism, III. evolutionism, IV. a relativistic "intuitionism," V. inability to grasp metaphysical and cosmological principles and the realities of the Universal domain, VI. a mockery (latent or overt) of the sacred, VII. a prodigal dearth of spiritual imagination, VIII. no eschatological understanding, IX. a pseudo-mysticism in the form of a "cosmic consciousness."[2]

Let us consider these charges in relation to Eckhart Tolle who, in many respects, follows in the footsteps of the figures with whom Perry was concerned—quite self-consciously so in the case of Krishnamurti. On the basis of the book in front of us, the charges most easily sustained are IV, V, VII, VIII, and IX. The case is more complicated with reference to I and to III, while he can be declared (more or less) innocent of VI—though some will think this lenient.

The most disabling limitation of Tolle's work, from which much else inevitably follows, is "the inability to grasp metaphysical and cosmological principles": thence, no real understanding of either Intellection or Revelation, no comprehension whatever of the multiple states of Being, not even a glimmer of understanding of Tradition or orthodoxy, no awareness of the metaphysical basis of the "transcendent unity of religions." As Frithjof Schuon and others have so often insisted, there can be no effective spiritual therapy without an adequate metaphysic; this is to say that an efficacious spiritual method must be rooted in a doctrine which can never be exhaustive but must be sufficient. To put it even more simply, a *way* of spiritual transformation, such as is provided by all integral traditions, must be informed by an adequate *understanding* of Reality. In the case of Eckhart Tolle we have neither doctrine nor method—only a jumble of ideas, perceptions, and reflections, some insightful, some attractive, many no more than the prejudices of the age dressed up in "spiritual" guise. Throw in a few passing nods towards a het-

---

[2] Whitall Perry, "Anti-Theology and the Riddles of Alcyone," *Studies in Comparative Religion*, 6:3, 1972, p. 186.

erogeneous collection of techniques ransacked from Zen, yoga, Sufism, Christianity, and modern psychology. Tolle's work actually confronts us with a case of what Schuon has called "the psychological imposture" whereby the rights of religion are usurped, the spiritual is degraded to the level of the psychic, and contingent psychic phenomena are elevated to the boundless realm of the Spirit. This kind of psychism, infra-intellectual and anti-spiritual, is endemic in New Age movements. And, to be sure, whatever distinctive features Tolle's work might evince, it belongs firmly in this camp.

No doubt some people have found a measure of guidance and temporary relief from their immediate problems in Tolle's books, though it is difficult to imagine them leading to any long-term transformation. After all, one does not harvest figs from thistles. Perhaps Tolle's books, for all their limitations, have served to direct some seekers towards deeper and more authentic sources of wisdom. This is to take the most charitable view possible. On the other hand, there is a good deal here to set off the alarm bells. Consider, for instance, this claim, one which has doubtless been swallowed whole by many Tolle enthusiasts:

> This book [*The Power of Now*] can be seen as a restatement for our time of that one timeless spiritual teaching, the essence of all religions. It is not derived from external sources, but from the one true Source within, so it contains no theory or speculation. I speak from inner experience. . . (p. 10).

A review of this scope does not allow us to dismantle this claim, nor to demonstrate its implications and possible ramifications—though these should be clear enough. In our time there have been many who have laid claim to some essential wisdom, surpassing traditional religious forms. By now we should be wary of all such claims when they are apparently based on nothing more than "inner experience" and when traditional criteria are either flouted or ignored. Tolle's work as a whole should be subjected to the most severe interrogation in the light of Tradition.

Review by Harry Oldmeadow

Revisioning Transpersonal Theory:
A Participatory Vision of Human Spirituality

By Jorge N. Ferrer

Albany, NY: State University of New York Press, 2002

A decade has passed since Jorge Noguera Ferrer first published his widely acclaimed book *Revisioning Transpersonal Theory*. Ferrer is a transpersonal psychologist from Spain, who has resided in California for a number of years. As its title indicates, the book sets the goal of significantly revising the postulates of transpersonal psychology, of removing elements that at some point may have helped in its development, but that today—according to the author—are obstacles that impede the advancement of this discipline.

The goal thus outlined is, certainly, ambitious, but the result—beyond the impact that the work may have had inside the transpersonal circle, where it has not been received without criticism[1]—is in the best of cases, of a much smaller import than expected. Some of the criticisms that Ferrer raises in his book are only partially justified, and we believe that they do not have the weight that he attributes to them, while we find others directly erroneous or unjustified. However, the major shortcoming of the book is noticed in the author's programmatic proposal. We find it poorly described and barely articulate, too little for a work that virtually attempts to relaunch transpersonal psychology as a whole. The book, as it was published in 2002, is presented, thus, as a premature work; perhaps it would have been preferable to compose a more modest book that would be in line with the state of his investigations then.

The first half of the book is dedicated to the criticism of transpersonal psychology. This is not the place to make a presentation of this discipline: it will be enough to say that the discipline was founded at the end of the 1960s by authors such as Stanislav Grof, Anthony Sutich, Abraham Maslow, and Miles Vich and it is defined by the *Journal of Transpersonal Psychology* (the authorized organ of this school), as "the study of humanity's highest potential, and with the recognition, understanding, and realization of unitive, spiritual, and transcendent states of consciousness."[2]

The deconstructive part of the book is centered on three main fronts:

1. Experientialism: transpersonal and spiritual phenomena understood as individual, inner experiences;

2. Empiricism: the necessity of an empirical foundation for transpersonal investigation;

3. Perennialism: the belief in knowledge, liberation, and spiritual goals of universal character.

The axis of the critical part of the book is centered on this last item, represented by the diverse variants of the perennial philosophy, which Ferrer considers as the "foundational frame-

---

[1] "I do believe that Ferrer's book basically marks the end of the transpersonal movement; with relativistic pluralism, no matter how dialectically presented, there is simply nowhere to go. Postmodernism is dying a slow and fitful death; increasingly scholars are moving from pluralism to integralism, in my opinion. The insuperable difficulties of Ferrer's book are a condensation of three decades of postmodern wrong turns, or so it seems to me" (Daryl S. Paulson, "Daryl Paulson on Jorge Ferrer: *Revising Transpersonal Theory*, Jorge N. Ferrer, posted online via the Shambhala website: http://wilber.shambhala.com/html/watch/ferrer/index.cfm/).

[2] Ferrer quotes other short definitions of the subject on page 16 of his book.

work of the transpersonal theory" (p. 138). The analysis of this review will therefore focus on this last point,

Before fully entering into the topic, it is necessary to make a couple of clarifications. The first is that perennialism (as Ferrer acknowledges) is far from being a homogeneous movement: although Frithjof Schuon and the perennialist or traditionalist school are the most eminent representatives of this philosophy, there are many other thinkers considered as perennialists as well, many of whom have been influential in the transpersonal paradigm (this too is not a homogeneous block), but whose work diverges in important aspects from the one traced by René Guénon, Frithjof Schuon, and Ananda K. Coomaraswamy, to mention only the founders of the traditionalist school. This is the case, for example, of Aldous Huxley, a popularizer of the perennial philosophy who proposed a neo-Advaita form of spirituality having nothing to do with traditional Hindu *dharma* or the *sanātana dharma* for that matter.

The second clarification is that, although perennialism has been very important for transpersonal psychology, the inverse can hardly be said. Transpersonal psychology incorporates methods and concepts that are flatly rejected by perennialism, among them the first two points that Ferrer criticizes: experientialism and empiricism. Empiricism involves basing knowledge (transpersonal, in this case) on the empirical sciences, that is, using the empirical method of testing, a method that entered into crisis years ago in the social sciences, and even in the most classical sciences, such as physics. Experientialism, for its part, postulates individual spiritual experiences as a benchmark—something that is not only difficult to ponder because of its own nature, but also is potentially dangerous for the spiritual development of the individual. The search for "experiences" taken as a benchmark, leads, ultimately, to empiricism and the necessity of finding a material, tangible, and quantifiable substratum for the spiritual world.

Some of the main objections that Ferrer makes in regards to perennialism are:

1. It reifies the Principle, the cause, presenting it as something pre-given and objective, in the frame of an aprioristic philosophy.

2. It privileges certain characteristics of the Principle over others (non-dual over dual, impersonal over personal, etc.).

3. Since it conceives the Principle as pre-given, it gives way to essentialism and a hierarchization of spiritual ways, obliterating the fruits of each one within their own contextual frame.

The answer that Ferrer gives to these problems, in the second part of the book, is the "participative vision," a route that avoids the subject-object contradiction by simply abandoning Cartesian logic for an integrative vision that recognizes the uncertain nature of the Principle. It thus binds the multiple, dynamic, dialectical, multidimensional, and malleable aspects of the "Mystery" (according to Ferrer's terminology), without fearing the ensuing oppositions and contradictions that this would seem to reveal.

In his perspective, Ferrer locates the emphasis not so much in the object (divine) or in the subject (human), but in that network of—multiple, always changing—relationships that is established between both of them. It is a performative, enactive spirituality; that is, a spirituality that arises in the subject's (individual, group, geographical space) lived action with the Mystery.

Leaving aside for a moment Ferrer's criticism of perennialism, it is necessary to say that it is a positive move to highlight the dynamic, active, and unfixed aspect of spiritual life.[3] Cartesian

---

[3] Let us stress, nevertheless, that recovering these aspects does not necessarily require discarding perennialism. A recent book, *Mitos, Ritos, Símbolos. Antropología de lo Sagrado* [Myths, Rites, Symbols: Anthropology of the Sacred] (Buenos Aires: Editorial Biblos, 2008), by anthropologist and Egyptologist Fernando Schwarz, presents a

dualism is harmful for metaphysics, as Ferrer well observes, and it is one of the fundamental criticisms of the modern world by perennialism, as Ferrer also recognizes. Nevertheless, we find that, paraphrasing Schuon, in acknowledging the aspect of immanence, Ferrer loses sight of transcendence. Ferrer focuses his attention mainly on the methodical aspects of the spiritual life, and does not deal much with the doctrinal aspect (perhaps for fear of falling into dogmatism).

By reading the strong criticisms of the perennialist conception of the Absolute, the reader awaits to see what Ferrer proposes in its stead. The author says little on this causal Principle, which he prefers to call the Mystery. He adds to it the adjective "indeterminate," and on occasion others like "malleable" or "dynamic," but little more are we told of it. It is understandable that Ferrer abhors definitions that would limit the limitless, according to his point of view; in any event, he has not solved the problem satisfactorily.

Many of his criticisms surface by analyzing purely doctrinal concepts as if they were univocal and unidirectional methodical prescriptions. This assimilation (we do not dare to say "confusion," because we suppose that Ferrer knows the difference between doctrine and method) is what allows him to make, in all logic formulations (given this previous assimilation), most of his criticisms of perennialism. We will pass now to a detailed analysis of these points.

1. The Principle as a Pre-given and Objective Entity

According to Ferrer, the Principle of which perennialism speaks is presented as an object (reification) that the subject should reach. This conception, which at the same time solidifies the Principle, limiting it, gives too passive a role to the subject who, on the other hand, Ferrer conceives as co-creator.[4] In the first place, it is necessary to say that, as long as the individual is identified with his egoic nature, the Principle (personal or impersonal) is presented with all the force of an absolute object. If it is accepted that man is limited and that he is surrounded by limits, then that which is limitless (although only a concept) is imposed upon him, in first instance, as something external, strange, objective.[5] The Principle is necessarily presented as

---

"participative" perspective kindred to that of Ferrer (by means of the concept of "creative imagination," taken from Sufism, via Henri Corbin), although in the frame of a small work that incorporates the contributions of perennialism.

[4] Which reminds us of Angelus Silesius' sentence in *The Cherubinic Wanderer*: "I know God cannot live one instant without Me: / If I should come to naught, needs must He cease to be" (Angelus Silesius, "Oneness with the Divine," in *Selections from the Cherubinic Wanderer*, trans. J.E. Crawford Flitch [London: George Allan & Unwin, 1932], p. 128). We believe that the sense of this sentence is something quite different from the meaning Ferrer would grant it.

[5] Clearly, this is not always the case. In spite of the objective condition of being immersed within existence and multiplicity, there are traditional societies—such as the indigenous peoples—in which it is understood in a much clearer way that the Mystery is present in the universe. A recent book presents a similar perspective to that of Ferrer, where the active, real, and lived presence of the Principle in the world is spoken of: "The stones, the hills, the lakes, the Earth, the Moon, the stars, Venus, they don't represent the gods, but rather they are gods, as literal and repeatedly the indigenous texts say. . . . Characteristic of the indigenous theology is the idea of the extended presence of the sacred in the world. . . . The indigenous vocation to specify the sacred in its diverse instances and manifestations comes from the conception that the places of the universe, as well as the times, are governed by different sacred forces" (Luis A. Reyes, *El Pensamiento Indígena en América* [Indigenous Thought in America] (Buenos Aires: Editorial Biblos/Desde América, 2008), pp. 104-106, reviewer's translation). Also, several decades back, there is a similar explanation, in which the conception of an external and superior Principle, outside of the

transcendent to the "external man," in the words of Schuon. But being objective does not mean that the content of the principle is constituted in a collection of particularities that the human being should gather. Second, it is curious to highlight that one of the distinguishing characteristics of the Principle is that it is "indeterminate," the preferred word that Ferrer fortuitously wishes to use to designate the Mystery.

Third, Ferrer seems to forget that there are other ways to designate the Principle, which can change its axis from transcendence and the object to immanence and the subject. From this aspect of immanence and the subject, the Principle is called the Self.[6] This does not change things much for Ferrer, since he would affirm that they are simply swingings between two sides of a dualist and/or Cartesian logic. But it is necessary to understand[7] that, by force, speech is lineal and presents limits for what is simultaneous and homogeneous.

2. The Non-dual, Monist, Metaphysics of Perennialism

In the same line of what he calls "the Myth of the Given," Ferrer denounces the fact that, although perennialists qualify the Absolute as ineffable and unqualifiable, they privilege a non-dual metaphysics, so that this Absolute is not truly neutral or unqualified.[8] This critique is understandable from Ferrer's position, which posits a plurality of valid paths, but with different spiritual *goals* (*nirvana, samadhi, unio mystica*, etc.), so that a non-dual metaphysics would not necessarily be superior to a dual one. It is more difficult, nevertheless, to reconcile this posture with his own definition about the Mystery.

If Ferrer criticizes monism (in the sense that the Principle must be One), why does he speak of "the" Mystery? If Ferrer does not understand—as he has said in a recent interview to this

---

world, is relativized. Surprisingly, the author is Ananda K. Coomaraswamy, one of the founders of perennialism: "Natural or artificial objects are not . . . arbitrary 'symbols' of such or such a different or superior reality; but they are . . . the effective manifestation of that reality: the eagle or the lion, for example, is not so much the symbol or the image of the Sun as it *is* the Sun under one of its manifestations (the essential form being more important than the nature in which it manifests itself)" (quoted in Frithjof Schuon, *The Transcendent Unity of Religions* [Wheaton, IL: Quest Books, 1993], p. 67).

[6] When Schuon begins his chapter, "The Modes of Spiritual Realization", from *The Eye of the Heart: Metaphysics, Cosmology, Spiritual Life* (Bloomington, IN: World Wisdom Books, 1997) thus: "It has been said that there are as many paths to God as there are human souls," (p. 121) he is in fact speaking of the indefinite possibilities that the spiritual path can offer.

[7] Ferrer himself—like the perennialists—recognizes the temporary nature of speech: "it will surely be only a question of time before its limitations [those of the participative vision] emerge (especially if it is reified or taken too seriously!)" (p. 187).

[8] In a similar line of reasoning, Ferrer critiques perennialism's choice of *Advaita Vedanta* as the best exposition of universal metaphysics. This is seen as contradictory with the view that all religions are true and share the same essence. Ferrer mentions Schuon in *Esoterism as Principle and as Way*, trans. William Stoddart (London: Perennial Books, 1990), when he asserts that "the perspective of Shankara is one of the most adequate expressions possible of the *philosophia perennis* or sapiential esoterism" (p. 89). The same statement, in fact, is made by Schuon on numerous other occasions ("The Perennial Philosophy," in *The Unanimous Tradition: Essays on the Essential Unity of All Religions*, ed. Ranjit Fernando [Colombo: The Sri Lanka Institute of Traditional Studies, 1999], pp. 21-24; "René Guénon: A Note," in *René Guénon: Some Observations* [Hillsdale, NY: Sophia Perennis, 2004], pp. 6-10; "The Vedanta" and "Gnosis: Language of the Self," in *Language of the Self* [Bloomington, IN: World Wisdom Books, 1999], pp. 19-41, 201-217). Again, when presenting himself as a defender of other spiritual paths, Ferrer seems to forget that one speaks here of doctrinal expositions and not of spiritual paths (in fact, Schuon practiced Islam and not Hinduism).

reviewer[9]—why it is considered that a non-dualist philosophy is nearer to the Principle than a dualist one, then why does he choose the "indeterminate" adjective to qualify the Mystery? Is not dualism more determinate than non-dualism (or a personal Being in front of an impersonal one)? This critique is all the more curious since Ferrer declares—with some reservations—that he feels closer to the mystic *apophatic* ways—the *via negativa* (p. 190), whose most important traditional representatives are of a non-dualist character.

The criticism, however, becomes understandable when we see that Ferrer is attempting to preserve the honesty and virtue of the diverse spiritual paths, without putting them into uncomfortable hierarchies. In this way, Ferrer is clearly part of the "leveling" mentality so much in fashion during the last decades, whose democratic standardization he submits to. This leads us to the last critique to be analyzed here.

3. The Hierarchies of the Spiritual Paths

Presenting hierarchical degrees of spiritual realization appears to be a problem for Ferrer in two senses: in the first place, it would be a perceived lack of honesty in the face of the supposed universality and unity of religions; second, and more importantly, it does not recognize the value of each spiritual path, promotes intolerance, and favors certain spiritual paths (such as *Advaita Vedanta*) to the detriment of others, without truly justifying this predilection.

Perennialism recognizes different paths within the religious traditions, which can be categorized in a very general way as: the path of action, the path of love, and the path of knowledge.[10] In Hindu terms these are: *karma marga, bhakti marga,* and *jñana marga.* These different paths correspond to so many different ways to approach the Divine, and followers of each path usually present their own path as the best. But perennialism does not so much deal with making rankings of spiritual traditions (either among religions or within a single religion), but in recognizing those that come closer to the indeterminate Principle. From this point of view, it is pertinent to say that the path of knowledge (*gnosis*), independently of the religion in which it appears, is the superior one, because it conceives the Principle with a lesser degree of determination (or limitation) than other paths.[11]

But it is erroneous to think that one religion is preferred to another,[12] or to believe that the recognition of the doctrinal superiority of *Advaita Vedanta* necessarily implies that other spiritual paths are inferior.[13] The adequacy of the diverse spiritual paths is justified by their own

[9] "Todo puede vivirse como un crecimiento espiritual" ("Everything can be lived as a spiritual growth"), *Uno Mismo*, October 2007, Buenos Aires, for the entire interview see the following link: http://www.desdeamerica.org.ar/pdf/Nota%20Jorge%20Ferrer.pdf.

[10] See Antoine Faivre and Jacob Needleman (eds.), *Modern Esoteric Spirituality* (New York: Crossroad, 1995), p. 459.

[11] The different types of spiritual methods are in agreement—in a general way—with as many different conceptions of the Principle: most personal forms are usually nearer the path of action while the impersonalist ones are nearer the contemplative paths.

[12] While this is not perhaps the case for exponents of transpersonal psychology, perennialism rejects anything like a "supra-religion," or the adoption of one religion above others, precisely because it recognizes that religions are appropriate messages for different human receptacles (the diverse peoples and cultures of humanity). Each religion is sufficient and offers some path of union, although necessarily in diverse ways.

[13] Again, there is an "admixture" here of the doctrinal and methodical aspects.

existence: to admit a doctrinal superiority of a path does not imply a denial of different religious paths, whose messages are all that they should be for the human receptacles where they have appeared. Ultimately, the degree of union with the Divine is something only to be judged by God.[14]

On the other hand, without being obliged to fall into essentialisms, it is somewhat difficult to deny altogether the differences of individual spiritual capacities, verifiable in practice. However this is not an obstacle for those who abide by the perennial norms that affirm both human differences and corresponding differences in the traditions themselves, so that each human being could, in principle, reach spiritual integration, as the "transcendent unity of religions" postulates.[15]

The Participative Vision

Regarding the emphasis, in the participative position, placed on the active and relational individual's role,[16] Ferrer seems to believe that interiority implies passivity. But this is not the case. Even when one speaks of passivity—in the Zen tradition, for example—or of no action (i.e. *wu-wei* or "actionless activity"), this should be understood as an opposite attitude to self-centered action (even when an ascetic attitude is favored); so that passivity is actually positive.[17] If one speaks of interiority, it is not necessary to imagine a semi-naked anchorite meditating in a hermitage. Several centuries ago it was said by the anonymous author of *The Cloud of Unknowing*: "It is very necessary to have much care of understanding the words that are said with spiritual intention, so that you don't conceive them materially, but spiritually. . . ; and it is specially convenient to be careful with the concept of 'interiority' and the concept of 'elevation'."[18]

Instead of conceiving spiritual realization as the correspondence (or union) of the subject with an Absolute object, Ferrer proposes, as criteria of validity, the emancipatory quality, free of egoism, that occurs in multidimensional processes that encompass every level of the person (the contemplative one as much as the emotional, sexual, and moral ones, among others). That is to say, "By their fruits you will know them". But those are exactly that, fruits, effects, and not the cause. Is it perhaps necessary to think that there is not a cause that leads to emancipation at

---

[14] This is how there are saints in "exoteric" (according to perennialist terminology) ambiences, and people that did not achieve realization—or even perverse ones—in gnostic or esoteric ambiences.

[15] This reminds us of an episode between Saint Thérèse of Lisieux and Pauline, her elder sister (and later spiritual instructor): "One day I expressed surprise that God does not give an equal amount of glory to all the elect in Heaven—I was afraid that they would not all be quite happy. She sent me to fetch Papa's big tumbler, and put it beside my tiny thimble, then, filling both with water, she asked me which seemed the fuller. I replied that one was as full as the other—it was impossible to pour more water into either of them, for they could not hold it. In this way Pauline made it clear to me that in Heaven the least of the Blessed does not envy the happiness of the greatest" (Saint Thérèse of Lisieux, "A Catholic Household," in *The Story of a Soul*, ed. Thomas N. Taylor [New York: Cosimo, 2007], pp. 42-43).

[16] Just in passing, let us mention a note: "About the distinction 'person-individual,' Guénon considers it equivalent to the distinction of the Self and the I. One can see that the person is considered here as a *relationship* with the Principle" (Antoine Faivre and Jacob Needleman (eds.), *Modern Esoteric Spirituality* [New York: Crossroad, 1995], p. 455, italics in the original).

[17] A positiveness not in a relational sense, but in a total sense, without opposites. In the same way, the *via negativa* is intrinsically positive, as Pseudo-Dionysius the Areopagite says at the end of his treatise, *Mystical Theology*.

[18] Ch. LI (London, 1922), edited by John Watkins.

every human level? And if the creative participation "emancipates individual spiritual choices from external religious authority" (p. 185), then who allows us to assess our actions as more or less egoic? How to know that a certain erotic communion is emancipatory, and not just sinking us more fully in an ocean of egoity? Is it the human individual who can verify it outside spiritual authority? It is as if the unrealized self that is traveling the path can observe itself according to the goal of realization. The same shortcomings that we find when Ferrer speaks of the Mystery can also be observed when he speaks of the "I." His obstinate desire not to be caught within hardening definitions, makes him place these terms on a nebulous and ambiguous plane which, in the end, obscures his entire theoretical proposal or should we say *revision*?

The path to the ego's transcendence must begin with a negation; one cannot speak of co-creativity and fullness without having overcome the limitation of terrestrial existence. And when this emancipation is achieved, there are no limits, and for that reason there is nothing that the person could do that would hinder this transpersonal condition; the liberated one does what he or she wants (only there is no identification with an "ego"). A Chinese sage of Zen Buddhism has said it in a masterful way: "Before a man studies Zen, to him mountains are mountains and waters are waters; after he gets an insight into the truth of Zen through the instruction of a good master, mountains to him are not mountains and waters are not waters: but after this when he really attains to the abode of rest, mountains are once more mountains and waters are waters."[19]

In our opinion, Jorge N. Ferrer's theoretical proposal masked as a method of transcendence appears to simultaneously contextualize everything, conflating ego-emancipating practices with participative experiences of the Mystery. To advocate Ferrer's method is to purportedly go beyond Cartesian dualism, which would be an impossible escape as one would only be further enmeshed in the subject-object straightjacket. Considering only the methodical aspect in general, it seems unattainable—from Ferrer's proposal—to distinguish what a true realization is from that which is not, when egoic limitations are muddled with transcendence (i.e. the confusion of the psychic and the spiritual)—such a participatory vision is irremediable. We recall from the traditional wisdom that the mountains are the same at the beginning as at the end, in the same way that the Self (*Ātmā*) is the same with regards to the multiple states of being, but there is a definitive path that leads to this realization so that the same actions are lived as a different, fuller, and more integral reality.

Review by Nahuel Sugobono

---

[19] Ch'ing-yüan, quoted in Whitall N. Perry (ed.), *A Treasury of Traditional Wisdom* (London: Simon & Schuster, 1972), p. 886; recently reissued under a new title, *The Spiritual Ascent: A Compendium of the World's Wisdom* (Louisville, KY: Fons Vitae, 2008).

Integral Psychology:
Consciousness, Spirit, Psychology, Therapy

By Ken Wilber

Boston, MA: Shambhala, 2000

Ken Wilber's book *Integral Psychology* is an ambitious, if not confusing and at times wooly, attempt to forge a rational approach to the mystery of an integral psychology of man. Sound intriguing? Indeed, one would hope, within these pages and based on the promises of the title and subtitle, to take a pail to the well of profound inquiry into a true psychology of man, hoping to find that the deepest recesses of the well contain not only reflected sky from the heavens above, but also the sparkling waters of some subterranean water table that draws upon a variety of remarkable ideas intended to ennoble the mind and heart with their clarity, insight, and depth. After all, when it comes to an exposition of such nebulous terms as consciousness, spirit, psychology, and therapy, which is what the subtitle promises, people have relied down through the ages on the revelatory texts of the religions to provide timeless insights into the perennial mysteries that confront humanity, including the questions of origins, purpose, and final end of humanity, rather than relying solely on the thinking and research of modern scientists and secular philosophers who like nothing better than to investigate the true nature of reality based purely on human speculation and their research into the physical world of matter.

We recall the claim of Stephen Hawking, in his best-selling book *A Brief History of Time*, when he expressed the hope to find a complete theory of everything that would bring together the classical world of Newtonian physics with the modern world of relativity and quantum indeterminacy. Later in 2004, Hawking was to retract the claim, not wishing to be associated with the notion that a "theory of everything" would have to be devised based on the purely physical aspects of reality and leaving aside the inward dimension that we all experience, and which scientists are unable to verify on their own terms.

The echoes of the perennial philosophy and other artifacts of a universal spirituality hover on the distant shores of modernity like sirens beckoning the wary, modern-day Ulysses into the tempting realms of a holistic and more traditional spirituality that embraces human psychology, consciousness, the soul, and much more. Wilber's effort represents a bold attempt, according to the back cover, "to honor and embrace every legitimate aspect of human consciousness" within the fold of his own unique world philosophy. As he says without hesitation in his introductory note to the reader, he wanted to write a history of psychology because "Someone has *got* to tell" (p. ix).

When innocent readers pick up a book, they have every expectation that the cost of the book will be justified in a reading experience worth paying for. Book reviewers have no such luxury and must come to terms with the value of a book in light of its intended readership. In critical inquiry, then, I must ask myself who the intended readership might be for Wilber's obviously extensive effort to present such a portentous theme as an integral psychology of man for future humanity, a psychology that embodies the established truth of the *religio perennis*, together with the latest findings of modern science regarding the workings of the mind and the intricacies of human consciousness. Those readers who are accustomed to the likes of a Henry David Thoreau, who takes his readers by the hand and brings them clear to the edge of the horizon before leading them back home with a smile on their faces, may be disappointed by the detailed, dry, often trendy, and sometimes pretentious attitude that lurks behind Wilber's attitude and writing style. Let us not forget Thoreau's friend and Concord compatriot, Ralph Waldo Emerson, whose essays read like a stroll through some celestial garden as he speaks of the "golden man" who is only half the expression of himself, the other half being "what lies within." Finally, the great perennialist master, René Guénon, comes to mind, who presented primordial and metaphysical principles from the great religious traditions for a modern humanity cast adrift on a sea of uncertainty and doubt regarding the great questions that confront us. His writing style comes across as detached and unconditional, but delivered with a modesty raised to the level of the traditional courtesy of a devoted soul. Many years later, his writings still shine in the afterglow of their own inner light, illuminating the prevailing darkness like a jack-o'-lantern hovering over the surface of some deadly marshland.

Wilber acknowledges early on the likes of Gustav Fechner, William James, and James Mark Baldwin, all of whom have taken part in the initial development of a "science of psychology" that was on speaking terms with the wisdom of the traditional ages, men who envisioned an integral view "that attempts to include the truths of body, mind, soul, and spirit, and not reduce them to material displays, digital bits, empirical processes, or objective systems" (p. xi). His stated goal is to present what he calls a "daylight view" of a science of psychology that integrates the best of both worlds, the revelatory truths embedded within the traditional and perennial philosophies of the great world religions, together with the latest findings of a modern science. The daylight view regards the whole universe and all of its material components as "inwardly alive" and "conscious." He sheepishly backs off initially from any grand design of integration, claiming early on that the book is meant to be "a beginning, not an end," a mere "outline form" of his overview of an integral psychology that can serve as the basis for further research and discussion. As such, the book itself contains about 190 pages of narrative text and a further, nearly 100 pages of detailed charts and explanatory notes, to flesh out what he calls a brief outline of his subject matter.

The book itself is broken into three main divisions. In Part One, entitled "Ground: The Foundation," Wilber opens his argument and bravely attempts to lay the foundation of his principles, ideas, and theories into some preliminary and cohesive order in order to prepare the reader for what lies in wait further on in the book. He acknowledges that most modern researchers stop short of acknowledging the higher, transpersonal, and spiritual levels of spirituality that are traditionally associated with the great world religions. He admits that "the bleakness of the modern scientific proclamation is chilling" (p. 55) and refers to the perennial philosophy as the "wisdom of premodernity" (p. 9) as if it were a form of wisdom that no longer applies within the modern world.[1] There is a studied effort of the author's part to create his own world. One regularly comes across such phrases as "in my own system" and "we call this" such-and-such when he wants to identify something with his own unique branding. In referring to the concept of the "self" by way of explanation, he writes "I call the first the *proximate self*. . . , and the second the *distal self*. . . . The both of them together—along with any other source of selfness—I call the *overall self*."

This calls to mind the three clear characterizations of the soul within the Islamic framework that draw their legitimacy from the Quran and that are considered precious, revelatory insights.

---

[1] He cites Plotinus, Shankara, Fa-tsang, and Lady Tsogyal as examples of perennial philosophers!

The first of the three degrees of soul that exist within man is called in Quranic terminology the *nafs al-ammarah* or "the soul that commands to evil" (12:53). This is the aspect of soul that is inclined toward the evil alternative, or in modern terms the passionate and egocentric soul. The second aspect of soul is identified as the *nafs al-lawwamah* or "the soul that blames" (76:2). This is the aspect of the soul that we understand today as human conscience when the soul blames itself, is aware of its own imperfections, and serves as the inner voice that persuades a person to repent and turn away from any shortcomings and evils. The third degree of soul is called in the Quran the *nafs al-mutma'innah* or "the soul at peace" (89:27). This is an aspect of soul with the potential for perfection and enlightenment resulting in the peace that is the *conditio sine qua non* of the abiding spirit. It is the soul reintegrated into the Spirit and at rest in the certainty of an essential and revealed knowledge. By way of concession to the religious traditions, Wilber concludes this opening section by stating that "this extraordinary rupture between pre-modernity and modernity—spiritual and material—needs to be confronted head on" (p. 56). He admits that "we cannot have an integral view of the levels of consciousness if modernity and modern science denies the existence of most of them" (p. 56).

In Part Two, entitled "From Premodern to Modern," the author traces the evolutionary history of psychology from the pre-modern era down to modern times. In the very first paragraph, he states that an integral psychology would need to include the spiritual dimension of humanity; but he seems to regret that the great world religions—and he names Christianity, Judaism, Islam, Buddhism, Hinduism, Taoism and unnamed indigenous religions—"are part of the legacy of premodernity" (p. 57). He envisions the need for a reconciliation of both "religious" premodernity and "scientific" modernity regarding their attitudes toward spirituality if an integral psychology truly wishes to embrace the enduring insights of both perspectives. In tracing a history of progression through the various systems of thinking and philosophy, he hopes "to take the enduring insights from both and jettisoning their limitations" (p. 57). He doesn't believe there is any other way to bring about an integral approach to the exposition of a true psychology of man. In this section, he identifies and includes summative remarks about some important modern pioneers of an integral approach to the "Kosmos," such as James Mark Baldwin, Jürgen Habermas, Sri Aurobindo, and Abraham Maslow.

In Part Three, entitled "Fruition: An Integral Model," Wilber attempts to honor both pre-modern and modern thinking by drawing upon their selected insights in suggesting his own postmodern approach to an integral psychology. As major contributions to the postmodern era, he cites the fact that the world is in part a construction as well as an interpretation, that all meaning is context-dependent, and that contexts are endlessly holonic. He states categorically: "All of these can be summarized, in the most general fashion, by saying that where modernity differentiated the Big Three, post-modernity would integrate them, thus arriving at an inclusive, integral, and non-exclusionary embrace" (p. 171). He calls this not only the heart of a constructive postmodernity, it is also "the heart of any truly integral psychology and spirituality" (p. 171). I must confess that as a valiant reader willing to wade through a lot of difficult concepts and alien jargon, I was hoping at this point to begin to see a movement toward the makings of a synthesis out of which an integral psychology could truly be born, at least as a "beginning" as ground for further discussion. As I determinedly made my way through the final sections of the text, however, I found myself increasingly confused, if not totally lost amid words, phrases, concepts, and theories that made no sense to me on their own, much less as elements of a unified theory of psychology. One of his complaints about postmodernism was that its differentiations often slid into dissociations so that its postmodern integral embrace often slipped into "aperspectival madness" that amounted to the denial of qualitative distinctions of any sort, leading to the denial of holarchies altogether. "And since the only way you get holism is via holarchies, in denying the latter, postmodernity effectively denied the former, and thus offered the world not holism but heapism: diversity run amok, with no way to integrate and harmonize the pluralistic voices" (p. 171). Needless to say, as what I call an "innocent" reader, I felt myself mired in a hopeless sea of linguistic heapism in its own right.

At this point, I found myself longing for the clear, simple, yet profound prose of the likes of René Guénon, who wrote of spiritual and metaphysical principles as if they came second nature to him and addressed to a humanity waiting to be enlightened. Four adjectives come to mind that may help characterize his unique style: exactness, intelligibility, harmony, and purity. His writing displays a conviction and certitude that is distinctly Guénon, an intelligibility that is the language of spiritual intelligence, a harmony of composition that is integral of purpose and consistent through the main body of his remarkable *oeuvre*, and his purity of style follows a line of argument that is intellectual, intelligible, and clear. For all of that, a self-assured and erudite quality passes on to the reader the implicit certitude of his thinking.

It takes some doing for the innocent reader to become familiar with Wilber's rarefied jargon, in which he seems to be using a creative approach to developing a body of symbolic terminology that may not suit every mentality, particularly when the symbols themselves have no universal and/or self-evident application, whereas the beauty of traditional symbols is that their universality touches the hearts of everyone. Similarly, the use of symbolic language runs the risk of losing its effectiveness if it is not grounded within a universal tradition that sinks its roots within one of the revelatory scriptures of the religious traditions. For example, Wilber launches quickly at the outset of this work into a reference to the Great Nest of Being—alternatively called throughout the work the Great Holarchy of Being and Knowing—which he inexplicably prefers over the more traditional and universally understood phrase the Great Chain of Being, used down through the ages by all the major religions that partake of the perennial tradition. The cosmos is not good enough as a point of reference but that it must be written with a capital K as in *Kosmos*, raising the question how he would refer to the study of cosmology. He refers to the Great River, the Great Rainbow, and the archeology of the self, which he calls the great navigator of the waves and streams that outline waves of development from matter to body to mind to soul to spirit, streams of development involving cognition, morals, identity, worldviews, values, etc. Towards the end of the book, his pen seems to take wings as he refers to such things as the Great Play, the Ocean of One Taste, the Big Three (the Good, True, and Beautiful), the Great Liberation, and the Original Face, calling to mind the Quranic reference to the *wajh* (countenance) of Allah, as in "Wherever you turn, there is the face of God" (2:115). The grandeur of the phraseology, together with the insistent use of capitals, presupposes a kind of universality to the jargon that they simply do not contain, in the same manner as we might use the words Cosmos, Revelation, Tradition, Nature and the like as universally accepted concepts that relate directly to humanity because they bear the stamp of eternal truth, having been extracted, as in a true archeology, from the revelatory scriptures of the great world religions.

On the one hand, one cannot help but admire the sincerity which seems to permeate Wilber's determination to bring together an integral psychology of man from the many disparate elements at his disposal from pre-modernity, modernity itself, and postmodernity. However, the end result of his efforts is that the reader is awash in an alien jargon that has little meaning and no true context. For example, he writes of the inherent contradiction of the agenda of postmodernity in this way: "The very stance of postmodern pluralism—relying as it does on postformal vision-logic and integral-aperspectival cognition—is itself the product of at least five major stages of hierarchical development (sensorimotor to preop to conop to formop to postformal)" (p. 171). Whereas words traditionally had a symbolic flavor that were designed to convey a meaning that was universally understood by all, the danger in this kind of writing is that it is far too specialized and so wrapped up within the internal world of the author that good intentions perhaps get lost amid a world of words, in some instances with words that are made up by the author ("heapism") that leave the reader afloat on a sea of incomprehensibility. The end result is an alien coinage that has very little value for the average reader.

Whether it be the unique use of language that often distorts rather than enhances the intended meaning, and because the ideas presented within this work seek to establish a synthesis of meaning across the broad expanse of history from a wide variety of disparate worldviews, including metaphysical, spiritual, new age, scientific, and the like, the book comes across as highly speculative, over-extended, and pretentious, attempting to bring together, through theory and speculation, ideas from many traditions and eras that would form the basis of further research, discussion, and speculation, all cast within the guise of bold assertions that have no basis in traditional thinking. For all of its purpose and intent, the reader is left with a series of complicated theories, focused areas of research, and multi-purpose charts from disparate sources and worldviews without knowing which pocket to place them in for future reference.

By contrast, one comes away from reading Guénon's work thinking that the thematic essence of his views on metaphysical knowledge could lie comfortably in a thimble as a secret treasure awaiting discovery, since everything he wrote seems to trace its inspiration back to the existence of a primordial point of departure that finds its true source in pure knowledge, as if arriving at this realization would enable a person to cross the unbreachable divide and thus transcend, in principle at least, the duality of this world. He poses the question himself in his *Studies in Hinduism*: "What is the origin of these traditional metaphysical doctrines from which we have borrowed all our fundamental ideas?"[2] He answers by stating there is no origin on the human plane of existence that can be determined "in time," calling into question even the concept of "origin." "The origin of tradition, if indeed the word 'origin' has any place at all in such a case, is as 'non-human' as is metaphysics itself."[3] In his mind, "metaphysical truth is eternal"; everything else is subject to change and contingency.

Integral Psychology's final chapter, entitled "The Integral Embrace," certainly promises through its title some kind of movement toward a synthesis of ideas from those that have been laid out in exotic and complicated detail through the narrative and in the charts and explanatory notes at the end. The integral embrace is none other than a synthesis of the best of the pre-modern, modern, and postmodern worldviews that would lead the way toward an integral psychology of man and the cosmos. However, what the reader is left with are sentimental, pseudo, and downright immature comments that on the surface sound like they should have promise, but that actually leave the reader with an unpleasant aftertaste. For example, Wilber urges us modernites "to pause for a moment, and enter the silence, and

---

[2] René Guénon, *Studies in Hinduism*, trans. Henry D. Fohr, ed. Samuel D. Fohr (Hilladale, NY: Sophia Perennis, 2004), p. 100.

[3] Ibid.

listen very carefully, the glimmer of our deepest nature begins to shine forth, and we are introduced to the mysteries of the deep, the call of the within, the infinite radiance of the splendor that time and space forgot" (p. 190). This gets better, or worse, as the case may be. Elaborating on his pet theory of consciousness evolution, he writes: "As the average mode of consciousness continued historically to grow and evolve—and because evolution operates in part by differentiation-and-integration—the perception of the Great Nest became increasingly differentiated and integrated on a widespread, cultural scale (and not just in a few individual pioneers)" (p. 191). The reader is left with the knowledge that "this is the dawning of the age of vision-logic, the rise of the network society, the post-modern, aperspectival, internetted global village." And even better: "Evolution in all forms has started to become conscious of itself" (p. 193). Assertions such as these—and they abound within this work—do little to solve the inherent mystery that lies within the heart of both humanity and the cosmos. On the contrary, they run the risk of making a mockery of the true aspirations of an integrated spirituality that has always formed the backbone of the perennial philosophy.

One important point that is overlooked or perhaps never even considered within this work is the fact that an "integral psychology" already exists within the perennial philosophy of the great world religions in which humanity's true nature is identified as a mirror reflection of the names and qualities of the Supreme Being. What the great world religions have repeatedly emphasized is that we live within the pattern and texture of a fabric that reflects the natural order and harmonies of the universe that are given evidence both within the soul of humanity— what Wilber repeatedly refers to as the self—and are reflected as well within the heart of the natural order. In our essence, we are not a fluid sea of untold depths and unmapped turmoil and we are not solid rock full of rough edges and shaded caves; we are instead a fabric of infinite realities that wind their way through an endless tapestry of threads passing through each other in peaks and troughs that highlight the course of a life with ribbons of certainty to illuminate the mystery of living within a given individual destiny.

A modern approach to the formation of an integral psychology would serve itself well by using the principle of unity that is found at the backbone of the perennial philosophy. The great world religions already contain within the fabric of their philosophies an integral psychology of Man, Nature, and the Universe as an interconnected reality within a single universal source. The psychology of the human being requires an inner, integral tapestry made possible by virtue of the golden thread of perennial truth that is woven into the very fabric of existence. Perhaps this mystery is the true point of departure in our journey of return to that mythical land beyond the celestial horizon, where "Spirit is still, but it sings sweetly and universes are born."[4]

Review by John Herlihy

---

[4] *The Essential Swami Ramdas*, ed. Susunaga Weeraperuma (Bloomington, IN: World Wisdom, 2005), p. 18.

Acknowledgments

I. Critique

Frithjof Schuon, "The Psychological Imposture." New translation by Mark Perry.

René Guénon, "The Confusion of the Psychic and the Spiritual." In *The Reign of Quantity and the Signs of the Times*, trans. Lord Northbourne (Ghent, NY: Sophia Perennis, 2004), pp. 235-240.

Titus Burckhardt, "Traditional Cosmology and Modern Science: Modern Psychology." In *Mirror of the Intellect: Essays on Traditional Science & Sacred Art*, trans. and ed., William Stoddart (Albany: State University of New York Press, 1987), pp. 45-67.

William Stoddart, "Situating the Psyche." Previously unpublished.

Philip Sherrard, "The Science of Consciousness." *The Scientific and Medical Network Newsletter*, No. 48 (April 1992), pp. 5-8.

II. *Theoria*

Harry Oldmeadow, "The Not-So-Close Encounters of Western Psychology and Eastern Spirituality." In *Journeys East: 20th Century Western Encounters with Eastern Religious Traditions* (Bloomington, IN: World Wisdom, 2004), pp. 309-334.

Samuel Bendeck Sotillos, "The Impasse of Modern Psychology: Behaviorism, Psychoanalysis, Humanistic, and Transpersonal Psychology in the Light of the Perennial Philosophy." Previously unpublished.

Huston Smith, "The 'Four Forces' of Modern Psychology and the Primordial Tradition: Interview with Samuel Bendeck Sotillos." Previously unpublished.

José Segura, "On Ken Wilber's Integration of Science and Religion." *Sacred Web*, 5, pp. 71-83.

Donovan Roebert, "The View of Selfhood in Buddhism and Modern Psychology." Previously unpublished.

John Herlihy, "Profile of Unfinished Man: Unveiling a Sacred Psychology of Humanity." Previously unpublished.

Whitall N. Perry, "Drug-Induced Mysticism: The Mescalin Hypothesis." In *Challenges to a Secular Society* (Oakton, VA: Foundation for Traditional Studies, 1996), pp. 7-16.

Charles Upton, "Drug-Induced Mysticism Revisited: Interview with Samuel Bendeck Sotillos." Previously unpublished.

III. *Praxis*

Ananda Kentish Coomaraswamy, "On Being in One's Right Mind." In *What is Civilization? And Other Essays* (Ipswich: Golgonooza Press, 1989), pp. 33-41.

Lord Northbourne, "Being Oneself." In *Looking Back on Progress*, ed. Christopher James 5th Lord Northbourne (Ghent, NY: Sophia Perennis, 2001), pp. 58-62.

Seyyed Hossein Nasr, "The Integration of the Soul." In *The Essential Seyyed Hossein Nasr*, ed. William C. Chittick (Bloomington, IN: World Wisdom, 2007), pp. 73-84.

Marco Pallis, "Some Thoughts on Soliciting and Imparting Spiritual Counsel." In *The Way and the Mountain* (Bloomington, IN: World Wisdom, 2008), pp. 79-108.

Tage Lindbom, "Love." In *The Tares and the Good Grain or the Kingdom of Man at the Hour of Reckoning*, trans. Alvin Moore, Jr. (Macon, GA: Mercer University Press, 1983), pp. 109-119.

Book Reviews

Harry Oldmeadow
The Power of Now: A Guide to Spiritual Enlightenment, by Eckhart Tolle. In Harry Oldmeadow, *Touchstones of the Spirit: Essays on Religion, Tradition, and Modernity* (Bloomington, IN: World Wisdom, 2012), pp. 183-188.

Nahuel Sugobono
Revisioning Transpersonal Theory: A Participatory Vision of Human Spirituality, by Jorge N. Ferrer. Previously unpublished.

John Herlihy
Integral Psychology: Consciousness, Spirit, Psychology, Therapy, by Ken Wilber. Previously unpublished.

Notes on the Contributors

Titus Burckhardt (1908-1984) was a German Swiss and one of the leading Perennialist writers of the twentieth-century. He was the great-nephew of the famous art-historian Jacob Burckhardt and the son of the sculptor Carl Burckhardt. He was an early childhood friend of Frithjof Schuon, sharing a common intellectual vision that lasted a lifetime. His writings present an exceptional blend of accessibility and penetrating insight into the metaphysical, cosmological, and symbolic dimensions of the world's plenary traditions. He acted as a specialist advisor to UNESCO, for the preservation of the unique architectural heritage of Fez, Morocco. Burckhardt immersed himself in the Arabic language and assimilated the principal classics of Sufism, translating axial exponents such as Ibn 'Arabi and Jili. He was a frequent contributor to the journal *Studies in Comparative Religion* and author of landmark works such as *Sacred Art in East and West* (1958) and *Alchemy: Science of the Cosmos, Science of the Soul* (1960).

Ananda K. Coomaraswamy (1877-1947) was one of the great art historians of the twentieth-century whose multifaceted writings deal primarily with visual art, aesthetics, literature and language, folklore, mythology, religion, and metaphysics. His most developed works adeptly expound the perspective of the Perennial Philosophy by drawing on a detailed knowledge of the arts, crafts, mythologies, cultures, folklores, symbolisms, and religions of both the East and the West. Along with René Guénon and Frithjof Schuon, Ananda Coomaraswamy is considered as a leading member of the Traditionalist or Perennialist school of comparative religious thought. The broad scope of Coomaraswamy's voluminous writings can be sampled in *The Essential Ananda K. Coomaraswamy* (2004).

René Guénon (1886-1951) was a French metaphysician, writer, and editor who was largely responsible for laying the metaphysical groundwork for the Traditionalist or Perennialist school of thought in the early twentieth century. Guénon remains influential today for his writings on the intellectual and spiritual bankruptcy of the modern world, on symbolism, on spiritual esoterism and initiation, and on the universal truths that manifest themselves in various forms in the world's religious traditions. The quintessence of Guénon's *opus* is to be found in works such as *Man and His Becoming According to the Vedanta* (1925), *Crisis of the Modern World* (1927), and his masterpiece, *The Reign of Quantity and the Signs of the Times* (1945).

John Herlihy (b. 1945) was born in Massachusetts and educated at Boston University and Columbia University in New York City. He is the author of numerous books such as *Modern Man at the Crossroads: The Encounter of Modern Science and Traditional Knowledge* (1999), *Borderlands of the Spirit: Reflections on a Sacred Science of Mind* (2005), and *Wisdom of the Senses: The Untold Story of their Inner Life* (2011). Herlihy currently works as the Director of the English Language Center at the University of Sharjah in the United Arab Emirates.

Tage Lindbom (1909-2001) was one of the intellectual architects of the Swedish welfare state, but later in life adopted the perspective of the Perennial Philosophy and became a strong opponent of secularism and modernism. Having completed a doctorate in History at the University of Stockholm in 1938, he was for many years director of the Labor Movement Archives and Library, housed in the headquarters of the Swedish Labor Movement in Stockholm. Close to the very center of decision-making, Lindbom helped conceive and implement "the Swedish model."

He was the friend of prime ministers, cabinet ministers, and labor leaders. He also served on public boards and commissions dealing with cultural questions. Two of his books have appeared in English, *The Tares and the Good Grain* (1983) and *The Myth of Democracy* (1996).

Seyyed Hossein Nasr (b. 1933) is University Professor of Islamic Studies at the George Washington University, Washington D.C. and is President of the Foundation for Traditional Studies (FTS), the central organ for *Sophia: The Journal of Traditional Studies*. The author of over fifty books and five hundred articles, he is one of the most important and foremost scholars of Islamic, Religious and Comparative Studies in the world today and he is also a leading member of the Traditionalist or Perennialist school. Nasr almost single-handedly arranged for the founding, in 1974, of the Imperial Iranian Academy of Philosophy, which attracted many Iranian and foreign scholars from diverse parts of the world who later become among the most respected specialists in their fields. A volume in the Library of Living Philosophers series has been dedicated to his thought. Nasr delivered the well-known Gifford Lectures that later turned into his work, *Knowledge and the Sacred* (1989), considered by many to be his most comprehensive statement of his philosophical position. Two other substantial works are *The Encounter of Man and Nature: The Spiritual Crisis of Modern Man* (1968) and *The Need for a Sacred Science* (1993).

Lord Northbourne (1896-1982), born Walter Ernest Christopher James, was the 4th Baron Northbourne of Kent, England. He was an agriculturist, educator, translator, and writer on both agriculture and comparative religion. He was educated at Oxford and was for many years Provost of Wye College—the agricultural college of London University. Lord Northbourne was a keen agronomist, and wrote an influential book *Look to the Land* (1940). In this book, Northbourne introduced the term "organic farming" to the world, as well as the concepts related to managing a farm as an "organic whole." He translated into English seminal works of the Perennialist school and was an early contributor to the journal of *Studies in Comparative Religion*. Many of these essays were later included in his books *Religion in the Modern World* (1963) and *Looking Back on Progress* (1970).

Harry Oldmeadow (b. 1947) is Coordinator of Religious Studies in the Department of Arts, La Trobe University, Bendigo, Australia. He studied history, politics, and literature at the Australian National University, obtaining a First Class Honors degree in history. In 1971 a Commonwealth Overseas Research Scholarship led to further studies at Oxford University. In 1980 Oldmeadow completed a Masters dissertation on the Perennialist or Traditionalist school of comparative religious thought. This study was awarded the University of Sydney Medal for excellence in research and was later published under the title, *Traditionalism: Religion in the Light of the Perennial Philosophy* (2000). He has written other important works such as *Journeys East: 20ᵗʰ Century Western Encounters with Eastern Religious Traditions* (2004) and his most recent, *Touchstones of the Spirit: Essays on Religion, Tradition, and Modernity* (2012). He currently resides with his wife on a small property outside Bendigo.

Marco Pallis (1895-1989) was a Renaissance man: a gifted musician, composer, mountaineer, translator, and a widely respected author on Tibetan Buddhism and the Perennial Philosophy. He was a distinguished member of the Traditionalist or Perennialist school of comparative religious thought. His eloquent writings focus on Buddhist doctrine and method, but are noteworthy for their universalist outlook. He personally knew many of the influential Tibetan Buddhist teachers that came to the West, including Chögyam Trungpa, who asked Pallis to write the foreword to his seminal book, *Born in Tibet* (1966). Pallis published three books devoted primarily to tradition, Buddhism, and Tibet: *Peaks and Lamas* (1939), *The Way and the Mountain* (1960), and *A Buddhist Spectrum* (1980) and was also a regular contributor to *Studies in Comparative Religion*.

Whitall N. Perry (1920-2005) was one of the few individuals who not only met but knew René Guénon, Ananda K. Coomaraswamy, and Frithjof Schuon first hand. He met Coomaraswamy at Harvard in the 1940s, lived in Egypt from 1946 to 1952 developing close ties with René Guénon, and was a close associate of Frithjof Schuon while living in Switzerland and moved with Schuon to the United States in 1980. Upon Coomaraswamy's recommendation, he embarked upon a seventeen-year labor to compile the spiritual wisdom of the ages in an encyclopedic anthology, entitled *A Treasury of Traditional Wisdom* (1971), which is considered by many to be a key work in the Perennialist canon. Besides being a regular contributor to *Studies in Comparative Religion* he is the author of *The Widening Breach: Evolutionism in the Mirror of Cosmology* (1995) and *Challenges to a Secular Society* (1996).

Donovan Roebert (b. 1959) is an artist and writer on Tibetan Buddhism as well as interreligious matters. He is the founder and coordinator of the South African Friends of Tibet and teaches weekly classes in Buddhist theory and practice, including meditation. He is the editor of *Samdhong Rinpoche: Uncompromising Truth for a Compromised World, Tibetan Buddhism and Today's World* (2006) and author of *The Gospel for Buddhists and the Dharma for Christians* (2009). Roebert lives in Hermanus, South Africa.

Frithjof Schuon (1907-1998) is a foremost spokesman of the Traditionalist or Perennialist school and is a philosopher in the metaphysical current of Shankara and Plato. He traveled to North Africa in 1932 to meet Shaykh Ahmad al-Alawi, a providential encounter that marked a turning point in his life. He had a profound interest in the North American Indians and in 1959 had the opportunity to attend a Sun Dance and was adopted into the family of Chief James Red Cloud, a grandson of the great chief known to history. He developed a deep friendship with Thomas Yellowtail, an important medicine man and a leader of the Sun Dance religion and was in contact with Black Elk through Joseph Epes Brown, who at the time was living with the Lakota holy man. He was also in contact with H.H. the 68th Jagadguru of Kanchi, who accepted the dedication to him of Schuon's book, *Language of the Self* (1959). Schuon has written more than two dozen books on metaphysical, spiritual, artistic, and ethnic themes and exerted the greatest influence on Perennialism in the twentieth century. He was also a prolific poet and gifted painter. Some of his most noteworthy works are *The Transcendent Unity of Religions* (1953), *Logic and Transcendence* (1975), and *Esoterism as Principle and as Way* (1981).

José Segura (b. 1944), a poet and a novelist, holds a Ph.D. with a specialty in traditional interpretation of Spanish Medieval and Renaissance texts. He is equally dedicated to applying the principles of the *Philosophia Perennis* to biblical Christianity and the arts. He has recently taught literature at the University of Central Florida, and is currently working on the recovery of the code present in the Hebrew Old Testament and behind the Greek text of the New Testament, a code which—if correct—drastically alters the accepted configuration of the text and yields an unexpected interpretation of the Western Revelation. He resides in Málaga, Spain.

Philip Sherrard (1922-1995) was an English author and scholar educated at Cambridge. Among the works for which he is best known is his collaboration in the translation of the *Philokalia* (together with his collaborators Kallistos Ware and Gerald Palmer). The combination of his interests in metaphysics, theology, art, and aesthetics led to his participation in the review *Temenos*, of which he was one of the founders in 1980. He was also recognized as a leading voice in situating modern attitudes and behaviors on the environment within a Christian framework. He is the author of *The Eclipse of Man and Nature: An Enquiry into the Origins and Consequences of Modern Science* (1987), *The Sacred in Life and Art* (1990), and *Human Image, World Image* (1992). The town of Limni on the island of Evia in Greece became his permanent home.

Huston Smith (b. 1919), renowned authority on the world's religions, is Thomas J. Watson Professor of Religion and Distinguished Adjunct Professor of Philosophy, Emeritus, Syracuse University. For fifteen years he was Professor of Philosophy at M.I.T. and for a decade before that he taught at Washington University in St. Louis, Missouri. Most recently he has served as a Visiting Professor of Religious Studies, at the University of California, Berkeley. Huston Smith was profoundly struck by the writings of Frithjof Schuon and knew many of the traditionalists personally. Smith himself acknowledges his indebtedness to the Perennial Philosophy as the bedrock of his work. His book *The World's Religions* (formerly *The Religions of Man*, published in 1958) has sold several million copies and has been the most widely used textbook for courses on comparative religion for many years. He is also the author of significant books such as *Forgotten Truth: The Primordial Tradition* (1976), *Beyond the Post-Modern Mind* (1982) and *Why Religion Matters: The Fate of the Human Spirit in an Age of Disbelief* (2001).

William Stoddart (b. 1925) was born in Carstairs, Scotland, lived most of his life in London, England, and now lives in Windsor, Canada. He studied modern languages and medicine in the universities of Glasgow, Edinburgh, and Dublin. He was an associate of Frithjof Schuon and Titus Burckhardt and translated several of their works into English from the original French or German. For many years he was assistant editor of the journal *Studies in Comparative Religion* (originally published in London, England, and now resuscitated, in print and on-line, by World Wisdom Books of Bloomington, Indiana). Pursuing his interests in comparative religion, Stoddart traveled widely in Europe (including Mount Athos), North Africa, Turkey, India, Sri Lanka, and Japan. Stoddart's books include *Outline of Hinduism* (1993, later republished as *Hinduism and Its Spiritual Masters* in 2007), *Outline of Buddhism* (1998), and *Outline of Sufism* (2012, formerly titled *Sufism: The Mystical Doctrines and Methods of Islam* in 1976).

Nahuel Sugobono (b. 1973) is an author and journalist who specializes in popular science and comparative religion. He studied anthropology at the University of Buenos Aires. As a journalist, his writings have appeared for almost 20 years in major Argentinean publications. As a writer, he has published more than 15 books of Indian myths and legends from Argentina and other parts of the American continent. Sugobono lives in Buenos Aires, Argentina.

Charles Upton (b. 1948) is a poet, activist, and prolific writer on esoterism, comparative religion, "metaphysics and social criticism," and mythopoetic exegesis, whose books include *The Science of the Greater Jihad: Essays in Principial Psychology*, *The System of Antichrist: Truth and Falsehood in Postmodernism and the New Age*, and its forthcoming sequel *Vectors of the Counter-Initiation: The Shape and Destiny of Inverted Spirituality*. Charles Upton and his wife Jennifer Upton, who is also a writer on topics of tradition, live in Lexington, Kentucky.

Note on the Editor

Samuel Bendeck Sotillos was born in 1972 in Hamburg, Germany and came to the United States at an early age. His paternal side of the family is from the Middle East and his maternal side is from Spain. He received his BA in Religious Studies with a focus on Psychology from Arizona State University, Tempe and went on to receive an MA in Education from Vermont College of Norwich University, Montpelier, Vermont and an MA in Psychology from the Institute of Transpersonal Psychology, Palo Alto, California. He has travelled throughout the world to visit sacred sites, and had contact with noted spiritual authorities. He has worked in the field of mental health with diverse populations covering the broad spectrum of disorders in many types of psychiatric settings, with clients struggling with substance abuse issues, grief and loss, terminally ill clients in hospice care and at risk children and youth, as well as homeless populations for a number of years. He is a Board Affiliate of the Association for Humanistic Psychology (AHP) and has published in numerous journals including *Sacred Web, Sophia, Parabola, Resurgence* and the *Temenos Academy Review*. He currently lives in the California Central Coast.